KEY TO THE ICONS

As you read this printed text or the unbound version online, you will see icons for the online activities that correspond with the content of the text. The various online activities are **only** available by going online to *Communication Unbound.* Your instructor will likely make assignments for those particular online activities that you might do in your class or offer a menu of choices for completing some of the activities.

Learning Objective: Covers the detailed content in each section.

Think About This: Critical thinking questions are designed to function as a message/chat board for class discussion.

Online Journal: A diary format allows you to explore communication issues on your own. You can either print the journal or save it to disk for future reference.

Video View: A video clip is followed by critical thinking questions to print or e-mail to yourself or your instructor.

Web Activity: An activity directs you to one or more Internet sites where you can explore a variety of communication topics and issues. You can print or e-mail the results to yourself or your instructor.

Rapid Review: Short questions in multiple-choice, true-false, and fill-in-the-blank formats allow you to quickly check your understanding of each section. Immediate feedback is given online.

Assessing Your Skills: Self-assessment activities measure a variety of communication competencies.

Practice Test: Multiple-choice and true-false questions are submitted for immediate scoring with answer feedback.

COMMUNICATION unbound

www.ablongman.com/doyle

Terrence Doyle

Northern Virginia Community College

PEARSON

Boston   New York   San Francisco
Mexico City   Montreal   Toronto   London   Madrid   Munich   Paris
Hong Kong   Singapore   Tokyo   Cape Town   Sydney

Executive Editor: Karon Bowers
Series Editor: Brian Wheel
Senior Development Editor: Carol Alper
Series Editorial Assistant: Jennifer Trebby
Marketing Manager: Mandee Eckersley
Media Production Supervisor: Matt Dorsey
Multimedia Project Manager: Tim Smith
Production Assistant-Media: Charles Morin
Composition Buyer: Linda Cox
Manufacturing Manager: Megan Cochran
Manufacturing Buyer: JoAnne Sweeney
Editorial-Production Administrator: Karen Mason
Photo Researchers: Carol Alper, Deborah Brown, Katharine S. Cook, Karen Mason
Cover Administrator: Linda Knowles

For related titles and support materials, visit our online catalog at www.ablongman.com

Between the time Website information is gathered and then published, it is not unusual for some sites to have closed. Also, the transcription of URLs can result in unintended typographical errors. The publisher would appreciate notification where these errors occur so that they may be corrected in subsequent editions.

Library of Congress Cataloging-in-Publication Data
Unavailable at Press Time

ISBN 0-205-35874-8

Printed in the United States of America
10 9 8 7 6 5 4 3 2 1   09 08 07 06 05 04

Photo Credits:
Module One: PhotoDisc/Getty Images, Corbis Royalty Free, PhotoDisc/Getty Images, Digital Vision; Module Two: PhotoDisc/Getty Images, Corbis Royalty Free, Digital Vision, PhotoDisc/Getty Images; Module Three: © Allyn & Bacon, PhotoDisc/Getty Images, Nova Development, Nova Development; Module Four: Courtesy of Bernard and Aimee Doyle; Module Five: Digital Vision, PhotoDisc/Getty Images, Photo-Disc/Getty Images, PhotoDisc/Getty Images; Module Six: Digital Vision, PhotoDisc/Getty Images, © Allyn & Bacon, Digital Vision; Module Seven: © Allyn & Bacon, PhotoDisc/Getty Images, © Allyn & Bacon, © Allyn & Bacon.

"And—beauty of beauties—

to find a soul in journey with me!"

Dedicated to John S. Rebstock

BRIEF CONTENTS

CONTENTS

2 Language and Perception   39

3 Nonverbal Communication and Listening 67

4 The Self and Relational Communities 97

5 Interpersonal Communication 127

6 Professional Communication 169

7 Public Speaking   211

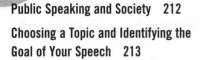

LIST OF ONLINE ACTIVITIES

If you want to make reference to content in the hard copy of your textbook as you are working online with one of the activities, use this list of online activities to locate the proper page number in your hard copy text that corresponds to the activity you are working on.

Think About This

Online Journal

Web Activity

Video View

Rapid Review

Practice Tests

Multiple Choice and True-False Questions follow the Summary of each module:

Assessing Your Skills

PREFACE

What Is *Communication Unbound*?

Communication Unbound introduces a whole new concept for the way the introduction to communication course is taught and learned. This new "unbound" product provides all the content, learning activities, and pedagogy for the basic communication course in an exciting and active format—online!

Communication Unbound is rich with interactive resources—video, web activities, study quizzes, an electronic journal, and more—to enrich and enhance learning. The modular format of *Communication Unbound* encompasses all the topics that instructors would expect to see in a traditional text and allows the instructor to choose an individualized course of instruction. To offer you as much flexibility as possible, you can choose to read the basic text content of *Communication Unbound* in its "unbound" format online or use it in conjunction with the hard copy companion version that you are reading now, and then use the additional online features to reinforce and apply concepts.

You may also be taking your introduction to communication class in one of a variety of course formats. Some schools will use *Communication Unbound* for traditional face-to-face classes that meet two or three times a week. At other schools the classes meet entirely (or nearly so) in the online environment. Web-intensive classes may use a combination of face-to-face meetings with significant online instruction. Regardless of how your course is taught, the content and format of *Communication Unbound* provides you with great flexibility.

A Unique Perspective

Communication Unbound introduces the concept of "relational community" as a common thread that ties together the three main types of relationships covered in this text: interpersonal, professional and small-group communication, and speaker-audience. While its primary focus is the application of communication principles to communities we relate to on a face-to-face basis, *Communication Unbound* also explores how we build relational communities through electronic channels of communication in a way that only this type of online text and its interactive activities can—by the direct experience of going online. Concepts are introduced and then backed up by theoretical, research-based information. You learn by applying these concepts to the practical situations illustrated in the many rich examples of communication situations: real people you can identify with, public figures, characters from contemporary and classical movies, and historical figures. At the end of major sections a series of *Implications for Communication*, summaries of the practical applications of the concepts taught, help you integrate what you have learned with your everyday communications.

As you read the online version of *Communication Unbound*, you will be invited to become an active participant. On many of the text web pages, you will see icons that take you to the *Online Journal*, *Video View* clips and activities, *Web Activities*, and

Think About This discussion items, all of which allow you to offer your thoughts and reflect on your own communication experiences. If you are reading the bound version, an icon in the margin will let you know that an online activity is available to accompany the passage. No matter how you choose to access the content, you will be part of a rich online relational community that will help you learn and apply effective communication skills.

A Unique Organization

As you will see when you begin reading *Communication Unbound*, it appears somewhat shorter than other textbooks you may have used and is organized into seven modules rather than chapters. Each module is set up to integrate several themes about communication. You may read the text in the order that the modules appear or in a different order that is more appropriate for your class.

Module One: Views of Communication   We start by defining *communication* as the process of creating meaning, and we examine three different, yet interrelated views on communication. First, you will read about the *transmission view*, which focuses on communication as a process of sharing information. Next, there is a discussion of the *symbolic view*, which emphasizes the use of verbal and nonverbal symbols and the processes of perception and listening. The third part of the module deals with the *relational view* and emphasizes the development of relational communities for interaction at various levels: intrapersonal, interpersonal, professional and small group, public speaking, and mass-mediated.

Throughout this module (as well as the others that follow) we explore *face-to-face interaction* and *computer-mediated communication*. We will emphasize the importance of face-to-face interaction as our primary channel of communication, while at the same time recognizing how different types of electronically mediated communication can be used to construct alternative and complementary channels of interaction. As you move through this course, you will also have opportunities to practice skills for communicating, whether in face-to-face interactions or online.

Module Two: Language and Perception   This module begins by identifying ourselves as members of one or more speech communities. That is a group of people who use unique verbal and nonverbal elements of language. In this module we will also emphasize the integration of verbal and nonverbal communication. However, the primary focus of Module Two is on verbal aspects of language and application of language rules. Another major focus of Module Two is perception, and we will see the interplay between using symbols and forming perceptions.

Module Three: Nonverbal Communication and Listening   The third module extends the discussion of language we began in Module Two by providing further consideration of ways that verbal and nonverbal elements are integrated. We will see that it is basically impossible to use words without nonverbal communication. This module also builds on the discussion of perception begun in Module Two with a consideration of listening skills. The particular focus on listening in this module—and throughout the book as a whole—is an exploration of listening as a process of creating meaning.

Module Four: The Self and Relational Communities   In Module Four, we will explore how we define ourselves in light of five views of self-concept. We will also see the interplay between individuals and relational communities. This will invite you to see how your relationships with friends, family, romantic partners, and even our society as a whole have had an impact on how you see yourself and how you communicate with others.

Module Five: Interpersonal Communication   The discussion of interpersonal communication in this module focuses principally on personal relationships with friends, family members, and romantic partners. The module begins with a consideration of how these contexts of interpersonal communication can be defined and proceeds to examine how relationships emerge. We will also explore ways to deal with relationship issues.

Module Six: Professional Communication   This module also focuses on interpersonal communication with special reference to the workplace and within large organizations such as a corporation. It begins with a discussion of interviewing, proceeds to examine small-group communication and leadership, and concludes with a discussion about how to plan and conduct formal group presentations.

Module Seven: Public Speaking   You will learn strategies for presenting informative and persuasive speeches here. The organization of the module is set up to provide practical guidance in creating and presenting speeches. This is a step-by-step process of choosing a topic and identifying a speaking goal, analyzing an audience, assessing the speaking situation, researching speech content, organizing and outlining a message, and relating to the audience with effective delivery.

Navigating Communication Unbound

You can easily access the content in *Communication Unbound* in a number of ways, depending on your personal preferences, learning style, and study habits.

Navigating the Content Online

You can start with Module One and complete each module in order, stopping along the way to do the particular activities your instructor assigns. When you click on an activity icon, a new window will open and tell you how to proceed. When you have finished an activity, submit your work, close the window, and you will be returned to the main text. An electronic "bread crumb" trail will help you trace your steps.

- You can go to the *Module Outline*, where you can click on the heading of your choice and go straight to that section.
- You can click on a *Learning Objective* to go to the section that covers that material.
- You can read the module straight through (in the print or online version) and then go back to the activities you plan to do by clicking on them in the navigation bar on the left of the screen. You will also find a complete listing of the online offerings in the list of features following the table of contents in the printed version.
- At the end of each activity you will be given the options to send a copy of your answers to questions raised in the activity as an e-mail to yourself, your teaching assistant, or your instructor. Check the boxes for each person you want to receive your results. If you and your recipients prefer to receive your results as an attachment, select either plain text in a MIME attachment or (for Netscape or Internet Explorer e-mail) html in a MIME attachment. If you and your recipients prefer to receive your results in the body of your e-mail message, select either plain text or (for Netscape or Internet Explorer e-mail) html. Experiment to see what works best for you.

■ We recommend that you set up a paper folder for the pages that you print and/or an electronic folder to organize your e-mail submissions by module, so that you can easily refer back to them later as you move on to other concepts or prepare for exams. Be sure to keep all your work so that you can refer back to it later in the course.

As you use and become familiar with *Communication Unbound*, and use the various assets, you will discover the path that suits you best. Click on the "Help" button if you run into problems.

Navigating the Online Activities

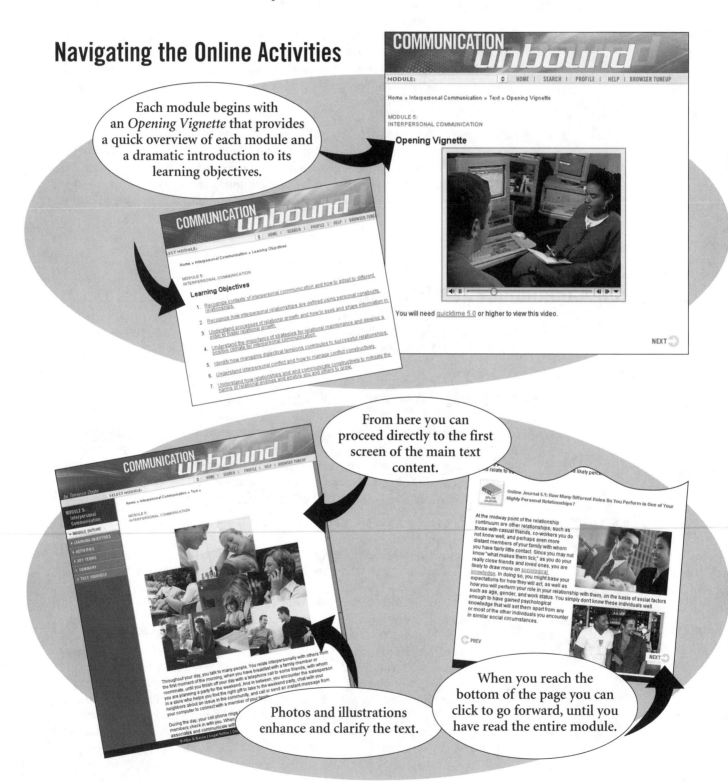

Each module begins with an *Opening Vignette* that provides a quick overview of each module and a dramatic introduction to its learning objectives.

From here you can proceed directly to the first screen of the main text content.

Photos and illustrations enhance and clarify the text.

When you reach the bottom of the page you can click to go forward, until you have read the entire module.

Clicking on the *Online Journal* icon takes you to an electronic diary that allows you to explore communication issues on your own and to make personal applications of course concepts to your life. While intended principally for the you to record private thoughts, your journal entries may become part of a portfolio to be submitted as a graded project.

As you progress through the modules, you will be asked to refer back to your *Online Journal* entries from time to time.

Home » Interpersonal Commu...
Relationships

MODULE 5:
INTERPERSONAL COMMUNICATION

Online Journal
5.2: Formality and Informality in Interpersonal Relationships

Your Online Journal should be saved to your hard drive or to disk so you may review and edit your thoughts when needed.

You need to save one file for all 7 modules. If you have not already saved module 5's online journal, you should do so now and then open in your word processor and complete this journal assignment. If you have already saved this file, open it and find this numbered activity.

Online Journal

Online Journal 5.2
Formality and Informality in Interpersonal Relationships

Think about the various kinds of interpersonal situations in which you communicate and how you develop formal and informal styles of communication with the various relationships in your life. First, fill in the name of a person with whom you relate for each category and check off the most appropriate box on the formal/informal style continuum.

Then, provide examples that illustrate how you communicate with that person in formal or informal ways.

1. A very good friend that you have known for a long time.

| Very formal | Somewhat formal | Formal or informal, depending on the situation | Somewhat informal | Very informal |
| 1 | 2 | 3 | 4 | 5 |

Describe several characteristic situations that illustrate how you interact with this person formally or informally. Elaborate on some of the rules of the relationship that govern how you communicate formally or informally by considering such things as the meanings and expectations for using verbal versus nonverbal expressions.

MODULE 5:
INTERPERSONAL COMMUNICATION

Interpersonal Communication May Be Formal or Informal

Irrespective of how personal they are, our interpersonal relationships also vary in their level of formality. Think about the casual style of communication you fall into with peers and friends, and then contrast it with the style of communication you use with an employer or teacher. Some communication situations call for using more formal types of speech acts. Recall from the discussion in Module One how Searle (1969) explains a speech act as a type of utterance that is used in a specific situation in order to accomplish a communicative goal. Interpersonal communicators follow rules as they perform speech acts. Whether we communicate formally or informally, then, will be governed by the rules that govern a particular situation and relationship. Clearly, expectations of formality do not generalize across relationships.

Online Journal 5.2: Formality and Informality in Interpersonal Relations

Susan provides an interesting example of the personal yet formal style of interaction that governed her relationship

A screen will come up that allows you to write your journal entries as a Word file and then save them directly to disk on your computer. You will be able to use your word processor for easy access when you need to work with the files again.

THINK ABOUT THIS

5.5: How are the rewards and costs of self-disclosure weighed using social exchange theory?

Social penetration theory is premised on social exchange theory. Put differently, individuals are motivated by the goals of maximizing rewards and minimizing costs.

Social exchange theory was articulated by Homans (1958). He examined how people make choices in human relationships by weighing the rewards or benefits of being in the relationship against the costs of doing so. It is somewhat like the balance sheet that an accountant studies, in which assets and liabilities are identified and considered against one another to determine equity, or final value. Using this metaphor, every relationship has certain liabilities, or costs, as well as certain assets, or rewards. When the rewards exceed the costs, there is equity in the relationship and the partners are motivated to stay in it. But when the costs exceed the rewards, the partners are likely to consider other alternatives, such as leaving the relationship entirely or initiating relationships with others.

When applying social exchange theory to self-disclosure, Altman and Taylor (1987) examined how people make judgments about sharing information about themselves on the basis of the costs and rewards of doing so. Every self-disclosure has certain costs as well as certain rewards or payoffs.

1. Think of a particular situation in which you decided to make a significant self-disclosure. In making that decision, what were some of the rewards that you perceived would come to you? Describe the situation in general terms. You need not go into specific detail about what information you shared. Instead, describe what you saw as the rewards of self-disclosing.

Most people that I know don't hesitate to announce to the world if they

When you click on a *Think About This* icon, a screen opens that poses critical thinking questions for discussions—either in a classroom or through the virtual discussions—or both, depending on the course design.

5.11: How did Laverne and Vivien adopt protective responses in

1. According to Paul and Paul (1994), conflict situations worsen when we follow the path defensive and close ourselves off from our partner. Paul and Paul identify three differe protect ourselves in this situation:

• An *indifferent* stance, in which we withdraw or passively resist our partner
• A *controlling* stance, in which we try to change the other, perhaps using tactics
• A *compliant* stance, in which we give in out of fear of rejection and disapproval

Which types of self-protective stances did Laverne and Vivien adopt in the "battle of the they said.

It looks to me like Vivien was definitely using a controlling stance. Some of Vivien's language seemed to indicate control, such as calling Laverne's wanting a new computer stupid.

Laverne seemed to be using a combination of controlling and being indifferent. So, Laverne blamed Vivien for being uptight, but then drew from the

The questions are designed to elicit a range of possible responses so that you can examine different points of view, read the perspectives of others, and recognize how and why communication experiences differ from one person or community to another.

MODULE 5:
INTERPERSONAL COMMUNICATION

Video View
5.5: Happily Ever After

Background: View the footage from the ABC Good Morning America program: "Happily Ever After: A Wedding in Times Square" (*Good Morning, America*, 2002). Assess the themes of each of the stories in light of Sternberg's (2000) perspective on love stories. For instance, Molly and Darren (the two clowns) presented a skit in which she loses her engagement ring down the drain and he is the comic plumber who comes to the rescue. Or, the image of "best buddies," is the theme as Tad and Jaime tell their story.

You will need quicktime 5.0 or higher to view this video.

1. How would you tell the story of a romantic relationship in which you've been involved using any of the themes from the couples in the "Happily Ever After" series or other themes that are unique to your situation? Briefly narrate the story and highlight its themes.

The *VideoView* icon leads you to a video clip followed by critical thinking questions. Video examples feature different types of communication situations: students presenting speeches or role-playing in interpersonal and small-group contexts, historic speeches, and segments from broadcasts on ABC News programs such as *Good Morning America, 20/20,* and *Nightline,* which deal with communication-related topics.

...super...   ...will be on CD-ROM and of
                                                    BROWSER TUNEUP

1. How would you tell the story of a romantic relationship in which you've been involved using any of the themes from the couples in the "Happily Ever After" series or other themes that are unique to your situation? Briefly narrate the story and highlight its themes.

> The Tad and Jamie story certainly resonated with me because my relationship with Pat grew out of a longtime friendship. And like their story, there was this same kind of "aha" experience when I realized that "Wait a minute, I don't feel the same way toward Pat as do all of the rest of my friends." And the something more turned out to be a mutual feeling! Here is what happened.

2. Describe the themes in the "Happily Ever After" stories or in your own. For instance, the story of Molly and Darren portrays the complementary roles of crisis (losing the ring) and heroic rescue. The story of Tad and Jaime emphasizes images of excitement. How do the themes of the stories point to expectations or attitudes about ... relationship ... and/or roles that each person performs?

The *Web Activity* icon will take you to the Internet where you can explore a variety of communication topics and issues. Many of the Web Activities can serve as a starting point for writing assignments or for group discussions.

Web Activities
5.10: Types of Interpersonal Conflict

Purpose: The goal of this activity is to recognize that there are many types of conflict and that they may be expressed in a wide range of types of communication situations aside from personal communications. At the same time, we can also appreciate how some of the principles of conflict management that we've explored in this text apply to a wide range of conflict situations, and how we can learn principles from the study of other types of conflict that apply to interpersonal communication.

Locate the Conflict Management and Conflict Skills page developed by Nan Peck.

1. Choose the links from the navigation bar for:

    *   "Conflict 101"
    *   Personal Conflict
    *   Family and Friendships

    After you have reviewed the contents of these pages and followed some of the links that are on the pages, address the following question:

    *   What attitudes and viewpoints did you learn about conflict in personal interpersonal relationships that you can apply to your own interpersonal relationships?

Conflict Management and Communication Skills

Conflict Home Page
Conflict 101
Personal Conflict
Family & Friendships
Civic Life
Professional
Intercultural
International

Peck Home Page
E-mail Nan Peck
Link to Northern VA Community College

Updated on May 1, 2002
Nan Peck, Asst. Professor
Speech Communication
Northern Virginia
Community College
Annandale, Virginia, USA

How do you manage conflicts in your personal life?

For many of us, conflict is something that we dislike and try to avoid. Our parents might have told us, "If you can't say something nice, don't say anything at all." We may have interpreted this to mean that we ought to say nothing when we're upset, frustrated, or not in agreement with someone else.

Others of us enjoy conflict and find that it is healthy and desireable. We might promote conflicts to stimulate thinking, feelings, or our nervous systems.

In meaningful relationships, conflict is inevitable, so we have reason to learn to manage it better. This website looks at conflict through a communication lens. How can we talk and listen with others so that we meet our needs, realize our goals, and promote goodwill between parties?

There are several ways to look at conflict. The categories along the left side of this page focus upon some of the relationship contexts in which we encounter conflict.

Source: Used by permission of Nan Peck, Northern Virginia Community College

MODULE 5:
INTERPERSONAL COMMUNICATION

Rapid Reviews

5.4: Relational Development and Information Exchange

Directions: For each of the following items, fill in the blank with the appropriate word.

1. Uncertainty reduction theory suggests that communicators use any of three communication strategies to learn about others: a _____ observation strategy, in which they watch how others act; an active information-gathering strategy, in which they find out information from third-party sources; and a direct interaction strategy, in which they deal directly with the person about whom they want to learn more.

2. Uncertainty reduction theory examine others in an effort to _____ an_____ uncertainty, an interpersonal commu_____ others.

3. Self-disclosure can be defined as th_____ about oneself.

MODULE 5:
INTERPERSONAL COMMUNICATION

5.2: Defining Interpersonal Relationships

Directions: Answer each of the following questions true or false.

1. We use personal constructs in order to develop our expectations of w

   ◉ True
   ○ False

2. While each individual develops personal constructs that are unique culturally shared assumptions and values about the meaning of co

   ○ True
   ◉ False

3. Data from the U.S. Census Bureau found that the proportion of ho

You can quickly check your understanding of each section by clicking on a *Rapid Review* icon to answer short questions in multiple-choice, true/false, matching, and fill-in-the-blank formats.

RAPID REVIEW

Summary: 83% Correct

83%

17%

0%

Of 6 questions, here are your results:
■ 5 correct or not graded
■ 1 incorrect
☐ 0 unanswered

Submitted on 25/Oct/2003 at 09:15:32 EST

1. Correct   We use personal constructs in order to develop our expectations of what constitutes an interpersonal relationship.
Your Answer: True

Click on the *Assessing Your Skills* icon to review the skills discussed in each module and help you to identify strengths and areas for personal growth in communication competence.

ASSESSING YOUR SKILLS

Assessing Your Skills

5.3: Understanding Processes of Relational G and Share Information in Order to Foster Growth

Assess how well you understand the processes of relational growth and ho share information in order to foster relational growth. To begin, rate each st section by checking off the appropriate box on the agree/disagree continuu

1. I recognize how telling narratives is meaningful for sharing informatio growth.

   ○ ○ ○ ○ ○
   Strongly Disagree 1 2 3 4 5 Strongly Agree

2. I am comfortable using uncertainty reduction strategies to gather infor others and to allow others to gather information about me.

   ○ ○ ○ ○ ○
   Strongly Disagree 1 2 3 4 5 Strongly Agree

3. I examine both the costs and rewards of self-disclosing information ab

   ○ ○ ○ ○ ○
   Strongly Disagree 1 2 3 4 5 Strongly Agree

4. I make appropriate choices about sharing breadth and depth of informa myself, especially in terms of the developmental phases of a relationsh

   ○ ○ ○ ○ ○
   Strongly Disagree 1 2 3 4 5 Strongly Agree

5. I recognize that self-disclosures communicate relational messages in a sharing information.

   ○ ○ ○ ○ ○
   Strongly Disagree 1 2 3 4 5 Strongly Agree

1. Answered   I am effective in the process of encoding by being competent in choosing verbal and nonverbal codes to express the content of messages I want to transmit.

   ○ ○ ○ ○ ○
   Strongly Disagree 1 2 3 4 5 Strongly Agree

Your Answer:
I think that I am able to communicate well in a great number of different types of situations, although I am certainly most comfortable and competent when I am talking with someone in an informal and one on one type of circumstance rather than in public speaking.

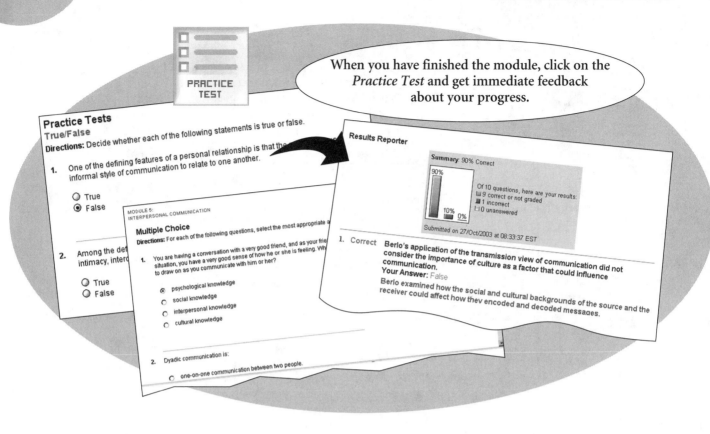

When you have finished the module, click on the *Practice Test* and get immediate feedback about your progress.

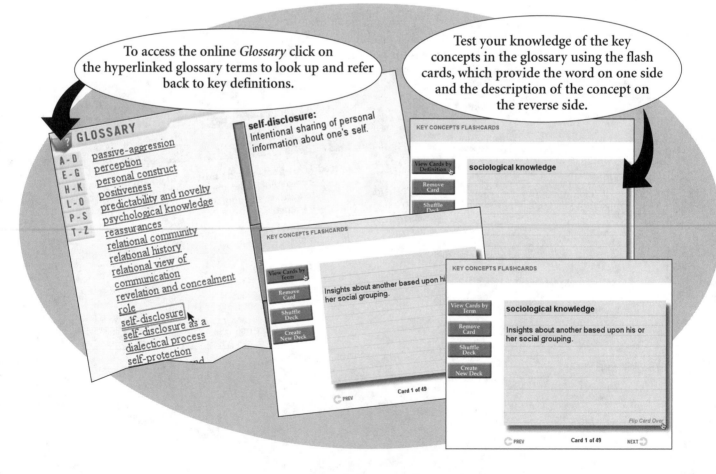

To access the online *Glossary* click on the hyperlinked glossary terms to look up and refer back to key definitions.

Test your knowledge of the key concepts in the glossary using the flash cards, which provide the word on one side and the description of the concept on the reverse side.

Getting Started: Logging On to *Communication Unbound*

Insert the CD that comes under the flap of this book into your computer's CD drive. Log onto the Internet and, when prompted, enter your individual access code that is provided with your CD. Then follow the on-screen instructions to begin.

Set up your profile so that you can e-mail your work to one or more of the following options: instructor, TA, other, or yourself, by filling out the information in "Preferences."

1. You **MUST** click on the **E-mail Results** button in the *Results Reporter* in order to send your results to your instructor.

2. Enter all e-mail addresses carefully.

3. We do not save a copy of your results. **Always e-mail a copy of your results to yourself.** If you would like to print a copy of your results, click on the Results Reporter content frame and then either click on the Print icon in your browser's tool bar or select Print from the File menu of your browser.

4. Due to the large volume of e-mail our server handles, *Communication Unbound* e-mail is batched and sent out at thirty-minute intervals. Depending on when you send your results to our server for e-mailing, it may take up to thirty minutes for your results to arrive in your instructor's e-mail. In the event that an error occurs in e-mailing the results, our server will attempt to resend the e-mail for up to three days.

Type the full name and e-mail address of all persons to whom you want to send your results. If you don't enter the correct e-mail address in this space, your results will not be delivered.

In addition, if you want to be on the mailing list for this site, click on the "mailing list" icon found on the front page of the site and fill in your name and e-mail address. There are separate lists for students and instructors. We use mailing lists to alert you to changes to *Communication Unbound*, author or guest speaker hosted iChat events, or other items directly related to your textbook. We do not use mailing lists for marketing or "spam" e-mail purposes.

Supplements

- **Instructor's Manual/Test Bank.** A complete manual for instructors offers a wealth of ideas for tailoring the unique electronic offerings of *Communication Unbound* for traditional, online, or web-intensive course formats. Included are ideas for getting the course started, suggested syllabi, lecture outlines, ideas for online and in-class assignments, discussions, role-plays, and group and individual activities. A "Module-at-a Glance" grid lists all the materials you can choose from. A selection of multiple choice, true-false, and essay questions are available for each module for testing.

- **Computerized Test Bank.** The test questions are available electronically through our computerized testing system, TestGen EQ. The fully networkable test generating software is now available in a multi-platform CD-ROM. The user-friendly interface enables instructors to view, edit, and add questions; transfer questions to tests; and print tests in a variety of fonts. Search and sort features allow instructors to locate questions quickly and arrange them in a preferred order.

Acknowledgments

I want to thank the editorial and production staff at Allyn and Bacon, especially Karon Bowers, Executive Editor; Brian Wheel, Series Editor; Mandee Eckersley, Marketing Manager; Carol Alper, Senior Development Editor; Karen Mason, Editorial-Production Administrator; Matt Dorsey, Media Production Supervisor; and Susan Freese, Copyeditor. I also appreciate the valuable feedback from reviewers and focus group participants who made comments about this book as it was being developed, including:

Leonard Assante, *Volunteer State Community College*
Doug Brenner, *Glendale Community College, Maricopa*
Tracy H. Frederick, *Southwestern College*
Renea B. Gernant, *Concordia University*
Trudy L. Hanson, *West Texas A&M University*
Carol M. Heinemann, *DeVry University*
Christine K. Holland, *University of North Florida*
Paul Lakey, *Abilene Christian University*
Judy Litterst, *Saint Cloud University*
Shirley W. Maase, *Chesapeake College*
Thomas J. Mickey, *Bridgewater State College*
Tushar Raman Oza, *Oakland University*
Nan Peck, *Northern Virginia Community College*
Jeff Ritter, *La Roche College*
Danny R. Robinette, *Eastern Kentucky University*
Ken Robol, *Halifax Community College*
Douglas Rosentrater, *Bucks County Community College*
Sarah Stout, *Kellogg Community College*
Sue Strohkirch, *Fort Hays State University*
Kristen P. Treinen, *Minnesota State University, Mankato*
David Martin Wadle, *Miami Dade Community College, Wolfson*
Alan Zaremba, *Northeastern University*

Along the way of writing this book, I also drew on the feedback from my current and former students at Northern Virginia Community College, George Mason University, and the University of Northern Iowa.

My personal appreciation is also deeply felt for many expressions of support from my primary relational communities: my friends, my family, my children Meaghan and Brendan, and especially my partner John.

I am also most appreciative of the feedback that you can offer me about *Communication Unbound* and your experiences as a student or instructor as you use it. Feel free to contact me at my college. The address is Terrence Doyle, Liberal Arts Division, CM 304, Northern Virginia Community College, 8333 Little River Turnpike, Annandale, Virginia 22003-3796, or simply send an e-mail message to tdoyle@nvcc.edu

Terrence Doyle
Northern Virginia Community College

Views of Communication

Learning Objectives

After reading the module and participating in the activities, you will be able to:

1 Understand the definition of communication as the creation of meaning, and recognize three different views of how meaning is created.

2 Understand how the transmission view of communication focuses on information exchange.

3 Understand how the symbolic view focuses on how meaning is created with symbols.

4 Understand how the relational view focuses on the creation of meaning in the context of relationships.

VIDEO VIEW

TAKE AN INVENTORY of how you communicate in a typical week. Each day, you probably relate to friends and family members, colleagues at work, and classmates at school. In this text, we will use the term **relational community** to examine how we interact in a variety of personal, social, and cultural contexts and in a range of types of **communication situations**, or circumstances. We will also see how relationships are created and sustained at various levels, including interpersonal communications, professional relationships, and small-group communications as well as in public speaking situations and as mass-mediated types of communication situations.

A relational community may include a team in a workplace or an audience of people assembled to hear a speaker. The people you meet when you go online in the virtual space of a chat room or a bulletin board discussion are further examples of relational communities. Some relational communities are quite small, whereas others can be very large.

The communities you join will also have a wide range of purposes and goals. Throughout your week, you may combine forces with other members of a group to make decisions, to work out problems, or simply to socialize.

Communication as the Creation of Meaning

LEARNING OBJECTIVE
1.1

ONLINE JOURNAL
1.1

THINK ABOUT THIS
1.1

Communication can be defined broadly as the process of creating meaning. This module introduces that definition of communication and looks at three different yet interrelated views of how meaning is created. Watzlawick, Beavin, and Jackson initially referenced these views in their book *The Pragmatics of Human Communication* (1967). As depicted in Figure 1.1, each view of the communication process has a different primary focus:

■ *Transmission view:* How information is exchanged between a source and a receiver.
■ *Symbolic view:* How meanings are symbolized. Symbols are vehicles of conception and used to achieve communicative goals.
■ *Relational view:* How a relational community provides the context for shared meaning and how communication is used to create and sustain relationships.

In this module, we will explore how each of these three views of communication offers a different perspective on how meaning is created. We will also see how each view corresponds with the other two views.

Think of exploring these different views as being similar to the way you would examine a piece of sculpture in an art gallery. As you study a statue, you are likely to walk around it. From each vantage point, you will get a different angle of vision, a different perspective of the whole. You may also move closer to the statue so that you can concentrate on the fine detail of a particular element, or you may pull back to take a more expansive view. Taking in each perspective is necessary to gain a fully rounded understanding, since no single perspective provides the view of the statue as a whole.

As an introduction to the three views of communication, consider the following communication situation and how each provides different insights and points of focus.

relational community The personal, social, or cultural context in which communicators interact with one another.

communication situations The wide range of situations and circumstances in which most of us communicate each day.

communication The process of creating meaning; involves exchanging information, using symbols, and creating and sustaining relationships.

Each view of how meaning is created has a different primary focus yet corresponds with the other two.

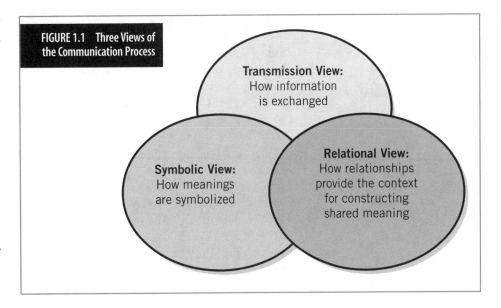

FIGURE 1.1 Three Views of the Communication Process

Transmission View: How information is exchanged

Symbolic View: How meanings are symbolized

Relational View: How relationships provide the context for constructing shared meaning

A Duck in a Noose: A Puzzle from Three Views

In October 2002, people living in and near Washington, DC, experienced a series of sniper attacks. Someone was shooting people at random as they went about their day-to-day business. During the midst of the shootings, a telephone hotline was established so that law enforcement officials could receive information from the public that might help them solve the case. At one point, news reports indicated that the alleged sniper or snipers themselves were calling the hotline. The snipers apparently used the hotline to make specific requests.

Chief Charles Moose of the Montgomery County Police Department, who headed the law enforcement effort to capture the perpetrators, appeared on television to respond to these messages that were presumed to come from the snipers. Much of what he said seemed to make little sense on its surface and was probably understandable only to the snipers—and perhaps to Moose and his associates. What do you make of Moose's statement to the snipers?

> You asked us to say, "We have caught the sniper like a duck in a noose." We understand that hearing us say this is important to you. However we want you to know how difficult it has been to understand what you want.

If we look at this example from the perspective of the *transmission view of communication,* we will see that it involves an exchange of information. The exchange was initiated with the phone calls to the hotline from someone presumed to be the sniper and to whom Moose responded. The transmission view explains how communicators (or in this case, the presumed sniper) send information as coded messages through one or more channels of communication (in this case, the telephone hotline). Moose responded by using the medium of television as a channel of communication.

As we puzzle over the meaning of the phrase "We have caught the sniper like a duck in a noose," we can also shift perspectives to apply principles from the *symbolic view of communication.* The symbolic view sorts out how communicators create meaning using verbal and nonverbal symbols, like the "duck in a noose" metaphor, along with nonverbal cues, such as Moose's tone of voice or facial expressions. Symbols are used to communicate concepts and relay intentions through spoken or written words and their accompanying nonverbal expressions. We use symbols as tools in order to make sense of our own thoughts and feelings as well as those of others.

Some commentators interpreted the "duck in a noose" metaphor as expressing the perception held by the sniper that he or she was invulnerable to being caught. Commentators probed the sniper's intent in asking Moose to repeat the riddle and wondered if what the sniper sought was an admission from Moose in his television appearance that law enforcement officials would be unable to catch him or her.

Exploring the incident from the *relational view of communication* provides us with yet another interpretation. Moose's reference to his wanting to understand the sniper could be interpreted as an attempt to open the door to further communication with him or her. Perhaps on both sides, the hotline phone calls and Moose's response to them were interactions intended to form a relationship. The sniper may have been communicating his or her desire to be understood, and Moose's response indicated a willingness to deepen lines of dialogue with the sniper. The relational view of communication examines how we form and sustain relationships. And in this situation, Moose sought a relationship in hopes of gaining other clues for solving the case.

Implication for Communication: Creating Meaning

Communication Is Complex   As the "A Duck in a Noose" scenario illustrates, communication is a complex process involving many factors. No single perspective is likely to give us a fully rounded understanding of how we communicate. Nor will we develop competence to become more effective communicators if we consider the communication process from only a one-dimensional view.

In this text, we will explore three dimensions: the transmission, symbolic, and relational views. At present, we will give primary attention to the transmission model of communication. This module will provide only a brief overview of the symbolic and the relational views, but they will be discussed more fully in later modules.

The Transmission View: How Information Is Exchanged

transmission view   A theory for describing, explaining, and evaluating how information is conveyed or exchanged between communicators.

message   Information that is organized in symbolic form or in accordance with the rules for using a system of signs; a message is comprised of content and codes.

source   The speaker or writer who originates the message; according to the transmission view of communication, the person or group who originates the message.

LEARNING OBJECTIVE
1.2

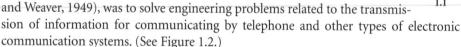
WEB ACTIVITY
1.1

Shannon and Weaver introduced the **transmission view** of communication in the late 1940s. The original goal of their work, which was developed in their Mathematical Model of Communication (Shannon and Weaver, 1949), was to solve engineering problems related to the transmission of information for communicating by telephone and other types of electronic communication systems. (See Figure 1.2.)

Since the 1940s, the notion that communication is a process of sending **messages** has been widely embraced. For instance, the view of communication as information flow is at the heart of the definition of *communication* in the *Columbia Encyclopedia* (2001), which describes communication as an act of *sending* someone a message, as though it were a process of transferring or transporting an idea from one mind to another mind.

The basic concepts of Shannon and Weaver's model have been applied to other forms of human communication beyond the telephone. Among scholars in speech communication, Berlo offers the most widely used application of the transmission view of everyday interaction, including face-to-face communication. His *The Process of Communication* (1960) analyzes the relationship between the **source**, or the person who

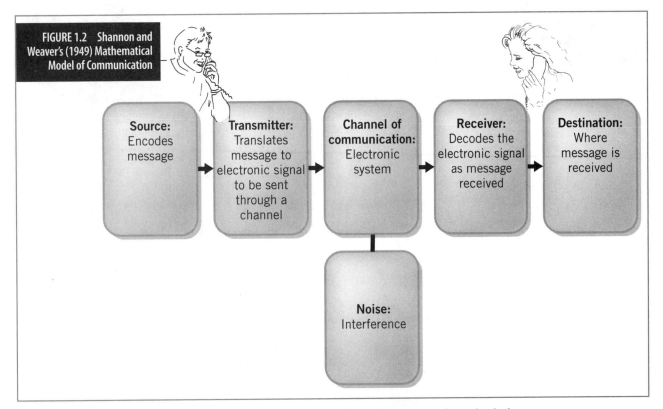

FIGURE 1.2 Shannon and Weaver's (1949) Mathematical Model of Communication

The original Shannon and Weaver model was used to analyze the flow of information through telephone systems.

originates a message or a sequence of messages, such as a speaker or a writer, and the **receiver**, or a listener or reader.

Consider from your own experience how you can have in mind an idea that you want to communicate. You also can have a sense of who should receive that message. Next, you will determine the best way to get in touch with the other person, such as making a phone call, writing a letter, or speaking face to face. You might also make decisions about how to phrase your ideas and how best to express yourself using nonverbal communication.

The model that is depicted in Figure 1.3 is based principally on the work of Berlo and others who have studied human communication. We will explore the process of information exchange by focusing on four aspects of the transmission view:

- *Sending and receiving messages:* How messages are encoded and decoded
- *Messages and channels:* How messages are composed and structured in order to be transmitted through a channel of communication
- *Feedback and feedforward:* How the communication system becomes interactive
- *Communication environment and noise:* How communication occurs in a context and how communicators overcome interference

receiver The listener or reader who interprets the message; according to the transmission view of communication, the person or group who receives the message.

Sending and Receiving Messages

Sources and Encoding As noted earlier, the *source* is the person or persons who originate a message or a sequence of messages. A speaker or writer is a source, for example. You are the source when you initiate a conversation with a friend, present a speech to

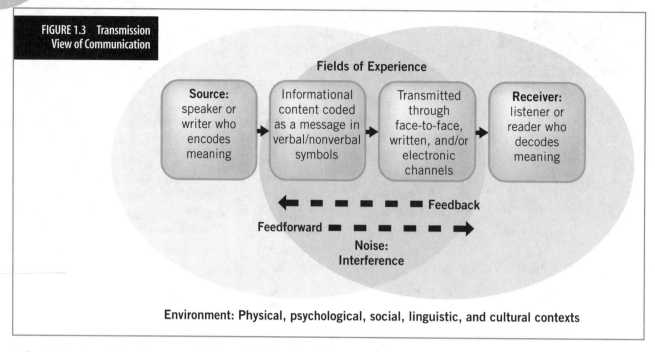

FIGURE 1.3   Transmission View of Communication

Berlo (1960) adapted the Shannon and Weaver Model to describe human interaction.

VIDEO VIEW

1.1

encode/encoding The act of creating a message by putting ideas, thoughts, and feelings into codes; according to the transmission view of communication, how the source creates the message using a symbolic form or system of signs.

codes Electronic signals that are used to transmit information through a channel of communication; verbal and nonverbal systems of symbols that are used for encoding and decoding messages.

your colleagues at work, write an essay for one of your courses, pen a friendly letter to a family member, or communicate with a classmate or instructor by way of an e-mail message. In each of these instances, you **encode** a message that can be understood by the other person. **Encoding** is the act of creating a message by putting ideas, thoughts, and feelings into codes.

Codes are transmitted through channels of communication. When Shannon and Weaver (1949) developed their version of the transmission model, they defined *codes* as electronic signals that were used to transmit information. In particular, they studied how speech spoken into a telephone is converted into electrical signals that can be transmitted along telephone lines. These researchers were not concerned with communication as a process of creating meaning.

The subsequent versions of the transmission model that we use in communication studies consider how codes are used to transmit meaning. Codes include verbal and nonverbal symbol systems that speakers and listeners use to communicate meaning. The verbal and nonverbal aspects of communication are integrated with one another for creating meaning, however.

This integrated approach has been described by a number of communication theorists. Bavelas and Chovil (2000) explain how face-to-face communication includes various visible acts of meaning, such as facial displays, hand gestures, and body movements, which are used along with verbal communications and are integral to the whole message that a communicator creates. To this list of visual acts of meaning, we might also add the vocal cues that accompany words as a speaker uses tone of voice and qualities of speech, such as rate, pitch, vocal quality, and tone. Bavelas and Chovil suggest that communicators integrate the verbal and nonverbal elements of speaking in much the same way that they grammatically combine the parts of a sentence with the rules of syntax.

As users of a language, we know how to organize the sequence and structure of words in a sentence because we have learned the rules of *syntax* for combining words to make sentences. Just as we observe the rules of *linguistic* syntax for integrating parts of a sentence, Bavelas and Chovil propose that we follow rules of *communicative* syntax when we use verbal and nonverbal elements together.

Further support for the integrated approach to verbal and nonverbal communication is found in studies by Buck and VanLear (2002). They explain how words are combined with a range of types of nonverbal communication. Sometimes, nonverbal expressions are intentional, while others are spontaneous and thus separate from purposeful communication, such as coughing to clear your throat, which typically lacks communicative intent. Displays of emotion may also be expressed spontaneously and without conscious intent, while others are staged in such a way to appear as if they were spontaneous. Even so, many instances of symbolic communication combine verbal and nonverbal elements.

Receivers and Decoding　　Next, examine how the message is received and **decoded** by the receiver who listens to a message or reads it. Successful communication occurs when the receiver decodes the message as the source encoded it. For Shannon and Weaver (1949), the test of successful decoding was to see how closely the electronic signal on the receiving end of the telephone line corresponded to the electronic signals as they were encoded at the source. As Shannon (1948) explains:

> The fundamental problem of communication is reproducing at one point either exactly or approximately a message selected at another point. Frequently the messages have meaning; that is they refer to or are correlated with certain physical or conceptual entities. These semantic aspects of communication are irrelevant to the engineering problem. The significant aspect is that the actual message is one selected from a set of possible messages.

A humorous advertising campaign conducted by a cell phone company serves as an apt example in which the message reproduced at the receiving end was not an exact reproduction or similar enough to the source's message for successful communication. In the ad, a rancher uses his cell phone to call an animal supplier to buy *two hundred oxen*. On the receiving end of the telephone, the supplier decodes the rancher's message as *two hundred dachshunds*. The misunderstanding is attributed to faulty transmission over inferior phone systems.

Yet when we switch to consider ways that meaning is communicated in verbal and nonverbal symbol systems, we redefine decoding to encompass how a receiver *interprets* the coded message. Misunderstandings can then be analyzed as problems of interpretation, and not just as engineering problems.

Field of Experience　　Shramm's (1954) concept of the **field of experience** adds another element that helps us adapt the transmission model for use in studying how meaning is created. Shramm observes that when two people interact, each person brings to that event a whole set of life experiences based on his or her personal background and culture. These experiences shape how that person perceives the world and are reflected in a range of personal points of view.

We communicate more effectively with another person when we have experiences in common. We can then encode messages based on the assumption that our receiver's field of experience aligns with ours. Successful communication, according to Shramm, is based on "building up commonness." On the other hand, we miss the mark in a dramatic way when we have little or nothing in common with the other person with whom we are communicating. For instance, this may occur when another person is speaking to us about an unfamiliar subject or uses a vocabulary that is hard to interpret. This situation can be illustrated by considering the problem of what might be called "fedspeak."

decode/decoding　According to the transmission view of communication, how the receiver receives and interprets the message sent by the source.

field of experience　The set of life experiences, based on one's personal background and culture, that he or she draws on to encode and decode messages; shapes how that person perceives the world.

1.2

Alan Greenspan, who served as the head of the U.S. Federal Reserve Board, starting with the presidential term of George H. W. Bush, and continuing into the administrations of Bill Clinton and George W. Bush, was once described as the second most important leader in the United States. This is because the head of the Federal Reserve Board is the chief spokesperson for establishing monetary policy. The words of the Federal Reserve Chair can have an enormous impact on stock markets around the world and shape the views of other economic policymakers in the United States. However, when most of us read or hear one of Greenspan's statements, we are likely to find it difficult to decode if we do not share a field of experience that includes the technical knowledge of markets and economics.

1.2

Field of Experience and Culture   A significant part of a person's field of experience is the cultural background that he or she brings to a communication situation. A *culture* is a system of knowledge and a way of looking at the world that is shared by a relatively large group of people. Aspects of that system of knowledge include shared beliefs, values, and attitudes. Since cultures develop over time, members of a culture share in the history and tradition of their culture and pass the knowledge of that culture and its way of perceiving the world to other members.

At first, we may think only of our *nationality* as defining our culture. Yet we can probably also identify a range of other ways to define our membership in a culture. For example, religion, ethnic or racial heritage, gender, sexual orientation, and social class are all meaningful ways of defining the cultural group with which we relate.

Cultural background has a huge impact on how we encode and decode messages, especially when we communicate with people from different cultures. The classic television program *I Love Lucy*, starring Lucille Ball, which first aired in the 1950s and has seemingly been in reruns ever since, featured an intercultural marriage that was the source of many conflicting yet humorous situations. While Lucy's background was middle class and reflective of mainstream culture in the United States, the character of Ricky, her husband, who was portrayed by Desi Arnaz, had the background of an immigrant from Cuba.

Viewers of *I Love Lucy* may recall an ongoing bit of comedy that was derived from this aspect of their relationship. When Ricky expressed his ideas in English, his second language, Lucy's responses would highlight the differences between his pronunciation and hers. At other times, and especially when Ricky wanted to communicate strong feelings, he would switch from English to encode his thoughts in Spanish.

1.2

In fact, the cultural and social differences between Ricky and Lucy were probably greater than language. Since each of the fictional characters on *I Love Lucy* came from a different cultural background, he or she brought to the communication situation a unique set of cultural and social attitudes.

1.3

These attitudes shape how we interpret one another. A recent report, entitled "Getting under Our Skin," which was broadcast on the ABC news program *20/20*, explored some of the ways that racial differences in the United States produce communication problems. The program examined the view of author Lena Williams (2000), who wrote the following in her book *It's the Little Things: The Everyday Interactions That Get under the Skin of Blacks and Whites:*

> An innocent gesture can be misconstrued as a calculated insult. An entire race can be maligned or stereotyped by the inconsiderate actions of one. We form impressions and judge one another based on brief encounters or on what we believe, or are led to believe, we know about the other group. (pp. 13–14)

The subtitle of the program asks the meaningful question "Are everyday gestures racially charged?" To answer this question, the producers at *20/20* commissioned a marketing firm to conduct an interracial focus group, whose members shared examples of how they interpreted gestures and verbal statements—often, in dramatically different ways and in many instances as implying racial attitudes.

As an illustration, an African American member of the focus group described irritation at seeing a white motorist lock the doors of her car as she pulled up to a stoplight near where he was standing. The action signaled to him an accusation—that she thought he would try to break into her car.

Messages and Channels

The second focus for examining the transmission view of communication is to see how messages are sent through channels. The **channel** of communication can be defined as the medium of transmission used by the communicator. Thus, the communicator not only encodes the message using communication codes, but he or she also selects the channel through which it will be transmitted.

For example, in the sniper case, previously cited, the sniper's preferred channel of communication with law enforcement officials was to make phone calls to the public hotline. In addition, the sniper left a note on a tree near one of the shootings.

Depending on the channel of communication that we employ, the symbolic code for encoding a message will vary. The most obvious effect is the ratio of verbal to nonverbal communications.

Face-to-Face Communication as Standard Bavelas, Hutchinson, Kenwood, and Matheson (1997) developed the *Integrated Message Model* to explain how face-to-face communication affords the greatest opportunity to integrate the **verbal code** with the **nonverbal code**, whereas writing and text-based electronic communications, such as e-mail messages, emphasize the verbal component over the nonverbal. These authors also note how face-to-face communication affords a greater level of immediacy between communicators and so opportunities for spontaneous interaction and collaboration.

Bavelas et al. think that face-to-face communication should be regarded as the standard for making comparisons to other types of communication systems, since it is the first mode of communication that people learn. In addition, these authors offer a three-dimensional model of communication that emphasizes the three distinctive features of face-to-face communication:

- Unrestricted verbal expression
- Substantial use of meaningful nonverbal acts
- Instantaneous collaboration between speaker and listener in ways that allow for immediate feedback and adaptation

As Figure 1.4 indicates, this model for face-to-face communication as a standard of interaction is organized as a cube.

When we use the face-to-face channel, elements such as tone of voice, facial expression, body language, and spatial proximity are used along with words. Moreover, since a channel of communication is a point of contact between a sender and a receiver, any of the human senses can be employed as part of the channel of face-to-face communication. The face-to-face channel thus opens the possibility of communicating with touch, smell, taste, and warmth along with the hearing and seeing. Indeed, we can communicate with all of our senses.

Since other forms of communication are less comprehensive than the face-to-face channel, we may need to make adjustments when we communicate using them. For instance, a writer needs to compensate for the limited

channel The medium of transmission used by the communicator; may be an electronic medium, such as the telephone; radio or television; the Internet; or face-to-face communication.

verbal code A rule-governed system of symbols codified as a spoken language that is used by members of a relational community.

nonverbal code A rule-governed system of symbols expressed behaviorally by members of a relational community; includes physical, vocal, spatial, thermal, olfactory, and tactile components.

Bavelas et al. (1997) observe how face-to-face communication maximizes the impact of verbal and nonverbal integration and allows for collaborative feedback. When a communicator uses writing or most forms of electronic communication, it is important to compensate for parts of the cube that are less prominent or absent.

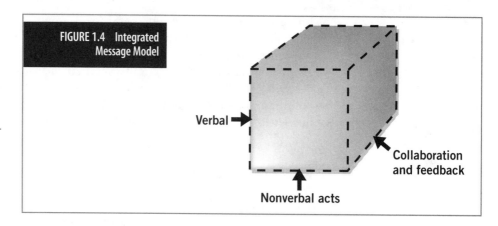

FIGURE 1.4 Integrated Message Model

Verbal

Collaboration and feedback

Nonverbal acts

range of nonverbal elements (for example, the graphical aspects of writing, such as type font, paper quality, etc.) and the lack of immediacy that characterize this form of communication. Both of these qualities clearly lessen the degree of collaboration and interaction that is possible with the receiver. According to Bavelas et al., a writer can compensate for this limitation by taking special measures to use clear language, to provide examples, and to rephrase ideas.

Feedback, Feedforward, and Interaction

Feedback and Interaction   **Feedback** is the interpretation of meaning and response that the receiver makes to the source. Watzlawick, Beavin, and Jackson (1967) explain that when communicators provide feedback in an ongoing exchange, each affects the other. Feedback may be verbal or nonverbal.

ONLINE JOURNAL

1.3

Think about the last face-to-face conversation that you had with a friend. Each of you probably used verbal and nonverbal behaviors to communicate feedback, such as making eye contact to show that you were paying attention and following what was being said, head nodding to express agreement, smiling to show appreciation, plus a variety of audible responses, as well. Even when you talk on the telephone, consider how you listen for feedback from the other person. Vocalizations like "ah-hah" and "hmmmm" generally indicate that the other person is listening. A sigh or a long silence may indicate that he or she is distracted or even annoyed. Even the lack of an overt response through silence is itself a form of feedback

Communication becomes interactive as the speaker and listener provide feedback to one another, which makes their communication a two-way flow of information, rather than a one-way process of sending messages from source to receiver. If we think of communication as only flowing in one direction as the original Shannon and Weaver (1949) model suggested, the receiver may be perceived as a passive recipient. However, when we consider feedback to be an integral part of the communication process, the receiver and the source are actively involved in communication. Both are shaping the event.

In addition to making both the source and the receiver active participants in the communication process, providing feedback gives each a measure of control over the interaction. Watzlawick, Beavin, and Jackson (1967) note that feedback can force change in the relationship between and among communicators.

An example of how listeners use feedback to change interaction is turn-taking during a conversation. Suppose you are listening to a friend. Your feedback, whether in verbal or nonverbal form—or both—can signal to your friend that you want to take your

feedback   The response that the receiver makes to the source.

turn at speaking. You may deliberately clear your throat, for instance, or take on a particular facial expression that says you want to speak. In larger groups, the feedback process for gaining the floor may be more formalized. For instance, a listener in the audience may use a raised hand to ask the person chairing the meeting to yield the floor. Such feedback provides a "red light" of sorts when it has the impact of getting another person to stop talking. At other times, a listener may display an attentive face and a head nod—feedback that says "Keep on talking." Doing so is sort of like the listener giving the speaker a "green light" to keep going.

Ekman and Friesen (1969) have introduced the concept of conversational **regulators**: types of nonverbal signals we send to one another to govern the flow of conversation, back and forth. Regulators are like traffic signals that control the flow of traffic at a busy intersection. We use regulators to indicate who has the floor in a communication situation and to indicate when we want to take our turn at speaking.

Sometimes, feedback can have the intent of silencing a speaker. For instance, when Michael Moore was awarded an Academy Award for best documentary in 2003 for his film *Bowling for Columbine,* he received a standing ovation as he strode to the platform to retrieve his Oscar. The awards ceremony was held in March, at the start of the war in Iraq waged by the United States and Britain. Although award recipients had been instructed not to make political statements during their acceptance speeches, Moore decided to use his speech to denounce the war. (His movie had focused on problems of violence in U.S. society.) The immediate feedback from the audience was a chorus of booing, and the director of the awards ceremony had the orchestra play music in an effort to drown out Moore and get him to leave the stage.

Feedforward   An effective communicator may also anticipate the type of response that a *receiver* will make. Richards (1976) has developed the concept of **feedforward** to describe how we make adjustments in advance of encoding a message. Here is how it works: As we think about what to say, we anticipate how the other person is likely to react. We may, for instance, estimate whether he or she will be receptive to what we want to say or have the background, such as a sufficient shared field of experience, to understand our meaning. At times, we may also have a hunch that a listener could take what we are saying the wrong way.

1.5

And so, in our minds, we adjust how to express ourselves so that we are most likely to be understood and to get the kind of reception that we intend. In some situations, we may also verbalize our feedforward with a kind of setup or preview of the main message. For instance, we may lead into a critical statement to someone by first saying, "I hope you take this the right way." Or when offering a hypothesis, rather than a final judgment, we might say, "This is my best guess."

Immediate and Delayed Interaction   Feedback and interaction are often immediate. During face-to-face interaction, we see the other's responses as we are talking. Feedback in those settings may also be expressed in words, as our verbalizations with one another overlap in a continuous flow of give and take. At other times, however, the feedback is delayed. The source transmits the message to the receiver but his or her feedback comes later, such as in an e-mail exchange or "phone tag" situation.

Communicating by way of the Internet has led to development of the terms *synchronous communication* and *asynchronous communication.* Sometimes, we communicate in the here and now, which is synchronous time. **Synchronous communication** occurs when the source and receiver are communicating without a significant delay between their sending and receiving of a message. When we are involved in face-to-face communication, such as a conversation with a friend or while giving a speech before an audience, we are doing synchronous communication. A live chat over the Internet is

regulators   Types of nonverbal signals that communicators send to one another to govern the flow of conversation, back and forth; enable adjustments in the pacing of interaction and taking turns as source and receiver.

feedforward   The adjustments that are made in advance of encoding a message; an approach to anticipating how a message will be received.

synchronous communication   Communication in the here and now; occurs when the source and receiver are communicating without a significant delay between their sending and receiving of a message.

also considered to be synchronous. In this case, the exchange of messages may be delayed very slightly but not significantly so.

By contrast, **asynchronous communication** occurs when a lapse of time occurs between when the sender transmits a message and when the receiver decodes it and provides feedback. For example, the letter you send to your friend that gets a response a week later is an example of asynchronous communication. When you leave a message in a business associate's voice mailbox and await his or her return phone call, your communication is asynchronous.

1.4

Some communication models also use the term **transaction** to describe the type of conversation in which we simultaneously play the roles of source and receiver. Transaction applies most directly to circumstances in which we are a speaker and a listener at the same time, especially in face-to-face communication. When people converse face to face, they may overlap one another's statements and demonstrate by way of nonverbal communication their immediate feedback. In this way, we are the receiver of feedback at the same time that we are the source who is speaking.

Feedback as Intentional or Unintentional   Feedback may also differ in terms of how deliberate or intentional it is. We have all likely thought about how we want to react to someone in a given situation. Yet at other times, perhaps even most times, we offer feedback without being consciously aware of how we are reacting. These may be spontaneous reactions that seem to "blurt out" rather than being thought out.

1.3

Communication Environment and Noise

The **environment** is the physical, psychological, social, linguistic, and cultural situation in which communication takes place.

Sometimes, we communicate in a comfortable *physical environment*. Consider how the design of a room, the style and arrangement of furniture, and even aesthetic features such as color, light, and decoration can enhance your comfort in communicating. You have probably tried to communicate in physically uncomfortable spaces, as well. It is more difficult to speak in a noisy environment, and it is harder to listen if the temperature of a room is too hot or too cold. Some environments are peaceful and calming, while others bombard our senses with numerous distractions.

1.5

The level of physical comfort and the aesthetics of a space may further influence our feelings and motivation to communicate. We may also be affected by how formally a physical space is designed. Consider how the floor plans of many homes include a formal living room and a more casual and informal family room. Public spaces will also vary dramatically in their level of formality.

Along with the concrete circumstances of physical space, we may also think of communication as occurring in social, linguistic, and cultural environments. Each of these environments has an impact on the process of communication, which we may take for granted. Yet if we have stepped outside of our day-to-day environment to interact with people who speak a different language or dialect or whose culture or social group membership differs from our own, we have most likely experienced how environments of communication can differ dramatically. Those differences require that we make adaptations in how we communicate.

Often, the failure to adapt results in an impediment to or breakdown in communication, which is labeled in the transmission model of communication as **noise**. According to Shannon and Weaver (1949) a communication system will not be completely free from noise. There is always, in their view, a ratio of successful transmission of information rel-

VIDEO VIEW

1.4

asynchronous communication Occurs when a lapse of time occurs between when the sender transmits a message and when the receiver decodes it and provides feedback.

transaction The type of conversation in which one simultaneously plays the roles of source and receiver; often characteristic of face-to-face communication.

environment The physical, psychological, social, linguistic, and cultural situation in which communication takes place.

noise According to the transmission model of communication, an impediment to or breakdown in communication.

1.5

ative to an amount of noise that interferes. Successful communication occurs when the amount of noise can be reduced. The concept of noise may include any of the following:

- Electronic noise in the channel of communication
- Physical noise in the environment
- Internal noise, such as semantic, psychological, social, or cultural factors residing in the source or receiver of communication

1.5

When Shannon and Weaver (1949) developed their version of the transmission view, they assessed noise in the channel of communication and in the electronic process of transmission itself. Remember that these researchers were concerned with the transmission of information through telephone systems. They used the term **channel capacity** to capture the concept of how much information could be transmitted through a system. Their principal concern was with **electronic noise** that interfered with the transmission of information through an electronic system. When there is a great deal of static on a phone line, as, for instance, in the example of the oxen versus dachshund illustration noted earlier, there is a problem with the signal-to-noise ratio of the transmission. The amount of noise is too great for the signal to be effectively communicated.

Just as electronic noise can affect communication, **physical noise**—that is, competing background noise, like music or loud talking—presents another external source of communication interruption. Suppose you are trying to converse with a friend at a loud party. You might try shouting to be heard over the din, before you ultimately resign yourselves to the futility of trying to speak with one another over the loud physical noise. Again, the concept of the signal-to-noise ratio explains how the greater amount of physical noise drowns out the signal.

Electronic and physical noise each represents instances of external noise. Shannon and Weaver's idea of noise has been broadened to *internal* forms of noise, as well. These forms of noise might be thought of as residing within the source or the receiver or both.

Semantic noise arises out of language differences and misunderstandings. Semantic noise interferes with communication, for example, when a non-native English speaker asks if he can "pass away" rather than "pass by."

Cultural noise arises when cultural expectations are not met in communication. For example, an older Asian immigrant accustomed to great respect for age may be unable to hear any form of disagreement from younger, Americanized family members.

1.6

Social noise occurs when people communicate differently from one another because they have been socialized into groups that operate somewhat like cultures. Thus our age, gender, social class, race, sexual orientation, ethnic identification, or religious background can affect how we communicate.

Psychological noise occurs when our feelings, attitudes, values, and beliefs interfere with communication. Some of the common types of psychological noise are manifested in our bias or prejudices. When we are overcome by overly strong feelings that keep us from being an effective speaker or listener, our abilities to communicate can be compromised.

1.4

Implications for Communication: Exchanging Information Effectively

Assess the Effectiveness of Your Communication   In most of our day-to-day encounters with people, we focus on the content of our communication: the thoughts and feelings that we are expressing and those of the people to whom we are listening. And that is certainly how it should be most of the time. Yet when we study the process of

---

channel capacity   The amount of information that can be transmitted through a given channel of communication.

electronic noise   Interference with the transmission of information through an electronic system.

physical noise   Interference with communication that comes from competing background noise, like music or loud talking.

semantic noise   Interference with communication that stems from language differences and misunderstandings.

cultural noise   Interference with communication that occurs when cultural expectations are not met in communication.

social noise   Interference with communication that occurs when people communicate differently from one another because they have been socialized into groups that operate somewhat like cultures.

psychological noise   Interference with communication that occurs when one's feelings, attitudes, values, and beliefs interfere with communication.

communication, as we are doing in this course, it is valuable to pull back from the communication process to examine it. In this way, we can deliberately focus on how we communicate in order to gain personal insight about our competence and how to improve in this area.

Throughout this course, we will explore how to develop various competencies for effective communication. As a starting point for enhancing your own effectiveness, take stock of the kinds of communication situations in which you feel you are successful.

Assess Your Skills and Abilities   Berlo (1960) suggests that a source and a receiver will be more or less successful in communicating with one another based on the knowledge and skills that each possesses. How adept they are at communicating will also be reflected by their relative comfort level in communicating in various types of situations. Surely, we have all had the experience of feeling comfortable in expressing ourselves—when the right words just came to us and we delivered them with confidence and perhaps even style. Yet at other times, we may have found it hard to come up with just the right thing to say or the right way to say it. We may have struggled for quite some time and even felt a measure of stress with our difficulty in encoding ideas.

We are not all equally comfortable in communicating in various channels of communication. Some of us may be more comfortable when communicating in face-to-face, interpersonal contexts, while others of us may prefer to express ourselves in writing, on the telephone, via the Internet, or in a more formal situation, such as participating in a meeting or giving a speech before an audience.

What are some of the circumstances in which you are most successful as a source? The National Communication Association (NCA) commissioned the Roper Organization to survey people in the United States to learn their views about communication. This study, entitled "How Americans Communicate," was conducted in the summer of 1998. A sample of 1,001 Americans was interviewed over the telephone. The NCA study found that as many as 62 percent of the respondents said that they were very comfortable communicating most of the time.

1.6

Identify which areas of day-to-day communication are most comfortable for you. One way that you can reinforce your communication competence is to affirm those areas in which you are especially strong. At the same time, you can identify areas in which you are not as strong and then set goals for improvement.

As you move through this course and examine various contexts of communication, you can also reflect on how you can carry over skills from one area to another. For instance, building confidence to communicate interpersonally in conversation can help you in a public speaking or an interview situation if you perceive that more stressful communication situation as being somewhat like a conversation.

Build Common Fields of Experience   An effective communicator also strives to discover how his or her own field of experience overlaps with that of another person. Shramm's (1954) phrase "building up commonness" bears repeating. It points to the value of being active and intentional in the way that we establish common ground with others. We can build up commonness by sharing information about ourselves and learning about others. Doing so makes us better able to understand each other more clearly.

Building up commonness also points to a kind of mindset that an effective communicator can adopt, in which he or she is aware of when and how another communicator is coming at a communication situation from a different field of experience.

Adapt to Differences in Culture and Social Background   Our ability to encode and decode the messages of others is also enhanced when we are able to communicate comfortably with people whose culture is different from ours. Many of us live in communities that are very diverse. We work with people with a wide

1.7

range of skills and backgrounds and go to school with classmates who come from around the globe.

A report from the U.S. Census Bureau indicates that the United States is becoming an increasingly diverse nation. The 2000 census found that 28.4 million people residing in the United States were born in another country (Lollack, 2001). That figure represents 10.4 percent of the total U.S. population. This finding represents an increase from the 1990 census, in which just under 20 million people, or 8.6 percent, of the people residing in the United States were found to have been born in another country.

Adapting to cultural differences also applies to recognizing racial and ethnic differences. The NCA (1998) study also found that Americans feel slightly more comfortable and effective when communicating with another person from their own racial group. Nearly three-fourths of the respondents in the study indicated that they were very comfortable communicating with someone of the same racial group. When communicating with someone from a different racial group, 65 percent of respondents felt that they communicated very comfortably across racial lines. When asked the corresponding question about the effectiveness of their communications, 62 percent of those interviewed reported that they were very effective at communicating with someone from their own group. This compared to the assessment of 52 percent who thought that their communicating with people from other racial groups was very effective.

Other variables of social background—such as gender, sexual orientation, economic background, and the like—may represent challenges when we communicate with people who differ from us. Perhaps the most useful approach to successfully adapting to these differences is to acknowledge them, rather than ignore them. Acknowledgment can lead to dialogue and exploration of how another person's or group's field of experience shapes the way they think and communicate about things. Learning about differences can lead to actually appreciating diversity, rather than seeing it as an obstacle.

Recognize How the Channel Affects the Message and Its Reception When we apply the transmission view to human communication, such as interpersonal relationships and public speaking, our primary concern is with the practical choices that communicators make from among the different channels of communication available. We will improve our chance of being successful if we consider how the channel of communication affects how a given message is encoded and decoded.

Bavelas et al. (1997) urge us to think of face-to-face dialogue as the standard for communicating because it permits the greatest use of verbal and nonverbal communications as well as the greatest immediacy for feedback and interaction. When we use other forms of communication, we need to make special adaptations to accommodate for what is lacking.

For instance, written communication and some forms of electronically mediated communication lack the full presence that comes with face-to-face, verbal involvement. Writing and some asynchronous forms of electronic communication also lack the immediacy of feedback and interaction. An effective communicator needs to compensate for these missing elements.

ASSESSING YOUR SKILLS

1.1

Adjust to Various Communication Situations Successful communicators make adjustments in how they develop messages, especially by being receptive to the *feedback* provided by others and by using *feedforward* to anticipate how a message will be received. In his development of the feedforward concept, Richards (1976) placed primary emphasis on ways that we can deliberately think about and develop conscious communication strategies to overcome possible difficulties. We will also be more effective if we can recognize various types of noise and know how to adapt our communication to avoid interference.

RAPID REVIEW

1.5

The Symbolic View of Communication: How Meanings Are Symbolized

LEARNING OBJECTIVE
1.3

The **symbolic view** of communication provides a second way of understanding how communication is a process of creating meaning. It is not a complete departure from what we have explored already in discussing the transmission view. Instead, the symbolic view offers a change of focus by centering our attention more deeply on how communicators use symbol systems to create meaning.

To understand this change of focus, in which we are moving from the transmission view to the symbolic view, think about watching a movie and how we get a different perspective when the film cuts from a wide-angle view of the scene to zoom in for a close-up of just one part. Also recall the metaphor of walking around the statue and looking at it from more than one position. Along with circling the entire statue, you can also gain understanding by looking closer at just one part of it. A visitor to the Accademia Gallery in Florence, for instance, can look at the full size of Michelangelo's David and walk its full circumference. At the same time, the visitor can manipulate the computer program for the Digital David, which zooms in on specific parts of the statue.

It is also useful to note that the symbolic view of communication is more rooted in a philosophical framework than the transmission view, which is a scientific explanation of communication. The symbolic/philosophical approach puts more emphasis on the study of communication as a humanistic field.
Philosophers of language, who created the theories that comprise the symbolic view, give more attention to how learning and using symbols are distinguishing characteristics of being human. Burke (1966) notes in his definition of *humans* that we are the "symbol-using (symbol-making, symbol mis-using) animal" (p. 16). Thus, the symbolic view emphasizes how meaning resides in the *users* who create language and its possible meanings, rather than in the messages or codes that are communicated. Along these lines, Chandler (1995) makes this observation:

> Meaning-making is not central in transmission models. It is widely assumed that meaning is contained in the "message" rather than in its interpretation. But there is no single, fixed meaning in any message. We bring varying attitudes, expectations and understandings to communicative situations. Even if the receiver sees or hears exactly the same message which the sender sent, the sense which the receiver makes of it may be quite different from the sender's intention.

Meaning-making and sender intention are central to the symbolic view. We can see this by developing two main points:

- Symbols are vehicles of conception.
- Speech acts achieve communicative goals.

Symbols as Vehicles of Conception

Symbols for Conceptualization   Langer (1942) has developed the definition of **symbols** as "vehicles for the conception of objects." As she explains:

> Symbols are not proxies for their object but vehicles for the conception of objects. To conceive of a thing or a situation is not the same thing as to "react toward it" overtly, or to be aware of its presence. In talking about things, we
> have conceptions of them, not the things themselves; and it is the conceptions, not the things, that symbols directly "mean." (p. 61)

---

symbolic view   A theory of how communication is a process of creating meaning; focuses on how communicators use symbol systems to create meaning.

symbols   Vehicles of conception; enable humans to form conceptions that are abstractions of experiences and to generalize from one situation or circumstance to another.

Symbols enable humans to form conceptions that are abstractions of experiences and to generalize from one situation or circumstance to another. We use words and nonverbal symbols to distinguish and label what we perceive, to think about those things, and to describe our experiences to others. Symbols serve as tools for communicating and creating meaning.

When we consider how symbols are vehicles of conception, rather than entities to which we merely react, we recognize that symbols do not usually elicit single behavioral responses. One symbol can have many different meanings. We can illustrate this point by considering how the family dog might learn a behavioral response to a phrase such as "Do you want to go out?" Many of us who own dogs use such a phrase to signal to Fido that it is time for his evening walk! Fido has one reaction that behaviorists call a *conditioned response*. But Fido does not think conceptually about going out. He simply makes a tail-wagging response.

Some additional reflection on the "duck in a noose" example that we considered at the start of this module will shed more light on Langer's view. When symbols are seen as tools, we free ourselves from thinking that words and nonverbal expressions refer only to concrete objects. For instance, the phrase "a duck in a noose" symbolizes an abstract image: that it is impossible to catch a duck in a noose. In other words, the sniper may have been asking Chief Moose to say, "I can't catch you."

1.11

CBS news commentators (October 24, 2002) explained at the time that the image of a duck in a noose was probably based on a Cherokee folktale entitled "The Rabbit, the Otter and Duck Hunting." In the story, a rabbit boasts to an otter that he can catch a duck by wrapping its neck in a noose made of tree bark. But the duck turns out to be craftier than the rabbit. With the noose around its neck and the rabbit holding onto the straight end of the rope, the duck flies high into the air—so high that the rabbit is forced to let go. The rabbit falls and becomes trapped in the trunk of a tree.

While the Cherokee folktale was the most commonly accepted interpretation of the expression, there were others. Tim Noah (2002), who writes a column for *Slate*, invited his readers to submit their interpretations. Upon receiving this information, Noah reported 11 alternative interpretations, each representing a different conception of the image.

Parts of a Symbol   Another way of explaining how symbols are used to form and communicate our conceptions is provided by Saussure (1916). He notes that symbols (which he actually calls *signs*) have two dimensions: a surface level and an underlying conceptual level. When we listen to another person

1.12

speak, we hear the surface form of the message, as it is communicated in the words and accompanying nonverbal expressions. But at the same time, there is a deeper, underlying form, which constitutes the speaker's conceptions. Saussure labels these two components the *signifier* and the *signified* (see Figure 1.5).

The **signifier**, which can also be referred to as the *sound image*, is perceived on the surface. It is what the listener hears and observes in its outward physical form. The second part is the **signified**, which is the *concept* to which the signifier refers.

To illustrate the relationship between the surface forms of words and nonverbal communications and their underlying meanings, consider an imaginary dialogue between Jim and Carlos, as they talk about the game of *football*—or is it *soccer* or *fútbol?* In this dialogue, suppose that Jim has lived in the United States for his whole life and speaks English as his native language, while Carlos has recently arrived in the United States from Mexico. Spanish is his native language, though he is very familiar with English, since he studied it before he came to the United States.

When Jim talks about *football,* he is conceptualizing the game as it is played in the National Football League in the United States (see Figure 1.6). But when Carlos listens to Jim, he hears something that sounds like his sound image for *fútbol,* the Spanish word

signifier What the listener hears and observes in its outward physical form; is perceived on the surface; can also be referred to as the sound image.

signified The concept to which the signifier refers.

Contemporary views of the model use it to analyze verbal or nonverbal symbols.

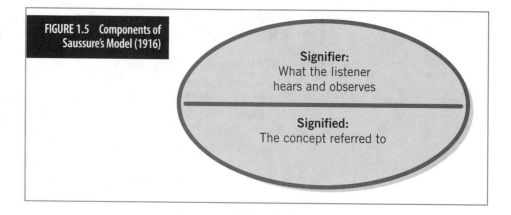

FIGURE 1.5   Components of Saussure's Model (1916)

Signifier:
What the listener hears and observes

Signified:
The concept referred to

for the game Jim's speech community calls *soccer* (see Figure 1.7). Clearly, the sound images of *football* and *fútbol* are close enough on the surface that Jim and Carlos may both think they are talking about the same thing. But will they have the same concept at the deeper level of meaning? They may not. As Carlos listens to Jim, he may think, "Jim is talking about fútbol Americano, not fútbol!"

Signifiers can be used to refer to a host of possible concepts that can be signified. You have observed that, no doubt, when you have looked at the wide range of synonyms that a dictionary lists for a particular word. Even within the same language, for instance, there are many possible conceptions for the word *chair*. We can conceive of a chair as a literal object or as a person who holds authority in a group. We can speak of the act of moderating a group meeting as *chairing* it or refer to an honorary title for a professor, such as the Boylston *Chair* of Rhetoric.

Yet few of us will have difficulty making sense out of the word when it is used. That is because as communicators, we are active sense-makers. As listeners, we participate in

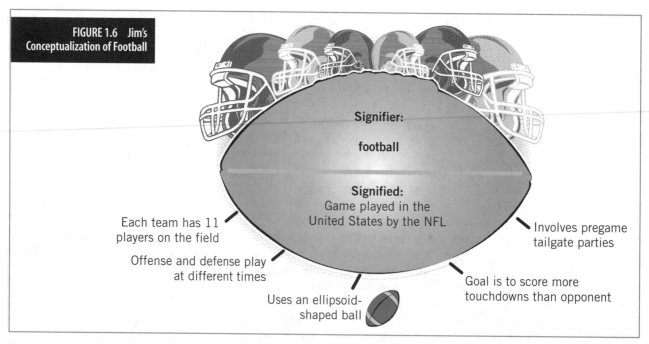

FIGURE 1.6   Jim's Conceptualization of Football

Signifier:

football

Signified:
Game played in the United States by the NFL

Each team has 11 players on the field

Offense and defense play at different times

Uses an ellipsoid-shaped ball

Involves pregame tailgate parties

Goal is to score more touchdowns than opponent

Components of a sign as Jim uses the signifier *football*.

Components of a sign as Carlos uses the signifier *fútbol*.

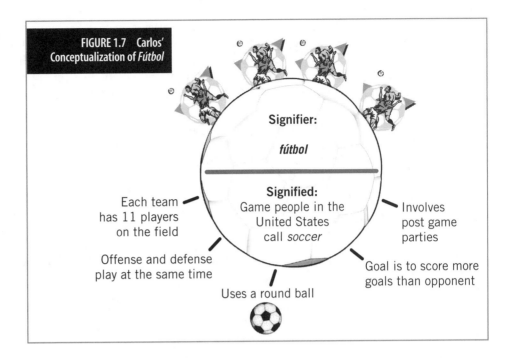

FIGURE 1.7 Carlos' Conceptualization of *Fútbol*

Signifier:

fútbol

Signified:
Game people in the
United States
call *soccer*

Each team
has 11 players
on the field

Involves
post game
parties

Offense and defense
play at the same time

Goal is to score more
goals than opponent

Uses a round ball

the process of creating the meanings that speakers intend. This concept of collaboration between speakers and listeners in creating meaning will be developed further as a part of the relational view of communication.

The Arbitrariness of Meanings   In addition to describing the signifier (or sound image) and the signified (or concept), Saussure (1916) also explains that the association between the parts of a symbol is arbitrary and thus the meanings for symbols are also arbitrary. By that, Saussure means that there is nothing inherent in a word or nonverbal expression that creates its meaning.

Apply this concept of arbitrariness to the different meanings for *football*. There is nothing inherent in the word or within the object itself that creates the connection between the two. By convention, people who speak English in the United States agree that the word *football* is used to talk about a certain kind of game as well as the ball used to play that sport. Indeed, the signifier *football* could just as well be used to signify any number of concepts, if members of a relational community would agree to call other games or experiences *football*. The agreements that we make about the meanings for symbols are *rules*.

Rules as Guidelines   Wittgenstein (1958) uses an appropriate metaphor to describe how communicators use rules when he compares communicating to playing a game, such as football or soccer. To be able to play a game, each participant has to follow the rules that define the moves, goals, and strategies of the game and that set the guidelines for how to play the game appropriately. The rules of a game also apply to the meanings of the symbols that are used for playing it.

WEB ACTIVITY
1.13

Wittgenstein uses another illustration from playing cards. The Queen of Spades is a symbol that means something different when playing the game of Hearts than when playing another game, like Contract Bridge. Each game has its own distinctive goal and rules for the kinds of actions that have to be performed to play it.

1.6

We can apply the card-playing analogy to many of our everyday language "games." The meaning of a phrase such as "You are really looking good today" will depend greatly on the context in which it is used. Between two friends, the expression would be considered a compliment, but in a workplace situation, it could be seen as an expression of sexual harassment. Saussure's (1916) principle of arbitrariness also applies here. There is nothing intrinsic to the phrase itself that makes it a compliment or an instance of unwanted sexual attention. The attributions of positive versus negative meanings are constructed by symbol users in keeping with the rules of particular communicative situations.

Sometimes, the rules for using symbols are fairly inflexible. Lawyers in a courtroom, for instance, when they present an argument or a petition are likely to need to use very precise legal language to be in accord with the rules of the Court. Yet, at other times, there is a great deal of flexibility. Perhaps, it is much like playing a game of "pickup" basketball in which the rules of play are created and negotiated by the participants rather than being the formal league rules that govern stricter ways of playing the game.

Wittgenstein (1958) teaches that we learn how to play different types of language games when we learn the rules for how to communicate in particular types of situations. His metaphor of using language as though playing a game is a foundation for *speech act theory.*

1.6

The Communicative Goals of Speech Acts

VIDEO VIEW
1.6

Searle (1969) describes how we use **speech acts** to perform actions that are intended to achieve specific goals, such as making a promise to do something and asking someone's forgiveness as part of an apology. Each performance is organized around an intention that the communicator is trying to achieve, and it includes a sentence or set of sentences and communicative behaviors that fulfill the requirements of performing a particular kind of speech act. The performance of the speech, like the way we play a game, is governed by *pragmatic rules.*

speech act An utterance communicated to perform an action that is intended to achieve a specific goal, such as making a promise to do something; organized around an intention that the communicator is trying to achieve and includes a sentence or set of sentences and communicative behaviors that fulfill the requirements of performing the act.

constitutive rules Establish what behaviors must be performed in order to accomplish an intended communicative goal; what a speech act counts as in a given circumstance.

regulative rules Govern what kind of communication behavior is appropriate or inappropriate in a given situation.

Pragmatic Rules Searle (1969) outlines two types of pragmatic rules that govern how we perform speech acts, especially in ways that enable us to achieve our communicative goals and to adhere to the norms and expectations of a specific communication situation:

WEB ACTIVITY
1.14

- **Constitutive rules** establish what a speech act means. Searle observes that constitutive rules "create and define forms of behavior" (p. 33) that must be performed in order to achieve the communicative goal of a type of speech act.
- **Regulative rules** govern what kind of communication behavior is appropriate or inappropriate in a given situation.

To illustrate how these two types of rules apply, think about a particular type of speech act, such as telling a joke. The *constitutive rules* offer guidelines that define what it means to tell a joke. So, a joke deals with subject matter that lends itself to humorous treatment. Joking is typically expressed with a tone of voice and types of physical behaviors that say "I'm being funny." And the joke teller presents the joke in a way that builds up the humor, culminating with a punch line or surprising twist. A constitutive rule for telling a joke identifies each of these elements and establishes how the speaker must perform it so that his or her utterance counts as a joke.

Along with constitutive rules, speakers also need to observe *regulative rules,* which govern when, where, and how it is appropriate to tell a joke. Certain off-color topics might satisfy a constitutive rule for telling a joke but offend listeners and thus violate a regulative rule. So, too, certain gestures may fit perfectly with a constitutive rule for telling a joke but be perceived as crude in a given situation and thus in violation of a regulative rule.

We can examine the constitutive rules for making an apology by using a hypothetical situation. Vivien and Laverne are two fictitious characters that we will refer to throughout the book. They have a rather rocky relationship, one prone to misunderstanding and miscommunication. At present, Vivien has gone a step too far in criticizing Laverne and feels obliged to make an apology. In our example, let's suppose Vivien perceives that Laverne has been hurt as a result of an argument they have had. In the course of that argument, Vivien, feeling a great deal of frustration over the impasse between them, made a blunt statement to Laverne: "You are being such an idiot!" Laverne understood this as an insult, rather than a statement of frustration on Vivien's part.

As soon as the words were out of Vivien's mouth, Laverne used that hurt facial response that Vivien can recognize from their prior communications. It is the look that Laverne often uses in response to feelings of being insulted. So, a spontaneous blurting out on Vivien's part was interpreted by Laverne to be an insult.

VIDEO VIEW

1.7

Suppose it is now the next day, and Vivien wants to make an apology. Vivien says to Laverne: "I am sorry." And from there, Vivien continues: "I didn't mean to put you down. I was feeling frustrated. I really will try to be more careful with my words, because I recognize that they can be hurtful." If you were Laverne in this communication situation, would you accept the apology?

In this example, Vivien's statement "I am sorry" and the accompanying explanation might fit some of the constitutive rules for an apology. When someone apologizes we expect him or her to do certain things such as take ownership of the behavior and offer some kind of explanation. Other specific actions that are part of the apology may include a direct request for forgiveness and perhaps promising not to repeat the offending behavior. Along with the verbal statements of the apology, Laverne might also discern whether Vivien used nonverbal communication that sounded and looked sincere.

Along with constitutive rules, a speech act is also governed by regulative rules that govern what kinds of communication behaviors are appropriate or inappropriate in a given communication situation. Searle (1969) notes, "Regulative rules take the form of or can be paraphrased as imperatives" (p. 34). One of the regulative rules in this hypothetical example involving Vivien and Laverne might be stated as follows: Each must be respectful of the other and avoid the use of verbal and nonverbal expressions that might be interpreted as communicating disrespect.

Different kinds of situations call for different rules. In one situation, we understand that using a careful and formal style of speech is appropriate, while in another, we know that it is perfectly fine to be less formal. The same symbol—whether a part of the verbal code or the nonverbal code—may be polite and appropriate in one circumstance and rude and inappropriate in another. Likewise, some topics of communication are appropriate in certain circumstances but not in others.

Many regulative rules reflect social attitudes and cultural norms. What is proper in one culture or social group may be out of bounds in another. For instance, it is often considered appropriate to use a colloquial expression such as "I'm stuffed" after you have eaten a full meal at someone's home in the United States, especially if it is an informal situation. However, in Australia, the same expression would be regarded as improper and even rude. For Australians, "I'm stuffed" is a slang expression for saying you are tired or bored.

Along with governing face-to-face communication, regulative rules apply in various channels of communication. Just as there are rules for appropriateness in spoken conversation, so, too, there are rules for writing and communicating online.

WEB ACTIVITY

1.15

Effects of Speech Acts   Austin, whose philosophy of language influenced Searle's development of speech act theory, captured the practical nature of the speech act with the title of his seminal book, *How to Do Things with Words* (1962). The emphasis should be placed on the word *do* in the title because speech acts *perform actions.* They are used to achieve ends or goals.

1.7

Austin observes that many speech acts have the effect of producing changes in how we perceive situations or define relationships. This is the case for many rituals in which we participate. In a heterosexual wedding ceremony, for instance, the presiding officer utters the phrase "I pronounce you husband and wife" after both have declared their intention to be married to the other. The words, as part of the larger ritual, produce a change in the relationship. Or consider how you have experienced the more informal situation of defining another person as a friend. Such a naming ritual is frequently done as a mutual act of defining the other. Each of these is a kind of naming ritual that involves performing speech acts.

Speech act analysis can also be used to understand public communications. For instance, the U.S. Constitution and historical practice require a formal declaration of war in order for the United States to go to war. A declaration of war might be regarded as an elaborate speech act. The constitutive rules for the speech act—which have been established by constitutional provisions, legal precedent, and historical tradition—stipulate that the president must describe a state of enmity that exists between the United States and another country and thus justifies going to war.

1.16

One of the most often cited examples of this type of speech act is the "Day of Infamy" speech that President Franklin D. Roosevelt delivered before a joint session of the U.S. Congress on December 8, 1941. Roosevelt began the speech by referring to the bombing of Pearl Harbor and other military attacks on U.S. military forces on December 7. He also faulted the Japanese government for beginning hostilities and concluded with the declaration that a state of war existed.

Regulative rules govern public speaking and public discourse, as well. The appropriateness of the content and style of what public speakers can or should say is governed by the regulative rules prescribed for a particular situation. For instance, on the floor of Congress, regulative rules discourage verbal behaviors such as name-calling and accusing fellow members of lying.

1.17

Implications for Communication: Creating Meanings with Symbols

Understand That "Meanings Are in People, Not in Words"
Learning concepts from the symbolic view of communication deepens our understanding of how messages are encoded and decoded. Moreover, it further cautions us to realize that meaning is not contained in the communication code but in the communicator who employs words and nonverbal symbols. To use a phrase from the study of *general semantics,* another theory that is part of the symbolic view, "Meanings are in people, not in words."

1.18

To become more effective communicators, we need to resist the idea that words and nonverbal expressions have inherent meanings. Moreover, we need to recognize that since others have different concepts for words and nonverbal expressions, we should adopt an attitude of flexibility about what others mean or intend when they communicate with us. Sometimes, we will need to communicate about the intended meaning of another's or our own symbols.

Watzlawick et al. (1967) describe this kind of talking about talking as **meta-communication**. They explain that meta-communication is used "when we no longer use communication to communicate but to communicate *about* communication" (p. 40). Meta-communication about symbols is used when we ask others to clarify what

meta-communication   Communicating about communication; may be used to explore the underlying assumptions, values, background, and motivations for how we communicate.

kind of association they are making between the signifier they use and the underlying concept that they mean. As speakers, we meta-communicate about our symbols when we specify how we are making an association between the signifier of our symbols and what is being signified.

1.2

Observe Rules for Using Symbols Rules establish patterns of behavior that communicators are expected to perform. We learn the rules by observing communication situations and seeing how the game of communication is being played. Doing so requires being mindful to the patterns of behavior that the rules prescribe. Competent communicators are able to discern the rules for particular kinds of speech acts as well as the contexts in which to use those speech acts for achieving communicative goals. In the second and third module of this text, we will explore further aspects of how rules govern verbal and nonverbal codes.

1.7

Rules are also observed in relationships. We turn next to how the relational view of communication explains the formation of relational communities.

The Relational View of Communication: Relational Contexts for Creating Meaning

1.4

The **relational view** of communication focuses on how relational communities are created and how they provide a context for members of a community to share meaning with one another. In this section, we will explore some of the ways that a relational community is formed. We will also define a relational community more formally shortly by developing a model.

The *relational community model (RCM)* reflects the insights of a number of communication scholars who focus on relationships as a primary way of studying how people communicate. Among the contributors is Stewart (1999), who emphasizes how **collaboration** is a key element in the relational view of communication when he defines *communication* as "processes humans use to construct meaning together" (p. 16). Communicating, in this sense, is not doing separate acts of encoding and decoding but rather a shared activity.

1.8

In expressing a similar idea about collaboration, Fisher and Adams (1994) use the metaphor of two people dancing. In this regard, communication is not the steps made by an individual but the shared movement of two or more people relating to one another. Fisher and Adams extend the metaphor of a dance by observing that each member of the relationship follows patterns, or dance steps, that he or she knows how to perform in relationship to one another.

Pearce and Cronen (1980) present a similar perspective on how meaning is collaboratively created in their *coordinated management of meaning (CMM)* model. These authors observe how meaning is coordinated as communicators understand the content of their interactions in light of the rules for performing speech acts in various types of recurring and similar episodes (or types of communication situations) that they have experienced before in their relational history. In addition, communicators make sense of one another by drawing on the personal history each brings to the relationship and cultural knowledge.

1.7

relational view A theory of communication that focuses on how relational communities are created and how they provide a context for members of a community to share meaning with one another.

collaboration The shared activity of creating meaning; a key element in the relational view of communication.

Galvin and Cooper (2003) note three principles about relational communication that are pertinent to how relationships are created and how a relational community provides the context for the collaborative construction of meaning by its members. The first principle is that "it is through talk that people define their identities and negotiate their relationships with each other" (p. 2). As applied to the evolution of a relational community, we can think of the relationship as being an outcome of communication between parties.

The second principle that Galvin and Cooper outline is that a shared communication culture provides relational partners with "a shared vision of reality, or a shared worldview, which includes unique communication patterns" (p. 2). That vision of reality is constructed by communicators when they interact with one another, and it provides the basis for their being able to make sense of one another.

And the third principle is that relationships change. According to Galvin and Cooper:

> Relationships develop a life of their own. After the early interactions, relationships reinvent themselves through the amount and type of participant involvement. Relationships experience various stages of development as they deepen and, in some cases, become less powerful or end. (p. 2)

The Relational Community Model

Figure 1.8 outlines five key elements of the relational community model:

- *Relational contexts:* We enter relationships on various levels, including intrapersonal, interpersonal, and professional and small-group communications along with public speaking and mass-mediated communications.
- *Relational rules:* Members of a relational community observe unique constitutive and regulative rules that govern their relationship.
- *Relational histories:* Members of a relational community understand relationships to develop unique relational histories.
- *Relational and content messages:* Members of a relational community define the relationship through communicating relational messages.
- *Relational roles:* Members of a relational community mutually define one another's roles in the relationship.

Relational Contexts   We create relational communities in a variety of communication contexts. Although these contexts of communication share certain

1.8

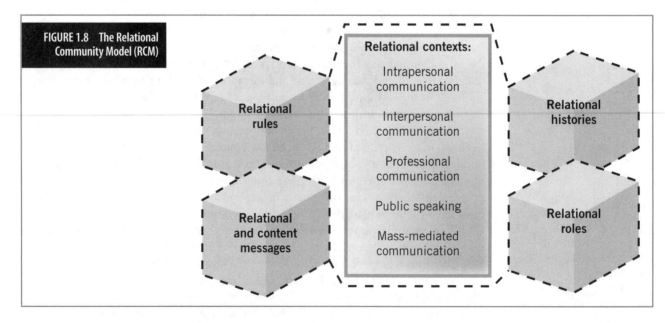

FIGURE 1.8   The Relational Community Model (RCM)

Relational rules

Relational and content messages

Relational contexts:
Intrapersonal communication
Interpersonal communication
Professional communication
Public speaking
Mass-mediated communication

Relational histories

Relational roles

Depicts the interrelationships among the five qualities that define a relational community.

characteristics, it is also useful to distinguish how each involves unique aspects of communicating and relating:

- *Intrapersonal communication:* Communication within oneself that occurs by way of interior dialogues. Thinking, feeling, observing, and forming perceptions; planning how and what to say; and reflecting on what someone else has said are everyday examples of intrapersonal communication. Through intrapersonal communication, an individual constructs an image of self and self-esteem.
- *Interpersonal communication:* Communication between people in a relationship that has been mutually defined as more or less personal, exclusive, and informal. Relationships with friends, lovers, and family members are the most common interpersonal relationships. Clubs and recreational groups that have a primary aim of social interaction are also a form of interpersonal relationship.
- *Professional communication:* Communication in the workplace that is aimed at achieving work-related goals. Interviews and working in small groups, as well as relationships within a large organization, all reflect common types of professional relationships.
- *Public speaking:* Communication between a speaker and audience that is guided by principles of rhetoric for the creation and evaluation of formal presentations. Speeches that intend to share information, to persuade, or to entertain are common examples.
- *Mass-mediated communication:* Communication with a very large and usually impersonal audience with messages that are commonly transmitted by way of an electronic channel of communication such as broadcasts on radio and television or on the Internet.

Intrapersonal Communication   You might at first resist the idea that **intrapersonal communication** has much to do with being a member of a relational community. After all, intrapersonal communication is commonly defined as "communication with oneself" (DeVito 1986, p. 171). Yet intrapersonal communication is also relational. How we assess ourselves and create a sense of personal identity does not happen apart from communicating with others in our various relational communities. How we think and feel about things is also greatly affected by our interactions with those in our relational communities.

Intrapersonal communication is also symbolic, since the interior dialogue we carry on inside our own heads can be thought of as a type of **inner speech**. The Russian linguist Vygotsky (1962) describes inner speech as a type of symbolic communication that takes place within oneself. Vygotsky observes how we use the language that we acquire from the members of our immediate community as a tool for gaining self-awareness.

Nicholl (1998) elaborates on Vygotsky's theory by explaining that "language provides the framework through which we perceive, experience, and act." We thereby create meaning by using symbols. And although we construct meaning intrapersonally, we do this using the symbols of the relational communities with which we identify ourselves.

An example of how we form perceptions and reflect on our experiences can be seen in the film *Cast Away,* which depicts the experiences of a person marooned on an island. A unique element of the dialogue of the movie is the type of inner speech of the main character, Chuck Noland (played by Tom Hanks), as he talks aloud with a symbolic character, Wilson. In fact, Wilson is a volleyball. Thus, out of his profound need for interaction and to be a part of a relational community, Noland creates a partner with whom he can talk about being on the deserted island. The volleyball, Wilson, bears a comical face that Noland has drawn with his own blood. Noland's thoughts, feelings, fears, and efforts to solve problems are the gist of his conversations with Wilson.

We also use the inner speech of intrapersonal communication to structure our experiences and to anticipate communication situations. For example, a public speaker plans a speech to an audience by thinking about what to say, and we anticipate conversations with others and may even rehearse, at least in part, what we might say.

intrapersonal communication Communication within oneself that occurs by way of interior dialogues.

inner speech The interior dialogue an individual carries on inside his or her head.

1.8

After a conversation or communication event, we also reflect on past communications. Have you ever come out of a meeting or ended a conversation doing a kind of instant replay, in which you go over in your mind what you thought just transpired? How many times have you replayed a certain dialogue with a friend? Have you thought about how a formal speech was received? In each of these occasions, you were communicating intrapersonally.

1.9

Writers, movie makers, and dramatists portray intrapersonal communication as planning and instant replay in literary form. Think about the last time you watched a television program or a movie in which the director had a character in the story think aloud. Woody Allen's classic movie *Annie Hall,* which stars Diane Keaton along with Allen, features intrapersonal communication within the midst of conversation. Allen uses the movie techniques of voiceovers, flashbacks, and a split screen to show the inner thoughts of his character, Alvy Singer, and those of Annie, played by Keaton.

Moments of intrapersonal communication have also been featured in popular television programs, such as the *Wonder Years, Malcolm in the Middle,* and *Friends.* Even Shakespeare featured intrapersonal communication in his tragedies, using the soliloquy to present a moment of meaningful self-reflection for characters such as Hamlet and Macbeth.

Intrapersonal communication may also result in a kind of self-regulating. Mead (1934) conceptualizes two dimensions of self that he calls the **I** and the **Me.** The I is the part of the self that thinks and acts, sometimes impulsively and at other times with creativity and insight. The I may also act in socially undesirable ways as a result of its impulsiveness. The Me is the part of the self that has internalized the expectations and norms of the larger societal or interpersonal relational community of which one is a member. The Me is thus the socially conscious dimension of the self that seems to conform to society and to behave in ways that are normal and appropriate. In applying Mead's constructs of I and Me to intrapersonal communication, consider the kinds of interior dialogues you have within yourself. When the I dimension of self does something that is out of line, the Me dimension provides internal feedback and correction.

As intrapersonal communicators, we also set expectations for ourselves. Merton (1948) has coined the phrase **self-fulfilling prophecy** to describe the idea that when we create an expectation for ourselves or for other people, we later communicate and otherwise act in ways that fulfill that expectation.

I   The part of the self that thinks and acts, sometimes impulsively and at other times with creativity and insight.

Me   The part of the self that has internalized the expectations and norms of the larger societal or interpersonal relational community of which one is a member.

self-fulfilling prophecy   The idea that when we create an expectation for ourselves or for other people, we later communicate and otherwise act in ways that fulfill that expectation.

interpersonal communication   Communication between people in a relationship that has been mutually defined as more or less personal, exclusive, and informal.

interpersonal relationships   Personal relationships characterized by interaction between people who share a substantial amount of information about one another that has been communicated over the course of a relatively long relational history.

1.10

Think about the last time that you created such an expectation for yourself. For instance, perhaps you had to give a speech in a class or at work, and as that day approached, you told yourself that it was going to be a dreadful experience. In making this self-fulfilling prophecy, you may have set yourself up for failure. You will likely do better by going into communicating experiences with positive expectations of success. The interior dialogue that shapes that kind of self-fulfilling prophecy involves telling yourself that you feel confident and well prepared for the presentation.

1.9

Interpersonal Communication   If you were to take an inventory of the various people you relate to on a daily basis, you would count many different relationships that involve **interpersonal communication**. Some of these are relatively one dimensional—for instance, your relationship with a family physician, with whom communication is mostly confined to discussing matters of your health. Other more significant relationships will be multidimensional. You may think of the same person, for instance, as your friend, your lover, and your spiritual mate—even a professional co-worker if you work together in the same office or in a family business.

Interpersonal relationships come into being as the parties involved mutually define the relationship itself. We thus define ourselves as friends, as lovers, or as members of a family. In a separate module of this text that deals with interpersonal relationships, we will examine in more detail how this process of mutual definition of a relationship is communicated.

We can distinguish our different interpersonal relationships by considering three aspects of interpersonal communication. These include the degree of formality we use in communicating with one another, how personal the relationship becomes, and the number of people in the relationship.

Professional Communication The third context for creating relational communities is **professional communication**, which encompasses work-related interactions such as interviewing, small-group communication, and communication within a large corporate or public sector organization. A key feature of professional communication is the pursuit of common goals that is embraced by members of the organization and its various small groups.

Many professional relationships share some of the aspects of interpersonal communication, as described in the last section. Interpersonal communication in the workplace probably varies greatly along the dimensions of how personal we are with one another and how formally we communicate. Since the work environment is organized around accomplishing work-related tasks, it is fruitful to consider how work relationships are organized in accordance with principles of **small-group communication**.

In the work environment, small-group communication is organized to achieve the goals of solving a problem or making a decision. Sometimes, the function of a group is to accomplish a specific task. Groups develop structures—such as norms for interaction, roles, and leadership—that enable members to collaborate effectively. Members of small groups also relate to one another socially.

Public Speaking **Public speaking** is the fourth level of communication. A speaker often strives to achieve the goal of sharing information or of persuading an audience. At other times, a speaker may seek to entertain or to respond to the expectations of a ceremonial occasion.

On a day-to-day level, we may need to do a formal presentation at work or attend a job-related conference that includes making a public presentation. In our personal lives, we also attend public gatherings and participate in ceremonies that mark the rites of passage of our lives. We make toasts to congratulate the happy couple at a wedding or a commitment ceremony. We mark milestones in our lives and in the lives of those around us with parties to welcome new births, to celebrate birthdays, and to honor anniversaries. We experience losses and participate in rites of grieving. Many of our occasions for public speaking involve a face-to-face channel of communication, although a speech may also be broadcast through an electronic channel of communication.

Public speaking is also relational. An effective speaker develops a rapport with his or her audience members and engages them on a relational level to participate in thinking about a subject. A ceremonial speech, for instance, can develop and reinforce a deep sense of community between the speaker and the audience and among audience members, as well.

A pertinent historical example of a speech that fostered a sense of community was President Ronald Reagan's eulogy to the crew of the space shuttle *Challenger*. On January 26, 1986, all seven members of that crew died when the rocket that was launching the shuttle into space exploded. Reagan presented two speeches at the time. First, on the day of the disaster itself, he went on television to make a speech of tribute to the crew. A few days later at a memorial service, he eulogized them, praising them as heroes and extolling their character, courage, and fortitude. Those assembled at the memorial service included family members and the extended audience of television viewers, who shared a sense of profound grief.

VIDEO
VIEW

1.9

professional communication
Communication in the workplace that is aimed at achieving work-related goals.

small-group communication
Communication among members of a group that is organized to achieve the goals of solving a problem or making a decision.

public speaking Communication between a speaker and audience that is guided by principles of rhetoric for the creation and evaluation of formal presentations.

1.11

A distinguishing characteristic of public speaking is that speakers typically present a somewhat formal talk that is addressed to an audience of many listeners. An effective public speaker also plans what he or she is going to say so that the presentation fulfills the expectations of an audience and of the type of speaking situation.

In Module Seven, we will examine some of the principles and steps for planning a speech. These principles of effective speaking are based on the field of communication studies called **rhetorical theory**. In addition to developing concepts that guide the practice of public speaking, rhetorical theory provides a philosophical and ethical foundation and methods for the critical examination of speech texts. Along with learning to speak well, our study of rhetorical concepts in Module Seven will provide not only guidelines for being an effective speaker but also for becoming an effective listener of public discourse. Doing so requires applying standards of critical thinking as an audience member.

1.10

The study of public speaking will guide you in becoming a better citizen of your community. Consider the way that public discussions and debates are held in your immediate community. At the state and national levels of government, policies are publicly formulated that deeply influence how we live our lives. Public communication is also at the heart of the U.S. judicial system. Indeed, some of the earliest fully developed textbooks, created in ancient Greek and Roman communities, were written for advocates who needed to present arguments in a court of law.

Mass-Mediated Communication   Another distinctive form of public communication is addressed to a mass audience. Traditional media have included print sources, such as magazines, newspapers, and books, as well as programs that are broadcast through electronic channels, such as radio and television. Recent developments in the mass media can be found on the Internet, where an individual can address a worldwide audience by participating in an online forum or posting a message to a bulletin board.

The common characteristic of these types of **mass-mediated communication** is the size of the audience that can be reached through the use of a technology of communication. Indeed, the audience can be the whole population of the world. McLuhan (1964), a media critic, has developed the term *global village* to capture the idea that we can be linked to people all over the world, thereby creating a relational community on a mass level.

1.12

1.19

McLuhan's work emphasizes the impact of traditional electronic media, such as radio and television. He notes that our daily access to broadcasts from distant places provides an almost instantaneous sharing of information. Communications that used to take days to be transmitted from one country to another can now be communicated instantly. In recent years, we have experienced dramatic examples of how mass communication can be instantaneous—namely, with the reports surrounding the September 11 crashes into the World Trade Center and the Pentagon and the subsequent period of grief and shock that overtook the nation. Many of the reports and images that originated in New York, in particular, were broadcast worldwide as the events were happening.

Another recent example is the coverage of the war in Iraq in 2003. As often happens at a time of war, parties on the different sides of the conflict represent points of view that reflect their own biases and perspectives—sometimes amounting to propaganda. The most recent communication developments, which integrate the Internet transmission of news with traditional mass-mediated communications such as radio and television, permit viewers around the globe to receive contemporaneous reports from different points of view. So, along with American news reports of the war in Iraq, it was possible to view reports from Great Britain and from other European countries as well as from various parts of the Middle East.

rhetorical theory   The set of concepts that guide the practice of public speaking; also provides a philosophical and ethical foundation and methods for the critical examination of speech texts.

mass-mediated communication Communication with a very large and usually impersonal audience with messages that are commonly transmitted by way of an electronic channel of communication.

The development of the Internet in the last part of the twentieth century provided still another means for members of the global village to communicate with one another. While the traditional mass media require a very expensive setup of broadcasting equipment and access to band-width frequencies that channel broadcast signals, the Internet provides a low-cost medium of communication for individuals and organizations. Consider how the web page you might place on the World Wide Web could communicate your message to anyone in the world. Similarly, you can communicate with a mass audience through online forums such as bulletin boards.

While the online forum can be a type of mass communication, when communicators interacting online do not know one another personally, some forms of **computer-mediated communication** on the Internet are also interpersonal. Markham (1998) identifies three different metaphors to describe the way people interact on the Internet. The first metaphor, which corresponds with the transmission view of communication that we discussed earlier in this module, examines computer-mediated communication as a *tool* for gathering or sharing information. If your primary use of the Internet is to do research for class projects or to read news reports online, for instance, the principal metaphor that characterizes your online experience is the tool for exchanging information. Along with this metaphor, Markham also explores the metaphor of the Internet as a *place* where people go in order to interact with others. This metaphor, she explains, is expressed when people think of computer-mediated communication as taking place in a virtual space or when people interact with one another as members of virtual communities. The language of using the Internet such as creating a *home page* or the use of spatial imagery that is communicated when Internet communicators talk about going into a *room* represents the concept of computer-mediated communication as a space. The third metaphor that Markham offers is captured in the title of her book, *Life Online* (1998). This metaphor, which she calls *being online,* suggests that people construct a sense of themselves, creating an identity and a way of being online. With the third metaphor of being online, communicators construct a reality that encompasses the online experience. The self and relationships are embodied through images and textual features that are made available through the technology.

There is also controversy about whether computer-mediated communication enhances or undermines interpersonal relationships. A study with the provocative title "Internet Isolation," conducted by Nie of the Stanford Institute for the Quantitative Study of Society and Erbring of the Free University of Berlin, examined the social implications of Internet use. Nie and Erbring (2000) found that individuals who spend more than five hours per week interacting with people on the Internet spend less time involved in other, perhaps more personal types of interpersonal communications.

WEB ACTIVITY
1.20

However, a second study conducted by Cole (2000) of the UCLA Center for Communication Policy, entitled "Surveying the Digital Future," found that communicating online may nurture interpersonal relationships, especially in friendship and family interactions. Similarly, a survey by the Pew Research Center (2002), as part of its series of studies on the Internet and American life, found that as many as 84 percent of Internet users regularly communicate with friends and family using e-mail messages and increasingly turn to the Internet as a way of discussing serious issues with the people who are close to them. The same study also found an increased use of e-mail in the workplace.

Communication researchers Flaherty, Pearce, and Rubin (1998) have also explored how an individual's motivations to communicate might relate to how and why he or she uses the Internet or face-to-face communication. Flaherty and associates discuss certain *interpersonal motives* for looking at why we relate to others and *media motives* that might be our reasons for using forms of mass communication. In terms of interpersonal motives, individuals are motivated to communicate

THINK ABOUT THIS
1.8

computer-mediated communication Communication that uses a computer as the channel through which the message is transmitted; used as a tool to transmit information, as a place for interacting with people, or for constructing a way of being online.

for many reasons: to feel a sense of inclusion and belonging in relationships, to experience affection or to assert control, to relax, to escape, or simply to feel pleasure. Flaherty et al. also discuss individuals' particular media motives, such as to achieve social interaction, to pass time or to shift time, to follow habit, to seek information, to entertain, and to meet people.

Now that we have surveyed the five types of relational contexts, we will examine the theme that relational communities are governed by rules. We will see that members of relational communities develop unique constitutive and regulative rules that govern their relationships.

1.11

ONLINE JOURNAL
1.13

Relational Rules   Just as rules govern speech acts, rules also govern relationships. *Relational rules* are used to define relationships and to establish the norms and expectations people have of one another.

Constitutive Rules   **Constitutive rules for relationships** establish patterns of communication behavior and reflect how members define the nature of their relationship. To illustrate this point, think about how you relate to one of your best friends. Constitutive rules define the nature of that relationship by establishing repeated patterns of behavior that you and your friend perform together. Suppose you have a rule in your relationship that establishes that every Saturday morning, you will play a round of tennis together. Additionally, your friendship might be defined as being very intimate through sharing personal information about one another. Another rule of your relationship might establish the expectation that each party will make meaningful self-disclosures of information to one another.

Regulative Rules   **Regulative rules for relationships** establish the boundaries of what is appropriate versus inappropriate. As noted in the discussion of speech acts, regulative rules govern our sense of being polite and needing to conform to the dictates of social etiquette. When we apply the concept of regulative rules to relationships, a similar principle is involved. Moreover, what is appropriate in one relationship may be out of bounds in another.

VIDEO VIEW
1.10

Rules and Relational Contexts   Relational rules are observed in each of the relational contexts that we outlined earlier in discussing the relational community model (RCM), not just the interpersonal context. For instance, members of a small group observe constitutive rules that define the patterns of communication that characterize the group. How many of us, for instance, have belonged to a study group whose goal was to help one another learn a subject? Work-related groups and teams are similarly governed by rules that identify the task that the group members are to perform. In a separate module of this text, we will explore how groups are structured.

Although the communication between a public speaker and his or her audience may be somewhat formal, this is a unique type of relationship. To illustrate this idea, think about the number of times during a week that you are involved in some type of public speaking situation. In a religious ceremony, for instance, you have a relationship with the person doing a sermon. At work, you relate to a person giving a briefing or conducting a meeting. At school, the teacher who is giving a lecture to a class communicates from the context of an academic relationship. And in each of these contexts, you may also have a relationship with the others in the audience. You may relate to other worshipers in the pews, to co-workers assembled around the conference table, or to the classmates seated around you in accordance with the rules that constitute and regulate each type of public speaking event.

constitutive rules for relationships
Establish patterns of communication behavior and reflect how members define the nature of their relationship.

regulative rules for relationships
Establish the boundaries of what is appropriate versus inappropriate.

In sum, relational rules govern various types of communication contexts. Along with rules, relational communities in various types of relational contexts also share unique relational histories. This is the third aspect of the RCM.

Relational Histories   A **relational history** emerges out of the recurring types of communication situations that the members of a relationship repeat as part of their pattern of interaction. Baxter and Montgomery (1996) emphasize the significance of continuity as a critical element for the evolution of a relationship and its shared understandings. Even though we interact with another person in a unique moment of time, we draw on our relational history to perceive continuity from our past. We make sense of a present moment of dialogue with another person by drawing on shared history. To explain this idea further, Baxter and Montgomery compare communication to performing improvisational styles of jazz. Musicians who play music together are able to draw upon previously used musical forms and create a spontaneous new form in the current moment.

Personal Constructs and Recurring Patterns   Whereas each communication situation is a unique moment, we also create what Kelly (1996) calls **personal constructs** to capture how a given situation seems similar to a previous one. Our constructs enable us to assign meanings to situations and to anticipate events that are part of a history of similarly constituted communication situations. Kelly explains:

1.14

> Since events never repeat themselves, else they would lose their identity, one can look forward to them only by devising some construction which permits him to perceive two of them in a similar manner.... The recurrent themes that make life seem so full of meaning are the original symphonic compositions of a man bent on finding the present in his past, and the future in his present. (p. 83)

We can make sense out of the present moment and one another by drawing on the relational history we share. Wood (1999) has defined a similar concept that she calls a *relational culture,* which is an "ongoing process through which partners create common understandings of who they are, how they operate, and what rules, values, beliefs, and so forth are appropriate in their private world" (p. 256).

In Module Five, we will return to the concept of relational history to see how interpersonal relationships emerge, especially as relational partners self-disclose information about themselves and create patterns of interaction for sustaining the growth and well-being of their relationship. And when we discuss small-group interactions in Module Six, we will also see how the members of a group share relational histories with one another.

A public speaker who shares a relational history with members of his or her audience can also draw on insights gained from prior experiences of relating to that audience to develop effective strategies for speech making. Audience members also make sense of what a speaker is saying by recalling earlier statements that he or she made.

Relational and Content Messages   The fourth component of the RCM is drawn from Watzlawick et al.'s (1967) axiom that every communication has a relational and a content dimension. These authors explain that the **content dimension** of a message is the sheer information that is exchanged. The **relational dimension** of a message communicates attitudes and feelings that each party has about the relationship along with content. Watzlawick et al. elaborate that relational messages "are about one or several of the following assertions: 'This is how I see myself.... This is how I see you.... This is how

---

relational history   The cumulative set of experiences shared by members in a relational community; develops out of the recurring types of communication situations that members repeat as part of their pattern of interaction.

personal construct   A means of assigning meaning to a situation by perceiving how it is similar to a previous situation; enables people to assign meanings to situations and to anticipate events that are part of a history of similarly constituted communication situations.

content dimension   The sheer information that is exchanged in a message.

relational dimension   Communicates attitudes and feelings that each party has about the relationship along with content.

VIDEO VIEW

1.11

I see you seeing me'" (p. 52). Burgoon and Halle (1987) isolate as many as eight different types of relational messages:

1. *Immediacy/affection messages:* Communicate a sense of involvement, attraction, warmth, interest, and enthusiasm or the lack of these qualities.

2. *Similarity/depth messages:* Seek to move the conversation to a deeper level, one at which communicators share interests, concerns, values, and backgrounds; doing so leads to greater friendliness in communication.

3. *Receptivity/trust messages:* Express sincerity, honesty, openness, and willingness to listen or the lack of these qualities.

4. *Composure messages:* Communicate relaxation and comfort, as well as personal poise and composure in an interaction, or the lack of these qualities.

5. *Formality messages:* Make interaction formal or move communication to a more casual level.

6. *Dominance messages:* Attempt to persuade, control, win favor, seek approval, or gain dominance in a conversation or the lack of these qualities.

7. *Equality messages:* Treat the other as an equal, expressing cooperation, or the lack of these qualities.

8. *Task orientation messages:* Communicate the intention to focus on a task at hand or the willingness to communicate about personal or social matters along with or instead of being task oriented.

Sometimes, relational messages are communicated quite explicitly. Lovers may declare their affection for one another, or a supervisor may assert authority over employees in a direct manner. In family interactions, a member of the family may directly state the prerogatives of his or her role. A dramatic scene in the film *Tortilla Soup,* a story about a Mexican American father and his three daughters, depicts the way that the father, Martin Naranjo (played by Hector Elizondo), is challenged by his youngest daughter, Maribel (whose role is performed by Tamara Mello). Contrary to her father's wishes, Maribel prefers not to go to college. She insists that she would rather spend time discovering herself, rather than pursuing an academic career. The scene illustrates how each party in the father/daughter relationship is asserting power. When Maribel stakes her claim to independence from her father's authority, he responds by reasserting it.

Unlike the example from *Tortilla Soup,* there are times when relational messages are not as explicitly stated. Implicit relational messages are sometimes not put into words but expressed more subtly through nonverbal communication.

Symmetrical and Complementary Relationships   Watzlawick et al. (1967) also observe that relational communication patterns reflect whether partners in a relationship see themselves as being equal or unequal. This is stated in another axiom from their model: "All communicational interchanges are either symmetrical or complementary, depending on whether they are based on equality or difference" (p. 70).

Symmetrical relationships involve a mirroring of communication behavior and reflect the sense that communicators treat one another as equals in exercising control and power. According to Watzlawick et al., partners in healthy symmetrical relationships communicate acceptance of one another and express feelings of mutuality, trust, and respect by treating one another as equals. Partners in a marriage or two co-workers might hold equal status positions, such that each has a voice in the type of shared decision making that they do. Neither would likely assert dominance over the other or be submissive to the other. In such a symmetrical relationship, there is equal give and take.

symmetrical relationship   A relationship that involves a mirroring of communication behavior and reflects the sense that communicators treat one another as equals in exercising control and power.

The second type of power arrangement is a **complementary relationship**, which is based on differences in power and control. Like the symmetrical relationship, this power dynamic evolves over a period of time, as partners establish their power roles relative to one another. Watzlawick et al. (1967) explain that there are two different positions in a complementary relationship: One individual assumes the position that is superior, or "one-up," in relation to the position held by his or her partner, and the other individual assumes the corresponding inferior, or "one-down," position.

Sometimes, positions in a complementary relationship are established by culturally defined roles or the expectations of a given relational community. Thus, the dependent relationship between parents and young children and the system of status and rank within a hierarchical organization like the military both establish a complementary pattern. That is, both parties in collaboration create a complementary pattern. As Watzlawick et al. explain:

> One partner does not impose a complementary relationship on the other, but rather each behaves in a manner which presupposes, while at the same time providing reasons for the behavior of the other: their definition of the relationship. (p. 69)

To put this matter another way, one party acts the superior role in tandem with the enactment of behaviors of submission on the part of the other. This is a pattern of behavior that is performed consistently over a period of time. Consider the metaphor of relationships as a dance in which one dancer is dominant by leading and the other follows for the duration of the ball.

1.15

Whether the relationship is symmetrical (equal) or complementary (unequal), partners in the relationship will interact with consistent and recurring patterns of communication that reflect how they relate to one another as equal or unequal parties. At the same time, healthy relationships are not completely static. Change occurs as relationships grow and partners renegotiate the definition of the relationship. Perhaps the most vivid example of this is the way that a healthy relationship between a parent and child evolves as the child grows to be less dependent on his or her parents. Complementary relationships that fail to change become rigid and may damage the members of the relationship. Watzlawick, Beavin, and Jackson illustrate this with the example of a mother and child. Mother and child complement one another in their different roles:

1.12

> After all, there can be no mother without a child. But the patterns of a mother child relationship change with time. The same pattern that is biologically and emotionally vital during an early phase of an infant's life becomes a severe handicap for his further development, if adequate change is not allowed. (p. 108)

Relational Roles   Implicit in the way that we define relationships and the relational rules that govern a relationship is the creation of a set of roles that each member of a relationship performs. This leads to consideration of the fifth part of the RCM: relational roles.

A **role** is a pattern of behavior that is performed by playing the part called for in the relationship. A way of thinking about roles is to draw on a drama metaphor, in which the characters in a play perform their parts as written by the playwright in the script. In various types of communication situations, roles are mutually defined and negotiated by the parties in the relationship. We play our roles in tandem with another person, who plays his or her corresponding role.

Roles and Relational Histories   The roles that we perform are not static. As a relationship emerges over time, its members participate in a process of ongoing negotiation

complementary relationship   A relationship that is based on differences in power and control; one partner assumes the position that is superior, or "one-up," and the other partner assumes the corresponding inferior, or "one-down," position.

role   Patterns of behavior performed by individuals in a relationship; roles are mutually defined by members of a relational community or cultural group.

1.16

and redefinition of their own roles and the roles performed by one another. For instance, Baxter and Bullis (1986) have observed from their research that points of transition, or *turning points,* mark the changes in a romantic relationship. Turning points are perceived and interpreted by the parties to the relationship. The classic comedy *When Harry Met Sally,* which stars Meg Ryan and Billy Crystal, depicts the growth of a relationship through different turning points of friendship and romance. Consider how at each turning point the fictional characters Harry and Sally assume different roles and define new identities for one another as friend or lover, antagonist or confidant.

Relationships among group members can also undergo a process of redefinition. The long-standing favorite television program *Friends* provides another illustration of turning points in a relationship among members of a group. Recall how Chandler and Monica initially knew one another as fellow members of an ensemble of friends but later became lovers and ultimately married one another. Among members of a group, the changes in relationships are oftten more complex than is the case when two partners in a couple redefine roles. In *Friends,* for example, when Chandler marries Monica, his relationship with his long-time roommate, Joey, also has to be redefined. Chandler's relationship with Ross, who is Monica's brother, is affected, as well. Hence, when Monica marries Chandler, Ross becomes Chandler's brother-in-law.

Roles in Small-Group Communication We also define our roles in work-related, small-group encounters, sometimes jockeying for position within the group. Thus, members of a group might undergo a kind of negotiation process to earn a leadership role.

Bormann (1969), who developed a model of leadership emergence in small groups that we will detail further in Module Six, notes that "the role a person takes is worked out by the individual and the group together" (p. 206). Bormann's point echoes the views of Watzlawick et al. (1967) about how symmetrical and complementary relationships are defined mutually, rather than through unilateral action on the part of a single member. Indeed, Bormann finds from his empirical studies about leadership emergence that when a contender for the leader role acts too forcefully and in a unilateral manner to seize leadership, other group members will commonly reject that person's bid for leadership.

Faithful viewers of the so-called reality television program *Survivor,* broadcast on CBS, may recall examples of this rejection. Overly aggressive members of the group ran a high risk of alienating other tribe members if their aggressive grab for leadership was not consented to by the others.

Cultural Expectations of Roles How we define our roles may also be affected by cultural expectations of the larger society. In Module Four, we will return to this theme with a consideration of how individuals construct a sense of identity by interacting with the members of their culture. As we learn our culture, we acquire a value system, a set of beliefs, ways of perceiving our status relative to others, and rules for expressing ourselves.

1.9

Implications for Communication:
Creating Meaning through Relational Contexts

Adopt an Attitude of Collaboration and Mutuality If we adopt the perspective that communication is like a dance in which each member of a relationship does his or her steps in tandem, we will see that collaboration and mutuality lead to interdependence. In various relational contexts such as interpersonal, professional, public, and mass-mediated we interact with others in ways that mutually affect one another. The rules that guide interaction and roles that we perform are mutually defined and negotiated through communication with others.

Recognize the Uniqueness of Each Relationship   Each relational community of which we are a part is unique. It is governed by its own rules, which establish expectations for its members. Successful relational communication requires that we exercise mindfulness and employ meta-communication in order to understand and fulfill the expectations of unique relational rules.

Recognize the Patterns of Communication That Constitute a Relational History   Each member of a relational community shares its unique history. Past experiences guide members of a relational community and enable them to make sense of a present communication situation in light of their relational history. At the same time, effective relationships are not static but adapt as they mature. Doing so requires a measure of flexibility and openness to dealing with new situations. Effective communicators are able to adjust to new circumstances. This may involve a renegotiation of the meaning of the relationship itself along with its rules and the roles that its members perform. In Modules Four, Five, and Six of this text, we will return to this theme of adaptation and growth, seeing how managing change is an essential competence for success in various types of relationships.

1.10

1.13

1.3

Summary

In this module, we have explored three different, yet interrelated, views of communication. The transmission view describes communication as the exchange of information between those who send and receive messages. The source encodes a message and transmits it through a channel to a receiver who decodes. The process becomes a two-way communication as the receiver provides feedback. A source also anticipates by way of feedforward. Communication occurs in an environment and noise may disrupt or interfere with the successful transmission of information.

According to the symbolic view of communication, communication is a process of constructing meaning. Communicators use verbal and nonverbal symbols as vehicles of conception. In order to communicate a conception, we establish an association between the external form of a symbol, the signifier (or sound image) of a symbol, and its underlying concept, the signified. Symbolic communication is governed by rules. Rules for using speech acts help achieve certain communicative goals.

The relational view of communication examines the collaborative process of creating relational communities that provide the context for meaning. There are five contexts of relational communication: (1) intrapersonal communication, which is self-reflective interior dialogue or inner speech; (2) interpersonal communication, which we use to mutually define ourselves and relationships and to communicate with others about whom we have different degrees of personal involvement and depths of knowledge; (3) professional communication, which we use to communicate to achieve common work-related goals; (4) public speaking, in which we enter into relationships with others as a speaker or as an audience member; and (5) mass-mediated communication, in which we communicate using various forms of media, both traditional and contemporary.

In each context, members of a relational community mutually define the nature of their relationship and develop a relational history—that is, the sum of shared experience they have with one another—in order to actively make sense of one another's meanings. In a manner similar to how symbolic communication is governed, relationships are governed by regulative rules that govern the appropriateness of communication and constitutive rules that establish patterns of communication and roles that members perform.

References

Austin, J. L. (1962). *How to do things with words.* London: Oxford University Press.

Bavelas, J. B., & Chovil, N. (2000). Visible acts of meaning: An integrated message model of language in face-to-face dialogue. *Journal of Language & Social Psychology,* 19, no. 2, 163–194.

Bavelas, J. B., Hutchinson, S., Kenwood C., & Matheson, D. H. (1997). Using face-to-face dialogue as a standard for other communication systems. *Canadian Journal of Communication,* 22. Available online: <www.wlu.ca/~wwwpress/jrls/cjc/BackIssues/22.1/bavel.html>. Accessed May 17, 2002.

Baxter, L. A., & Bullis, C. (1986). Turning points in developing romantic relationships. *Human Communication Research,*12, 469–493.

Baxter, L. A., & Montgomery, B. M. (1996). *Relating: Dialogues and dialectics.* New York: The Guilford Press.

Berlo, D. (1960). *The process of communication.* New York: Holt, Rinehart, and Winston.

Bormann, E. G. (1969). *Discussion and group methods: Theory and practice.* New York: Harper and Row.

Buck, R., & VanLear, C. A. (2002). Verbal and nonverbal communication: Distinguishing symbolic, spontaneous, and pseudo-spontaneous nonverbal behavior. *Journal of Communication,* 52, no. 3, 522–542.

Burgoon, J. K., & Halle, J. L. (1987). Validation and measurement of the fundamental themes of relational communication. *Communication Monographs,* 52, no. 1, 19–41.

Burke, K. (1966). *Language as symbolic action.* Berkeley: University of California Press.

CBS News. (2002). Coverage of sniper shooting. Broadcast October 24, 2002. Available online: <www.cbsnews.com/stories/2002/10/24/national/main526811.shtml>. Accessed June 21, 2003.

Chandler, D. (1995). *The transmission model of communication.* Available online: <www.aber.ac.uk/media/Documents/short/trans.html>. Accessed June 11, 2001.

Cole, J. (2000). *Surveying the digital future.* Available online: <ccp.ucla.edu/ucla-internet.pdf>. Accessed June 14, 2001.

Columbia Encyclopedia, 6th ed. (2001). Available online: <www.bartleby.com/65/co/communi-catn.html>. Accessed June 25, 2001.

DeVito, J. A. (1986). *The communication handbook: A dictionary.* New York: Harper and Row.

Ekman, P., & Friesen, W. V. (1969). The repertoire of nonverbal behavior: Categories, origins, usage and coding. *Semiotica,* 1, 49–98.

Fisher, B. A., & Adams, K. L. (1994). *Interpersonal communication: Pragmatics of human relationships.* New York: McGraw-Hill.

Flaherty, L. M., Pearce, K. J., & Rubin, R. B. (1998). Internet and face-to-face communication: not functional alternatives. *Communication Quarterly,* 46, 250.

Galvin, K. M., & Cooper, P. J. (2003). *Making connections: Readings in relational communication.* Los Angeles: Roxbury Press.

"Getting under Our Skin" [Television program]. *20/20.* ABC News. Broadcast June 23, 2003.

Kelly, G. A. (1996). A brief introduction to personal construct theory. In B. H. Burchett, S. A. Friedley and S. C. Looney (eds.), *Interpersonal communication: A reader* (pp. 73-101). New York: McGraw-Hill.

Langer, Susanne K. (1942). *Philosophy in a new key: A study in the symbolism of reason, rite and art.* Cambridge: Harvard University Press.

Lollack, L. (2001). Foreign-born population in the United States. *Current population reports.* Washington, DC: U.S. Census Bureau. Available online: <www.census.gov/population/www/socdemo/foreign.html>. Accessed: March 23, 2002.

McLuhan, M. (1964). *Understanding media: Extensions of man.* 2nd ed. New York: Signet Paperback.

Markham, A. N. (1998). *Life online: Researching real experience in virtual space.* Walnut Creek, CA: Alta Mira Press.

Mead, G. H. (1934). *Mind, self and society.* Chicago: University of Chicago Press.

Merton, R. K. (1948). The self-fulfilling prophecy. *Antioch Review,* 8, 193–210.

National Communication Association (NCA). (1998). How Americans communicate. Available online: www.natcom.org/research/Roper/how_americans_communicate.htm. Accessed June 20, 2003.

Newport, F. (2001). *Black-white relations in the U.S.: 2001 update.* Available online: <www.gallup.com/poll/specialreports/pollsummaries/sr010711.pdf>. Accessed June 15, 2002.

Nicholl, T. (1998). *Vygotsky.* Available online: <www.massey.ac.nz/~ALock/virtual/trishvyg.htm>. Accessed December 7, 2001.

Nie, N., & Erbring, L. *Internet and society: A preliminary report.* Available online: <www.stanford.edu/group/siqss/press_Release/preliminary_Report.pdf. Accessed June 14, 2001.

Noah, T. (October 24, 2002). What's a "duck in a noose"? Part II. *Slate.* Available online: <slate.msn.com/id/2073137/>.

Pearce, W. B. & Cronen, V. (1980). *Communication, action and meaning: The creation of social realities.* New York: Praeger.

Pew Research Center (2002). *Getting serious online: As Americans gain experience, they use the web more at work, write e-mails with more significant content, perform more online transactions, and pursue more serious activities.* Available online: <www.pewinternet.org/reports/toc.asp?Report=55. Accessed May 17, 2002.

Richards, I. A. (1976). *Complementarities: Uncollected essays.* Cambridge: Harvard University Press.

Saussure, Ferdinand de. (1916). *Course in general linguistics.* New York: Philosophical Library.

Searle, J. R. (1969). *Speech-acts: An essay in the philosophy of language.* London: Cambridge University Press.

Shannon, C. E. (1948). A mathematical theory of communication. *The Bell Systems Technical Journal,* 27, 379–423. Available online: <cm.bell-labs.com/cm/ms/what/shannonday/shannon1948.pdf> Accessed June 28, 2003.

Shannon, C. E., & Weaver, W. (1949). *The mathematical theory of communication.* Urbana: University of Illinois Press.

Shramm, W. (1954). How communication works. In W. Schramm (ed.), *The process and effects of mass communication.* Urbana: University of Illinois Press.

Stewart, J. (1999). Communicating and interpersonal communicating. In J. Stewart (ed.), *Bridges not walls* (pp. 16–44) Boston: McGraw-Hill.

U.S. Census Bureau. *Language use.* Available online: <www.census.gov/population/www/socdemo/lang_use.html>. Accessed December 7, 2001.

Vygotsky, L.V. (1962). *Thought and language.* Cambridge: MIT Press.

Watzlawick, P., Beavin, J. H., & Jackson, D. D. (1967). *The pragmatics of human communication: A study of interactional patterns, pathologies, and paradoxes.* New York: W. W. Norton.

Williams, Lena. (2000). *It's the little things: The everyday interactions that get under the skin of blacks and whites.* New York: Harcourt, Inc.

Wittgenstein, L. (1958). *The blue and brown books.* New York: Harper and Row.

Wood, J. T. (1999). *Relational communication: Continuity and change in personal relationships.* Belmont, CA: Wadsworth.

Language and Perception

Learning Objectives

After reading the module and participating in the activities, you will be able to:

1 Understand how members of a speech community use language and how verbal codes are governed by rules.

2 Understand how verbal codes are governed by phonetic rules.

3 Understand how verbal codes are governed by semantic rules.

4 Understand how verbal codes are governed by syntactic rules.

5 Examine perception as receiving information and focusing attention.

6 Examine perception as organizing and interpreting information.

UIDEO VIEW

WE ARE BORN INTO COMMUNITIES of meaning. Kenneth Burke (1966), a prominent communication theorist who has written on the subjects of literary criticism and rhetoric, observes that the capacity to use symbols is a defining characteristic of being human. We are, he observes, bodies that learn language.

Burke's definition invites us to explore a range of meanings for the word *body*. In part, it suggests the physical nature of speaking symbolically when we communicate using verbal and nonverbal forms. It may also bring to mind the concept of a *corporate body* that includes others in a **relational community** who share the same language and who learn to communicate with the symbols of their community. In addition, the reference to *body* could invite us to consider how human beings are biologically equipped to learn and use language. Communicating with symbols is inherent to the human situation.

In Module One, we explored how communication is a process of creating meaning. We observed that meaning is created through the exchange of information according to the *transmission view of communication*; that meaning is constructed with verbal and nonverbal symbols according to the *symbolic view of communication*; and that meaning is shared within the context of relational communities according to the *relational view of communication*. In this module, we will focus on the symbolic view with special reference to how speakers and listeners use language and create meaning as they form perceptions.

In Module One, we also introduced the idea that communication involves the use of verbal and nonverbal codes. Moreover, we observed that these two codes are integrated when communicators interact. Recent theorizing about language use by Bavelas and Chovil (2000) and Buck and VanLear (2002) challenge the common dichotomy used to distinguish nonverbal communication from verbal communication. Namely, Bavelas and Chovil observe how speakers and listeners integrate both types of communication as they carry on a conversation. Buck and VanLear note that if any meaningful distinction is to be made, it is to distinguish *intentional* communicative behavior from spontaneous and *unintentional* communicative behavior. The former is symbolic communication, which may include verbal and nonverbal elements that merge with one another, while the latter, spontaneous use includes nonverbal behavior, which is frequently used to express feelings. This particular aspect of the nonverbal behavioral expression of feelings will be one of the topics for Module Three.

In Module One, we also introduced Langer's (1942) definition of *symbols* as "vehicles of conception." When we define symbols in this way, we are concerned with how words and nonverbal expressions are used as tools or strategies for creating meaning. Speaking, writing, thinking, feeling, forming perceptions, reading, and listening are all examples of using symbols as vehicles of conception for creating meaning.

In this module, we will also emphasize the connection between language and perception, especially as we examine how we use words and nonverbal symbols to distinguish and label the things that we perceive, to think about things, and to talk with others about our experiences. When we describe our perceptions to others, we use symbols to share our thoughts about what we have observed.

In the first part of this module, we will explore how **language** is a rule-governed system of symbols and observe how verbal components of language are governed by linguistic rules. Linguistic rules are guidelines that govern pat-

WEB ACTIVITY

2.1

relational community The personal, social, and cultural context of human communication.

language A rule-governed system of verbal and nonverbal symbols used by members of a speech community to create meaning.

40

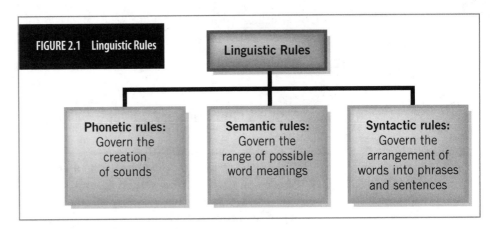

FIGURE 2.1 Linguistic Rules

Linguistic Rules

Phonetic rules: Govern the creation of sounds

Semantic rules: Govern the range of possible word meanings

Syntactic rules: Govern the arrangement of words into phrases and sentences

Linguistic rules are guidelines that govern patterns of communication in order to make them meaningful to speakers of a language.

terns of communication in order to make them meaningful to speakers of a language (see Figure 2.1). **Phonetic rules** govern the sounds we create linguistically, **semantic rules** govern the range of possible meanings for words, and **syntactic rules** govern the arrangement of words into phrases and sentences. Module Three will further explore how rules govern nonverbal aspects of language. In this module, we will also observe how we use language as members of a speech community.

Speech Communities

A **speech community** is a group of people who share a **dialect**, or a variety of a language (Gumperz, 1972). One type of speech community may be represented by the large group of people who speak your native language, such as American English or Spanish or Vietnamese. On a smaller scale, other speech communities are found in specific geographic regions within a country. These different varieties of language are referred to as *regional dialects*.

Awareness of geographic differences in language use will be greater for people who have moved from one part of the country to another or who travel from region to region. Bob, whose work caused him to move from Michigan to Washington, DC, describes how awareness of having a dialect is a matter of perception:

> Until fairly recently, I always thought that I didn't have an accent. I was born and raised in a rural part of Michigan. Growing up, I had an aunt, uncle, and cousins who lived in Alabama. Whenever I saw them, I was always amused by the way they talked. They had a heavy southern accent and pronounced "*you all*" as "*yawl*." To me, they had an accent. I didn't.
>
> However, when I moved to the DC area, occasionally someone would ask me where I was from. They would say that I had a little bit of an accent. I didn't know what they where talking about. I would tell them I'm from Michigan, and they would say, "*I thought so.*"
>
> I have also come to discover a few words that folks around here use differently than I do. The one that comes to mind right off is the word *pop*. When I first moved here, I would ask someone if they wanted a pop and they would look at me as though I were crazy. Here, everyone says *soda* or *Coke* to refer to Coke, Pepsi, etc. Back in Michigan, if

phonetic rules Guidelines that govern the creation of sounds of a language.

semantic rules Guidelines that govern the range of possible meanings for words.

syntactic rules Guidelines that govern the arrangement of words into phrases and sentences; grammatical rules.

speech community A group of people who share a given variety of a language, or dialect.

dialect A variety of a language; demonstrates systematic differences in how speech is spoken; may differ by geographic regions or correspond to differences in social or cultural groupings.

you hear someone say that they want a *soda pop*, you would look at them as though they were being uppity.

There are other words that we pronounce differently, such as *Illinois* and *New Orleans*. However, I still don't think I have an accent—at least, I don't hear it.

Speech Communities as Social Groupings

2.1

As Figure 2.2 illustrates, there are many forms of speech communities, not just geographic ones. A speech community may be determined by membership in a social or cultural group, such as a racial or ethnic group. And the dialect spoken in a speech community may be influenced by the fact that some of its members continue to speak more than one language; for example, elderly members may still use their native language from another country. Membership in a speech community can also reflect a person's level of education as well as other noticeable cultural and demographic factors. In some communities, for instance, there are differences in how people speak that are based on gender. Whether people reside in a rural area or in a city may also be a factor in determining speech community membership.

2.2

Even a circle of friends or a group of people of the same age can comprise a speech community, as long as its members observe the rules for using a distinct language variety. Baxter and Montgomery (1996) describe how people in close relationships develop their own *private message systems*. They explain:

Private message systems of relational meanings emerge in close relationships that often bear little resemblance to public language rules. A simple example is the use of endearing nicknames, which often seem anything but endearing to outsiders. (p. 158)

Along with the unique understandings for words, Baxter and Montgomery describe how people in a relational community also develop a private message system for nonverbal expressions. A certain facial expression or posture as well as a distinctive roll of the eyes, for instance, can be understood to hold specialized meaning for friends,

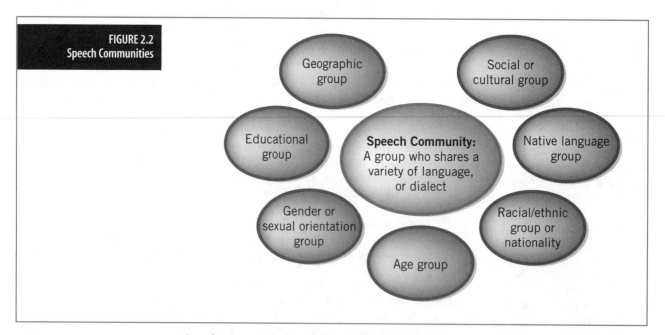

FIGURE 2.2
Speech Communities

Speech communities may be large or small and are characterized by any number of qualities.

romantic partners, family members, or a team at work—but not for outsiders. Private message systems enable members of a relational community to bond with one another, creating a shared identification with one another that separates the "us" of the relationship from others who are not as closely connected.

Think about the different speech communities that you belong to and how the members of each one speak in ways that are distinctive to that particular community. Each group likely has characteristic ways of making the sounds of certain words and perhaps even some very distinctive meanings for certain words. Membership in a speech community that has its own dialect makes the use of language fundamental to relationships. As Gergen (1999) explains:

2.1

> Language and all other forms of representation gain their meaning from the ways in which they are used in relationships. What we take to be true about the world or self, is not thus a product of the individual mind. The individual mind (thought, experience) does not thus originate meaning, create language, or discover the nature of the world. Meanings are born of co-ordinations among persons—agreements, negotiation, affirmations. (p. 48)

RAPID
REVIEW
2.1

Implications for Communication: Understanding the Role of Dialects and Speech Communication

Recognize and Respect Language Differences   Everyone speaks a dialect of some kind, and many people switch back and forth from one dialect to another, as we will see shortly. An effective communicator appreciates how his or her own dialect, as well as the dialects that others speak, reflects membership in a speech community. Yet many of us have the tendency that Bob described—to perceive others as being different—and miss the fact that we speak a dialect, too. Language diversity is a fact of life for many of us. Listen to your classmates or your co-workers; you are likely to hear a wide range of different dialects.

Learn to Use Language by Listening   As we learn to use language, we become more competent at listening well. At times, doing so may require deliberate effort at tuning into sounds that are not used in our own speech community. We can also learn to listen to the speech of others by understanding the differences between one dialect and another.

Phonetic Rules: The Sounds of Language

LEARNING
OBJECTIVE
2.2

Members of a speech community draw on their knowledge of the sounds of their language to acquire the *phonetic rules* for producing and interpreting sounds as meaningful speech.

Phonemes as Distinct Sounds of a Language

> **phonemes**   The particular sounds that make up a language; the sounds produced in accordance with the phonetic rules that describe the distinctive features of a language.
>
> **articulation**   The production of the distinctive sounds of a language.

ONLINE
JOURNAL
2.3

The particular sounds that make up a language are **phonemes**. Each phoneme of a language can be described with what linguists identify as the distinctive features for **articulation** of a certain sound. We articulate each sound at a specific point in our mouths. In addition, the articulation of some sounds includes a distinctive feature such as vibrating our vocal folds while others do not. For instance, we make some sounds (such as the sound of /v/ in *vocal*) by vibrating our vocal folds, whereas for others (say, the /f/ in *fold*), we do not make such a vibration. When the vocal folds are vibrated, a phoneme is described as a *voiced* sound; if the vocal folds are not vibrated, it is an *unvoiced* sound. Determining whether sounds are voiced or unvoiced is just one of the ways that linguists distinguish *consonants.* There are other distinctions among sounds as well that can be used to identify how each phoneme is articulated. You could study those in more depth in a linguistics course, however.

Some linguists also study the acoustical properties of spoken sound. They apply concepts from physics to measure the properties of each sound and the shape of sound waves that are formed. The particular frequency and duration of each phoneme can be described and measured in terms of its particular acoustic dimensions that correspond with how the sound is produced in the process of its articulation.

Vowel sounds can be distinguished, in part, by the size and shape of the speaker's mouth opening as well as by the location in the mouth where they are made. That is to say, some vowels are produced higher or lower in the mouth and others are toward the front, the back, or the middle of one's mouth. Again, these systematic differences in how sounds are produced reveal the distinctive features of each vowel in accordance with the phonetic rules for the sound.

Hearing Phonemes   Early in life, we learn to recognize the distinctive set of sounds that the people in our environment use for meaningful communication. We tune in certain sounds and tune out others. We recognize a certain set of sounds as components of our native language, such as English or French. We also learn to recognize how patterns of sounds are formed to create words, phrases, and sentences. We may hear other vocal sounds, such as someone coughing, but we differentiate them as being something other than meaningful language.

Phonetic Filter Hypothesis   Dupoux and his associates (1997) explain this ability to identify meaningful speech sounds with the **phonetic filter hypothesis**. According to this hypothesis, when we apply such a filter, we are more likely to hear and recognize the sounds of our native tongue. Not only that, but we may also distort or even add sounds that are not articulated so that what we hear conforms to the patterns of our native language. By nine months of age, children learn to tune into the particular sounds of their native language.

You may be able to relate to this idea of selectively perceiving sounds as meaningful if you have ever tried to learn a new language or even pronounced words from another language that have been introduced into your own language. In those situations, you likely imposed sounds of your own language in pronouncing the new words. Simply ask a native French speaker to say the word *champagne*, and you will be able to discern how English speakers have imposed the phonetic rules of English onto that French word.

How you make meaningful speech sounds is related to the sounds that you hear. When you have internalized the phonetic rules for your language, you recognize which acoustic properties of those sounds are meaningful and which are not.

As an illustration of this, consider how speakers of *tonal languages*, such as Chinese and Vietnamese, are able to make fine distinctions between sounds based on subtle changes in the speaker's tone of voice. Even a slight change in tone may indicate an altogether different word. Linh Anh, whose native tongue is Vietnamese, explains it this way:

The Vietnamese language has six different tones of voice. For example in my dialect of Vietnamese, we say *má* for the word *mother* with a rising tone. If the tone goes down in

phonetic filter hypothesis Suggests that we recognize the phonemes that are part of our primary language and filter out or distort sounds that are not part of that language.

saying *mà*, that is the word *but*. The tone goes up and down slowly when you want to say *mā* to mean a *tomb*. But if you make the up and down tone fast as with the word mä, it is describing a *horse*. In my dialect from the south of Vietnam, we say *mả* with the sound in the back of our throat to talk about *young rice plants*, but people in the central part of Vietnam use that tone for *mother*. When you just say ma without a change in tone, you are saying *ghost*.

Pronunciation and Dialects

Pronunciation   The number of phonemes in a language is fairly small. For instance, most speakers of English in the United States use between 40 and 42 distinct sounds. Yet, the ways in which people pronounce them can vary considerably. **Pronunciation** is how individuals actually make sounds and say words as they speak. In everyday use, our pronunciation is one of the elements of the dialect we speak.

When we pronounce words, we combine the various phonemes from our language. Of course, not every phoneme is completely sounded out. It is commonplace, for example, for speakers to drop or de-emphasize some sounds. We hear this especially when we are speaking informally such as when most of us drop the /g/ sound at the end of a word that ends in /ing/. So, we would say I am *goin'* rather than I am *going*. Even in formal speech, we are likely to place less emphasis on certain sounds in a word when they are located in a syllable of a word that is not accented.

We might also think of pronunciation as the range of recognizable ways that phonemes can be articulated. For instance, the vowel sound in the words *dog* and *how* is the same phoneme even though it is pronounced in different ways by people from different geographic areas of the United States who speak different dialects. Differences from one dialect of the same language can usually be understood so long as they fall within a range of acceptable ways of pronouncing the sound. Thus, when you communicate with an English speaker from a speech community that is different from yours, you will probably understand him or her.

The recent film *Bend It Like Beckham* illustrates an interesting mix of dialects of English and the variations in how people pronounce English words. The film, set in London, tells the story of Jesminder Bjamra, a teenager who is simply called Jess by her friends (or *mates*, to use the British colloquial term) and fellow soccer (or *football*) teammates. Jess's family lives in a middle-class neighborhood in London. Their native country is India, and thus Jess's parents and older members of the Indian community with whom they associate speak English with a more pronounced Indian accent than do younger members of the community. Jess and her sister carry only a slight trace of an Indian accent because they have lived most of their lives in London. We also see interactions among Jess, her sister, and their extended network of friends—some of Indian origin and some not—as they speak the British slang that's appropriate to their age group. Added to the mix is the character of Joe, Jess's coach, whose dialect reflects the fact that he comes from Ireland. All of the characters in the story speak English and can understand what one another are saying by accommodating to the pronunciation differences of their dialects.

Legacy of Dialects   Dialects are surprisingly durable. For instance, a person who drops the final /r/ from words may do so for a lifetime, even after relocating to another region of the country where the /r/ is pronounced. Similarly, a person who learned a dialect of English in a specific part of Great Britain— say, the Cockney dialect in urban London—or in any of the countries that once comprised the British Empire is likely to maintain aspects of his or her dialect after moving to another English-speaking country. Sometimes, the systematic differences in dialects

pronunciation   How we actually make sounds and say words as we speak; in everyday use, demonstrates what dialect we speak.

may endure for a number of generations. This is evidenced in various parts of the United States, where the influence of other languages is strongly felt for a long time.

Some speakers purposely change their dialect as part of an effort to acclimate themselves to new circumstances. It is very difficult, however, to completely change a dialect, especially as we grow older. Moreover, in many respects, it may not even be desirable to make a complete changeover.

Irish dramatist George Bernard Shaw, who lived most of his life in England but still spoke with a Dublin accent, explored the issue of changing one's dialect in the satirical play *Pygmalion*, which was adapted for presentation as a musical comedy in the United States as *My Fair Lady*. Shaw's pointed criticism is aimed at the arrogance of Professor Henry Higgins, an aristocratic expert in English phonetics and social dialects, who attempts to change the lower-class Cockney dialect spoken by a young woman he encounters, Eliza Doolittle. With a great deal of hard work, Eliza is able to make dramatic changes in her speech—enough so that she can be presented at a high-society gathering as a duchess.

2.4

Yet as Eliza learns, a change in one's speech comes at a great cost: losing one's bond with her community of origin as well as sacrificing one's personal identity and integrity. When we lose our dialect, we lose a significant piece of ourselves. If we are to make changes, it would be wise to be judicious about how and when to change.

Shaw's *Pygmalion* theme has been repeated in other films to illustrate the difficulties of a language makeover. The recent film *The Princess Diaries*, for example, narrates the story of 15-year-old Mia, who learns that she is the heir-apparent to the throne of a small kingdom named Genovia, which is located somewhere in Europe. Mia has grown up in San Francisco. So before assuming her new royal role, she must be groomed to learn a whole new way of speaking and behaving that fits with the demeanor and expectations of her grandmother, Queen Clarisse Renaldi, whose throne Mia will inherit.

2.1

Implications for Communication: The Role of Language as Sound

Accommodate Differences   Some speakers also learn how to make minor adaptations in order to de-emphasize aspects of their dialect as they move from one communication situation to another. Some may even develop more than one dialect to use in different communication situations. You might have one style of speech to use in your home and other informal settings and another to use in public or in communication situations that call for a more formal approach than that used at home.

2.1

In a presentation to teachers in California, which you can view online by clicking the Video View icon, Orlando Taylor observes that communicators who can speak more than one dialect or variety of a language gain power. Taylor also confronts a dilemma that societies face: the desirability of having commonality in our use of language so that we can understand one another, yet at the same time recognizing the value of preserving diversity. Taylor argues that schools hold a special responsibility of empowering students to be able to use the language of the school, which is the standard for a given community, while at the same time teaching respect for language differences.

2.2

Acknowledge Judgments of Differences   Unfortunately, we live in an environment in which prejudice is embodied in racial and ethnic stereotypes associated with the speech of certain groups of people. Those who speak dialects associated with a certain racial or ethnic group, nationality, gender, sexual orientation, social class, age, or religious affiliation may experience discrimination.

Massey and Lundy (1998) found that prospective renters in Philadelphia who made telephone calls to inquire about rental properties were more likely to be discriminated against if they used a dialect of English that Taylor (1990) calls *Black vernacular English*, which has also been called *Black English* or *Ebonics* in news reports and popular parlance. The discrimination took several forms: being treated with less courtesy, being charged higher sales fees, receiving less attention and responsiveness from sales agents, and even being denied access to rental housing altogether.

WEB ACTIVITY
2.5

The fact that discrimination occurs has been recognized in U.S. public laws, as well. For example, the Civil Rights Act of 1964 and Title VII of the Immigration Reform and Control Act of 1986 have been applied by the courts to rule that an employer may not discriminate in the workplace on the basis of an employee's accent without demonstrating that the accent interferes with his or her job performance. Similarly, workplace rules that require the speaking of English only cannot be enforced legally unless this restriction can be proven to be a business necessity.

THINK ABOUT THIS
2.2

Learn the Standard for Your Community   There is no one completely correct standard for speaking English in the United States. The people are simply too diverse. There are, however, preferred ways of speaking in a given community and in order to satisfy the requirements of a communication situation. At times, we may need to adapt to a certain type of communication situation and adjust the way that we speak to enhance communication with our listeners.

There are practical tools for learning how to articulate the sounds of English. Along with listening carefully to the people in your environment, you can use the guides for pronunciation found in dictionaries. Dictionaries use a system of markings that are referred to as *diacritical markers* to guide the pronunciations of words.

WEB ACTIVITY
2.6

Make Accommodations as a Listener   Listeners as well as speakers should make accommodations to ensure effective communication. Moreover, this might even be thought of as the listener's responsibility as a participant in a dialogue that is truly collaborative.

THINK ABOUT THIS
2.3

Indeed, as an active participant in the process, the listener has several responsibilities. He or she needs to make a special effort to understand a speaker by keeping an open mind and being tolerant of differences. The listener's responsibilities also include providing helpful feedback that enables a speaker with roots in a different speech community to make the kinds of adjustments necessary for successful communication. To be most effective, that feedback should be constructive, rather than critical.

ASSESSING YOUR SKILLS
2.2

RAPID REVIEW
2.2

Semantic Rules: Words and Meanings

LEARNING OBJECTIVE
2.3

Semantic rules govern how we create meaning for the words we use. Cherry (1966) explains that words do not have fixed meanings that can be contained in a dictionary. When we look up a word in the dictionary we are discovering how people commonly use that word when they speak or write. The word *dictionary* comes from the same Latin root as the word "to speak," *dictio*. In a sense it provides guidance for pronouncing words when we speak and using words so others can understand what we say. Cherry continues: "the dictionary supplies phrases more or less synonymous with the word, as judged by common usage" (p. 71). Common usage changes over time and thus dictionaries reflect the current and past trends in how communicators speak particular words to create meaning. The meaning is in the communicator who uses a word, not in the dictionary. In fact, dictionaries are continually being rewritten to keep track of how people create new meanings for words. McKean (2002), explains how we create *neologisms*. Neologisms reflect the dynamic quality of language use and the way that individuals and groups create new words, often on the basis of old words. For instance, she sites the example of the contemporary term "humongous" as just such an example of a neologism. It is probably constructed, she notes, by combining three words "huge," "monstrous," and "ginormous." What, you will ask is ginormous? It's another word for gigantic.

Denoting Meaning

We create meaning by using words on two levels: to denote meaning and to connote meaning. The *American Heritage Dictionary* (2000) defines *denotation* as the "act of denoting." When we speak *denotatively*, we use words to refer to concepts and categories of experience. The *American Heritage Dictionary* also describes a **denotative meaning** as the "most specific or direct meaning of a word, in contrast to its figurative or associated meanings." The most commonly used denotation is usually found among the initial entries for a word in the dictionary.

As a rule, when a communicator uses a particular word, he or she expects that other members of the speech community will have a common set of experiences as to what category of object or concept that word is used to denote. Denotative meanings, according to DiVesta (1974) "consist of inclusive features (attributes that define what a concept is) and exclusive features (attributes that define what a concept is not)" (p. 69).

One way of thinking about denoting meanings is to imagine categories of meaning as boxes. *Inclusive features* specify what things can be put in the same box, and *exclusive features* exclude things from a certain box. For instance, if we look up the word *dog* in the dictionary, we will find the commonly shared denotative meanings of the word. Since the dictionary defines words by using other words, the definition of *dog* might mention the fact that dogs are *canines*. That is a category, or box, of animals that includes dogs, wolves, foxes, and any other wild or domesticated animal that is in the canine family of mammals. But human beings are excluded from that box, at least on the denotative level. The dictionary entry governs the range of possible denotations—what is in the box and what is not.

Hierarchies of Abstraction   Katz and Fodor (1963) explain that members of a speech community develop mental categories of word meanings that they call **semantic features.** Semantic features comprise a set of attributes or characteristics of our mental categories. Each of the conceptual categories we use for thinking is also made up of a set of semantic features that we apply to the world around us. Based on our experiences, we are able to group things and ascribe common characteristics to the items in a given category, or denotative "box."

Since the conceptual categories that we create can be broad or narrow, it is sometimes useful to see how we create a hierarchy that establishes levels of abstraction. For instance, categories that are very broad are more abstract. Abstractions can be fit into a hierarchy of successively narrower categories. As we move from the highest point in the hierarchy to the lowest, the meaning becomes progressively narrower and more concrete.

Condon (1975) illustrates the hierarchical nature of categories of abstraction by considering how we play the game Twenty Questions. When you play the game, you start out by asking about the broad category of the thing under consideration: "*Is it an animal, mineral, or vegetable?*" you ask. Each of these three broad conceptual categories

denotative meaning   The objective or specific meaning of a word; typically among the first definitions found in a dictionary entry for a given word.

semantic features   The mental categories of word meanings developed by members of a speech community; the set of attributes or characteristics of those categories.

could be thought of in terms of its different semantic features. Whether a thing is an animal, mineral, or vegetable is an abstract category at a very high level of abstraction since it applies to a very broad range of things. However, as you play the game, you can eliminate two of them. Then, you are only working with one category of meaning. Within a category such as animal, you might next move to the question such as *"Is it a human animal?"* And if your partner in the game says, *"No, I am not thinking of a human animal,"* you will respond by asking if the animal is *"found in the wild"* or *"is it domesticated?"* With each question, you are getting at a smaller category of meaning within the broad category of things that are animals. You are moving step by step to lower levels of abstraction. Suppose your partner with whom you are playing Twenty Questions is thinking of her dog named Rover. *Rover* represents the concrete name of the particular dog.

2.3

Connoting Meaning

Along with using words to *denote* meaning, words are used to *connote* meaning, as well. In everyday use, a word may connote or imply a wide range of meanings that are not captured or governed by the rule that establishes its denotative meaning.

So, sometimes we think outside the box and use the word *dog* in more ways than indicated by the primary denotative definition in the dictionary. For instance, suppose you respond to your friend's good fortune by saying "You lucky dog!" The semantic rule for *dog* on the denotative level would prohibit calling a person a *dog*, but on the connotative level, you can use the word figuratively to imply some kind of association between the affability and positive experiences of a dog's life to good fortune.

VIDEO
VIEW

2.3

Connotation and Affective Meaning   A **connotative meaning** evokes the attitudes and values associated with a word. In this sense, connotative meanings are more personal than denotative meanings and may be rooted in the unique experiences of an individual or a group. According to Chandler (2001), a connotation is the emotional level of meaning that is associated with the attitudes and values we hold. Connotative meanings, according to Barthes (1987), also reflect the cultural value system of a community that is embodied in its myths and ideologies.

Connotation and Cultural Myths   Myths represent the ideologies that are shared by many members of a cultural community. Let's illustrate this point with a common example.

THINK
ABOUT THIS

2.4

When we use the word *car*, the denotative meaning we assign to it refers to the qualities of an automobile and how it is used as a vehicle for personal transportation. Alongside that conventional denotation are culturally shared connotations. In that regard, we might look at the love affair that many Americans have with their cars and how a cultural ideology has developed that evokes a whole set of values, such as individual freedom and the convenience of personal travel by car. This ideology is expressed in the mythic images that are used in advertising and in films that depict cars. For instance, consider how many names for cars have a Western theme: *Mustang, Wrangler, Cherokee, Durango,* or *Laredo*. These words evoke the myth of the American Frontier and connote images of adventure, conquest, rugged individualism, and manly cowboys galloping across the open plains.

While connotations may be shared by many members of a culture, there may also be differences. Consider how much we differ as individuals and as members of the diverse relational communities that make up our larger community of language users.

connotative meanings   The emotional level of meaning of a word; associated with the attitudes and values we hold.

These differences are rooted in our individual experiences, attitudes, and values and may or may not fit the perspective of the cultural myth. Suppose, for instance, that you use a bicycle as your preferred mode of transportation. Suppose further that protecting the environment is basic to your personal value system. To you, the connotative meaning of car may suggest environmental waste and destruction. In your mind, a *car* is a *gas guzzler*.

The Semantic Triangle

Ogden and Richards's (1923) concept of the **semantic triangle**, which they introduced in their book *The Meaning of Meaning*, also provides a useful way of recognizing how denotative and connotative meanings are constructed (see Figure 2.3). The purpose of the semantic triangle is somewhat like that of Saussure's (1916) model, which was intended to identify the arbitrary connection between a signifier and the signified, which we explored in Module One.

The semantic triangle has three parts:

1. a referent, which is an object of reference
2. a symbol that stands for the referent
3. a reference, which includes the whole set of experiences that a language user brings to a communication situation

Note that the reference may include all of our memories and associations with the referent, or the thing that is the object of reference, including our subjective responses and feelings about it and the connotations we ascribe to the symbol that refers to the object.

As illustrated in Figure 2.4, consider the American flag to be the *referent*, or object of reference. On the semantic triangle, we can diagram the flag as the first point. At the second point of the triangle, we can place the *symbols* that stand for the flag, such as the phrase "Old Glory"; the colors red, white, and blue; or the title "The Star-Spangled Banner."

2.8

At the third point of the triangle is the *reference*. The reference for the American flag is a whole set of emotions that the flag evokes based on our past experiences. Perhaps we remember from early childhood our experiences in school or in community organizations of declaring "The Pledge of Allegiance" to the flag, which articulates powerful patriotic sentiments. We may also have learned lessons about the history of the flag and even revere it as a sacred symbol. Using Barthes's (1987) terminology, we can see that a cultural myth surrounds the flag, given the values and feelings it evokes.

The semantic triangle provides a useful way of recognizing how denotative and connotative meanings are constructed. The referent is the object of reference, the symbol is what stands for the referent, and the reference includes the whole set of experiences that a language user brings to a communication situation.

Source: Based on Ogden and Richards (1923).

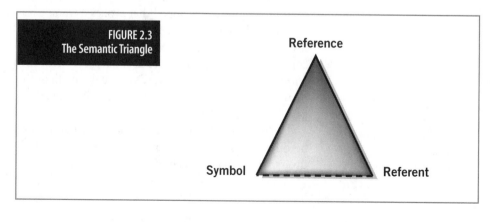

FIGURE 2.3
The Semantic Triangle

Reference

Symbol   Referent

The semantic triangle can be used to diagram the relationship between the linguistic symbol "Old Glory" and the flag itself as the referent. The reference includes the associations and experiences evoked by the flag.

Source: Based on Ogden and Richards (1923).

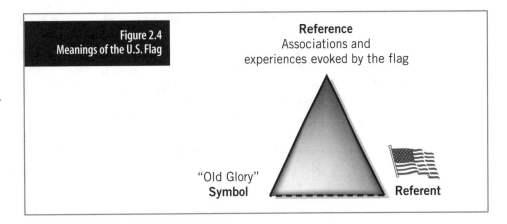

Figure 2.4 Meanings of the U.S. Flag

Reference
Associations and experiences evoked by the flag

"Old Glory" **Symbol**

Referent

Meanings Are in People Ogden and Richards's (1923) semantic triangle also enables us to identify individual and group differences in meaning. As illustrated with the earlier example of the various connotative meanings of the word *car*, we may have different references for objects such as the flag or different connotations for a phrase such as "Old Glory." Think about your own values and feelings toward the American flag. Compared to others, are you more or less likely to have a sense of reverence for the flag? What emotional associations do you have with this symbol?

In recognizing that people differ in how they create meaning, Richards (1936, 1976) and others subscribe to the concept that words do not have inherent meanings. In other words, meaning does not reside in the word itself but in the people who use the word. This means that the connection between a word and its meaning is arbitrary.

As we differ from one another in terms of the unique experiences that shape our references for words, so, too, we differ in terms of the connotative meanings we ascribe to symbols. As members of relational communities, we also share certain kinds of experiences that enable us to agree on the range of possible meanings for a given symbol.

VIDEO VIEW

2.4

Meanings and Communities In a diverse society with many relational communities, people do not always agree on word meanings, for they have had different experiences and thus formed different points of reference for symbols and objects. Consider the controversy that arose when Zayed Yasin (2002) used the Arabic concept of *Jihad* as the central theme of his commencement address at Harvard University on June 6, 2002.

WEB ACTIVITY

2.9

Yasin's original title for his speech was "My American Jihad" (shown in Figure 2.5 in Arabic). His words provide a dramatic example of how words may evoke significantly

Figure 2.5 The Words *My American Jihad* in Arabic

الجهاد في أمريكا

semantic triangle A model for analyzing how denotative and connotative meanings are constructed; parts include a referent, a symbol, and a reference.

Yasin's speech about Jihad provides a dramatic example of how words can evoke significantly different connotations for members of different relational communities. (Note that words in Arabic are read from right to left.)

2.5

different connotations for members of different communities. Yasin, a student, was selected to be one of three speakers for the graduation ceremony (Healy, 2002). At the time, the tragic events of 9/11 were still very fresh in the minds of many members of his audience. For some of them—indeed, for many Americans—the word *Jihad* had been interpreted to mean "holy war" and was associated with a religious justification for terrorism. Yasin's goal in speaking was to offer an alternative definition from his perspective as a Muslim American. He said, "*Jihad* is a word that has been corrupted and misinterpreted; both by those who do and do not claim to be Muslim. And we saw last fall, to our great national and personal loss, the results of this corruption." He proceeded to define *Jihad* as "the determination to do right, to do justice even against your own interests" (Ferdinand, 2002).

Metaphors

A **metaphor** is used to make a comparison between two things by transferring the meaning of one to another. The word *metaphor* comes from a Latin term for "transfer." If you were to say "James is a sly fox," you would be saying that he is similar to a fox and transferring the concepts and feelings about slyness associated with foxes to the person named James. Thus, a metaphor is a symbolic use of language, not a literal one. Metaphors are sometimes called *figures of speech.*

Sometimes, a metaphor directly states the fact that a comparison is being made by using a word such as *like* or *as.* This kind of metaphor is called a *simile.* A person who is *quiet as a mouse* or *as slow as molasses* has been described using a simile.

2.6

2.7

Semantic rules govern the kinds of comparisons that can be made using metaphors. In order for a comparison to make sense, the speaker and listener must have the same kind of reference in mind—for instance, that mice are incredibly quiet or that molasses pours quite slowly.

Richards (1936) describes a metaphor as a kind of interaction between ideas: "When we use a metaphor, we have two thoughts of different things active together and supported by a single word, or phrase, whose meaning is a resultant of their interaction" (p. 93). And Langer (1942) describes a metaphor as a kind of logical analogy. In our minds, she observes, we have a "perception of common form" (p. 125) when we create a metaphor. The construction of a metaphor involves comparing new experiences to prior perceptions of things or events and finding some similarity between them. Langer further describes the use of metaphorical language as "striking evidence of abstractive seeing, of the power of the human mind to use presentational symbols. Every new experience or new idea about things evokes first of all some metaphorical expression" (p. 125).

We develop this capacity for creating and understanding metaphors early in life. For example, take Meaghan, now an adult, who has always regarded the Fourth of July as her favorite holiday of the year. Members of her family recall how she described her first fireworks display when she was two years old as *pretty thunder.* For Meaghan, fireworks were just a different kind of thunder that shared additional qualities of other pretty things that sparkled glittering colors.

2.7

metaphor Used to make a comparison between two things by transferring the meaning of one to another; a symbolic use of language, not a literal one.

Metaphors and Creativity   Langer (1942) provides several reasons for creating metaphors. Sometimes, we use a metaphor because we don't know a word to describe a new experience and thus need to rely on an old word or image. At other times, we use metaphors for emphasis. Poets and great orators use metaphors in this way to be creative.

2.10

At yet other times, the motivation for creating a metaphor is not to be eloquent but to avoid directly talking about a subject. In these situations, we have a word to communicate our meaning but don't want to say it. Instead, we talk around the subject by using a metaphor and describing the subject more indirectly. We say a person is "over the hill" instead of saying he or she is old.

Indirect expressions also include *euphemisms*. A person uses a euphemism to substitute a more polite or positively connotative expression for something that is thought of as being impolite or negative. Indeed, the word *euphemism* is formed from the Greek words for "good, " or *eu*, and "speech," *pheme*. A euphemism is thus "good speech."

Langer concludes that the ability to create metaphors is the "power whereby language, even with a small vocabulary, manages to embrace a multimillion things; whereby new words are born, and merely analogical meanings become stereotyped into literal definition" (p. 125).

2.8

Even so, there are some limits on metaphorical expression. We can judge a metaphor in terms of how well it conveys the desired meaning. As an example, consider how you might describe something as a "circus." Suppose you come home at the end of the day and your relational partner asks how your day went. You think of how busy you were and say "My day was a circus." In using that metaphor, you are tapping into a set of conventional associations that you and your relational partner probably share about the circus. Is it the frenetic atmosphere, in which so many things are going on simultaneously, or the feeling of fun and lightheartedness? If so, you and your partner would probably laugh together about how busy your day was. Suppose, however, that you faced a really serious problem at work or were involved in a car accident on the way home. Would you call either of those things a "circus?" Probably not. Neither evokes emotions of being lighthearted or fun. Among members of a speech community, there is a system of meaning that is governed by semantic rules—even with the creativity involved in constructing metaphors. These rules establish the range of possible meanings for a symbol, or conventions of meaning. When we have a convention, we recognize the importance of agreeing with the members of our relational community to share a given meaning.

Metaphors and Slang Groups of people in relational communities, both large and small, also use **slang**, or specialized expressions that are unique to a certain group. Members of a group who use slang develop unique and often creative vocabulary terms that are typically used in an informal conversational setting. For example, findings from the College Slang Research Project (Sanders, 2003), at California State Polytechnic University, Pomona, show that the word *dog*, with its alternate spellings of *dawg* and *dogg*, can be used to refer to a male friend. This is obviously not the denotative meaning of "canine" or "animal," which is known by the general population. Rather, it's a slang expression used by college students. According to Sanders (2003), *dog* is the third most commonly used slang expression among students.

2.11

2.5

Jargon Like slang, **jargon** is a set of expressions, even common expressions, that are understood principally by members of a certain group. You might, for instance, belong to a work group that has such a specialized vocabulary. Some hobby groups and special interest groups also create their own unique vocabularies. Musicians might refer to a scheduled performance as a *gig*, and jazz musicians, in particular, may call their instrument their *axe*. In the workplace, it is also common to find a whole vocabulary of jargon for a specialized field. Safire (2003) observes how the U.S. Defense Department introduced the term *embedding* as part of *Pentagonese* to describe the practice of having reporters covering the 2003 War in Iraq live alongside and travel with Army units.

2.4

2.3

slang Specialized expressions that are unique to a certain group; used especially for informal speaking.

jargon A set of expressions, even common expressions, that are understood principally by members of a certain group, especially in a professional or technical field.

Implications for Communication: Finding Meaning in Sound

Acknowledge That People Can Have Different Meanings for the Same Word   Just as there is no single way to pronounce many words, covering all contexts, there is no single meaning, considering both the denotative and connotative levels. Unfortunately, assuming that there is a single meaning often leads to misunderstanding. Richards (1936) refers to this as the **proper meaning superstition**.

Words have multiple meanings, so to communicate effectively, we need to recognize the range of possible meanings and how to adjust to specific situations. We also need to acknowledge that the people with whom we communicate may have different meanings than ours.

Recognize Relational Meanings for Symbols   Even in interpersonal relationships, such as in families or within the context of a small group of friends, relational partners can create their own private semantic rules, in which they identify a symbol as meaning something unique as part of the private message system of that smaller relational community. To illustrate this, consider how Thomas interprets the slang expressions used in his relational community:

> In my social life, my community is comprised mostly of African and Hispanic Americans from the New York City area. We are all big fans of hip-hop music from the New York area, which is a culture in its own, and it is reflected in the language we use. It is a social slang with an accent found in the northeastern part of the United States or a New York accent.
>
> The semantics involved in the slang that my friends and I use are based on hip-hop music. The slang words we use have totally different connotative meanings, most of the time. It may be very difficult for someone out of my speech community to understand a conversation between my friends and me. Here's an example:
>
> *Question:* "Yo did you bounce to dat new mix joint spot, or did you chill up in the cut last night?"
> *Answer:* "Nah sun, I tried ta peep dat joint but it looked mad whack, and da line was stupid long, so I just chilled at da crib."
>
> Translation:
> *Question:* "Hey, did you go to that new club, or did you relax at home last night?"
> *Answer:* "No, my friend, I tried to visit that club, but it did not seem that good, and the line was very long, so I just relaxed at home."

Use Words to Speak Clearly   Since words can have many possible meanings, expressing ourselves comes down to making choices about which words will be most effective. If our goal is to be understood, the clearest way to express our ideas is to use words in ways that other members of our speech community will understand.

Finding a shared meaning may sometimes be a matter of negotiating a common experience, especially when we speak connotatively or listen to someone speaking denotatively but at a high level of abstraction. In these situations, the listener may simply ask "What do you mean?"

Syntactic Rules: Language and Structure

Syntactic rules govern the arrangement of phrases and sentences. Thus, they also guide how we construct meaning, since each word in the syntactic structure of a sentence creates a context for interpreting each of the other words in the sen-

2.9

tence. The subject of the sentence, for instance, is understood in relation to the predicate. Even if we don't understand the meanings of the words, we can make a good guess based on the order in which they appear in a sentence.

Sentence Structure

You acquired the most common rules of syntax by learning the *grammar* of your language and how to string words together to form meaningful phrases and sentences. You know, for instance, that a meaningful English sentence requires at least a noun or pronoun for the subject and a verb for the predicate, even if one of these is implied, as in a one-word sentence like the command *Stop*. *Stop* is the verb and the implied subject is the pronoun *you*.

Word Order Along with the rule for determining what parts of speech must be present or implied to make a functional sentence, syntactic rules also govern the order of words. For instance, you have probably learned that when you are speaking English, a declarative sentence can be expressed in the active or the passive voice. It is the order of the words that makes the sentence active or passive.

So, using the active voice, a declarative sentence might read *Mary gave me that red book last night*. By putting the subject of the sentence before the verb, the active voice emphasizes the active nature of the event. The passive form of this same declarative sentence would be *That red book was given to me last night by Mary*. By changing the order of the words, emphasis is placed on the book, rather than on Mary's act of giving it to you.

Similarly, we know how to recognize the structure of a question or an exclamation. In this sense, syntactic rules also tell us what kind of response we are expected to make as a listener. We know we are expected to reply to a question or to respond to the emotion of an exclamatory sentence.

As we move around the globe, from one language group to another, the syntactic rules for the arrangement of words change dramatically. You have probably observed how the order of words in phrases and sentences differs in some languages. For instance, speakers of English know that in the phrase *that red book*, the adjective *red*, which describes a certain book, needs to go before *book*.

The order of the words that comprise a complete sentence also varies from one language to another. An English sentence typically follows the formula *Subject-Verb-Object (S-V-O)*. That is, the subject of a declarative sentence comes first, is followed by the verb and then the object. The sentence *Mary read that book* follows the S-V-O order. In contrast, consider the example provided by Rosario about word order for a sentence spoken in Tagalog:

> Tagalog is the language of the Filipino community. But depending on your location in the country and where you were raised, you might speak one of ten different dialects. The speech community I was raised in uses unique grammatical rules for arranging a sentence.
>
> For example, in English I would say, "Yesterday I saw an old friend whom I have not seen since I was a child." In Tagalog, I would say, "Nakita ko ang kaibigan ko kahapon, ng nuon pa." The word order translated into English is "Saw I a friend yesterday that's a while."
>
> No one, even if they spoke English, would understand this statement with a clear understanding of its exact meaning. This shows the differences between my two speech communities.

Agreement Within phrases or sentences, we also follow syntactic rules for *agreement* among words. For instance, in the phrase *that red book*, the words *that* and *red* are

proper meaning superstition
The fallacy that there is only one correct meaning for a word.

singular and refer to a particular book. Yet if Mary had delivered more than one book, we would expect a competent communicator to say *those red books*. *Those* and the /s/ on the end of *book* are both plural forms.

Again, differences in agreement can be found as we move from one language to another. In some languages, such as the Romance languages based in Latin, the endings of words designate whether they refer to masculine or feminine concepts. In Spanish, *book* is a masculine word, *libro*. The syntactic rules of Spanish dictate that most masculine words end with the sound /o/. And the rest of the words in the phrase, including *that* and *red*, must be in agreement as masculine forms. The masculine form for *the* is *el*, and the masculine word for *red* is *rojo*. So, a Spanish speaker talking about *the red book* would say *el libro rojo*. (Note that the rule for the order of an adjective and its noun is different in Spanish, too!)

In contrast, a feminine word in Spanish, such as *mesa*, which means "table," ends with /a/, which is sounded like "uh." A Spanish speaker would point to *the red table* and say *la mesa roja*, using *la* as the feminine article *the* and *roja* as the feminized form of the adjective *red*, using the same /a/ ending as with *mesa*.

2.5

Formal and Informal Syntax   Some situations call for a more formal style of speaking or writing. Public speaking and professional communication, for instance, often call for using complete sentences and correct grammar. But in more casual situations, it may be acceptable to use less traditional language. An informal speech may present abbreviated thoughts that are expressed in incomplete or ungrammatical sentences, especially when it's known that the person or persons in the audience will be able to supply the information needed to comprehend the ideas.

Vygotsky (1962) describes how this happens in dialogue:

> Dialogue always presupposes in the partners sufficient knowledge of the subject to permit abbreviated speech and, under certain conditions, purely predicative sentences. It also presupposes that each person can see his partners, their facial expressions and gestures, and hear the tone of their voices.

The same is true of some types of informal writing, in which we count on the reader to fill in information. The kinds of notes that you leave for the person with whom you live or the e-mail message you send to a close friend may appear very much like informal oral speech.

2.6

Writers use a much more elaborate style for most instances of formal writing in books and periodicals and in business and academic settings. Vygotsky notes that the writer often needs to provide more detail to be understood by the reader. Formal written texts are thus usually developed with complete sentences and in accordance to the conventions of traditional grammar.

Implication for Communication: Understanding the Rules of Language

Adjust to Different Situations   Syntactic rules govern how words are put together to form phrases and sentences. To become a competent member of a speech community, we must learn the rules for doing so in our particular dialect and language. We must also learn to adjust to different types of communication situations. Effective communicators know the syntactic rules for formal and informal communication situations.

In this section, we explored how communicators create meaning by using three types of language rules: Phonetic rules govern the patterns of sounds, semantic rules establish guidelines for word meanings, and syntactic rules guide the syntax for forming phrases and sentences. In the next section, we further explore the significance of symbols as vehicles of conception as we examine how people form perceptions.

Perception and Selectivity

LEARNING OBJECTIVE
2.5

Perception is the process of creating meaning that involves *receiving information* through one's senses and then *organizing and interpreting* that information in a meaningful way.

Receiving Information and Focusing Attention

The process of receiving information through the senses is called **sensation**. Simply put, sensation occurs when one or more of our sensory organs take in information. That does not mean, however, that we pay attention to every one of those sensory inputs. As we will see shortly, we make selective choices to attend to some of these sensations and to tune others out. If we tried to take in everything going on around us, we would be overwhelmed, for there is simply too much information. Even in a relatively quiet environment, there are many stimuli to which a person could attend. This is particularly pertinent to holding a conversation with another person in which you may tune out various sensations in the environment as you tune in your friend and what he or she is saying.

Selective Attention   Think about what you tune in as well as what you tune out if you are with a good friend at a restaurant having dinner and sharing a pleasant evening of conversation. If you decided to do so, you could take note of many things going on around you. You may hear the sounds of traffic outside, WEB ACTIVITY 2.12
of music being played in the room, of servers clattering dishes, or of other diners carrying on conversations. In that same dining environment, you may have a host of smells. Similarly, there will be visual stimuli all around you, such as the decorative details of the room and the various appearances of the other diners. Yet given all this, you will probably focus on your friend and what he or she is saying. If something else other than your friend does demand your attention, you are also likely to comment upon it. You've probably done this when you interrupt the conversation to say, "Oh, don't you just love this song!" or if something catches your eye, you may draw your friend's attention to it as well with a comment.

In situations like these, we make selective choices—on a conscious or an unconscious level—to tune in some things and tune out other things. In his *Principles of Psychology*, James (1890) discusses how we make choices to emphasize certain aspects of an ongoing stream of consciousness:

> Out of what is in itself an undistinguishable, swarming *continuum*, devoid of distinction or emphasis, our senses make for us, by attending to this motion and ignoring that, a world full of contrasts, of sharp accents, of abrupt changes, of picturesque light and shade. . . . Attention, on the other hand, out of all the sensations yielded, picks out certain ones as worthy of its notice and suppresses all the rest. (pp. 285–286)

perception   The process of creating meaning that involves receiving information through one's senses and then organizing and interpreting that information in a meaningful way.

sensation   The process of receiving information through the senses.

We are selective in making conscious and unconscious choices to pay attention to certain things. This is the concept of **selective attention**. In terms of the restaurant example, this is when we focus our attention on the conversation at hand. We may pay selective attention to the object of our perception that holds the greatest interest or appeal. For instance, we usually tune into objects that are high in intensity, such as bright colors, more often than to objects that are dull, such as muted colors. Likewise, a dynamic or moving object is more likely to win our attention than one that is static or still.

2.10

Personal Differences and Attention   The role we play as a receiver also affects where we focus our attention. For instance, our individual experiences, interests, needs, and values may cause us to assign special significance to some types of objects or events more than others. Consider how a police officer and a physician will attend to different things at the scene of a traffic accident. Each will focus on different details in keeping with his or her professional role.

It can be fascinating to see how different people experience the same communication event and come away from it with dramatically different perceptions. In part, those differences arise because each observer made different choices as a matter of selective attention. Those differences in attention can also lead to misunderstanding, especially when we assume that a person with whom we have shared an experience focused on the same things that we did.

A dramatic example of differences in selective attention can be observed in the 1993 film *The Joy Luck Club*, which recounts the stories of four women who emigrated from China as refugees after World War II. As the story begins, June, who is the narrator and the daughter of one of the four principal characters, is planning a trip to China. Her mother, Suyuan, has died, and the other main characters have told her that she has twin sisters who were left behind when her mother fled China. Each of the other main characters, however, tells a slightly different version of the story, reflecting their individual perspectives.

News reports also illustrate selectivity on the part of observers who can offer only a partial view of an event. The limited vantage point of reporters, camera crews, photographers, and editors impacts how audiences receive only part of the story. News sources are limited by their perspectives and may also articulate a bias. A particularly pertinent example of different perceptions of the news was illustrated by the coverage of the war in Iraq in 2003. During the war, journalists were "embedded" in army units. The reporters thus saw the war from the ground level and from the perspective of the troops in the field. But that did not mean that the reporter always had the "big picture" view of the war. At one point, Secretary of Defense Donald H. Rumsfeld (2003) commented in a press briefing:

> What we are seeing is not the war in Iraq. What we're seeing are slices of the war in Iraq. We're seeing that particularized perspective that that reporter, or that commentator or that television camera happens to be able to see at that moment. And it is not what's taking place. What you see is taking place, to be sure, but it is one slice. And it is the totality of that that is what this war is about and being made up of.

Implications for Communication: The Role of Perception

Understand That Perception Is an Active Process   Whether on a conscious or unconscious level, a communicator is an active agent who makes choices to tune in some things and

selective attention   The act of making conscious and unconscious choices to pay attention to certain things.

tune out other things. This sometimes requires an effort at concentration. When we are listening to another person speak or present at an event, for instance, we tune out what we don't find meaningful, such as background noise or activity. And we tune in those parts of the experience we think are meaningful.

2.5

Stimulate the Attention of Listeners   Speakers also share the burden of helping listeners be attentive. Effective communicators make special effort to gain the attention of their listeners. In Module Seven, we will explore this idea further, with special reference to the importance of attention as a factor of effective public speaking.

Organizing and Interpreting Information in Meaningful Ways

We also make choices about how to organize the information we perceive, arranging it into a pattern that seems to make sense. Langer (1942) observes that when we perceive an experience, "we promptly and unconsciously abstract a form from each sensory experience, and use this form to conceive the experience as a whole, as a 'thing'" (pp. 83–84).

Doing so is also an active process of perception. Suppose you go to a gallery to take in an exhibit of paintings or sculptures. When you observe a particular piece of art, you are likely to construct its form in your mind as you view it. While this is very much the case when we study a piece of abstract art, the same principle of constructing a form applies to representational art.

For instance, envision the famous painting by Leonardo da Vinci, the *Mona Lisa*. It seems simply to be a portrait of a woman. But as you look at her face, you make connections in your own mind about the lines of her eyes and the shape of her mouth and you even form your own impression of what she might be thinking or feeling. You observe these facial features in the context of the colors that da Vinci chose for the woman's clothing and for the background and use them to draw further conclusions about the meaning of the painting.

As with selective attention, people differ in how they organize information and draw conclusions. To understand this better, we will turn next to explore principles of organization and interpretation from Gestalt psychology.

Gestalt as a Perception of an Interconnected Whole   Psychologists have used the term *gestalt* to explain how we look for the forms of things. In other words, we perceive experiences not as isolated elements but as parts of an interconnected whole.

Like selective attention, our organization of experience is an active process of deciding where the connections exist among the elements of an event. Principles of organization include creating closure so that experiences will be whole, applying perceptual sets, and drawing on the categories we construct with language. In organizing the experiences that we comprehend, we build structures of meaning through language and draw on our personal constructs.

closure The strategy of filling in information that appears to be missing so that an experience will be a whole and meaningful pattern.

Closure   Gestalt psychologists introduced the concept of **closure** to explain how we fill in information that appears to be missing so that an experience will be a whole and meaningful pattern. We use the principle of closure as listeners, for example, when we fill in information that is implied but not stated by a speaker. And in everyday conversation, we listen by "reading between the lines" of what someone is saying.

2.7

Chomsky (1975) observes that a speaker or writer "naturally presupposes a vast background of assumptions, beliefs and conventions" (p. 30). When we consider this in light of the relational view of communication, we see how communicators fill in those things that are presupposed by drawing on the shared history with others in a relational community.

Perceptual Sets   Many times, we also bring to a situation a set of expectations that are based on our prior experiences. Sometimes referred to as a **perceptual set**, this is a previously determined view of an object or an event. When we apply a perceptual set to a given situation, we see what we expect to see.

2.11

2.14

To illustrate this concept, consider the optical illusion created by W. E. Hill in 1915 (see Figure 2.6), which is an image of an older woman or a younger woman, depending on your perceptual set. Hill (1915) referred to the two women in the image as his wife and his mother-in-law. If you approach it looking for a picture of the wife, you will likely see a young woman. If you change your view and expect to see an image of the mother-in-law, the picture changes to reveal an older woman. In each case you will draw on your perceptual set of what you expect either woman to look like.

2.12

We learn perceptual sets. One type of perceptual set is the **stereotype**, which is a way of grouping a whole set of people or events and then generalizing about the group as a whole. In applying a stereotype, we fail to make the distinctions that would allow us to look at people or events as being unique. Stereotypes may be created to make categorical judgments of people in terms of race or ethnicity, gender, sexual orientation, religion, age, social class, occupation, educational level, physical characteristics, physical abilities—or just about any human characteristic.

Regardless, a stereotype reflects the judgments we make about members of a group, in which we refuse to recognize or appreciate individual differences. Moreover, holding a stereotype can lead to having a distorted image of a certain group of people if we don't move beyond the generalization to see individuals and their unique qualities. As a type of perceptual set, a stereotype causes us to see people as fulfilling the expectations of the

perceptual set   A previously determined view of an object or an event based on past experiences.

stereotype   A way of grouping a whole set of people or events and then generalizing about the group as a whole.

FIGURE 2.6   **Drawing on Your Perceptual Set**

W. E. Hill's line drawing may be an image of an older woman or a younger woman, depending on your perceptual set.

Source: Hill (1915).

2.8

generalization we have made. Thus, if someone has the stereotype that members of a particular group are lazy, his or her perception of anyone belonging to that group will be biased, leading to a selective perception that further reinforces the stereotype.

Stereotypes may also be transformed into *labels*, or derogatory terms that are used to categorize whole groups of people. Labels have very strong connotations, so much so that we may refer to them as "fighting words." In some communities, new labels are created to replace negative labels. As an example, consider the language used to describe people with various physical and emotional disabilities has undergone a transformation in recent years. For instance, words such as *crippled* and *disturbed* have been eliminated from the vocabulary.

Semantic Categories and Perception   The semantic rules of language provide a category system for organizing and interpreting experience. In his discussion of the process of perception, Bruner (1975) observes how we isolate a new idea or object in an effort to fit it into a category that makes sense to us and then look for cues that reinforce and confirm that categorization.

2.13

Suppose that you see a round sphere and think that it is probably a ball. To be more certain, you look at it more closely and take in its details. In order to undertake this process of categorizing, you must already know the cues of shape, texture, and size that characterize various types of balls. When we see an object that fits one of our categories and its classifications, we say, as psychologist and philosopher William James remarked, "Hello, *Thingamabob*, again." James, you might also recall from our discussion above, also developed ideas about selective attention.

In our minds, we have created a set of semantic categories and subcategories. We then use that information to organize and interpret experiences, trying to find the right fit between experience and category. Perhaps you can relate to seeing something that you know you have a semantic category that it belongs in, but you still struggle to come up with the right word to describe it. During that momentary loss for the right word, it becomes a *whatchumacallit!* Your mind continues to probe its linguistic database until you finally can fit the experience of the *whatchumacallit* into the appropriate category.

Sometimes, the categorization of an experience is a matter of debate. In legal and political situations, for instance, our judicial and public discourse is aimed at drawing distinctions between concepts and using carefully selected words to create meaningful differences. These are not simple matters of semantic "hair splitting." The distinctions have profound consequences for how we perceive things and for how we respond to them.

For instance, the U.S. judicial system and laws establish definitional categories for responding to various types of legal matters. Legal terms differentiate a *felony* from a *misdemeanor*. But how does the law determine whether a certain criminal act should be treated as an *adult crime* or as a *juvenile offense*? Similarly, how do the courts define what constitutes *negligence* in an auto accident? When is an act legally justified as *self-defense*? Certainly, many areas of the law are open to interpretation.

Language choices can also have a powerful impact in shaping perceptions, especially when words are carefully chosen for the positive or negative connotations that they evoke. In politics, this is sometimes referred to as *spin*. Earlier in this module, we made the observation that connotations reflect widely

2.15

shared cultural attitudes and values. When political rhetoric becomes spin, words are selected in order to shape how audience members will perceive a political situation or event in a positive or negative light. For instance, language used by members of the Bush administration to describe the war against Iraq in 2003 was carefully chosen to create the perception, or spin, that the war was meant to be a war of liberation. Writing in the *New York Times,* Bumiller (April 20, 2003, p. 14) describes the rhetoric leading up to the war as a "public relations campaign" that was extremely successful. She observes the coordinated effort of the Bush White House and the Pentagon, in "shaping a positive battlefield narrative" when various members of the Bush administration spoke about the war, often repeating the same key terms and images. Bumiller concludes that the public relations campaign to promote the war was planned and coordinated by the White House Communications Office.

Personal Construct Theory While we share many meanings with others, perception is also subjective, since we don't all agree in every situation. Each person brings to a communication situation his or her unique life experiences. Kelly (1955) examines this matter of subjectivity with his *personal construct theory.*

2.16

Kelly explains that individuals form **personal constructs** similar to the way in which scientists test theories. That is, the scientist develops a theory and then creates a hypothesis to test the theory. Kelly suggests that when we make sense of the world around us, we use a similar process. Our theories are our constructs. Moreover, we use our constructs to anticipate how we will experience things or relate to others.

We also test our constructs in the "laboratory" of real-life experience. Suppose you have a construct about going to a party that you've developed on the basis of your entire life's experiences of going to parties. You may also have developed a set of judgments about going to parties. Kelly notes that these judgments are often expressed in the form of dichotomies, or opposing terms, called *bipolar evaluations.* So, you might have been to some parties that you enjoyed and to others that were not fun at all. Kelly would say that one of your personal constructs about parties is the dichotomy of *pleasurable/not pleasurable.* What other sets of bipolar terms would you apply to going to parties? Perhaps you might think of parties as being formal versus informal, work related or not work related, ostentatious or simple, large or small, intimate or not intimate.

Each of us will develop our own personal constructs for going to a party. After all, we will each draw on our own unique set of life circumstances and construe what it means to go to a party, based on that set of experiences. At the same time, we will find that others share some of the same kinds of experiences

2.8

that we bring to the event. Kelly calls this the *commonality corollary.* This is the extent to which an individual's constructs are similar to those of other people. Moreover, since we sometimes share perceptions based on shared personal constructs, we can also anticipate how another person will likely interpret experiences or events. Kelly calls this the *sociality corollary.*

Construct Theory and Cognitive Complexity Delia, O'Keefe, and O'Keefe (1982) have built on Kelly's work on personal constructs and developed their *constructivist model of communication.* The key concepts in this model are *cognitive complexity* and *person centeredness.*

2.14

Cognitive complexity relates to how many constructs an individual uses. People who are high in cognitive complexity are likely to have a greater number of constructs than those who are low in cognitive complexity. Thus, people who are high in cognitive complexity have deeper insights into others and about human nature in general as well as to the specific people in their environments.

Individuals who are high in cognitive complexity are also likely to develop the capacity of **person centeredness**. According to Burleson and Waltman (1988), person-centered people are able to understand the perspectives of others more clearly and thus become more competent in tailoring their communications to other people. The specific competency of being able to perceive concepts from another person's perspective is called **perspective taking**.

personal construct A means of assigning meaning to a situation by perceiving how it is similar to a previous situation; enables people to assign meanings to situations and to anticipate events that are part of a history of similarly constituted communication situations.

cognitive complexity A measure of how many constructs an individual uses; persons high in cognitive complexity likely have a greater number of constructs and more insight into others.

person centeredness The ability to understand the perspectives of others more clearly and thus become more competent in tailoring communications to other people.

perspective taking The ability to perceive concepts from another person's perspective.

When we have a relational history with another person or with a group of people, we are able to make fairly good judgments about how their personal constructs will be similar to or different from ours. However, these judgments are never foolproof. We can be way off in our assumptions of how closely we share constructs.

This is the problem that Bach and Deutsch (1970) refer to as *mind reading,* especially when relational partners read too much into one another's attitudes and motivations. When we go too far in trying to read another's mind, we may act on our assumptions as if they were facts. To ensure we are on firm ground with one another, it may be valuable to have a dialogue about our perceptions of one another's constructs. Like good scientists, we sometimes have to revise our hypotheses and theories.

2.6

2.6

Implications for Communication: Understanding Perceptual Differences

In summing up, we might explore some of the ways that perception differs from one person to another. Some of these differences can be accounted for on the basis of physical and physiological factors, whereas others can be traced to the influence of psychological, social, and cultural factors.

2.17

Understand Physical and Physiological Factors   Speaking is a physical and physiological act, and so is receiving information as an observer or listener. Information is transmitted as physical waves that are received through the various senses. People will differ in what they perceive in terms of how the raw data of communication are seen or heard. A person who is blind, for instance, will perceive the world differently from someone who is sighted.

Recognize That Psychological States Also Affect Perception   How we feel influences how we receive information and express ourselves. In any given communication situation, we are likely to receive a message and respond to another person differently, depending on whether we are in a positive or a negative frame of mind. How greatly we are aroused, either positively or negatively, by a situation will also influence how we take in information and interpret what we perceive.

2.15

Beyond the day-to-day mood swings that most of us likely undergo, our overall level of **emotional intelligence** may also affect our perception. Mayer and Salovey (1990) define *emotional intelligence* as "the ability to monitor one's own and others' feelings and emotions, to discriminate among them and to use this information to guide one's thinking and actions" (p. 189).

2.18

Goleman (1995) has made the concept of emotional intelligence popular with a best-selling book of the same name. His view is that people vary in their overall levels of emotional intelligence as it is expressed in self-confidence, awareness of their own feelings and the feelings of others, empathy, optimism, and the capacity to manage emotions.

Recognize That Social and Cultural Background Influences Perception   While physical, physiological, and psychological factors explain individual differences in perception, social and cultural influences help us see how our membership in groups affects how we create meaning when we form perceptions or listen to other people.

2.19

Standpoint theory, which has been described by Wood (1999), accounts for group differences in perception by examining how a person's position in a social system affects

emotional intelligence   The ability to monitor our own feelings and those of others, to discriminate among those feelings, and to use this information to guide our thinking and behavior.

standpoint theory   The theory that a society is organized in terms of a hierarchy of power and status, and depending on the status of a social group in that hierarchy, its members will enjoy certain rights and privileges.

perceptions of others. The premise of standpoint theory is that a society is organized in terms of a hierarchy of power and status. Depending on the status of a social group in that hierarchy, its members will enjoy certain rights and privileges. Typically, those at the top of the social hierarchy exercise more rights and privileges than those at the lower echelons.

American society, according to Wood, is differentiated in terms of race/ethnicity, wealth, gender, and sexual orientation. These are also the kinds of social groupings that we explore in this text as types of relational communities whose members share a framework of social and cultural knowledge.

Members of groups that are lower in status are likely to perceive themselves and situations differently. Wood uses an illustration from Hegel's writings about the relationship between a master and a slave. Hegel argued that each would perceive situations very differently. The slave, as a representative of a lower-status group, would more likely be attentive and thus have a fuller perception of the power differences between the slave class and the master class than would the master. Hegel's explanation is that the slave's survival depends on knowing how power arrangements work. The slave is more vulnerable and has a greater stake in understanding the dynamics of the relationship.

Wood adds that members of dominant groups may also have a limited and partial understanding of social arrangements due to their unwillingness to acknowledge the injustices that differences in social standing create. She observes, for instance, that members of black and white communities in the United States may have different perspectives on the legacy of slavery and racial prejudice and discrimination for this reason.

ASSESSING
YOUR SKILLS

2.7

RAPID
REVIEW

2.7

Summary

We are born into communities of meaning. Our speech communities may represent our cultural and social background as well our memberships in salient groupings. As a member of a given speech community, we learn its dialect and the rules for using it.

Communities develop phonetic rules for creating the sounds of language, semantic rules to guide word meanings, and syntactic rules for structuring phrases and sentences.

Communicators also create meaning by forming and testing perceptions. In the process of forming a perception, it is important to recognize how we make choices to focus on particular sensations and to exercise selective attention. Perception is not a passive process. As competent perceivers, we will also acknowledge how we organize and interpret experiences. In particular, we can take stock of how perceptions are formed on the basis of perceptual sets that establish expectancies; how information may be filled in with the practice of providing closure; and how semantic categories permit the organization of experience. Finally, we can understand how personal constructs are employed to make assessments and respond in a manner that is person centered.

Perceptions also vary from one person to another and from one kind of communication situation to another. People form perceptions on the basis of physical and physiological factors, at one level. Psychological factors, such as situational emotional experiences as well as an overall capacity of emotional intelligence, are influential, as well. Likewise, social and cultural factors affect perception in terms of how experience has been encoded in the language of a speech community and the social or cultural standpoint from which a person interacts with others.

References

American Heritage Dictionary. (2000). 4th ed. Boston: Houghton Mifflin.

Bach, G. R., & Deutsch, R. M. (1970). *Pairing: How to achieve genuine intimacy.* New York: Avon.

Barthes, R. (1987). *Mythologies.* New York: Hill & Wang.

Bavelas, J. B., & Chovil, N. (2000). Visible acts of meaning. *Journal of Language & Social Psychology,* 19, no. 2, 163–194.

Baxter L. A., & Montgomery, B. M. (1996). *Relating: Dialogues & dialectics.* New York: Guilford Press.

Bell, A. (1984). Language style as audience design. *Language in Society,* 13, 145–204.

Bruner, J. S. (1975). *Beyond the information given: Studies in the psychology of knowing.* Edited by J. M. Anglin. New York: W. W. Norton.

Buck, R., & VanLear, C. A. (2002). Verbal and nonverbal communication: Distinguishing symbolic, spontaneous, and pseudo-spontaneous nonverbal behavior. *Journal of Communication,* 52, no. 3, 522–542.

Bumiller, E. (2003). Even critics of war say the White House spun it with skill. *New York Times,* April 20, 2003, Section B, p. 14.

Burke, K. (1966). *Language as symbolic action.* Berkeley: University of California Press.

Burleson, B., & Waltman, M. (1988). Cognitive complexity: Using the role category questionnaire measure. In C. Tardy (ed.), *A handbook for the study of human communication* (pp. 1–35). Norwood, NJ: Ablex.

Chandler, D. (2001). *Semiotics for beginners.* Available online: <www.aber.ac.uk/media/Documents/S4B/sem06.html>. Accessed June 28, 2002.

Cherry, C. (1966). *On human communication.* 2nd ed. Cambridge, MA: MIT University Press.

Chomsky, N. (1975). *Reflections on language.* New York: Pantheon Books.

Condon, J. C. (1975). *Semantics and communication.* New York: Macmillan.

Delia, J. G., O'Keefe, B. J., & O'Keefe, D. J. (1982). The constructivist approach to communication. In F. E. X. Dance (ed.), *Human communication theory* (pp. 147–191). New York: Harper & Row.

DiVesta, F. J. (1974). *Language, learning, and cognitive processes.* Belmont, CA: Wadsworth.

Dupoux, E., Pallier, C., Sebastian, N., & Mehler, J. (1997). A distressing "deafness" in French? *Journal of Memory and Language,* 36, 406–421.

Ferdinand, P. (2002). Harvard student gives speech citing "Jihad." *Washington Post,* June 7, 2002, p. A3.

Gergen, K. J. (1999). *An invitation to social construction.* London: Sage.

Goleman, D. (1995). *Emotional intelligence.* New York: Bantam Books.

Gumperz, J. (1972). The speech community. In P. Giglioli (ed.), *Language and social context* (pp. 219–231). Harmondsworth, England: Penguin.

Healy, P. (2002). At Harvard, a word sparks a battle. Senior says his speech aims to redefine "jihad." *Boston Globe,* May 29, 2002. Available online: <www.boston.com/dailyglobe2/149/metro/At_Harvard_a_word_sparks_a_battle+.shtml>. Accessed July 16, 2002.

Hill, W. E., (1915). My wife and my mother-in-law. *Puck,* November 16, 11.

James, W. (1890). *The principles of psychology.* Available online:<psychclassics.yorku.ca/James/Principles/index.htm>. Accessed July 16, 2002.

Katz, J. J., & Fodor, J. A. (1963). The structure of a semantic theory. *Language,* 39, 170–210.

Kelly, G. A. (1955). *The psychology of personal constructs.* New York: W. W. Norton.

Langer, S. K. (1942). *Philosophy in a new key: A study in the symbolism of reason, rite and art.* Cambridge: Harvard University Press.

Massey, D. S., & Lundy, G. (1998.) *Use of black English and racial discrimination in urban housing markets*: New methods and findings. Available online: <www.ksg.harvard.edu/inequality/Seminar/Papers/Massey.pdf>. Accessed July 7, 2002.

Mayer, J. D., & Salovey, P. (1990). What is emotional intelligence? In P. Salovey & D. J. Sluyter (eds.), *Emotional development and emotional intelligence* (pp. 3–31). New York: Basic Books.

McKean, E. (2002). Neologizing 101. New York Times, Section 6, p. 1. August 25, 2002.

Ogden, C. K., & Richards, I. A. (1923). *The meaning of meaning: A study of the influence of language upon thought and the science of symbolism.* New York: Harcourt Brace and World.

Richards, I. A. (1936). *The philosophy of rhetoric.* London: Oxford University Press.

Richards, I. A. (1976). *Complementarities: Uncollected essays* (pp. 246–253). Cambridge: Harvard University Press.

Rumsfeld, D. H. (2003). Department of Defense briefing by Secretary of Defense Donald H. Rumsfeld, March 21, 2003. Available online: <www.centcom.mil/CENTCOMNews/transcripts/20030321.htm> Accessed July 17, 2003.

Sanders, J. (2003). The college slang page top 20 2003 college slang terms. Available online: <www.intranet.csupomona.edu/~jasanders/slang/top20.html>. Accessed July 17, 2003.

Saussure, F. de. (1916). *Course in general linguistics.* New York: Philosophical Library.

Safire, W. (2003). . . . And so embed. *New York Times*, March 9, 2003. Section 6, p. 22. Available online: New York Times on the Web.

Taylor, O. (1990). *Cross-cultural communication: An essential dimension of effective education.* Available online: <www.maec.org/pdf/taylor.pdf>. Accessed July 2, 2002.

U.S. Equal Employment Opportunity Commission (2002). Federal laws prohibiting job discrimination: Questions and answers. Available online: <www.eeoc.gov/facts/qanda.html>. Accessed October 13, 2003.

Yasin, Z. (2002). "Of Faith and Citizenship: My American Jihad." Commencement address given at Harvard University, June 6. Available online: <www.beliefnet.com/frameset.asp?pageLoc=/story/107/story_10725_1.html>.

Vygotsky, L. S. (1962). *Thought and language.* Cambridge: MIT Press.

Wood, J. T. (1999). *Relational communication: Continuity and change in personal relationships.* Belmont, CA: Wadsworth.

Nonverbal Communication and Listening

Learning Objectives

After reading the module and participating in the activities, you will be able to:

1 Examine how patterns of nonverbal behavior are integral to the process of communication.

2 Recognize how nonverbal communication may be symbolic, spontaneous, or pseudo-spontaneous.

3 Examine how nonverbal communication is used for the creation of relational meaning.

4 Examine listening as integral to communication.

5 Examine listening as a process of receiving information.

6 Examine listening as a process of constructing meaning.

7 Examine listening as a process of relating.

VIDEO
VIEW

I N 1984, THE POP STAR MADONNA SANG, "We are living in a material world." Over the years, the bouncy rhythms and refrains of the so-called Material Girl have been parodied with a variety of offbeat themes, such as "We are living in a liberal world" and "We are living in a high-tech world." In this module, we will explore how we are living in a material world (or worlds) of *communication*. We are material communicators who use nonverbal communication along with words as we speak and listen to one another.

In Module One, we explored the theme that *communication* is the process of creating meaning through the exchange of information between sources and receivers. We also saw how *communicators* assign meanings to symbols and interact with one another in the context of relational communities. In Module Two, we developed the theme that language, which includes verbal and nonverbal elements, is a vehicle of conception for creating meaning. And in this module, we explore the material world of communication, focusing on *nonverbal communication* and *listening*.

ONLINE
JOURNAL

3.1

At first glance, you may think that the principles of nonverbal communication and listening apply only to spoken dialogue in a face-to-face communication context. Bavelas, Hutchinson, Kenwood, and Matheson (1997) suggest in their *Integrated Message Model*, which we introduced in Module One, that face-to-face interaction with another is our first and most common form of communication. Yet, the same principles, that words and nonverbal symbols are integral to one another and that interaction requires the collaborative efforts of a sender and receiver, can also be applied to other contexts of communication, including written communications and electronically mediated interaction. Bavelas et al. explain that when we change the medium of communication, we adapt basic principles of spoken dialogue.

Just how communicators compensate and adapt in different kinds of communication situations is explained by *interaction adaptation theory* (Burgoon, Stern, and Dillman, 1995; Floyd and Burgoon, 1999). Namely, we make judgments in a given communication situation about what is *required, expected,* and *desirable.*

THINK
ABOUT THIS

3.1

Interaction adaptation theory also explains how communication is a process of reciprocity between relational partners. As we judge a situation, we take into account the person with whom we are communicating and what is required, expected, and desirable for that given relationship. You probably grasp this intuitively when you consider how in one relationship, it is absolutely vital to communicate face to face, but in another, it's best to communicate in writing, on the phone, or through another electronic channel, such as e-mail.

The first section of this module will examine the patterns of behavior that constitute *nonverbal communication.* In keeping with the theme of examining the material world in which we communicate, nonverbal patterns of behavior might be called *material language.* It is through nonverbal behavior that physical acts of communication are performed, that states of mind and feelings are given material forms, and that relationships are embodied.

RAPID
REVIEW

3.1

Nonverbal Communication: Material Language

Nonverbal communication is comprised of physical, vocal, spatial, thermal, olfactory, and tactile components—all of which we use when we interact with others. How we use these nonverbal patterns of behavior can be compared to how we use words: as members of speech communities and relational communities who share rules for communicating. And like verbal communication, nonverbal communication is governed by a set of rules.

Hall (1973) observes that nonverbal communication is an extremely important component of language that we often fail to acknowledge. He writes:

> Most Americans are only dimly aware of this "silent language" even though they use it every day. They are not conscious of the elaborate patterns of behavior which prescribe the handling of time, spatial relationships, attitudes toward work, play, and learning. In addition to our verbal language, we are constantly communicating our real feelings in the language of behavior. (p. ix)

To understand the importance of nonverbal communication, we will examine three basic features:

- How nonverbal communication creates the physical context of language
- How nonverbal behavior may be symbolic, spontaneous, or pseudo-spontaneous
- How nonverbal behavior is a way of communicating relational messages

Nonverbal Communication as the Physical Context of Language

When we speak or write, it's impossible to divorce our words from our nonverbal behaviors. As Jones and LeBaron conclude (2002), the verbal and nonverbal elements are inseparable. Thus, we can't speak without gesturing with our hands, taking on a certain posture, or using our voices to communicate nonverbally. And we can't write down words on paper or type them on a computer without using a visual, nonverbal system. In fact, Marhkam (1998) observes that when interactions online are confined to text, the text becomes an embodiment in cyberspace.

As the verbal elements of communication are used in conjunction with the nonverbal elements, the nonverbal elements also create the physical context for listening and understanding words. This is similar to the way that the syntactic structure of a sentence creates a context of meaning for each word. That is, each word in the sentence, such as the subject, is understood in relation to the verb. We interpret the sentence as a whole. In a similar vein, we understand spoken words in relation to the nonverbal symbols a speaker uses.

Behavioral psychologists, anthropologists, and researchers in communication distinguish various types of nonverbal behaviors that may be used in conjunction with words or in place of words:

- *Paralanguage:* Vocal nonverbal behavior that is produced through manipulation of the voice
- *Kinesics:* Physical nonverbal behavior, such as gestures, movements, tensions of the body, facial communication, and eye gaze
- *Haptics:* Use of touch
- *Proxemics:* Use of spatial distance and territoriality
- *Chronemics:* Meaning of time
- *Olfactics:* Perception of smells

- *Typography and graphics:* Physical representation of meaning
- *Artifacts:* Concrete objects and personal appearance

3.2

Paralanguage: Vocal Nonverbal Behavior   Studies of **paralanguage** consider how a speaker manipulates the vocal qualities of rate, pitch, loudness, intensity, silence, and voice variation. Paralanguage is most like the phonetic aspect of spoken words and how we use phonetic rules in the sense that the dynamics of voice are used in conjunction with the articulation of phonemes. But studies in paralinguistics also go beyond the articulation of individual sounds to examine how a number of vocal elements coalesce.

A person's patterns of paralanguage create a vocal "fingerprint," so to speak. Most of us can almost instantly recognize the voices of people with whom we interact regularly. As we listen, we discern the distinctive ways that they make phonemes and the characteristic rhythms and vocal tones they use. You may have a friend who has a unique way of pausing or raising or lowering vocal pitch. You may distinguish some of your loved ones for speaking quietly and others for speaking loudly. Some speakers are highly energized, and others are much more subdued. The distinctiveness of each person's voice may also reflect unique aspects of his or her physiology and carry traces of his or her dialect.

Voice verification technology can isolate and measure the paralanguage and the acoustic phonetic elements of a voice. For instance, when tape recordings of messages by Osama bin Laden were circulated to his followers and broadcast on Al Jazeera television after the 9/11 attacks, voice verification was used to discern whether the voice on the tape was authentic.

3.1

VIDEO VIEW
3.1

VIDEO VIEW
3.2

Kinesics: Physical Behavior   **Kinesics** includes physical nonverbal behavior, such as gestures, movements, and tensions of the body. Facial communication is also an important aspect of kinesics. Studies of facial communication isolate how particular parts of the face are expressive, with special reference to the eyes, eyebrows, and the area around the mouth. Facial communication is also studied to note how we disclose or mask our feelings.

Eye gaze is a prominent aspect of facial communication. We may look directly at someone or divert our eyes during an interaction, sometimes purposefully and at other times without conscious awareness. Our patterns of eye contact are also subject to cultural rules and norms. Whether we follow these rules or violate them can be interpreted as meaningful to listeners. In a given setting, we may thus view another person's eye contact favorably or unfavorably, depending on what we have learned about how to relate interpersonally or in small-group or public communication situations.

In their studies of people engaged in conversations, Bavelas, Coates, and Johnson (2002) have observed how speakers and listeners coordinate patterns of eye gaze. North American listeners commonly look at the speaker more than the speaker looks at them, until the speaker makes direct eye contact to create a *gaze window* of mutual eye contact that is used to secure a response.

3.3

Haptics: Use of Touch   **Haptics** is nonverbal communication through the use of touch. Studies about the communicative dimensions of touch explore it as one of the most elemental forms of communication. Touch is the first type of human interaction that humans learn, originating when a child leaves the womb and relates to the external world as a newborn. In later development, touch becomes associated with communication variables such as affection, intimacy, trust, power, and violence. Behavior studies in haptics also look at attitudes toward touch, especially attitudes about welcoming and resisting touch.

paralanguage   Vocal nonverbal behavior that is produced through manipulation of the voice.

kinesics   Physical nonverbal behavior, such as gestures, movements, and tensions of the body; facial communication is an important component.

haptics   Nonverbal communication through the use of touch.

Norms about touching are also explored in light of cultural attitudes and expectations. An Le describes the unique rules that govern touch in Vietnamese culture:

> It is rude in Vietnam if a younger person touches any part of an older person's body when they are talking. And when they shake hands, it is the older one who first presents his or her hand. Then, the younger must shake with both hands to show respect.
>
> It is also very impolite for anyone to touch another person's head, except for parents who can touch the heads of their own children. To Vietnamese people, the head is an important part of the body and a holy part of the spirit. It is how we pay our respect to Buddha and ancestors.

3.4

3.2

Proxemics: Use of Space   The term **proxemics** applies to how we organize the distance or physical closeness we want to maintain between ourselves and others and to the way that people stake out their *territory*. Hall (1959) has observed that people in the United States have an *intimate distance* of 6 to 18 inches, which is reserved for their closest relationships; a *personal distance* of $2\frac{1}{2}$ to 4 feet, which is comfortable for friends and casual acquaintances; a *social distance* of 4 to 7 feet, which is for impersonal relationships; and a *public distance* of 7 feet or more, which is for communications in public settings.

Hall has also explored how the distance people choose to maintain between themselves and others varies greatly from one cultural community to another. You may have lived in or traveled to another country in which the intimate or social distance was much different than in the United States—perhaps allowing more or less space. As an illustration, Stasia describes how space was organized very differently in the community in Eastern Europe where she lived the first fourteen years of her life. There the distances were much closer than in the United States. She observed her surprise when she first entered a classroom in the United States:

> It was intimidating to walk into the classroom for the first time. I thought to myself, what is going on here? Everyone is sitting at their own desk and the desks are so far apart. In the village that I had come from, the schoolroom was set up with students sitting on benches. There was another person right next to you.

Territoriality: Ownership of Space   Another spatial aspect of nonverbal communication is **territoriality**, which deals with how people claim ownership of physical space. Studies in territoriality describe how communicators carve out their spaces and incorporate aesthetic and design features to personalize them. Territoriality is closely related to the concept of the *environment* of communication that we discussed in Module One.

Linda, who works in a large corporation, observed how staff members in her office environment communicated territorial messages. Some of these were expressed in how they designed their spaces and added personal touches. Her reflections also underscore the idea that people may interpret territorial messages in different ways:

3.2

> In the workplace, employees often identify their territory by decorating their workstations with personal items, such as family photos and other personal artifacts. In my office, the director usually has an open door policy, which conveys the nonverbal message that "All are welcome." But if the door is closed, this conveys an ambiguous message.
>
> For example, the entire staff had just concluded a staff meeting held by the director. During the meeting, things discussed were not so favorable, and after the meeting, the director entered her office and closed the door. "What's going on?" was the question in the mind of staff members. One person perceived that the director was upset with the outcome of the meeting; another perceived that the director did not want to be disturbed.

proxemics   Nonverbal communication through the use of spatial distance; includes physical closeness and maintenance of zones of personal space.

territoriality   A spatial aspect of nonverbal communication that deals with how people claim ownership of physical space.

In actuality, the door was closed because the manager in the office next to the director was having a loud conversation. The director closed her door to protect her environment from their interaction. Then again, she may have needed some time out after the meeting, regardless of whether she was upset!

Chronemics: Meaning of Time   Studies in **chronemics** often take an anthropological focus to examine what *time* means within the context of a culture. These studies may focus on the cultural norm for being punctual or on time-related values, such as showing reverence for the past and upholding tradition, believing in the importance of living in the present, and emphasizing the need to plan for the future.

3.3

Hall (2000) describes several ways in which people use time. A *monochronic* use of time involves doing one thing at a time. In contrast, a *polychronic* use of time involves multitasking, or doing more than one thing at a time.

Olfactics: Perception of Smells   The study of **olfactics** examines how people exude and perceive smells. Smell, like touch, is a primal form of communication. There are also social and cultural norms related to smell that align with norms for personal hygiene and grooming. Olfactory studies examine these subjects as well as how fragrance and air quality affect the physical environment for communication.

3.5

How we respond to certain smells is very subjective and rooted in our individual life experiences. Particular fragrances often trigger memories and evoke spontaneous responses that can be positive or negative. Skip examines his negative reaction to the smell of roses, which usually evokes a pleasurable response:

3.4

> I know this will sound kind of weird to many, but I have a very negative visceral reaction any time I am around roses. I associate them with death. The roots of this response can be found in my childhood. In the town where I grew up, they had a custom of holding wakes whenever someone died. Atop the casket, there would be a huge arrangement of roses. When I smell roses, I smell the funeral home.
>
> A couple of years ago, I was dating a woman who had a favorite rose-scented perfume. I had to ask her not to use it. So on Valentine's Day, I give her a huge box of chocolates. Now they have the fragrance and taste that conjure up romance for me!

Typography and Graphics   When we think about nonverbal communication, we usually consider the range of physical behaviors used for speaking in the face-to-face channel of communication, such as tone of voice and body movement. Yet written communication—whether read on a computer screen, the display of a cell phone, or a page in a book—also includes nonverbal elements such as **typography and graphics**.

The arrangement of type and white space, the use of different type fonts, the colors used, the typewritten characters, and the physical texture of the paper are all elements of typography. Similarly, the graphics, or illustrations, added to a textbook or used in a multimedia presentation are also elements of nonverbal communication.

In the virtual space of the Internet, these elements of graphics and typography can be manipulated to add a nonverbal dimension to words. As communicators interact online, they create a physical representation of self that reflects their self-image. Online communicators can create visual icons of themselves, called *avatars*.

3.5

Artifacts: Meanings of Objects   A final aspect of nonverbal communication is **artifacts**. Personal objects—such as clothing, jewelry, tools, and things you carry—may also express messages. Sometimes we communicate with aesthetic objects, such as a work of art.

---

chronemics   Nonverbal communication related to the meaning of time.

olfactics   Nonverbal communication related to how people exude and perceive smells.

typography and graphics   Nonverbal aspects of communication that relate to how information is visually presented, whether on paper or onscreen; includes the arrangement of type and white space, the use of different type fonts, the colors used, the typewritten characters, and the physical texture of the paper and also the use of illustrations.

artifacts   Personal objects and aesthetic elements that are used to communicate nonverbally.

Implications for Communication: Understand Nonverbal Communication Holistically

Although we can separate these different types of nonverbal behaviors, they are rarely used in isolation from one another. Rather, as Jones and LeBaron (2002) observe, we use nonverbal communication *holistically*, understanding the interplay among nonverbal behaviors as well as how they are used effectively with words. Grove (1999) advises that we need to examine the total context in which nonverbal communication is used in order to use it accurately:

> Observers' judgments of what behaviors represent are more likely to be accurate when observers take into account the total context in which the behavior occurs and when those judgments are based on observation of whole sets or sequences of nonverbal behaviors. Stated another way, our judgments are more likely to be wrong when they are based on a single behavior in isolation from its context. (p. 113)

Recognize How Decoding Nonverbal Communication Is a Process of Forming Perceptions   In Module Two, we examined the process of forming *perceptions* as a two-step process of creating meaning that involves (1) receiving information through one's senses and then (2) organizing and interpreting that information in a meaningful way. The various components of nonverbal communication—tone of voice, kinesic behavior, touch, smell, sense of space, and awareness of time—are received by different sense organs of the human body, yet the meaning of the communication is created as the perceiver makes sense of the whole pattern, or *gestalt*. Again, we perceive an experience not as a set of isolated elements but as an interconnected whole.

As we do in exercising selective attention, we organize our experiences through an active process of deciding where the connections lie among the various elements. Principles of organization include creating closure so the experience will be whole, applying perceptual sets, and drawing on the categories we construct with language. Effective communicators recognize that their perception of the nonverbal world around them is an active process.

Recognize How the Physical Context May Be Congruent or Contradictory   The nonverbal code of language, like the verbal code, is governed by rules. One critical rule addresses how we expect verbal and nonverbal elements to reinforce one another. We might think of this as the **nonverbal congruency rule**.

Imagine that you are communicating with a loved one. Suppose that you are both recalling pleasant thoughts and memories from an enjoyable experience that you have shared. As you hear the other person's voice, you also observe his or her facial expressions, which reinforce the vocal tone and add impact to the words. As you listen, you also may observe the tensions, movements, and gestures (the kinesics) of the other person's body or of your own. The spatial distance between the two of you may also add to the *gestalt*. In addition, there will be elements of direct and intense eye contact and touch. Suppose, too, that you are seated comfortably in the pleasant environment of your own home and surrounded by objects and photographs that symbolize your shared memories. All of these elements cohere in a dialogue of sharing fond memories.

Yet at other times, the information the source communicates may be perceived by the listener as contradictory or incongruent. In other words, the parts don't fit together. Sometimes, this incongruence is not intended, but aspects of nonverbal behavior belie the spoken words. For instance, a speaker might try to mask his or her feelings by controlling

nonverbal congruency rule   The expectation that verbal and nonverbal codes will reinforce one another.

facial expressions, yet reveal those feelings by the movements of his or her eyes, which can't be manipulated with the same conscious control as other parts of the face. Likewise, the kinesic behavior that might be contained in an effort to appear relaxed will be contradicted by a tone of voice that reveals stress or anger.

When a speaker violates the congruency rule, we may feel a sense of confusion or even distrust in his or her motives, wondering what the real meaning is behind the message. Or we may judge his or her competence as a communicator, especially when we can't otherwise explain the incongruence.

3.3

But can we really tell when someone is being deceptive based on perceptions of particular nonverbal behaviors, such as fidgeting and blinking? Empirical research reported by Feeley and Young (1998) estimates that our ability to detect lies from specific nonverbal behaviors isn't all that good—only slightly more accurate than flipping a coin. The odds of detecting deception are higher when the listener takes in the whole pattern of nonverbal behavior and how it relates in context to the content of what the speaker is saying.

Park, Levine, McCormack, Morrison, and Ferrara (2002) outline a host of features beyond communication behavior that people use to detect untruths. These factors include information learned from third-party sources, physical evidence, confessions, and inconsistencies between statements and prior knowledge.

3.7

Identify Purposeful Contradiction   At times, the contradiction between verbal and nonverbal elements of communication may be deliberate. For instance, when we want to make a statement that is ironic or sarcastic, our mocking tone of voice, rolling of the eyes, or facial sneer may signal to the listener that our words are not to be taken literally. Similarly, when we make jokes, we use a variety of nonverbal expressions to cue the listener to take what we say as humorous.

Purposeful contradiction can also be exclusively nonverbal. Wearing white, high-top tennis shoes along with a black tuxedo may be done to create humor or perhaps to mock a serious occasion. Students who are graduating from high school or college often take this approach, combining the formality of the graduation robe with a humorous touch in terms of dress or demeanor. The message of graduation day incongruity says "Sure, this is a serious occasion, yet it's one of celebration, too."

3.2

Adapt to Different Channels of Communication   We use the fullest range of nonverbal communication behaviors when we are involved in a face-to-face interaction, whether we are the speaker or the listener. Yet nonverbal communication is also important in situations that are not face to face. Effective communicators are able to adapt as they move from one channel or medium of communication to another.

In a study that compared the use of face-to-face communication to other types of mediated interactions, Burgoon, Bonito, Ramierez, Dunbar, Kam, and Fischer (2002) found that many people prefer interacting in situations of close proximity with others, which draw on all of the elements of face-to-face dialogue, because doing so is more familiar than using mediated forms of communication. In addition, face-to-face communication creates interpersonal immediacy.

At the same time, Burgoon et al. found that the lack of nonverbal elements in face-to-face communication can actually be beneficial in some cases. For instance, some kinds of task-centered interactions enable communicators to focus more meaningfully on the verbally transmitted information in the absence of many nonverbal elements. A certain amount of interpersonal immediacy may be lost in this situation, but working on task may be enhanced.

3.1

We may also weigh the practical concerns of time, cost, and convenience in deciding whether to communicate face to face or through media. As a hypothetical example, consider the various ways you might communicate that you want to borrow money. What choices would you make in order to do so? First of all, whom would you ask for a loan? And would that choice make a difference in whether or not you made your request through face-to-face interaction? Would it matter how much money you wanted? Would it matter if it were a formal loan, say, from a bank or credit union, or a personal loan from a family member or friend?

Nonverbal Communication as Symbolic, Spontaneous, and Pseudo-Spontaneous

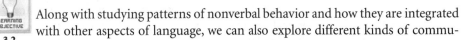

Along with studying patterns of nonverbal behavior and how they are integrated with other aspects of language, we can also explore different kinds of communication codes that are expressed nonverbally. A recent line of research suggests that some forms of nonverbal behavior operate very much in the same manner as verbal codes, while others differ. Buck and VanLear (2002) differentiate three categories of nonverbal communication:

- *Symbolic nonverbal communication* is used in the same way that speakers use words to convey intentions. Symbols are thus governed by social conventions. Some symbols are iconic and resemble the things they signify. Nonverbal symbols, like words, are encoded and decoded in the left hemisphere of the human brain.
- *Spontaneous nonverbal communication* includes involuntary displays that reveal emotions and motivations. Such communication is governed by the right hemisphere of the brain.
- *Pseudo-spontaneous nonverbal communication* includes voluntary efforts to intentionally withhold or express emotional states.

Symbolic Nonverbal Communication   **Symbolic nonverbal communication** is governed by a set of rules that is similar to the semantic rules that govern word meanings. As an example, consider the types of symbols that you would observe if you visited the U.S. Supreme Court chambers in Washington, DC.

3.6

The Chief Justice of the U.S. Supreme Court sits at the center among the eight other members of the Court. The Chief Justice pounds a gavel to call a session to order. These signs are symbolic expressions of the Chief Justice's role and authority. The black robes that the other members of the Court wear and the members' placement in the room, where they sit on a platform that is higher than anyone else, also symbolize the role of the Associate Justices. In addition, the Justices sit in order of their seniority, with the newest members sitting farthest from the center of the platform. Even when they are photographed outside of the court, the members are presented in order of status with more senior justices seated in the front row and junior members standing in a second row.

Consider additionally how we learn the rituals of a given relational community and a particular kind of communication situation. Some of our most common rituals are greeting rituals, in which the gestures are defined by the culture and the closeness of a relationship. To illustrate, LeBaron and Jones (2002) studied a videotape of the unexpected meeting of two friends in a beauty salon and charted the intricate pattern of nonverbal behaviors of two women re-establishing their relationship.

More complex rituals are exemplified by the traditions we follow in conducting a funeral, performing a marriage or commitment ceremony, celebrating a birthday, or

symbolic nonverbal communication Nonverbal expressions that have symbolic meanings; governed by social conventions.

marking an anniversary or retirement. Interpersonal communicators, as well as public speakers and their audiences, have learned the rules for performing the nonverbal behaviors expected in each of these situations. Moreover, most people can recognize the different rules for using nonverbal symbols as we move from one communication situation, culture, or relationship to another.

Nonverbal Symbols as Icons   Some nonverbal symbols are used as **icons.** What distinguishes an icon, according to Buck and VanLear (2002), is that it resembles the thing that it symbolizes. Thus, the "meaning of the symbol (as an icon) does not rely entirely upon social convention, but can be inferred from the nature of the symbol as used in context" (p. 525). Pictures, photographs, portraits, cartoons, diagrams, and maps can all be iconic.

For instance, a photograph or a painting of a scene may depict an event in the same way that a portrait of a person represents his or her face and physical characteristics. In the wake of the destruction of the World Trade Center, for instance, three firefighters were photographed raising a U.S. flag. That image became an icon of the whole event and captured a host of patriotic feelings. Indeed, it became an icon for the events of September 11.

WEB
ACTIVITY
3.7

Subsequent plans to memorialize the event with a life-size bronze statue created a controversy, however. The original photograph had depicted three white men raising the flag. Yet, as reported by Flynn (2002) in the *New York Times*, the plan for a bronze memorial was scrapped when firefighters learned that the design for the statue called for depicting a black and a Hispanic firefighter along with a white firefighter. The intent of that design was to symbolize racial and ethnic diversity in the New York City Fire Department. Flynn explains how "opponents of the statue had collected the signatures of more than 1,000 firefighters who objected to the design, saying it had sacrificed historical verisimilitude for political correctness." According to Flynn, who spoke with officials of the company that developed the plans for the life-size statue, the plan was to create a "symbolic representation" rather than a historic record of the event.

A schematic diagram shows the relationship among the components of what it represents. For example, many items are purchased unassembled and come with instructions that are supposed to show you how to put the pieces together.

A map is a visual rendering of the spatial organization of the place that it signifies. Perhaps you have drawn a map to guide someone who is driving to your house. The morning weather report on your local television station or on the web provides maps that trace the movements of weather conditions as they approach your community, complete with pictorial icons of bright yellow suns or gray clouds, depending on the forecast for the day's weather.

On election night, a national map portrays which candidate has won the electoral votes of each state using the convention of assigning a particular color to each political party. Those who watched the election coverage of the U.S. presidential election in 2000 will recall how the graphic depicting the state of Florida changed colors as the television networks reported that Florida's votes had been won by Vice President Al Gore, then by Governor George Bush, and finally declared the race too close to call. The icon for the state of Florida remained gray for almost two months.

Public speakers often use pie charts and bar graphs as icons to show the relative weights of statistics. Public speakers may also use clip art and photographs in a multimedia presentation as icons that signify certain points.

VIDEO
VIEW
3.3

icons Symbols that resemble what they signify.

ONLINE
JOURNAL
3.8

Hand gestures are also used as icons in everyday speech and in art forms such as dance and pantomime. Some icons communicate meaning completely without words, as is done in pantomime, while other icons are used with verbal expressions. For instance, as you describe how large something is, you

FIGURE 3.1   Emoticons

Emoticons are typewritten. Shown here is the emoticon for reading a book. Many emoticons are like this one and need to be read from left to right. To interpret it, you see the face of the reader on the left. The symbols usually used for greater than represent the covers of the book and the equal sign in the middle is for the pages of the book.

might move your hands apart to show the size. Visualize the gesture that often accompanies the verbal phrase "Fill my glass to the top."

3.9

The sounds of certain words can also serve as icons. The poetic device of **onomatopoeia** is used in everyday speech, as well as in literature, to express the meaning of a word by its sound. The sound produced by combining the various phonemes of the word *buzz,* for example, resembles the sound of a bee. When we identify a bird as a *cuckoo,* we produce a sound that's similar to that made by that type of bird.

An especially expressive speaker may also modify a sound within a word so it is articulated as a nonverbal vocal icon. For instance, drawing out the vowel in the word *long* and shortening the vowel in the word *snap* will make these words sound like what they mean. Do so in reading aloud this sentence: "I waited so *long* for the day to come and when it did arrive, it was over in a *snap.*"

You might add an iconic gesture to that phrase, too, perhaps snapping when you say the word *snap.* Perform the speech act of telling someone "Be quiet," and note whether you find yourself whispering the words, modeling quietness in your own speech.

Icons are not confined to spoken dialogue. When we write, we use typewritten and handwritten iconic images. For instance, messages posted on discussion boards of the Internet or shared by way of e-mail or instant messaging may include typographic icons called *emoticons* (see Figure 3.1). Sometimes, the software used for live chat conversations provides icons such as laughing, frowning, applauding, and asking a question. These icons can be very helpful to quickly offer feedback or comments about what is being exchanged verbally.

3.8

3.9

Based on an ethnographic study of interacting with people online, Markham (1998) describes how paralanguage is inserted into speech online by using keyboard strokes as well as the range of other nonverbal expressions that are displayed during a chat online:

> In addition to the computer inserting some of the paralinguistics, people seemed much more emotionally expressive than in face-to-face conversation, perhaps because they/we expressed their emotions. I wonder if this is because people are forced to use the emote command to create and show facial expressions or emotional actions such as laughing, crying, sighing, gesturing, and so forth. Using computer commands (typing "emote" or ":") and then writing out the desired emotions ("laughs," "Sighs deeply") may make participants more aware of emotional expressions as part of every conversation and as part of the presentation of self. Certainly, I am more aware that emotional and nonverbal communication was happening. (p. 48)

onomatopoeia An iconic use of language in which a word sounds like what it signifies.

Spontaneous Nonverbal Communication   While nonverbal symbols, including icons, are used intentionally, **spontaneous nonverbal communication** is involuntary, according to Buck and VanLear (2002). For instance, when you experience pain or fear, you have a spontaneous nonverbal response to the situation.

Spontaneous nonverbal signs cannot be separated from the underlying psychological states that evoke them. In this way, spontaneous nonverbal expressions might be likened to symptoms, for which there is a logical connection to the underlying cause. For example, physical signs such as a person's elevated body temperature signify that he or she has a fever and thus likely an infection.

Pseudo-Spontaneous Nonverbal Communication   Communicators sometimes try to mask their spontaneous nonverbal responses. To show this, Buck and VanLear (2002) use the illustration of a person who is hosting a party and experiencing a severe headache. The host may try to cover up the pain with an excessive display of smiling and good cheer. When a communicator imitates a certain feeling or attempts to mask a true feeling, he or she is performing **pseudo-spontaneous nonverbal communication**. In other words, he or she acts as if the feeling is real, when in fact he or she is putting on a type of emotional mask.

When we communicate in a stressful situation, we may manifest spontaneous signs of our nervousness. In a high-stress communication situation, such as having a job interview or giving a formal speech, those spontaneous responses may include vocalized pauses, physical rigidity, random movement, and fumbling with objects—all of which signify nervousness. Yet if a communicator gains a self-awareness of these signs of nervousness, he or she may display pseudo-spontaneous efforts to appear confident and composed. In fact, public speakers learn physical relaxation techniques that help them appear calm, even if they are churning away inside.

Implications for Communication: Distinguishing among Symbolic, Spontaneous, and Pseudo-Spontaneous Nonverbal Communication

ONLINE JOURNAL
3.10

Recognize and Adjust to Cultural Meanings   By distinguishing *intentional* symbolic uses of nonverbal communication from *spontaneous* and *pseudo-spontaneous* uses, we can appreciate the fact that much of what we know about how to communicate nonverbally is a reflection

WEB ACTIVITY
3.10

of our culture. Just as we recognize differences in the verbal code from one speech community to another, we can also identify meaningful differences in nonverbal communication that are rooted in the social and cultural groupings of language users.

Along with recognizing these differences, we can also adapt to differences. Martin provides an interesting illustration of learning to adjust to cultural differences after coming to the United States from Venezuela:

> In Venezuela, you don't use a curled index finger gesture to ask someone to come closer. In fact, it is an insult to use that gesture because it is used for calling an animal. When I first came to the United States, I felt angry when a co-worker used the gesture. I don't know whether I showed the anger on the outside, but I felt it inside as my spontaneous response. Now, I've gotten used to it and don't get upset.

Recognize How Nonverbal Communication Is Used to Communicate Emotions   In his classic textbook *The Principles of Psychology,* James (1890) writes, "Every passion in turn tells the same story. A purely disembodied human emotion is

THINK ABOUT THIS
3.5

spontaneous nonverbal communication   Nonverbal expressions that are made involuntarily and thus reflect the underlying psychological states that evoke them.

pseudo-spontaneous nonverbal communication   Nonverbal expressions that are intended to appear spontaneous; may involve imitating a certain feeling or attempting to mask a true feeling.

a nonentity" (p. 453). We embody emotions when we speak and write. We also may learn to feel the responses of our own bodies as we listen and read. The embodiment of feelings with or without words is an experience of nonverbal communication. Emotional expressiveness may be spontaneous or pseudo-spontaneous.

While words and nonverbal behavior are both important vehicles for expressing feelings, we use our whole bodies to experience feelings. Paralanguage, kinesics, and the use of space and touch all come into play in expressing our feelings. In a given communication situation, one or more of these elements might have an especially significant role.

At times, we find ourselves in situations that limit how freely and fully our feelings can be expressed. This may occur when we are expected to play a particular role or meet the demands of a communication situation that is governed by rules that prohibit direct statements of feeling. These are the kinds of situations that may invite us to use pseudo-spontaneous displays of feelings. For instance, upon being criticized by your boss in front of a group of co-workers, you would likely do your best to remain calm and in control, rather than react with hurt or anger.

At other times, we may choose to overstate our feelings. Grove (1999) discusses the rule of *intensification,* which occurs when we express more emotion than is really involved in the situation. This is something like the verbal strategy of hyperbole, which is used to overstate an idea or feeling. You may follow the rule of intensification, Grove observes, when you greet a guest effusively. At other times, we deintensify our feelings, especially when it is inappropriate to show emotion in a public setting. How freely we show disappointment, for instance, may be regulated by a given communication situation.

Express Feelings Openly When Possible   Johnson (1972) explains that we also learn to conceal our feelings by repressing them, disguising them, or distorting them. We are especially likely to limit our verbalization of feelings if we have internalized the rules and expectations of others. Although well meaning, other people may cause us to deny our feelings by encouraging us to "Cheer up" or with other comments that seem to say "You aren't entitled to feel that way."

Pollack (2000) points to differences in how boys and girls learn to express feelings and notes that boys are subject to cultural constraints of the so-called *boy code.* According to Pollack, "Boys are just as competent about their emotions as girls" (p. 3), but they have been placed in a cultural "straightjacket" that limits their emotional expressiveness.

Thus, hearing the emotional voices of boys—and men, as well—requires a different style of listening. The following guidelines are recommended for communicating with a boy or man:

1. Create a safe space in which he can express his feelings.
2. Provide a lot of time to listen to him, rather than rush him into an expression of emotion.
3. Offer alternatives to speech for communicating his feelings, such as writing, drawing, or communicating through action.
4. Listen without interrupting or judging him.
5. Show affirmation of what he says.

Nelson describes how learning as a child to mask his facial displays of feelings created misunderstanding in some of his adult relationships:

> For many years, I tried—and was largely successful—to mask my facial expressions. I learned that to show hurt, or anger, or excitement on my face was to open myself up to disappointment and hurt.

This was largely brought on because of my relationship with my parents. When I felt hurt and angry about something, I would keep as straight a face as possible. I figured if they were going to hurt me or make me angry, I certainly wasn't going to give them the satisfaction of seeing it affect me. Of course, this only caused more problems. My lack of facial expression only caused further rifts between my parents and me when I was growing up.

After I left home, I continued to mask my feelings. I eventually came to recognize this was a barrier to effective and healthy communication. When I was first dating and then engaged to my wife, she would occasionally ask me if something was wrong. I would, of course, reply that nothing was wrong—and follow up with "Why do you ask?" It bothered me that she could tell I was troubled with something, and I wasn't sure what to do about it.

Over time, I have learned to be more forthcoming in expressing my feelings—in words and without trying to hide behind a frozen face. But I admit that I still have a tendency to regulate my facial expressions with others, although I do so far less with my wife than before.

Sometimes, the people around us dismiss our feelings as insignificant or irrational, perhaps because they don't feel comfortable with their own feelings. When we are constrained from verbalizing our feelings, we may also communicate mixed messages. We might try to use verbal and nonverbal symbols or pseudo-spontaneous expressions to deny or distort the feelings but at the same time (and perhaps beyond conscious awareness) use spontaneous nonverbal expressions that communicate more authentic feelings.

Mehrabian (1972) has observed that when speakers express their feelings in mixed messages, their listeners tend to pay much more attention to the spontaneous nonverbal dimensions of communication than the words themselves—especially the visual aspects of kinesics, such as body posture, gestures, facial expression, and vocal tone. In those circumstances in which the words used to communicate feelings are unclear or contradicted by nonverbal expressions, Mehrabian has found that as much as 93 percent of the message is communicated through nonverbal communication and only 7 percent through verbal communication.

3.11

In another study, Ekman and Friesen (1978) found facial communication to be the focus of receivers in their perception of a speaker's feelings. These authors suggest that the face, and especially the eyes, communicates basic emotions such as fear, anger, enjoyment, surprise, sadness, disgust, and so on.

UIDEO
UIEW

3.4

Express Emotions in Public Speaking   Effective public speakers also communicate feelings. The Greek rhetorician Aristotle used the term *pathos* in his book *Rhetoric* to describe persuasion that is achieved by arousing the passions of the audience along with logical appeals and the development of the character of the speaker.

An impassioned speaker may express feelings through spontaneous as well as intentional use of nonverbal symbols or through a pseudo-spontaneous display. Fannie Lou Hamer, an advocate for voting rights, recalls that she was once described as "the angriest woman in Mississippi." In a speech for young people, she drew on her anger to develop a powerful appeal to support voting in elections.

3.2

Hamer's speech told her own story about growing up in Mississippi in the middle of the twentieth century, a time when African Americans were denied the opportunity to vote. She began with a rhetorical question: "Have you ever wondered what all this voting stuff is about?" For Hamer, fighting to win the vote was a courageous struggle to combat prejudice and discrimination. Today, many years after the civil rights movement of the 1960s, her narrative and her delivery in recounting the events of her struggle continue to evoke strong feelings—for her and her listeners.

3.3

Nonverbal Communication and Relational Messages

As explained by Watzlawick, Beavin, and Jackson (1967), the **relational dimension** of a message communicates attitudes and feelings that each party has about the relationship. Just as with other feelings, relational messages may be communicated explicitly in words or implicitly through nonverbal expressions.

Many different types of relational messages may be used to define the nature of relationships. While the number and range of types of messages vary, communication theorists and psychologists, including Mehrabian (1971), have emphasized three that are commonly expressed using nonverbal communication:

1. *Immediacy messages*, which communicate liking, affiliation, warmth, and closeness to others
2. *Responsiveness messages*, which show interest and attention to others
3. *Control messages*, which reflect how relational partners perceive their power and status vis-à-vis one another

Nonverbal Communication of Immediacy How do you communicate a desire for closeness or for distance? **Immediacy messages** communicate those feelings either verbally or nonverbally. Coker and Burgoon (1987) list a constellation of nonverbal behaviors that communicate immediacy—such as physical proximity, eye contact, touch, and body orientation—that are communicated reciprocally by partners in a relationship.

We also learn to communicate immediacy in ways that are appropriate and expected by taking cues from our culture and the relational history we have established with the other person. How we express immediacy will vary from one relationship to another. Thus, what is appropriate for communicating immediacy in one situation may be out of bounds in another.

In keeping with their interaction adaptation theory of communication, which we discussed in the first section of this module, Floyd and Burgoon (1999) observe how partners in a relationship match one another's feelings by using the same or similar nonverbal expressions. This matching is done in light of how partners judge the types of behaviors that are required, expected, and desirable in a given situation.

For instance, you may communicate closeness or distance by reducing or increasing the physical distance between yourself and another or by making the tone of your voice warmer or colder. Depending on the norms of your culture and the way your relationship has been mutually defined, you may also make more or less eye contact or feel more or less free to touch the other person.

When we move from one culture to another, we may also observe significant differences in how members assign meaning to nonverbal behaviors as expressions of immediacy and the associated feelings of warmth, closeness, and connection. In American culture, for instance, the practice of two adults holding hands in public is largely confined to heterosexual romantic partners. Gay or lesbian romantic lovers who hold hands in public risk homophobic comments or even violence in some situations. In other cultures, holding hands may signify friendship, rather than romance. As another example, some communities may encourage effusive hugging while others may discourage it.

Nonverbal Communication of Responsiveness **Responsiveness messages** demonstrate interest in and attention to other people. They may also communicate more than the

relational dimension The part of a message that communicates the attitudes and feelings each party has about the relationship; may be communicated explicitly through verbal language or implicitly through nonverbal language.

immediacy messages Relational messages that communicate a desire for closeness or distance.

responsiveness messages Relational messages that demonstrate interest in and attention to another person.

simple fact that you are listening. Indeed, relational messages may say a great deal about how you feel about yourself and the other person. Your degree of responsiveness may also imply feelings of respect, support, and confirmation.

People who communicate a sense of responsiveness to others are often perceived as being open, compassionate, sympathetic, gentle, and friendly. Conversely, a lack of responsiveness communicates aloofness, indifference, insensitivity, and lack of caring (Richmond and McCroskey, 1998).

Many of us recognize on an intuitive level that when someone is paying attention to us, we feel greater motivation to communicate with him or her. Attentive listening—coupled with nonverbal behaviors such as head nodding and affirming vocalizations, such as "ah" and "uh-huh"—may communicate support and encouragement. Indeed, we may feel that we are valued and respected by the responsive individual.

The converse is also true. Suppose you are feeling bored with a conversation, but rather than state that directly to your relational partner, you withhold eye contact, yawn, slouch in your chair, and adopt a posture of being listless. Since relational messages communicate attitudes toward others and make statements about how we see ourselves, the person whose nonverbal behavior manifests boredom may be saying "I think you are dull." Moreover, since relational messages communicate attitudes a person holds about himself or herself, when someone is unresponsive, he or she may be saying "I am too important to waste my time listening to you."

Nonverbal Communication of Control   **Control messages**, which communicate power and status, are the third major type of relational messages that may be communicated principally through nonverbal means. As with the other relational messages described in this section, messages about control can be communicated with or without words.

Power and control can be expressed through several nonverbal means, including vocal tone, physical behavior, and touch. Status level in a relationship can also be expressed through nonverbal communication with artifacts, territory, use of space, and even time management. For instance, someone who is chronically late may be asserting his or her desire to control the situation or establish his or her importance.

Implications for Communication: Understanding Relational Messages

Recognize How Nonverbal Relational Messages Signal Changes in a Relationship   Relationships grow and change over time, and key turning points are often marked by changes in the tone and quality of nonverbal communication between partners. Guerrero and Jones (2000) have explored how partners in romantic relationships assess the growth in intimacy on the basis on pleasantness of vocal tones, facial expressions, and attentiveness. These are all aspects of immediacy in a relationship.

Appreciate How Relational Messages Affect Perceptions of One Another as Well as of a Relationship   In addition to their primary function of defining the nature of a relationship, relational messages also affect how people form judgments of one another. In their research, Burgoon and Le Poire (1999) found that we form a positive perception of someone as pleasant on the basis of how he or she communicates relational messages nonverbally. In particular, when communicators use nonverbal behaviors that express qualities of immediacy, along with energetic and dynamic communication, they are more likely to be judged positively.

control messages Relational messages that communicate power and status.

Learn to Accurately Interpret Feelings of a Relational Partner   The partners in an interpersonal relationship also need to become competent in understanding one another's feelings and interpreting relational messages. In a study of married heterosexual couples, Koerner and Fitzpatrick (2002) found that couples experience greater relationship satisfaction when they can accurately decode one another's positive and negative feelings as relational messages. Positive relational messages are expressed with prolonged eye contact, close interpersonal distance, blushing, pupil dilation, and increased smiling and touching. Satisfied partners can accurately discern when these messages are meant to convey feelings about the relationship.

However, Koerner and Fitzpatrick (2002) also learned that interpreting negative nonverbal communication can be problematic. For instance, one partner's feelings of sadness or depression may be misinterpreted by the other as being a negative judgment of him or her or as displeasure with the relationship, when in fact, it may have little or nothing to do with the relationship or the partner. Terry describes the problem of misinterpreting depression as negative relational messages:

> One of the most important things to come out of the therapy that I did with my partner John was learning to recognize when he was experiencing depression. My tendency was to interpret his negative moods as his being unhappy with our relationship and me. The real eye-opener occurred one day in a session when our therapist turned to me and said: "Terry, this is not about you."
>
> Once I could understand that, I could stop asking myself "what is wrong with me, here?" I could understand that John's depression was not a reflection of his feelings about our relationship, and me. Instead it was what was going on in him. That enabled me to gain a better perspective on John and have a lot more empathy for him rather than feeling defensive if John was acting depressed.

When negative feelings are misinterpreted, the relationship may be undermined or a cycle of reciprocal negative feelings may be initiated. Effective relational partners can often clarify feelings by talking openly and frankly about their feelings and perceptions.

In sum, nonverbal communication can be expressed through a wide range of behaviors that create the physical context for communicating. We communicate nonverbal messages that listeners perceive with any of their senses: sound, sight, touch, warmth, smell, and awareness of proximity. We also use nonverbal behaviors along with or in place of words and in various contexts, such as face-to-face communication, written communication, and mediated communication. Finally, nonverbal expressions may be congruent or incongruent with the verbal parts of a message.

As a system of symbols, nonverbal behaviors are frequently understood in light of conventions that vary from one relational community to another and from one communication situation to another. The symbolic use of nonverbal communication expresses the speaker's intentions. Some forms of nonverbal communication are used to spontaneously and involuntarily communicate feelings. In communication situations and relationships, nonverbal communication is particularly significant for expressing feelings and relational messages.

ASSESSING YOUR SKILLS

3.3

In the final section of this module, we will examine an integral part of communicating in a material world: listening.

RAPID REVIEW

3.4

Listening

listening The process of receiving information, constructing meaning from it, and responding to a verbal or nonverbal message.

LEARNING OBJECTIVE

3.4

As defined by the International Listening Association (1996), **listening** is "the process of receiving, constructing meaning from, and responding to spoken and/or nonverbal messages." Each of these elements of listening can be defined using the following three-part definition:

■ *Receiving information:* Listening is sensory, in that we use all of our senses to perceive the verbal and nonverbal elements of a message. In addition, we focus on what is most meaningful in a given situation in terms of our goal of listening in order to comprehend ideas, to critically analyze ideas, to experience pleasure and aesthetic appreciation, or to relate to others.

■ *Constructing meaning:* Listening is the process of organizing and understanding the verbal and nonverbal elements of a message in order to interpret it. This is the process of decoding and assigning meaning by perceiving the whole structure of a message and (when appropriate) critically evaluating it.

■ *Responding:* Listening is interactive in that we respond by providing feedback in the give-and-take of dialogue with another.

Note that this three-part definition of listening parallels the discussion in Module One of the three views of communication: the transmission view, the symbolic view, and the relational view.

Listening to Receive Information

Think about your typical week and the range of listening activities in which you engage. News programs on the radio and television, lectures at school, training sessions at work—are all situations that require you to listen to ensure that you comprehend what is being said.

As true of the process of perception, discussed in Module Two, when we listen, we do not take in all of the information in our environment. We are selective. We tune into what is most meaningful, especially in terms of our goal in a particular communication situation. Sometimes, our purpose in listening is simply to understand information. At other times, we may use critical thinking to evaluate information. Moreover, we may listen for pleasure or to relate interpersonally with another person.

Goals of Listening   To sort out the differences among these goals of listening, consider how your focus as a listener varies depending on the communication situation. When you are listening primarily to comprehend information, such as in a class lecture or a workplace briefing, you may have to pay a lot of attention to the main points and how they are developed. In that situation, you must focus on the particular pieces of information you will need to remember for later use.

Sometimes, the goal of listening may be to analyze information through critical thinking. Suppose that you are listening to a sales pitch or to an argument. In either situation, along with listening for comprehension, you need to pay attention to the logic and validity of the speaker's message and assess whether he or she is credible.

Listening to understand and to evaluate stand in sharp contrast with the kind of listening we do when relating personally to another communicator. In such an instance of relational communication, you need to focus on the feelings of the other person along with the information being communicated. Your relational partner may need support and a compassionate level of empathy and understanding.

Lastly, your goal in listening may be to listen for enjoyment. Suppose you go to a play or a concert or watch a movie or television program for pleasure. When the goal of communication is enjoyment, you listen in order to appreciate the aesthetic form of the message. Pleasure is one of the major factors of human motivation.

Sometimes, it is just plain fun to listen! We enjoy the wit and repartee of good conversation. We appreciate the eloquence and creativity of someone else's language and how he or she uses nonverbal elements of communication. We follow our favorite musical group or attend the theater to enjoy a play or movie. We watch favorite television programs and laugh or cry when they move us to do so. In sum, we respond with pleasure to the beauty of forms.

3.8

Implications for Communication: Receive Information More Effectively

Tune Out Distractions   Some communication environments pose particular difficulties for focusing our attention. In these cases, a competent communicator will exert extra energy to focus on what is really important. Luke describes a difficult situation that many of us may be able to relate to:

> Sometimes it is impossible to listen well in my house. Five members of my family live there, and at least two stereos are on all the time. Usually, there is also a TV going, and there may be conversations and phone calls, too. We are always asking each other to repeat something or skipping over whatever we don't hear. Sometimes the noise is just so bad that I can't study for an exam.
>
> To focus attention and listen effectively, I try to reduce environmental distractions. It is considerate to turn off the television or turn down the music if someone wants to talk with you. Closing a window eliminates traffic noises from outside. Even when I can't eliminate distractions, I can usually reduce them or change my location to one that is more conducive to paying attention and good listening.

Become an Active and Involved Listener   To be effective listeners, we need to treat listening as an active process, in which we are physically and mentally engaged. Pearce, Johnson, and Barker (2003) distinguish among four types of listeners:

1. *Active listeners* are fully attentive and present physically as well as mentally. Active listeners expend energy in participating in an exchange with other people by using direct eye contact, alert posture, and a physical stance that communicates they are engaged in the communication.
2. *Involved listeners* follow what the speaker is communicating mentally but sometimes show less overt physical responsiveness. By being active and involved, listeners assume a sense of shared responsibility for communicating with another.
3. *Passive listeners* are unwilling to take any responsibility for the success of a communication. They assume that the whole responsibility rests with the speaker. Passive listeners are likely to complain that a speaker bores them. They also may pretend to listen by faking attention and thus send distorted feedback to the speaker.
4. *Detached listeners* are not only uninvolved mentally but shows signs of inattentiveness and boredom.

Clearly, it is hard work to be an active and involved listener. Jill describes how easy it is to slip into being a passive listener, especially when the discussion at hand does not directly relate to one's own concerns:

> I listen with the greatest effectiveness when the conversation is relationship oriented—talking with a family member, a friend, or even an acquaintance—or related to personal interests or activities that truly stimulate me.
>
> Recently, I've had a hard time being a good listener on the job because I sit through long meetings that involve large groups of people from many departments.

Also, much of the discussion is extremely technical or does not pertain directly to my role. In other words, it's much harder to stay focused when the material is not interesting to me personally.

I'm glad I recognized this issue in myself before anyone else did (like the boss!). Now I try to concentrate on what is being discussed, even though it seems like boring stuff, because sooner or later, it's going to be my job to develop a communication or training module related to all that boring stuff.

Examine Habits and Attitudes toward Listening   Nichols, a pioneer in the study of listening, has identified a set of habits and attitudes that make someone a poor listener, such as a passive and detached listener (Nichols and Stevens, 1957). Poor listening occurs as a result of any of the following behaviors:

1. Deciding in advance that the subject being talked about is uninteresting and unimportant, rather than approaching it with an open mind

2. Being mentally critical of the speaker's delivery and appearance, rather than concentrating on the content of his or her message

3. Overreacting in showing opposition to the speaker's idea, rather than listening to him or her objectively

4. Listening only for the facts, rather than identifying the speaker's central theme or message

5. Trying to outline everything the speaker says, instead of picking out the main points

6. Pretending to give the speaker your undivided attention, rather than giving him or her accurate feedback

7. Tuning out technical or intricate messages, rather than trying to understand difficult material

8. Reacting to emotional words and phrases, rather than considering such language in the context of the whole message

Listen with an Open Mind   Quianthy (1990) reinforces the need to keep an open mind in order to receive information effectively. Our perception of what another person communicates can be biased by our own personal, ideological, and emotional responses. We become more open minded when we examine ourselves honestly, recognize our own unique perspectives, and welcome others to articulate their own unique perspectives. An open-minded person can recognize the legitimacy of an alternative point of view by making a conscious effort to understand it.

This does not mean that we have to give up our own viewpoints. When we can recognize the integrity of our own views while acknowledging and valuing those held by others, we have developed a heightened sense of self-confidence. And when we have confidence in our own views, it is not necessary for others to agree with or conform to us.

Listening to Construct Meaning

In addition to receiving information, listening is also the process of constructing meaning. In Module One, we explored the idea of making meaning as a central aspect of the symbolic view of communication. As explained by Chandler (1995):

There is no single, fixed meaning in any message. We bring varying attitudes, expectations and understandings to communicative situations. Even if the receiver sees or hears exactly the same message which the sender sent, the sense which the receiver makes of it may be quite different from the sender's intention.

As discussed in Module Two, communicators use words to denote and connote meanings. The meanings of those words, and of the nonverbal language used along with them, resides in the users: the listener and the speaker. Listening is a matter of seeing how the various parts of a message cohere. We interpret words in conjunction with nonverbal communication. We listen to what is spoken on the surface and then probe our own minds to uncover the unspoken dimensions of what someone is communicating. This makes the construction of meaning an active process of making meaning.

Structure-Building Framework Theory   When we construct meaning as listeners, we may also build a structure of meaning in much the same manner as a carpenter builds a house: from the ground up. Gernsbacher's (1997) **structure-building framework** theory suggests that we receive and comprehend information by building cognitive structures.

Gernsbacher describes this as a three-part process. First, as we listen to someone or read a message, we build a foundation. Thus, receivers focus more on the beginning parts of a message, since that is when the foundation is being laid. Then, as new information is received, the listener or reader maps the new information onto the foundation. In this second part of reception, the receiver draws on his or her memory to connect the new information to the old and to determine the coherence of what is being communicated. When that new information does not seem to cohere with the existing foundation, the listener or reader takes the third step of constructing in his or her mind a new substructure, which branches off from the existing one.

3.5

Structure Building as Dialogue   Structure-building framework theory can also be used to explain how the organization of meaning is a collaborative process, in which the source and receiver both play active roles in building a framework of shared understanding. An effective speaker or writer will provide a foundation that guides the listener to make the connection needed for message coherence. As speakers or writers, we do this by including a sufficient amount of background information or providing an introduction to what we say or write. This enables the receiver to perceive the foundation for what follows. As the message continues, an effective writer or speaker also provides transitions and uses a meaningful structure for the progression of points.

In face-to-face forms of dialogue, the listener may also provide feedback about the coherence of the message. Suppose that Vivien and Laverne are having a conversation. It is late at night and Vivien says to Laverne, "I am so tired, but I have to stay up late tonight to finish this report for my sociology class. It looks like an all-nighter. I think I will go out for a jog."

If you were Laverne, would you think this is a coherent message? The first sentence lays the foundation, establishing Vivien's concerns about being tired and needing to stay awake in order to complete the sociology report. And the second sentence can be easily mapped onto the first: An all-nighter is going to be necessary to get the task done. But what about the third sentence? How can Laverne make sense of that? Does it follow from the rest of the structure? For the conversation to make sense, Laverne will need to build a new substructure that makes some type of connection.

Laverne might also provide feedback and say something like "I don't get it. How come you are going running? Won't that tire you out even more and make it more difficult to stay up?" And then Vivien might say, "Running will get me juiced, so I will stay awake better."

Then again, Laverne may not need to ask the question about running. Based on their relational history, Laverne may be able to fill in the missing information: that

structure building framework theory   A theory that suggests that we receive and comprehend information by building cognitive structures.

Vivien often goes for a jog to get energized. Like Laverne, we often fill in the unspoken information that we know about others from our relational history with them. In any event, the new substructure of the message is that going for a run *does* have a causal connection to the need to stay awake and do the all-nighter.

Writing and Collaborative Structure Building   Written communication is also collaborative in Gernsbacher's (1997) view. Even though the reader of the communication is not immediately present, an effective writer will anticipate how the reader will likely respond. On that basis, the writer will construct a message that has a good chance of being comprehensible.

Traxler and Gernsbacher's (1995) research about writing strategies has led them to offer two guidelines: The first is to learn from the reader's feedback, and the second is to anticipate how the reader is likely to respond. The latter guideline, they note, gives the writer the experience of "being in their reader's shoes."

Difficult Conversations   Some communication situations are more difficult than others and pose special challenges for listening to and understanding the feelings and position of others. Stone, Patton, and Heen (1999) use the term *difficult conversations* to describe those types of communication situations in which misunderstanding and tension occur, sometimes to the point of erupting into conflict. The difficulty may arise from the topic at hand—as when talking about politics, religion, sex, or morality—or when facing a dilemma for which there is no easy, clear-cut solution.

Difficult conversations often involve highly complex situations, in which each party has intense feelings that may even relate to his or her sense of self-esteem and identity. Such conversations pose special challenges for listening and finding common ground with others in order to construct meaning.

The recent controversy in religious circles about the participation of gay and lesbian people provides an example of a difficult conversation. In the United States, local and national churches have been confronted with the dilemma of how to incorporate gay and lesbian people into full membership: Should churches offer commitment ceremonies to bless gay and lesbian relationships? Should churches ordain gay and lesbian people as ministers or priests or open leadership positions to ordained or lay members who are openly gay or lesbian? Underlying these questions are assumptions about morality, the meanings of sacred texts, interpretations of church practice, and issues of justice, identity, and personal integrity.

ONLINE JOURNAL
3.17

In some churches, these issues of sexuality have festered and produced animosity and division, while in others, efforts have been made to foster dialogue and participants have listened to one another. Such dialogue and listening can take place at interpersonal, small-group, and public levels.

Implications for Communication: Construct Meaning to Enhance Understanding

Avoid Making Quick Judgments   Slow down! Take the time to listen to others. Ask yourself what they are *really* saying, rather than making quick judgments.

When we make up our minds too soon about what someone else means, especially when involved in a difficult conversation, we can get into trouble. Fran provides an excellent illustration of how feeling stress caused her to make a quick judgment:

> My husband, Mick, and I have a very equal relationship with one another. Since we both work and have heavy demands on our time—Mick doing volunteer work in our church and me finishing my degree—we have an even distribution of labor around our house.

We both do housework and alternate the two biggest household tasks from month to month. So, during a given month, one of us will do the shopping, errands, and cooking and the other will do the laundry and cleaning.

Last week, we had a classic misunderstanding that arose from my poor listening. I am supposed to do the laundry and cleaning this month, but my cleaning tasks have been put off because I've had a couple of tests and a paper to write. On Thursday, Mick simply said to me that he'd noticed I had not had a chance to do the laundry and that he was hoping to wear a particular white shirt that was in the laundry basket for a conference that he would be going to on Saturday.

But before he could even finish, I exploded. In hindsight, it was mostly because I was feeling so much tension about my schoolwork. Mick said, "Whoa! I'm just asking because I see you've been doing a lot of extra stuff for school, and I was going to offer to go ahead and do the wash."

I immediately jumped to the conclusion that he was being critical. I completely read that into what he said.

Just as creating meaning is a collaborative process, so is creating misunderstanding. An active listener assumes responsibility with the speaker for achieving a mutual understanding. One concrete way to make sure this happens is by checking understanding. Doing so is an easy process of giving feedback to the speaker about what you think he or she said and then asking for clarification.

Ask Questions   A competent listener takes his or her level of activity to still another level by asking questions of the speaker. Questioning the source can clarify and test understanding as you try to comprehend a message. Questioning also can deepen the dialogue about ideas. Indeed, some questions challenge the parties involved in a dialogue to re-examine their ideas and develop better positions.

Questioning can turn a difficult conversation into a learning conversation, in which the goal is to explore on a deep level what another person thinks and feels. Interpersonal dialogue and the collaborative work of small groups will be more effective if the parties engage one another by asking questions. When public speaking events include a forum for the audience to ask questions, a deeper and better understanding of ideas will occur.

Use Critical Thinking   Some communication situations call for using critical thinking. For example, we use critical thinking in order to interpret a message and identify a speaker's intention. If a speaker is attempting to persuade us to accept an idea or to change our behavior, critical listening is vitally important.

Adler (1983) suggests four key questions that an effective critical thinker will ask as he or she listens to a speaker's message:

1. What is the whole speech about?
2. What are the main or pivotal ideas, conclusions, and arguments?
3. Are the speaker's conclusions sound or mistaken?
4. What of it? What consequences follow from the conclusions the speaker wishes to have adopted? What are their importance or significance to me? (p. 97)

It is also important to distinguish facts from inferences. It may be useful to distinguish these two things. A *fact* can be verified. This is often done by directly observing it. Facts can also be verified by other observers. Many times, facts can be measured. We can thus make observations of facts and use statistics to quantify something. In contrast, an *inference* is a conclusion that someone makes on the basis of observed facts. Forming an inference involves arriving at a logical conclusion or making a judgment on the basis of facts. When a speaker states an opinion or leads the audience to draw a conclusion, an inference is being made.

WEB
ACTIVITY
3.14

ASSESSING
YOUR SKILLS
3.5

Listening to Relate

When we listen to another person as part of the building and maintenance of a relationship, we go beyond simply listening to understand or critically examine information or experience enjoyment. Listening engages us in relationships.

To differentiate relational listening from other types, think about the ways you might participate in the following situation: Suppose that your hobby is bird watching. You have trained yourself to perceive and distinguish the songs of various kinds of birds. As you wander along a wooded trail, you use these skills to identify the different types of bird songs you hear.

In this case, you are listening principally to gain information and to enjoy the wonder of bird songs as part of nature. You are also using all of the skills for forming accurate perceptions: focusing attention and listening for the patterns of meaning that represent the sounds of the particular variety of bird you are attempting to identify. Once you identify that bird, you draw out your binoculars to validate that your identification was correct. And if you are like many other bird watchers, you've probably hauled a guidebook or two along, which you can consult to further confirm your visual perception.

In the middle of the day, you sit down for lunch along the trail with your best friend, with whom you've shared a morning of listening to bird songs. Throughout the morning, conversation has been sparse but so much the better to focus on your task at hand: perceiving, distinguishing, and enjoying varieties of bird songs. Now, it's time stop listening to birds and to begin relating to one another. How does your listening change as you engage in a personal dialogue?

It's quite likely that your listening will now become an even more complex process. Listening relationally involves providing both a nonverbal and a verbal presence. You respond to one another nonverbally as well as verbally, taking turns speaking and listening. Perhaps the substance of your conversation will touch on personal feelings and involve recognition of one another's needs, motives, or desires.

Cooper (1997) has conducted a review of the literature on listening, especially in a managerial context and finds that listening as a participant in dialogue involves more than the cognitive activity that's done to form perceptions as an informational or appreciative listener. Rather, such listening is much more complex because it requires the listener to take in the intricate parts of a message and actively engage the speaker in order to support and relate on personal and social levels. This is *relational listening*. In contrast, Cooper observes that *informational listening* is simply listening with accuracy and "involves discriminating facts from opinions, analyzing facts to understand messages, and remembering significant details from conversations" (p. 77).

When we listen to another in the context of a dialogue, Cooper observes that we are listening to show support. That "includes giving attention to the individual and showing involvement with verbal and nonverbal behaviors as well as the ability to make the other person comfortable and undistracted while communicating" (p. 77).

Implications for Communication: Relate and Respond as a Listener

We can become more effective as relational listeners if we follow these five guidelines for relational listening:

1. Create a nonverbal presence.
2. Demonstrate attentiveness in order to deepen dialogue.

3. Respond to and acknowledge the whole message.
4. Take turns.
5. Sculpt mutual meanings.

VIDEO VIEW

3.6

ONLINE JOURNAL

3.18

Create a Nonverbal Presence and Sense of Responsiveness and Immediacy   In face-to-face communication, an effective relational listener creates a physical presence by using nonverbal communication that says "I am listening to you fully, here and now." This may involve orienting one's body and posture to indicate openness, using eye contact in accordance with cultural rules of propriety, adopting facial expressions and head nodding that show receptivity, and using vocal indicators of being present, such as "ah-hah" and "uhmmmmm."

Our nonverbal behavior can also show that we have taken the time to listen to the other person. This may involve a measure of self-monitoring and awareness of ways that we might inadvertently signal that we don't have the time to listen. For instance, if we glance at our watch or otherwise seem to be rushing the conversation, we may communicate a lack of responsiveness. By being relaxed and fully present in the moment with the other person, we can help him or her feel at ease and encourage his or her participation.

Verbalize Attentiveness in Order to Deepen Dialogue   The second guideline for relational listening builds on the first. Along with using our nonverbal actions to show that we are present, we can verbalize our attentiveness, or the fact that we are following what the other person is saying. Doing so may involve asking a few questions, especially to clarify what has been stated or to encourage the speaker to expand on what he or she said. It is important to use tact and discretion in asking questions, of course. Asking too many questions can cause someone to feel that he or she is being interrogated.

Along with using questions selectively, the listener can demonstrate attentiveness by paraphrasing what has been said. A simple **paraphrase** rephrases what the other person said. It is especially useful to paraphrase in order to check your comprehension of what that person said. Thus, one of the goals of paraphrasing is to allow the other person to verify that he or she has been understood.

Getting verification from the speaker may be very important when our goal in listening is to understand information as well as for relational listening, as in the case of getting directions or comprehending a complicated idea. When you paraphrase what another has said and he or she responds "Yes, that is exactly what I mean." Personal feelings might be affirmed, as well. In this regard, a paraphrase demonstrates compassion and empathy between listener and speaker.

We may also show that we are paying close attention to a speaker by drawing on our shared history. Effective listeners remember details from earlier conversations or shared experiences that relate meaningfully to the present dialogue. Sometimes, it is quite effective to recall those earlier details and observe how they seem to connect with the current dialogue. In fact, asking the other if he or she senses some connection between a prior event and the present moment may be an effective way of voicing these reflections.

To illustrate this point, let's use an example. Suppose that Laverne is telling Vivien about a sequence of frustrations that happened at work. As Vivien listens, a similar situation from an earlier conversation comes to mind. If you were Laverne, you might be affirmed if Vivien said to you, "Yes, it must be hard to deal with this situation all over again. It sounds like the frustration you felt with the same person last week."

Paraphrasing is a useful strategy in public discourse as well as in interpersonal communication. Paraphrasing is very valuable when people are debating one another, for instance. The typical pattern of a debate is that one party makes his or her argument, and then the second party offers his or her rebuttal. An important component of a rebuttal is making a clear, accurate, and concise paraphrase of the original position before presenting a counter-argument to rebut it.

paraphrase   To rephrase what another person has said; as an active listening strategy, allows checking comprehension and verifying common understandings and feelings.

Communicating online can also be enhanced with paraphrasing. Think about how you have participated in dialogue with others in online discussion forums, in which there is a give and take of different points of view. Just as with a debate, online communicators often paraphrase what someone else has written before writing a response.

It is challenging, however, to provide listener responses in online interaction. Markham (1998) shares these observations:

> I found it difficult to manage the basic elements of conversation such as taking turns at the appropriate time, nodding, or mm-humm-ing to imply "Go on, I'm listening." I couldn't give a questioning glance or wrinkle my forehead or frown lightly to let the other person know I didn't understand what they were getting at. I couldn't smile, chuckle, or laugh spontaneously. Indeed, if I wanted to react to something that I found amusing, funny, striking, or in some other way noteworthy without interrupting the flow of the story, I had to type something such as "emote smiles" or "emote grimaces understandingly." (p. 71)

Respond to and Acknowledge the Whole Message   The whole message of a communication often goes beyond the actual information that is transmitted. Along with listening to the content, we also respond to and acknowledge the relational level of communication, which can be expressed both verbally and nonverbally.

Listening to the whole message implies a deep level of respect for the other person and for his or her feelings. Johnson (1972) points out that many of us fail at being effective listeners, especially when the feelings that another person is expressing are interpreted as negative feelings or as complaints or criticisms directed toward us. We respond defensively to such remarks in an effort to protect ourselves. But by improving our listening competency, we can acknowledge our defensive reaction and need for self-protection. That means getting in touch with our own feelings and emotional responses.

Listening to the whole message also entails assessing the interplay of verbal and nonverbal aspects of communication. Listeners as well as speakers can be mindful of the *congruency* between verbal and nonverbal communication. As listeners, we need to be perceptive to those situations in which the nonverbal elements seem to be at odds with the verbal. Sometimes, that is a simple matter of recognizing the nonverbal cues of a speaker who intends to be ironic or sarcastic. But other times, when the reason for the inconsistency is not clear, it is a greater challenge.

In these circumstances, a listener might gently probe the matter. A simple and nonthreatening way to do this might be to provide feedback that says "It feels to me as if you have mixed feelings about this. How does it seem to you?"

VIDEO
VIEW

3.7

ONLINE
JOURNAL

3.19

Coordinate Turn Taking   For dialogue to be a genuine collaboration, each member must be able to participate actively as both a speaker and a listener. This is a matter of taking turns.

As we move from listening to speaking, it's important to ascertain that the other person has had the opportunity to express himself or herself fully. An effective listener picks up on nonverbal indicators that the speaker is ready to yield the floor. The listener can also ask for his or her turn to speak in order to determine if the speaker is ready to yield.

Taking turns is more than just shifting the roles of speaker and listener. It also involves maintaining the continuity of the dialogue. The listener's feedback needs to be relevant to what the speaker has said. Indeed, one of the markers of an insensitive listener is to make a follow-up reply that does not connect with the speaker's message.

Create Mutual Meanings   Stewart and Logan (1997) credit their colleague, Milt Thomas, with the metaphor of *dialogic listening* as a collaborative effort, in which partners in conversation are like two people working with a piece of clay: "Like clay, verbal and nonverbal talk is tangible and malleable; it's out there between people to hear, to record, and to shape" (p. 82). According to this metaphor, the parties to a dialogue sit on each side of the potter's wheel, both shaping and modifying the form of the clay. They are sculpting shared meaning.

3.10

3.16

Stewart and Logan suggest that we do this most effectively when we focus on shared meaning. Such meaning is not just internalized within one person, to be discovered and understood by the other. Rather, shared meaning exists in what is going on between the parties. As described by the authors, "Meaning is not just what's inside one person's head. Focusing on 'ours' prepares you to respond and inquire in ways that make it clear that getting to the meaning is a mutual process" (p. 83).

Dialogic partners who approach meaning in this way may use simple feedback techniques, such as *paraphrase plus*. In this technique, one partner rephrases what the other has just said and asks him or her to go deeper. They encourage one another to say more. Dialogue may then grow into a process of mutual discovery and an opportunity to create shared perspectives.

3.6

3.6

Summary

We communicate in a material world by using a wide range of nonverbal behaviors and also by practicing effective listening.

As members of speech communities, we learn how to use nonverbal communication along with verbal communication. Nonverbal communication encompasses a wide range of behaviors, including physical, vocal, spatial, thermal, olfactory, and tactile components. Like the verbal code of communication, nonverbal communication operates in accordance with norms and rules that create a system of meaning. Nonverbal communication is governed by rules of congruency. Congruent patterns of nonverbal communication create the physical context for using language.

Some forms of nonverbal behavior are used as symbols and thus can be interpreted in light of social conventions. Another variety of symbols, called *icons*, resemble what they signify.

Spontaneous nonverbal expressions differ from symbols in that they are involuntary. In addition, spontaneous nonverbal expressions reveal internal emotional states and motivations. Some communicators attempt to conceal spontaneous expressions or use pseudo-spontaneous expressions to mask their feelings or deliberately convey an emotion they want to communicate.

In various types of relational contexts, communicators understand the capacity of nonverbal behavior for communicating feelings and expressing relational messages. When our feelings are not expressed verbally, we often try to express them nonverbally. A competent communicator is skillful at perceiving the feelings of others and at checking his or her own perceptions about those feelings. Relational messages—especially those that communicate immediacy, responsiveness, and attitudes toward control—can be expressed nonverbally or verbally.

Listening is also an integral component of the communication process. Listeners receive information, construct meaning, and respond relationally. A competent communicator recognizes the need to be an active listener and to respond to various types of listening situations. Thus, he or she will receive and act on information differently whether the goal is to comprehend information, to reflect critically, to listen for enjoyment, or to relate to another person. In any event, listeners are competent receivers of information by focusing attention, tuning out distractions, and striving to be active and involved participants.

Listeners are also active in the process of creating meaning. Competent communicators collaborate with one another to build structures of meaning by laying a foundation and then mapping new information onto the old or by creating new, meaningful substructures of meaning. Effective communicators will also identify how some communication situations pose special difficulties, especially when the topic of communication is a problematic issue or one that poses a problem that is not easily solved. Special care is advised to avoid making quick judgments. In creating meaning together, communicators can be much more competent by asking questions and exercising critical thinking.

Particular competencies for relational listening include the following: creating a sense of nonverbal presence that communicates immediacy and responsiveness; verbalizing attentiveness through the judicious use of questions, drawing on relational history, and paraphrasing; responding to the whole message of another in ways that acknowledge emotional expressions and relational messages; turn taking in a way that enhances dialogue; and collaborating with a relational partner in order to sculpt mutual meanings.

PRACTICE TEST

References

Adler, M. (1983). *How to speak how to listen.* New York: Macmillan.

Alessandra, T. (1993). *Communicating at work.* New York: Simon & Schuster.

Bavelas, J. B., Coates, L., and Johnson, T. (2002). Listeners as co-narrators. *Journal of Personality and Social Psychology, 79,* 941–952.

Bavelas, J. B., Hutchinson, S., Kenwood C., & Matheson, D. H. (1997). Using face-to-face dialogue as a standard for other communication systems. *Canadian Journal of Communication, 22.* Available online: <www.wlu.ca/~wwwpress/jrls/cjc/BackIssues/22.1/bavel.html>. Accessed May 17, 2002.

Britton, N. J., & and Hall, J. A. (1995). Beliefs about female and male nonverbal communication. *Sex Roles, 32,* 79–90.

Buck, R., & VanLear, C. A. (2002). Verbal and nonverbal communication: Distinguishing symbolic, spontaneous, and pseudo-spontaneous nonverbal behavior. *Journal of Communication, 52,* no. 3, 522–542.

Burgoon, J. K., Birk, T., & Pfau, M. (1990). Nonverbal behaviors, persuasion, and credibility. *Human Communication Research, 17,* 140–169.

Burgoon, J. K., Bonito, J. A., Ramirez, A., Dunbar, N. E., Kam, K., & Fischer, J. (2002). Testing the interactivity principle: Effects of mediation, propinquity, and verbal and nonverbal modalities in interpersonal interaction. *Journal of Communication, 52,* no. 3, 657–678.

Burgoon, J. K., & Halle, J. L. (1987). Validation and measurement of the fundamental themes of relational communication. *Communication Monographs, 52,* no. 1, 19–41.

Burgoon, J. K., & Le Poire, B. A. (1999). Nonverbal cues and interpersonal judgments: Participant and observer perceptions of intimacy. *Communication Monographs, 66,* no. 2, 105–125.

Burgoon, J. K., Stern, L. A., & Dillman, L. (1995). *Interpersonal adaptation: Dyadic interaction patterns.* New York: Cambridge University Press.

Chandler, D. (1995). *The transmission model of communication.* Available online: <www.aber.ac.uk/media/Documents/short/trans.html>. Accessed June 11, 2001.

Coker, D. A., & Burgoon, J. K. (1987). The nature of conversational involvement and nonverbal encoding patterns. *Human Communication Research, 13,* 463–494.

Cooper, L. O. (1997). Listening competency in the workplace: A model for training. *Business Communication Quarterly, 60,* no. 4, 75–85.

Ekman, P., & Friesen, W. V. (1978). *Facial Action Coding System (FACS): A technique for the measurement of facial action.* Palo Alto, CA: Consulting Psychologists Press.

Feeley, T. H., & Young, M. J. (1998). Humans as lie detectors: Some more second thoughts. *Communication Quarterly, 46,* no. 2, 109–124.

Floyd, K., & Burgoon, J. K. (1999). Reacting to nonverbal expressions of liking: A test of interaction adaptation theory. *Communication Monographs, 66,* no. 3, 219–239.

Flynn, K. (2002). Firefighters block a plan for a statue in Brooklyn. *New York Times,* January 18, 2002. Section B, p. 4. Available Online: New York Times on the Web.

Gernsbacher, M.A. (1997). Two decades of structure building. *Discourse Processes, 23,* 265–304.

Grove, T. G. (1999). Nonverbal elements of interaction. In J. Stewart (ed.), *Bridges not walls: A book about interpersonal communication* (pp. 105–116). Boston: McGraw-Hill College.

Guerrero, L. K., & Jones, S. M. (2000). Responses to nonverbal intimacy change in romantic dyads: Effects of behavioral valence and degree of behavioral change on nonverbal and verbal reactions. *Communication Monographs, 67,* no. 4, 325–361.

Hall, E. T. (1959). *The hidden dimension.* Garden City, NY: Doubleday.

Hall, E. T. (2000). Monochronic and polychronic time. In L. A. Samovar & R. E. Porter (eds.), *Intercultural communication: A reader* (pp. 280–286). Belmont, CA: Wadsworth.

Hall, E. T. (1973). *The silent language.* Garden City, NY: Doubleday.

International Listening Association. (2003). Available online: <www.listen.org >. Accessed June 6, 2003.

James, W. (1890). *The principles of psychology.* Available online: <psychclassics.yorku.ca/James/Principles/index.htm>. Accessed July 16, 2002.

Johnson, D. (1972). *Reaching out: Interpersonal effectiveness and self-actualization.* Englewood Cliffs, NJ: Prentice-Hall.

Jones, S. E., & LeBaron, C. D. (2002). Research on the relationship between verbal and nonverbal communication: Emerging integration. *Journal of Communication, 52,* no. 3, 499–521.

Jourard, S. (1966). An exploratory study of body-accessibility. *British Journal of Social and Clinical Psychology, 5,* no. 3, 221–231.

Koerner, A. F., & Fitzpatrick, M. A. (2002). Nonverbal communication and marital adjustments and satisfaction: The role of decoding relationship relevant and relationship irrelevant affect. *Communication Monographs, 69,* no. 1, 33–51.

LeBaron, C. D., & Jones, S. E. (2002). Closing up closings: Showing the relevance of the social and material surroundings to the completion of interaction. *Journal of Communication, 52,* no. 3, 542–565.

Markham, A. N. (1998). *Life online: Researching real experience in virtual space.* Walnut Creek, CA: Alta Mira Press.

Mehrabian, A. (1967). Attitudes inferred from nonimmediacy of verbal communication. *Journal of Verbal Learning and Verbal Behavior, 6,* 294–295.

Mehrabian, A. (1971). *Silent messages.* Belmont, CA: Wadsworth.

Mehrabian, A. (1972). *Nonverbal communication.* Chicago: Aldine Atherton.

Nakamura, K. (1996). *About American sign language.* Available online: <www.deaflibrary.org/asl.html>. Accessed July 16, 2002.

Nichols, R., & Stevens, L. A. (1957). *Are you listening?* New York: McGraw-Hill.

Park, H. S., Levine, R. R., McCormack, S. A., Morrison, K., & Ferrera, M. (2002). How people really detect lies. *Communication Monographs, 69,* no. 2, 144–158.

Pearce, C. G., Johnson, I. W., & Barker, R. T. (2003). Assessment of the listening styles inventory. *Journal of Business and Technical Communication, 17,* no. 1, 84–113.

Pollack, W. S. (2000). *Real boys' voices.* New York: Random House.

Quianthy, R. L. (1990). *Communication is life: Essential college sophomore speaking and listening competencies.* Annandale, VA: National Communication Association.

Richmond, V. P., & McCroskey, J. C. (1998). *Communication apprehension, avoidance and effectiveness.* 5th ed. Boston: Allyn & Bacon.

Stewart, J., & Logan, C. (1997). *Together: Communicating interpersonally.* 5th ed. New York: McGraw-Hill.

Stone, D., Patton, B., & Heen, S. (1999). *Difficult conversations: How to discuss what matters most.* New York: Penguin Books.

Traxler, M. J., & Gernsbacher, M. A. (1995). Improving coherence in written communication. In M. A. Gernsbacher & T. Givón (eds.), *Coherence in spontaneous text* (pp. 216–237). Philadelphia: John Benjamins.

Watzlawick, P., Beavin, J. H., & Jackson, D. D. (1967). *The pragmatics of human communication: A study of interactional patterns, pathologies, and paradoxes.* New York: W. W. Norton.

The Self and Relational Communities

Learning Objectives

After reading the module and participating in the activities, you will be able to:

1 Recognize that the development of self-concept is a dynamic process that is rooted in self-reflection and involves interaction with others in relational communities.

2 Understand the pragmatic view of the self and the role of consciousness.

3 Understand the dramatistic view of the self and how self-concept is developed through the enactment of roles.

4 Understand the humanistic view of the self and the centrality of the self-actualizing tendency.

5 Understand the cultural dimensions view of the self and how self-concept is shaped by identifying with the value systems of individualism and collectivism.

6 Understand the relational view of the self and how various relational selves are constructed through relationships.

VIDEO VIEW

LEARNING OBJECTIVE
4.1

DO YOU HAVE A PHOTO ALBUM of pictures that tell the story of your whole life? If you do, perhaps some of the pictures show you standing by yourself, looking at the camera, smiling with the look and facial response you've created so that you will be seen exactly as you want to be portrayed. Other pictures are likely more candid shots—your image as it was caught by the eye of the camera at a given moment.

ONLINE JOURNAL
4.1

Alongside the shots of you alone are the group photos of you with the various **relational communities** you belong to. Observe the photos in which you are pictured with family members and friends, classmates and co-workers. Look at yourself at these different points in your life and see the roles that you have performed at different times.

For many of us, our photo albums also depict the important transition points of our lives. Take a closer look at the photos in your album and try to remember what was going on in your life. You will likely see how you have grown and changed over the years.

ONLINE JOURNAL
4.2

Our sense of self changes over time, especially as we participate in dialogues—with ourselves and with others—to achieve self-awareness. So, too, the roles we play and the feelings we have about ourselves change in different circumstances and relationships.

This module will examine how we construct a sense of self through relating to other people and how our **self-concept** affects interactions with others. Closely paired with self-concept is the notion of **self-esteem:** the evaluative dimension of self-concept that is expressed as both positive and negative judgments about the self. Our self-esteem reflects our own assessments of competence and the need for the recognition and respect of others. We grow in self-esteem through interacting with the people in our various relational communities.

ONLINE JOURNAL
4.3

As we explore how an individual creates a complex sense of self, we will examine five perspectives:

WEB ACTIVITY
4.1

- *The pragmatic view* explains how we gain self-awareness through self-reflection and by importing the perspectives of others we interact with.
- *The dramatistic view* explains how we play roles in our interactions with others and use strategies and symbols to present ourselves to others and to manage the impressions they hold of us.

WEB ACTIVITY
4.2

- *The humanistic view* explains how we experience self-esteem and seek to grow as individuals so that we can achieve our full potential as self-actualized persons.
- *The cultural dimensions view* explains cultural patterns and value systems that influence how we form a sense of self.
- *The relational view* explains how we construct a complex sense of self, perhaps even multiple selves, as a result of participating in different relational communities.

The Pragmatic View: The Self and Consciousness

LEARNING OBJECTIVE
4.2

The **pragmatic view of self** is rooted in a school of philosophy that emphasizes how individuals and communities form attitudes, beliefs, and ways of thinking. These ways of thinking lead to the development of consciousness and an awareness of the self. Among the most articulate earlier advocates of pragmatism were William James, a philosopher and pioneer in the academic study of psychology, and George Herbert Mead, one of the key figures in the development of the theory of symbolic interaction.

The Three-Part Theory of the Self

James (1890) identified three components of the self, which a person is able to understand through self-reflection and by taking stock of his or her personal history and interactions with others. In James's view, we can step back and see ourselves as objects of reflection. That assumes, of course, that we actually take the time to examine ourselves.

What we see through self-reflection is what James called the **empirical self.** The three components of the empirical self include the physical self, which James termed the *material me;* the self in relation to others, or the *social me;* and the self who thinks and feels and holds beliefs and values (including judgments about the self), or the *spiritual me.*

If we return to the photo album metaphor, we may look at the pictures to remember the events they chronicle and to make assessments such as "Look at me as a baby; what a beautiful child" and "Here you see me pictured in my scout uniform, looking so proud after having earned all those badges." We may look at the group photos and reflect "I was a real star in my class at school" and "People would tell me how beautifully I sang in the chorus."

4.1

The Material Me   How do you see your body? James (1890) termed the physical self the **material me:** that part of the self that encompasses perceptions of one's body as well as physical objects that are extensions of the self.

When you look at yourself in a mirror, you make a self-assessment of your appearance and observe the nonverbal artifacts of your physical self, such as your clothing and grooming. These are symbolic presentations of your self-concept, if the material me is considered in light of the symbolic view of communication (which we introduced in Module One). Other objects that you own, along with the house you live in, also are parts of your material me and may communicate symbolic messages. And even though James developed his theory of the self prior to the invention of the automobile, he would probably observe today that his theory applies to car ownership, as well. Namely, one of the primary goals of automobile advertising is to get us to identify with cars that enable us to express our identity and personality.

4.3

4.1

4.4

Contemporary social scientists have added to our understanding of how body image is a part of self-concept and how we evaluate ourselves to form our physical sense of self-esteem. Fox and Corbin (1989), for instance, have developed a scale that measures how people judge their physical image in terms of factors such as perceived competence in athletic events, body attractiveness, level of physical conditioning, physical strength, and feelings of physical well-being.

Molly states how important physical fitness is to her self-concept:

Being physically fit has always been something that has made me feel good about myself and have a good self-concept. However, when I was pregnant, I think that my self-concept was affected because I wasn't used to being so out of shape—literally!

Earlier in high school and when I first attended college, I was a cheerleader. I took a lot of pride in being a talented cheerleader and gymnast. As a freshman in college, I was put on the varsity cheering team, which is rare, and I was told before I even tried out that I had been chosen. So, when I decided to stop cheering in my third year, I had a drop in my self-esteem because of the lack of having that positive influence. I have

relational community   The personal, social, and cultural context of human communication.

self-concept   The mental image an individual has of himself or herself; based on self-reflection and constructed through communicating with members of relational communities.

self-esteem   The evaluative dimension of self-concept, which is expressed as positive and negative judgments about the self; reflects assessments of competence and the need for recognition and respect from others.

pragmatic view of self   The perspective that an individual gains self-awareness through self-reflection and by importing the perspectives of others he or she interacts with.

empirical self   What the individual sees through self-reflection; comprised of the material me, the social me, and the spiritual me.

material me   The physical self; the perception of self that involves one's body as well as physical objects that are extensions of the self.

since had to come up with other aspects of my life, like being a good mother, to give me a positive view of myself.

The Social Me   In describing the **social me,** James (1890) said that we have "as many social selves as there are individuals who recognize [us]" (p. 295). Examples of the social me include the self-perceptions of being in such roles as friend, lover, family member, and group participant. In each of these roles— and thus in the social situations they involve—we act in a manner that is consistent with the relationship and show a different self.

As we reflect about our various relationships, we also gain awareness of the feelings of being loved, admired, and appreciated by others. We may feel a very powerful need to be recognized, especially by the people we love the most, and we may seek to be honored.

James suggested that honor is a powerful motivator. Any group, he noted, might create a code of honor for its members, embodying the values they hold. A code establishes appropriate behavior for the group's members and establishes the standards by which they may win the approval and recognition of others.

The Spiritual Me   James (1890) defined the **spiritual me** as the "entire collection of my passing states of consciousness" (p. 297), which might include one's emotions, thoughts, desires, and intellectual ponderings. This sense of self is the awareness of our own mind—what we feel, what we think, and what we cherish. The spiritual me may be expressed as a philosophy of life, a vision of the world, or as a religious or spiritual commitment. It is the most abstract dimension of the self.

The spiritual me may also be thought of as a seeker. In discussing the idea of spiritual self-seeking, James identified how people strive for growth on intellectual, emotional, and moral levels. He also noted that many individuals might pursue spirituality in the traditional sense of examining the meaningfulness of life as being grounded in spiritual forces and values.

Implications for Communication: Self-Awareness

Recognize the Interrelationships of the Three Parts of the Self   In identifying the three parts of the self, James (1890) described the physical, social, and spiritual dimensions as being interconnected and occupying positions on a hierarchy. At the highest level is the spiritual me, and at the lowest level is the material me. The social me is in the middle.

To illustrate the interconnectedness of the three parts of the self, James observed that a parent and child have a social relationship and a material bond of shared physical characteristics based on a common genetic inheritance. He observed, moreover, that when a parent dies, a part of the child's physical self also dies.

When we are in a social relationship with another person, we might also feel a kinship based on our shared ideas, feelings, and values. Our spiritual growth may also be supported and nurtured by a relational community of fellow believers. In that case, spiritual self-seeking becomes an aspect of the social me as well as the spiritual me. The material and spiritual aspects of the self are also interconnected. Even the way we groom and dress ourselves can be used to signify our connection to others. Some members of religious communities, for instance, assume a style of clothing, called a *habit,* to signify their membership and commitment to a spiritual vision.

As a personal illustration of how all three parts of the empirical self interrelate, Peter describes his experience of body piercing:

social me The perception of self in relation to other people and the value placed on those relationships.

spiritual me The perception of self that is the awareness of one's own mind; includes emotions, thoughts, desires, and intellectual ponderings as well as values and moral judgments.

Some people may think that having a piercing is just a piece of jewelry stuck into your body. But that is not the view for many of us who have piercings. Beyond the outward cosmetic change, a piercing symbolizes membership in a group and a way of expressing the attitudes and feelings that go with being part of a way of life. It is even like a religious experience for some people.

View the Development of Self-Awareness as a Process   We develop self-awareness over the course of a lifetime by interacting with many people and experiencing a wide range of circumstances. Thus, our definition of self changes through a slow and gradual process of maturation.

To illustrate this process, we might explore the life story of Malcolm X (1992), as it was told to Alex Haley in *The Autobiography of Malcolm X*. This book also served as a source for Spike Lee's film *Malcolm X,* in which Denzel Washington portrayed the main character. The autobiography provides a narrative of Malcolm X's process of self-discovery.

The narrative begins with the person who was named Malcolm Little at his birth. On his journey of personal transformation, he next becomes known as Detroit Red, a street hustler. In a manner that bespeaks James's interest in the importance of the material me and its connection with the social me, we observe in the Detroit Red phase of the story the practice of "conking," which is the application of harsh chemicals to tightly curled hair in order to straighten it. Malcolm also adopts the "zoot suit" style of clothing to symbolize his membership in a group of street hustlers.

Later, after Detroit Red is arrested and sentenced to prison, he is known as Satan by fellow inmates. This man next finds his spiritual me through self-education, which includes a deep reading of Islamic writings. This leads him to become a Sunni Muslim and a member of the Nation of Islam. In these relational communities, he is known as El Hajj Malik El-Shabazz and ultimately as Malcolm X.

Malcolm's participation in the Nation of Islam also changes over the years. At one point, he is a dutiful member and one of its chief spokespersons for its philosophy of racial separatism. Over time, however, as he begins to challenge his own thinking and the leadership of the group, he becomes an advocate for racial unity, which leads to his dismissal from the group. A profound conversion of self next occurs during a pilgrimage to Mecca, which he recounts in a letter (Malcolm X, 1964):

> During the past eleven days here in the Muslim world, I have eaten from the same plate, drunk from the same glass, and slept on the same rug—while praying to the same God—with fellow Muslims, whose eyes were the bluest of blue, whose hair was the blondest of blond, and whose skin was the whitest of white. And in the words and in the actions and in the deeds of the "white" Muslims, I felt the same sincerity that I felt among the black African Muslims of Nigeria, Sudan and Ghana.

Develop Self-Esteem as a Realistic Self-Assessment   James (1890) defined *self-esteem* as "the ratio of our actualities to our supposed potentialities" (p. 311). Implicit in this ratio is a comparison, or formula (see Figure 4.1). On the bottom half of the mathematical formula is the sense of what we think we are capable of doing or being. That is our potential or pretension. We compare that potential to what we actually achieve, which is the top half of the formula. Someone with healthy self-esteem makes a realistic assessment of his or her potential so that what is actually achieved is close to or exceeds what is perceived as potential.

Some of us make fair and realistic judgments about ourselves and live up to our perceived potential. In such cases, we experience positive self-esteem. On the other hand, we may have an unrealistic view of self that oversteps what we are actually capable of

James (1890) defined self-esteem as the ratio between our actualities and potentialities. We have healthy self-esteem when we make a realistic assessment of our potential so that what we actually achieve is close to or exceeds what we perceived as potential.

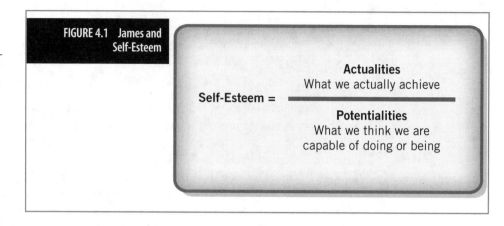

FIGURE 4.1   James and Self-Esteem

Self-Esteem =

Actualities
What we actually achieve

——————————————

Potentialities
What we think we are capable of doing or being

achieving. We may aim too high and end up feeling disappointed in what we really accomplish. The consequence of this is diminished self-esteem.

Suppose that a person of rather ordinary athletic competence sees himself or herself as having extraordinary athletic ability. James's theory would predict that this person will likely be disappointed in trying to compete against a more talented athlete. The loss is greater than simply being defeated on the athletic playing field. It involves a loss of self-worth, as well.

James's perspective speaks to the debilitating problem of *perfectionism* and its impact on self-esteem. The person who develops unrealistic expectations by thinking that he or she has to be perfect will find it extremely difficult to maintain high self-esteem. Perfectionism is an impossibly high standard—one that no one can consistently achieve. Since these expectations are unrealistic, they lead to repeated disappointments and a lowered sense of self-worth.

In sum, James's theory of the self invites us to think about our self-concept and to reflect about the self as a unified whole comprised of three parts: the physical, social, and spiritual. James's theory also enables us to understand how we gain awareness of ourselves on these three levels.

RAPID REVIEW

4.1

Symbolic Interaction

symbolic interaction theory
Term applied to George Herbert Mead's theory of communication to emphasize the importance of verbal and nonverbal symbols in the development of social relationships and identities.

significant symbols   The verbal and nonverbal expressions shared by members of a community that express a sense of collective meaning and identity.

Me   The part of the self that has internalized the expectations and norms of the larger societal or interpersonal relational community of which one is a member.

To see further how our awareness of self is affected by communicating with other people, we turn to Mead, another writer who developed the pragmatic view of the self. His view has been called **symbolic interaction theory.**

Mead made two principal contributions to the study of the self: (1) explaining the importance of **significant symbols** in how we each perceive the self and (2) elaborating on James's concept of the **Me** dimension of self. In particular, Mead identified how the inner voice of the Me articulates a societal perspective.

As we observed in considering the intrapersonal level of communication in Module One, Mead described the Me dimension of the self as an inner voice that communicates with the self in ways that reflect the social consciousness of the community as a whole. The Me thus functions as a kind of social critic and attempts to monitor behavior.

In an essay about social consciousness, Mead (1912) identified how a person's "inner consciousness is socially organized by the *importation* of the social organization of the outer world" (p. 406; emphasis added). In Mead's view, consciousness is imported as an individual learns the meaning of the significant symbols of his or her social world and the attitudes of others that are communicated through these verbal and nonverbal symbols.

WEB ACTIVITY

4.7

At birth, a child does not have a sense of identity nor does he or she have symbols for defining experiences. The individual learns significant symbols from other people in his or her relational communities. What are some of these significant symbols? Early in life, we learn names—our own name as well as the names of members of our family. At the same time, we learn the names that label the roles we perform, our gender, our social group, and our racial/ethnic identification. In terms similar to James's (1890) view of the social me, we learn to identify ourselves with the symbols of the various relational communities we belong to. And as we learn the names of things, we also learn the attitudes and values that are conventionally associated with them.

As individuals, we internalize, or take on, the viewpoints of others—their ways of defining us and the world around us and their ways of believing and valuing experiences. The inner consciousness of a person is thereby shaped by how significant symbols express the social consciousness of the relational communities he or she communicates with.

Mead (1934) explained the importance of social consciousness in this way:

> What goes to make up the organized self is the organization of the attitudes which are common to the group. A person is a personality because he belongs to a community, because he takes over the institutions of that community into his own conduct. He takes its language as a medium by which he gets his personality, and then through a process of taking the different roles that all the others furnish he comes to get the attitude of the members of the community. Such, in a certain sense, is the structure of a man's personality. (p. 162)

Mead distinguished two sources from which we internalize the perspectives and attitudes of others. First, he noted that we take on the views of *particular others,* such as family members, peers, lovers, and primary friends. And second, we take on the views of society at large, which he called the *generalized other.*

4.6

Particular Others Who are the people in your personal experience whose opinions count the most to you? Can you identify the people you have tried to model yourself after? Who has had the most impact on providing you with the words you use to define yourself and to make personal appraisals? Whose attitudes have you internalized?

Chances are good that this influence came from the members of your immediate family and peers when you were young. Sometimes, a teacher, a coach, a member of the clergy or a special neighbor will have had a substantial impact on the early development of your self-concept. Later in life, it is the people with whom you form your primary relationships, such as lovers and intimate friends, who become **particular others**—those individuals whose perspectives you continue to internalize as you define your self. Many times, these relationships with particular others have a long and enduring relational history.

The Generalized Other In addition to identifying the influence of particular others, we can see the impact of our culture at large. Mead referred to this as the influence of the **generalized other.** We internalize the attitudes, values, beliefs, norms, rules, roles, and expectations of larger relational communities when we import a sense of ourselves from our culture. As Mead (1934) explained: "The organized community or social group which gives to the individual his unity of self may be called 'the generalized other.' The attitude of the generalized other is the attitude of the whole community" (p. 154).

While the perspective of the particular other is communicated *interpersonally,* the perspective of the generalized other is often articulated through *societal structures,* such

particular others People with whom an individual has primary relationships, such as family members, lovers, and intimate friends, whose views he or she continues to internalize in defining the self.

generalized others The culture at large; the attitudes, values, beliefs, norms, rules, roles, and expectations of an individual's larger relational communities, which he or she internalizes in defining the self.

as the workplace, social and political organizations, schools and churches, laws and traditions, and so on. The perspective of the generalized other might also be heard in mass-mediated forms of communication, such as books and magazines as well as broadcast channels of communication such as the radio, television, and Internet.

Adhering to the views expressed by the generalized other provides a sense of social cohesion within a relational community and enforces a measure of conformity, as well. Again, as Mead (1934) explained:

> It is in the form of the generalized other that the social process influences the behavior of the individuals involved in it and carrying it on, i.e., that the community exercises control over the conduct of its individual members; for it is in this form that the social process or community enters as a determining factor into the individual's thinking. (p. 155)

Within a given society, its members may also organize into subgroups who have claimed a sense of shared self-identification. Each group, like society at large, communicates by way of its own set of significant symbols. As an illustration, Mead observed how people join political parties and thereby embrace, with varying degrees of loyalty, the ideology and symbols of the group.

4.8

4.3

4.7

The influences of generalized and particular others do not occur independently of one another.   They complement each other. Thus, viewpoints expressed in the symbol system of the generalized other are reinforced by the messages that are communicated personally to us by particular others. Consider, for instance, how you learned gender roles and developed expectations about forming romantic relationships. Your parents—along with other men and women in the various relational communities in which you were raised—likely served as the particular others whose attitudes you learned. You learned the language and nonverbal symbols of being male or female. You also observed the patterns of interaction that constitute romantic involvement.

You likely also learned about romantic involvement simply by observing the relationships of the particular others in your environment. For most people, the most common examples of romantic relationships are heterosexual relationships. Thus, specific attitudes are implicitly or expressly communicated, such as "You should fall in love," "You will be fulfilled in life if you become a parent and raise children," and "You may only fall in love with someone of the opposite sex."

At the same time, you experienced the impact of the generalized other. Literature, movies, television programs, and popular songs all reinforce images of and attitudes toward romantic relationships by depicting the culturally sanctioned version of love. Cultural traditions such as heterosexual marriage rites and laws that define a married couple as being heterosexual provide for the legal status of marriage and confer social and legal legitimacy as well as particular economic and legal privileges to married relationships such as rights of inheritance and provisions for medical decision-making. In this manner, a society establishes its expectations through the voices of particular and the generalized others.

4.4

Implication for Communication: Symbolic Interaction

Critically Assess the Impact of Others   Along with explaining how an individual constructs his or her self-concept by internalizing the attitudes of others, the theory of symbolic interaction also provides a method of critical analysis. We can use this theory to critique how interpersonal relationships with particular others and the social structures communicated by the generalized other affect our self-concept and self-esteem.

For the most part, we internalize the attitudes of others without being consciously aware of doing so. We often take for granted the attitudes and beliefs of our various relational communities, accepting them as truths without conscious examination or critical scrutiny. Yet attitudes and beliefs are not truths. They are perceptions.

Paul describes his experience of critically examining the perspective of the generalized other and of particular others:

> Everyone wants the perfect body and the perfect life. The problem is: What is perfect? My idea of the perfect body is influenced by the fitness magazines and what I have learned from friends and family members. My idea of the perfect life is making a lot of money to take my family on vacations. All of this is influenced by the environment around me. I should be focusing on what is perfect for me—not what is perfect for others.

Cathy reflects about her tendency to challenge the perceptions and expectations of others:

> Initially, it is easy to describe myself with labels: wife, mother, daughter, student, employee, and democrat. When I was younger, by default, I associated some of those roles with certain characteristics that seemed predetermined by the vague "they" of society. My parents had adopted the societal stereotypes, too. "They" said a wife should be a good cook; "they" said a mother should be strict; "they" said a student should be quiet in class. Since I didn't seem to live up to other people's expectations, I grew up always upsetting someone with my "insubordination."
>
> With adulthood came the freedom to be myself. Characteristics that best describe me are independent, strong willed, passionate, humorous, and, my own favorite, having common sense.

We can also evaluate the messages communicated from the mass media. For instance, critics of advertising point out that the size and shape of the typical fashion model, who is presented as the image of glamour and beauty, impacts how many people perceive their own body image—particularly women. This, in turn, can lead to lower self-esteem if the individual perceives the need to match this image. It may even contribute to the psychological and physical malady of *body image disturbance* and accompanying efforts to be thin by becoming bulimic or anorexic.

This experience was explained by student speaker Heath Rainbolt in a speech entitled "Body Image Disturbance." According to Rainbolt, it is only through a critical awareness of and rejection of the attitudes expressed in the symbols of advertising that we can conclude that we are at home in our own bodies—even when our appearance diverges from the idealized image found in advertisements.

VIDEO VIEW

4.2

In the same manner, members of minority relational communities can challenge the way that majority communities create labels that undermine self-esteem. An analysis of television programs by Gerbner (1998), which was done in conjunction with the Screen Actors Guild, found that members of some minority communities are often underrepresented in such programs relative to their size in the overall population of the United States. For instance, few characters of Asian descent are shown in television programs. Likewise, people of Hispanic background, the largest minority group in the United States, are shown in numbers significantly less than what they make up in the nation's population. African Americans are depicted in numbers that exceed their actual proportion of the population, but they are more likely to be portrayed as comic characters.

WEB ACTIVITY

4.9

What about other minority groups? How are physically and mentally challenged people depicted in the regular run of television shows? How are women still stereotyped in television dramas? How often are gay and lesbian characters

THINK ABOUT THIS

4.5

presented, and when they are, how are they portrayed? Namely, are they shown as being involved in meaningful romantic relationships? What images are presented of Native Americans and people from other ethnic groups and nationalities?

Burke (1967), whose studies have included a deep reading of Mead and his views on symbolic interaction, asserts that being able to conduct a critical analysis of symbols is a necessary life skill, or what he calls "equipment for living" (p. 293). When we acquire "equipment for living," we are able to understand the process of *naming:* how we each name our self and our experience and how others name us, too. Equipped with this knowledge, we, as members of relational communities, might ultimately claim the power to name ourselves in our own terms. Burke's studies of symbolic action have led to development of the dramatistic view of communication.

ASSESSING YOUR SKILLS
4.1

RAPID REVIEW
4.2

The Dramatistic View: Enacting Roles

LEARNING OBJECTIVE
4.3

Burke (1945) is credited with being one of the most influential contributors to communication studies in the twentieth century. His theory of communication, which he calls *dramatism,* treats human communication in terms of drama: namely, that communicators are social actors who enact dramatic roles as they relate to one another. Burke's theory of dramatism has been used to describe a wide range of communication situations and to analyze various types of discourse. With particular reference to self-concept, the **dramatistic view of self** focuses upon roles people perform as they interact.

A number of theorists have drawn on Burke's concept of dramatism. We will consider the work of two of them in this module: Goffman's model, which he calls *self-presentation,* and McCall and Simmons's *role-identity model.*

Self-Presentation

dramatistic view of self   The perspective that an individual plays roles in his or her interactions with others and uses strategies and symbols to present himself or herself to others and to manage their impressions.

role   Patterns of behavior enacted by an individual within the context of a particular relational community; the expectations for enacting a role are mutually defined by members of a relational community.

script   Establishes the sequences of action and behavior that each party performs in his or her role in a given communication situation.

audience   The spectators of a given communication situation; form impressions of the actors and the scene being played out.

Drawing on Burke, Goffman (1959) describes human interaction as a drama. We are on stage as we interact with others in the public arena of our lives as well as in our private, interpersonal relationships. Goffman uses several key terms to analyze the drama of everyday interaction.

The first of these terms is **role.** A role is a pattern of behavior that is performed by an individual in a relationship. Goffman explores how we learn to play a range of roles in a manner similar to how an actor learns the script of a play.

Just as the stage actor follows a script that has been written by a playwright, we may also follow different scripts for interacting in different communication situations. A **script** establishes the sequences of action and behavior that each party performs in his or her role in a given communication situation. As we play our part in a script, we also relate to the other actors in the drama. Each actor plays his or her part so that it is faithful to the script. Sometimes, we act much like a troupe of improvisational actors, making up our lines as we go and thus creating a script that is unique to a particular relationship and situation. At other times, we follow a much more defined script that has been constructed in accordance with cultural customs.

In every drama, there is also an **audience,** or the spectators of the situation. Like the audience that attends a play in a theater, the audience in a given communication situation forms impressions of the actors and the scene being played out.

To examine this concept of performing roles, consider how you play different family roles: perhaps daughter, sister, niece, cousin, and so on. Some of your family scripts stipulate how to perform these roles for the mundane stuff of everyday communicating. Other of your scripts stipulate how to play these roles while communicating on special occasions.

4.8

The family drama *Soul Food* provides an example of a three-generation African American family whose members gather each week for Sunday dinner. As in the film *Soul Food,* many of the scripts and the role performances are governed by cultural rules, such as the ritual of gathering each Sunday for dinner and the marriage ceremony of Bird, the youngest member of the family, which begins the film. Other parts of the weekly Sunday dinner script are unique to this family, such as how the sibling rivalry among the three sisters in the film is expressed.

4.3

Implications for Communication: Self-Presentation

Communicate to Create a Positive Impression   Goffman (1959) observes that as we play our parts in the drama, we also make choices in order to create positive impressions. As communicators, we want to be received well and to create the impression that we are credible and believable. Goffman refers to this as **impression management.**

4.10

The staging of a political performance is an apt example of impression management at work. During the debates in the presidential campaign of 2000, many political commentators critiqued the televised performances of Governor George W. Bush and Vice President Al Gore in the first of their three face-to-face debates, held in Boston a month before the election. In sum, Bush was perceived as being more affable and likable.

4.11

Critics observed that Gore attempted to present himself as being more competent and better informed than Bush. However, in doing so, Gore came across as being condescending. He was also faulted for interrupting Bush and for making faces in response to Bush's remarks. After the first debate, some critics concluded that while Gore may have won it on points related to content, he may have lost it in terms of how he presented himself. In the wake of that first performance, Gore's campaign staffers advised him of the need to present a warmer and more likable image.

In our own day-to-day interactions, we also make choices about how to present ourselves. Some of us may be able to relate to Melinda, who described her efforts to use impression management:

4.6

> I like to make good first impressions with people, especially with authority figures and elders. I use impression management on a regular basis and change it to fit the situation I am entering. As most people do, I act differently in different situations, but I usually try to maintain the same attitudes and beliefs. My techniques of impression management usually involve dressing up, doing my makeup, and getting myself psyched about a particular situation I am about to take part in. I also try to present a positive image by acting outgoing, being personable, and taking a personal, genuine interest in those around me.

Just as an actor rehearses a scene, we anticipate how to communicate and how to perform our roles. Consider how you might prepare to go to a job interview. How do you play the role of job seeker? How do you look and act the part, especially in light of the type of job you are seeking? What impressions do you strive to create in the minds of the people who are interviewing you? If you rehearse well, you might try to dress in a manner that is consistent with the role and that creates a positive impression. You might even do research about the company so that

4.12

impression management   Efforts by a person playing a role to control the perceptions that audience members hold of him or her.

you will be able speak with confidence about the nature of the work you would be doing if hired. And you will probably focus the content of your résumé to emphasize the ways in which you would be well suited to play a role in the company. Each of these is an example of impression management.

In addition, you may think through how you will be expected to follow the script for a job interview. Just as there is a script for a play, there is a standard way that a job interview proceeds. For instance, it usually begins with small talk. There are also expectations for how to respond to questions so that your answers are on target. Finally, there is a typical ending to a job interview, in which the timeframe for the decision is explained and so on.

Communicate to Construct an Online Persona   Communicating on the Internet creates a unique forum for constructing roles and managing impressions. Markham (1998) notes that since most of the communicating presently done on the Internet involves sending messages comprised of text, online interaction creates a unique opportunity as well as a challenge for creating an online persona.

An individual is, in one sense, freed from his or her physical body while interacting with others online. Hence, the presentation of one's self can be done through words alone, rather than including one's physical body. Markham writes that such an embodiment of self through text alone is particularly attractive for people who perceive their bodies as having been negatively judged or stigmatized.

At the same time, the lack of other types of nonverbal communication in online communication can also create negative impressions. For instance, in face-to-face communication, a harshly worded statement can be softened by using subtle forms of nonverbal communication, such as gestures and facial expressions. These nonverbal behaviors are not available for an online communicator, however.

In sum, Goffman's (1959) model offers a useful way of identifying how we perform roles in accordance with various scripts and how we adapt our performances to other actors and audiences. Goffman's model also provides a tool for self-reflection to consider how we make choices in order to manage the impressions that others have of us.

The Role-Identity Model

McCall and Simmons (1966) offer another perspective on how we perform roles with their concept of **role identity.** Specifically, we draw on our imagination to fashion idealized views of our various selves, and these idealized views have a significant impact on how we play roles and construct a self-concept. McCall and Simmons note:

> Role-identity . . . may be defined as the character and the role that an individual devises for himself as he likes to think of himself being and acting as an occupant of a particular social position. (p. 67)

Perhaps you have an image of what it means to be a good and faithful friend. Or maybe you have developed an ideal that you strive for to be a good student. If you are a parent, perhaps you have developed an ideal of what being a good and effective parent requires.

Each of these idealizations is an instance of the many imaginative views we hold of ourselves. Based on our idealizations, we envision how to play a part and how to be successful at it, and we rehearse the actions needed to play the role so that we can deliver a plausible performance. With the insights of an idealized view of our self, we may also

role identity   The character and role that an individual creates for himself or herself; generally indicates how an individual likes to think of himself or herself.

think about how others will respond to us. We may imagine their approval—or even their envy—for how we perform our roles.

The film *Jerry Maguire,* in which Tom Cruise plays the title role, illustrates the concepts of the role-identity model. In the film, Jerry serves as an agent for professional athletes. When the film begins, Jerry is disenchanted with his work. At one point, he describes himself as a shark in a business suit, rather than a friend who holds the personal needs of his clients foremost among his concerns. In other words, Jerry has created an idealized view of what it means to play the role of sports agent and feels that he is failing to live up to that view. This creates a crisis for him, which leads him to write a mission statement that articulates his idealized view of being a sports agent and then to set out on his own to perform that role.

McCall and Simmons observe that our idealistic views of self may be too lofty. At times, therefore, we experience frustration, even crisis, like the character of Jerry Maguire. Nonetheless, those views have an important impact on how we live our day-to-day lives. McCall and Simmons comment:

> The contents of a person's role-identities provide him with criteria for appraising his own actual performances. Those actions that are not consonant with one's imaginations of self as a person in a particular social position are regarded as embarrassing, threatening and disconcerting; if possible, they will be discontinued and superseded by actions more in keeping with one's view of self. (p. 69)

Role Legitimation   As we perform each of our roles, we are also aware of the audience members we can turn to for support. Receiving that support from others, in turn, creates a sense of legitimacy for how we play our roles. McCall and Simmons (1966) use the term **role legitimation** to describe the efforts we undertake to reinforce the legitimacy of the roles we play and to get support and affirmation.

 Social Exchange Theory and Role Identity   In addition to trying to fulfill our idealized view of how to perform a role, we are also motivated by the rewards that we gain by playing a particular role. McCall and Simmons (1966) base their idea of rewards on another theory of communication called **social exchange theory.**

As articulated by Homans (1958), social exchange theory explains how we make choices in human relationships by weighing the rewards and benefits of being in a given relationship in comparison to the costs. It is somewhat like the balance sheet that an accountant studies, in which assets and liabilities are compared to determine equity, or final value. Using this metaphor, every relationship has certain liabilities, or costs, as well as certain assets, or rewards. When the rewards exceed the costs, the relationship has value and the partners are motivated to stay in it. But when the costs exceed the rewards, the partners are likely to consider other alternatives—for example, leaving the relationship entirely or initiating relationships with others.

Implication for Communication: Role Identity

Choose the Roles That Are Most Gratifying   McCall and Simmons (1966) suggest that we choose to play some roles over others. They call this **role prominence.**

Think about the various roles that you have adopted in developing your self-concept. They are probably not all equally important, meaningful, or desirable to you. In fact, some may have huge costs that exceed the rewards you experience. Others may have such great rewards that you are willing to carry the burden of the costs.

role legitimation   An individual's efforts to reinforce the legitimacy of the roles he or she plays and to get support and affirmation from the members of his or her relational communities.

social exchange theory   The theory of behavior that suggests that individuals are motivated by efforts to maximize rewards and minimize costs.

role prominence   The notion that people choose to play some roles over others, particularly those roles that are perceived as more important and thus desirable to perform.

4.4

4.2

Once you have identified the various roles you play and how some of them are more or less desirable, you can construct a hierarchy of roles. Those roles at the top of the hierarchy have the greatest prominence. You are likely to feel supported in these roles by those around you who play their roles in ways that complement yours.

You are also likely to get the greatest rewards from playing the roles at the top of the hierarchy. The rewards for performing roles can take two forms: **Intrinsic gratification** is created within yourself, as for instance, when you judge that you have done something well and feel highly competent. You feel a sense of self-satisfaction and accomplishment that comes from within you. Other times, the rewards come from outside you, perhaps in the form of gifts or money. This is called **extrinsic gratification.**

4.7

Perhaps not surprisingly, the roles that we perform that have the greatest role prominence are played out in the relationships that we value the most. We thus have a greater stake in wanting to maintain and grow those relationships. Doing so fosters commitment to the specific identity and to the relational community associated with a given role.

In sum, McCall and Simmons provide a way of understanding how we select certain roles: We consider how each role fits the idealized view we hold of our self, which is encompassed in our role identity, and how we turn to other people for affirmation, support, and legitimation of that role. The theme of discovering the ideal self is also discussed in the humanistic view of the self and the work of Carl Rogers.

4.4

The Humanistic View: Self-Actualization

4.4

intrinsic gratification Rewards that come from inside the individual, especially as a sense of self-satisfaction resulting from perceptions of personal accomplishment and of being competent.

extrinsic gratification Rewards that come from outside the individual, such as gifts, material objects, and money.

humanistic view of self The perspective that individuals experience self-esteem and seek to grow as individuals so that they can achieve their full potential as self-actualized persons.

self-actualizing tendency The perspective that an individual is motivated to fulfill his or her full potential.

The **humanistic view of self** focuses primarily on how individuals create a sense of self-esteem that leads to self-actualization. The theoretical foundation of this view is humanistic psychology and especially the works of Rogers (1959), a psychotherapist whose thoughts on self-concept and self-esteem were developed through his interactions with clients involved in therapy.

4.14

The Self-Actualizing Tendency

The central concept of Rogers's view is the individual's motivation to fulfill his or her full potential, which he calls the **self-actualizing tendency.** Rogers believes that our motivation toward self-actualization comes from our very being as an organism. We are, he suggests, born to become who we are meant to be. This is the true and authentic self of a person who becomes self-actualized.

In a poem entitled "You Are There," Rebstock (2002) explores one of the central parts of the self-actualizing tendency: the idea that each person is uniquely created and thus motivated to become the person he or she is meant to be. Yet the world in which we are created is also a social world, in which the individual's path toward self-actualization may be thwarted by the pressures of social conformity and the desire to please others. This perception that one ought to fulfill the expectations of others can collide with the self-actualizing tendency. As expressed by Rebstock in the excerpts on the next page:

4.8

From the birth canal
    comes a being of exquisite uniqueness—
Formed of God's infinite love and creativity,
    One, of unnumbered variation.

The new being slips
    into the hands of a world that immediately
    swathes it in bonds of love,
Freighted with expectation.

We do not know how to love
    for love alone;
We are born to conform and not to Be.

The expectations—they come rarely from malice,
    but from human limitation.
We can know (and love) only so much.*

* This and the following excerpt are reprinted with permission of the author.

In the face of external pressures from the people in our relational communities, we must sometimes undergo a personal transformation to realize our true and authentic self. In the second half of his poem, Rebstock compares this transformation in spiritual terms to a process of being reborn:

Later, much later, and sometimes never,
    the being struggles to be born again—
To be God's created treasure
    rather than its conforming shadow.

It hurts, this rebirthing,
    because we know our own expectations
    far better than we can grasp
Infinite creativity.

And so the rebirthing stops sometimes,
    and we are beaten back
Into our expected places.

But I feel the contractions again,
    stronger this time,
    and they will not stop.

You—I—can't hold me back anymore.

And—beauty of beauties—
    to find a soul in journey with me!

Together, we face the unexpected.
Together, we stare the infinite "Yes" of God in the face.

"Yes, I will be!" we echo.
And we meet the world together.

4.11

Positive Self-Regard and Organismic Valuing   Rogers (1959) suggests that a vital part of self-esteem is **positive self-regard.** At the heart of positive self-regard are the realization of self-worth and an understanding of one's true potential. Positive self-regard is an important aspect of self-esteem, for it involves making evaluative judgments of ourselves and our efforts to seek the attention and recognition of others. By developing that sense of self-worth and by acknowledging our potential, we can perceive ourselves to have value, to be competent, and to be lovable.

To feel that sense of positive self-regard, we rely on two sources. First, we draw on ourselves, looking inward to tap our intuitive sense of what provides the source of our value. Rogers calls this a person's sense of **organismic valuing.** On an intuitive level, we understand ourselves and have a kind of inner knowledge of what is best for our own growth. In everyday language, we may speak of having a "gut feeling" or knowing in our "heart of hearts" what is best for us.

Our second source of positive self-regard is the people in our various relational communities who provide support and affirmation, such as our families, friends, and loved ones and even our culture at large. The positive feedback of these individuals tells us that we have worth—that we are valued and loved.

Marian writes about the importance of receiving positive feedback from others in developing positive self-esteem:

> Although my parents earned failing grades in terms of providing a sense of positive regard, my husband has become an important source of positive feedback for me. He was raised with much praise, and it has had a lasting effect on him: He owns and operates a successful mortgage and title company. His positive views have now had a direct effect on me.
>
> Still, I sometimes struggle with negative parental experiences in my past. I am now a parent of two wonderful young children and thankfully am able to recognize my parents' mistakes. I am parenting *my* children with the hope that they can benefit from a very positive upbringing.

positive self-regard   The realization of self-worth and an understanding of one's true potential.

organismic valuing   Looking inward to tap one's intuitive sense of what provides the source of his or her value.

conditions of worth   External criteria for achieving self-worth that are communicated to an individual as expectations that he or she must meet in order to be affirmed.

conditional positive regard   An affirmation that is rooted in conditions of worth established by others, which an individual must fulfill in order to be regarded as worthy, competent, and lovable.

unconditional positive regard   An affirmation that recognizes an individual's unique qualities and value without establishing conditions of worth.

Rogers observes that many of our interpersonal relationships help us to grow. Having meaningful people in our lives affirms the progress that we make and supports us in our efforts to realize self-worth. At other times, however, the expectations that others create for us may become standards that cannot be met.

Conditional and Unconditional Positive Regard   For good or bad, Rogers (1959) explains, the people around us create **conditions of worth,** or external criteria for achieving self-worth. These conditions of worth are communicated to us as expectations that we must meet in order to be affirmed.

While satisfying conditions of worth may make us feel affirmed, it results in a kind of affirmation of self that Rogers labels **conditional positive regard.** That is, we regard ourselves as being worthy, competent, and lovable only as long as we can fulfill the conditions of worth articulated by others. If we fall short of meeting those conditions, we may think that we are not worthy or good. Moreover, the conditions of worth may be unrealistic and thus ultimately impede us from reaching self-actualization.

Some of us, for instance, may have grown up in families in which the demands or expectations for how we were to behave established conditions of worth. In subtle or direct ways, we may have been told that we were good if we got good grades or acted politely. In our adult lives, we may also have been in relationships that offered love with strings attached: "Do or be this type of person and I will love you."

4.12

The opposite of conditional positive regard is **unconditional positive regard.** This type of response offers healthy feedback that recognizes our unique qualities and affirms our value without establishing conditions of worth. Relationships that express unconditional positive regard enable individuals to grow into their real selves and to move toward self-actualization. In Rebstock's (2002) poem, this is the "beauty of beauties—to find a soul in journey with me!" When we have such relationships, we feel affirmed for who we are, rather than compelled to meet other people's standards and expectations. We know that we are valued on our own terms.

Rogers's concepts about the self-actualizing tendency and the importance of receiving unconditional positive regard are illustrated by the characters in the film *October Sky*. Based on an autobiographical account entitled *Rocket Boys: A Memoir,* the film presents the story of Homer Hickam, Jr., who grew up in Coalwood, a small coal-mining town in West Virginia. While in high school, Hickam was inspired by the launching of the Russian spacecraft *Sputnik* to become a rocket scientist, although against the wishes of his father and in the face of fairly widespread opposition from many of the people in his relational communities of family, school, and town.

4.15

Rogers's concept of conditional positive regard can be applied to the story by examining the conditions of worth articulated to Homer by his father and by most of the members of his school: namely, that being a coal miner and an athlete were the most worthy and realistically attainable goals that Homer should aspire to achieve. A career in science or rocketry was seen as beyond the reach of a person growing up in the town of Coalwood.

Nonetheless, Homer did not lose sight of his own organismic valuing. He held fast to his dream. In addition, he received unconditional positive regard for his efforts from a small group of supportive friends who joined him in the project. He also won the affirmation of his mother and got help and encouragement from an inspiring math and science teacher. Homer and his friends eventually won the national science award, which ensured that each could leave the coal-mining town and go to college. For the real-life Homer Hickam, the dream also included the opportunity to work in the U.S. space program with NASA.

Implications for Communication: Self-Actualization

Identify Your Real Self   The path toward self-actualization begins inside one's self. True progress in awareness is attained when an individual understands what Rogers (1959) calls his or her **real self.** According to Rogers, that occurs when we view ourselves in light of our own unique self-worth and in accordance with our intuitive sense of organismic value.

You may dream, for instance, of a particular career as being very fulfilling and worthwhile. And every time you think of doing this line of work, you may feel energized in the manner that American author Joseph Campbell calls "following your bliss" (Campbell and Moyers, 1988). Doing that line of work and being that type of career person constitutes a tapping into your real self.

4.16

Unfortunately, we don't all find our bliss or live out what our sense of organismic valuing tells us is our real self. Sometimes, we find it especially difficult to realize the dreams and aspirations that make up our real self because we are trying to meet the expectations of others. Doing so sidetracks us from following our own sense of organismic value.

As we lose touch with living as our real self, we experience **incongruity,** and that creates an unrealistic type of existence. The self that is plagued by incongruity experiences a mismatch between the inner feelings of who he or she is meant to be and the outer expression of how he or she actually behaves. This individual enacts artificial roles and feels a sense of alienation, as he or she has lost

4.9

real self The sense of self-concept that is developed when an individual perceives himself or herself in light of his or her own unique self-worth and in accordance with his or her intuitive sense of organismic value.

incongruity A mismatch between one's inner feelings of who he or she is meant to be and the outer expression of how he or she actually behaves.

touch with the authentic person whose day-to-day life experiences would more closely match his or her internal life.

VIDEO VIEW
4.5

ASSESSING YOUR SKILLS
4.3

Recognize the Impact of Others   We gain self-esteem and are nurtured along the path toward self-actualization through our interactions with others and the quality of the feedback they provide. As noted earlier, interacting with other people may bring about growth in self-esteem by offering unconditional positive regard, or it may undermine personal growth and wholeness if the people with whom we interact create conditions of worth.

Thus, it is crucial to pick our friends and loved ones wisely, choosing those individuals whose feedback is meant to help us grow. The ultimate arbiter of self-esteem in the humanistic view of self is the individual. We each have the freedom to choose how we will affirm ourselves and how we will receive the assessments of others.

RAPID REVIEW
4.5

The Cultural Dimensions View: Cultural Values

LEARNING OBJECTIVE
4.5

Since the beginning of the modern era about 300 years ago, the goal of attaining individual independence and realizing one's unique identity has been widely held by most of the people living in the United States and other Western cultures. However, anthropologists and communication theorists, who study the influence of culture on communication, argue that this value is not universal. An alternative way of thinking about self-concept, especially as it is experienced in other relevant places around the globe, is the **cultural dimensions view of self.** This perspective suggests that cultural patterns influence how individuals form a sense of self by identifying with the values of individualism or collectivism.

Individualism and Collectivism

cultural dimensions view   The perspective that cultural patterns influence how individuals form a sense of self by identifying with the values of individualism or collectivism.

individualism   A cultural view that emphasizes the values of independence, self-direction, autonomy, and self-affirmation and in which achievement is considered a matter of individual merit.

collectivism   A cultural view that emphasizes the values of cooperation and group identification and in which achievement is considered a matter of group merit.

Hofstede (1980) distinguishes between *individualism* and *collectivism* as dimensions of cultural variability and observes how cultures differ from one another in terms of the general tendency of the population as a whole to identify with the values of individualism and collectivism. Hofstede also describes a cultural value system as being a kind of collective mental programming, much like the code used to program a computer. As noted in Figure 4.2, individualism and collectivism represent opposite ends of a continuum.

THINK ABOUT THIS
4.10

In cultures that embrace **individualism,** people are more likely to think of themselves as being autonomous and independent. People in individualistic cultures focus on the self as *I*.

At the other end of the continuum are cultures that embrace **collectivism.** They stress the importance of membership in a group or the *we*. This orientation leads members to value group cooperation and to identify strongly with the groups they belong to, such as family, company, church, and so on. In collectivist cultures, people believe in the value of working together toward the common purpose of strengthening the group. Maintaining the quality of relationships and group harmony are also centrally important concerns.

Joseph, a student who immigrated to the United States from the African country of Ghana, reflects about the differences between his experience of collectivism in Ghana and his experience of individualism in the United States:

FIGURE 4.2 Individualism/ Collectivism Continuum	

Individualism   **Collectivism**

Focus on *I*:   Focus on *We*:
Identification with   Identification with
values of autonomy   values of interdependence
and independence   and group harmony

Hofstede (1980) observed how cultural systems differ in terms of whether they identify with the values of individualism or collectivism. Individual variance can also occur within a single culture.

When I first got into this country, I was surprised to see how much emphasis was placed on the individual and personal achievements. In my culture, there is more emphasis on the family and the community. We do not say things like "my house" when talking about the family home; instead we say "our home." Credit for success in my culture goes to the family, not the individual who accomplished it—although within the family, we will congratulate the person for a job well done.

Now that I have been here for some time, I find myself using "I" a lot more in my conversations. The problem is that when I talk to my family back home, I have to correct myself all the time. Using "I" is considered arrogant and an act of separation from the group.

Individual achievements are not the main focus [in my culture]; rather the goal is the well-being of the family and the community. For example, if I see a kid behaving badly in this country, I just turn away and do not say anything. The norm here is that I should mind my own business. In my culture, there is no such thing as my own business—I can discipline a child who is misbehaving whether the parent is around or not. The thought is that the kid belongs to all of us, and if he turns out to be a problem, the entire society will suffer.

In short, in my culture an individual is not as important as the family or the community. Speaking too much about personal accomplishments is not encouraged. We prefer "our" and "us" to "I."

Direct and Indirect Styles of Communication   How we communicate goes beyond the use of pronouns such as *I* and *we*. Hofstede (1980) also explains that a *direct style* of communication is more likely to be valued in cultures that emphasize individualism. Communicators thus learn to be forthright, assertive, and bold. By contrast, in cultures that emphasize collectivism, an *indirect style* of communicating is more likely to be valued. This style helps to foster the goals of group harmony and enables people to avoid confrontation and perhaps conflict in interpersonal relationships.

Individualism/Collectivism and Individual Differences   While the values of individualism or collectivism likely predominate in a given society, individual differences also play a role in some situations. Within a given culture, there is a range of variance, even if the tendency is for most people in the society at large to be individualistic or collectivistic. Some members may feel less commitment to the value system that predominates within their culture. Figure 4.3 provides an illustration based on a hypothetical comparison of the cultural values in the United States and in Japan by Gudykunst and Kim (1997). As noted in Figure 4.3, people in the United States—on the whole—are more likely to

Gudykunst and Kim (1997) compare the cultural values of Japan and the United States, indicating the range of individual differences within each culture in identifying with individualism. In sum, U.S. culture places more emphasis on individualism than Japanese culture.

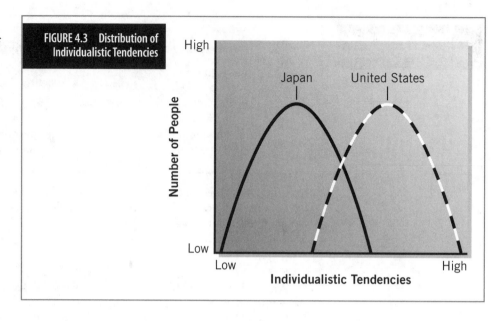

FIGURE 4.3   Distribution of Individualistic Tendencies

subscribe to values of individualism while most people in Japanese society identify with collectivism. But within each group there are differences that can be charted on a curve.

To label the differences within a culture, Triandis (1995) uses the terms *allocentric* and *idiocentric* as counterparts to *collectivism* and *individualism*. The term **allocentric** describes a person in an individualistic culture who subscribes to collectivistic values, and the term **idiocentric** describes a person in a collectivist culture who identifies with the values of individualism.

Vertical and Horizontal Dimensions

Triandis (1995) has also provided another set of factors for distinguishing among groups of people within individualistic and collectivist cultures by describing the vertical and horizontal perspectives embraced within a culture. People in groups that subscribe to a **vertical perspective** respect the importance of status and hierarchy. In contrast, people in groups with a **horizontal perspective** value equality; thus, they place less stock in social class and may downplay status differences.

4.11

4.14

When Triandis's vertical and horizontal perspectives are considered along with the continuum of individualism versus collectivism, four types of groups can be identified:

- Vertical/individualistic groups
- Horizontal/individualistic groups
- Vertical/collectivist groups
- Horizontal/collectivist groups

According to Triandis, members of a *vertical/individualistic group* are likely to be highly competitive and status oriented. Many large corporations in the United States illustrate this type of group. Members of such a group recognize a clear hierarchy of power and compete against one another to rise to the top. Moreover, getting to the top is rewarded as a matter of individual effort.

allocentric   Describes a person in an individualistic culture who subscribes to collectivistic values.

idiocentric   Describes a person in a collectivist culture who subscribes to individualistic values.

vertical perspective   A cultural view that respects the importance of status and hierarchy.

horizontal perspective   A cultural view that values equality, deemphasizing social class and downplaying status differences.

Triandis notes that this is not the case with all companies in the United States. Some combine values of individualism with a horizontal view that downplays the importance of a status oriented vertical structure in favor of a more egalitarian attitude. This is the kind of *horizontal/individualistic* model that Triandis found to be especially common among Australian companies.

There are also notable differences between types of collectivist cultures. For instance, corporations in India can be characterized as *vertical/collectivist groups* since Indian culture tends to value a hierarchical class structure and identify strongly with collectivism in terms of its focus on the ingroup relationships of members of the same caste. A kibbutz in Israel, by contrast, represents a *horizontal/collectivist group,* which is an egalitarian form of collectivism.

Implications for Communication: Cultural Values

Adapt to a Diverse and Changing World As with any aspect of self-concept and self-esteem, the way we define ourselves is a dynamic process. This is especially true in the contemporary world and for those of us who live in communities in which we encounter people from diverse backgrounds. Additionally, communities across the world are likely to be exposed to cultural differences as a consequence of developments in technology, travel, and communication. Not only do these developments facilitate contact with members of other groups, but they also break down the homogeneity of cultural experiences shared within a community.

Many of the communities in which we live have also undergone change due to immigration. An analysis of data from the 2000 U.S. census by Lollack (2001) indicates that 10.4 percent of the people counted in the last census were categorized as being "foreign-born," which means they were not citizens of the United States at birth. This represents more than 28 million people.

4.17

Many of these individuals are also recent immigrants to the United States. Census data reveal that the median length of residence for those who are foreign born was just 14.4 years. Almost 40 percent of foreign-born residents immigrated to the United States during the 1990s, and another 28 percent arrived in the 1980s.

Most of these immigrants came from countries that Hofstede (1980) would categorize as embracing a collectivist cultural perspective. According to the 2000 census data, 51 percent of foreign-born residents came from Latin American and Caribbean countries, most of which have collectivist cultures. The second-largest group of immigrants, just over 25 percent of the total, came from Asian countries, which also have collectivist cultures. European-born people constitute slightly more than 15 percent of the total immigrant population. Those coming from countries in Western Europe that have a tradition of emphasizing democratic political values and free market capitalism are more likely to embrace values of individualism. Eastern European cultures, according to Realo and Allik (1999), tend toward collectivism. The remaining 8 percent came from other regions of the world.

Adjust to Changing Family Dynamics The 2000 census data (Lollack, 2001) also indicate that cultural differences within families are growing, creating a particular challenge for many individuals. As many as one-sixth of the children counted (or 11.5 million children) reside in a household that includes one or more foreign-born adults. And of these children, almost 9 million were born in the United States and are thus classified by the U.S. Census Bureau as "natives." Thus, 78 percent of the children residing in households with foreign-born adults are themselves natives of the United States. Moreover, 41 percent of these children are under the age of 6 years.

The implications of these data for family communication are substantial. Namely, a significant number of the children in immigrant households have had little or no direct contact with the culture and the country of origin from which their parents came. These children have likely been acculturated into the American way of life and its value systems, which may differ substantially from the way of life and values embraced by their parents. Indeed, diversity in cultural views may be found not only among people from different nations, cultural groups, and neighborhoods but also among people within a single household.

The film *The Wedding Banquet* offers a humorous illustration of such a clash of cultures within a family. The movie presents the problems of an interracial gay male couple, Wai Tung and Simon. Wai Tung is a recent immigrant from Taiwan, which has a vertical/collectivist culture, and Simon is white and was born in the United States. They are the perfect example of an urban gay household. They are both urban professionals; Wai Tung is a businessman and Simon is a physician. They are also well integrated into an extended social network of gay friends. Although he is a recent immigrant, Wai Tung has become quite Americanized and has adopted the individualistic perspective of his lover's homeland.

All is fine for the couple, except for the fact that Wai Tung's parents, who still live in Taiwan, expect him to marry and produce children. This is a family obligation in a culture that stresses collectivism. In an effort to please Wai Tung's parents, Simon and Wai Tung develop a plan for Wai Tung to marry a Chinese woman named Wei Wei. She is at risk of being deported by U.S. immigration officials because she doesn't have a "green card," so marrying Wai Tung will solve her problems as well.

The plan is proceeding well until Wai Tung's parents decide to come to the United States for the wedding. During their visit, Wai Tung tries to move back and forth between two cultural worlds. In portraying this conflict, the film provides a poignant look at how Wai Tung confronts the inner struggle between the individualistic perspective of his new country and the collectivist attitudes of his parents.

The conflicts faced by the characters in *The Wedding Banquet* can also be understood in the light of the relational view of the self, which is the focus of the next section.

ASSESSING
YOUR SKILLS
4.4

RAPID
REVIEW
4.6

The Relational View: The Self—or Selves— in a Postmodern World

Connection and Autonomy

LEARNING
OBJECTIVE
4.6

In writing about the **relational view of self,** Baxter and Montgomery (1996) suggest that "'the Self,' in singular form, is a misnomer" (p. 159). Rather, they suggest, "people cocreate different selves with their parents, lovers, friends, spouses, children and other close associates" (p. 159).

Thus, instead of creating a single, coherent sense of self, we develop a **relational self:** a sense of self that allows for multiple selves. Baxter and Montgomery further elaborate that "one's identity is awash in the tides of different relationships, each one providing a crosscurrent version of who a person is or, more accurately, is becoming" (p. 159).

Baxter and Montgomery also describe the relational self in dialectical terms, or as a push and pull of opposing forces. Using metaphors from the physical sciences, they identify two types of forces: *Centripetal forces* pull elements to the center, causing a

relational view of self   The perspective that an individual constructs a complex sense of self, perhaps even multiple selves, as a result of participating in different relational communities.

relational self   A sense of self that allows for multiple selves to relate to different people and relational communities.

merging and resulting in connectedness, and *centrifugal forces* break down a unified whole into discrete parts, resulting in separation. To use more commonplace metaphors of kitchen tools, centripetal force is like a blender, which melds ingredients together as they swirl toward the center, and centrifugal force is like a salad spinner, which separates the moisture and debris from the lettuce as it spins. Dialectical theory claims that both forces are at work.

With respect to the construction of self, Baxter and Montgomery (1996) explain:

> The self is constructed out of two contradictory necessities—the need to connect with another (the centripetal force) and the simultaneous need to separate from the other (the centrifugal force). The centripetal-centrifugal dialogue is the indeterminate process in which the self is in a perpetual state of becoming as a consequence of the ongoing interplay between fusion and separation from others. (pp. 25–26)

The dialectical process of constructing a sense of self also applies to interpersonal relationships, as we will see in Module Five. There, we will explore the dialectical tension that Baxter (1994) calls **connection and autonomy.** *Connection* emphasizes our need to be close to others; we define ourselves in relation to others with whom we feel connected. Yet at the same time, there is a pull toward *autonomy,* as we experience the need for individuality and separation from others.

Many of us experience this type of dialectical tension in our family lives. We define ourselves in terms of our sense of connection (which is a centripetal force) as we adopt the attitudes and values of the family. We perform our family roles and follow its rules, as the family has established them. Our connection is further affirmed when we adopt the significant symbols of the family. We are connected.

At the same time, we assert individual autonomy and feel the need for separation (which is a centrifugal force). We seek a measure of independence from our families and claim our own space—quite literally with our nonverbal territory within the family's shared quarters. Likewise, we declare our independence in certain areas of thought and by adhering to our own values, individuating ourselves from other family members. We are autonomous.

As we will see in Module Five, healthy families are able to manage the dialectical tension between connection and autonomy—permitting family members to experience both.

Postmodernism

The idea of the relational self also draws on the notion of postmodernism articulated by Kenneth J. Gergen and others. In an interview in *U.S. News and World Report* (Sanoff, 1991), Gergen defines **postmodernism** as follows:

> Postmodernism is the product of an array of technologies that have saturated us with the voices of others. We are now immersed in an array of relationships in a way that has not existed at any other time in history. We take in views and values from all over the world. . . . In a sense, we become a local representation of an enormous array of others. The self is located outside us; as we move from one locale and relationship to another, we change. (p. 59)

At first, the idea that we define ourselves in relation to others may not seem particularly novel. After all, James (1890) indicated almost 100 years earlier than most postmodern writers that the self emerges in relationships with others. What distinguishes the postmodern view from the modern perspective that James described as the *social*

connection and autonomy An internal dialectic in which the contrasting value of togetherness or closeness is in tension with the value of independence.

postmodernism The perspective that living in today's technologically driven, fast-changing, and mobile world has altered people's sense of community and thus affected how they develop their sense of self. Postmodern thought rejects the concept of a stable core of identity.

me? James's view of the self was rooted in the idea that an individual has a stable core of identity. This stable core, Gergen (2000) observes, was developed through participation in a particular community during the modern era.

Yet in contemporary society, which is fast paced and mobile, that may no longer hold true. The traditional idea that a particular community serves as a stabilizing force, giving the individual a unified and coherent sense of identity, has given way to the postmodern experience of moving in and out of many communities.

The Erosion of the Essential Self   Living in the postmodern world, we experience what Gergen (2000) describes as "the erosion of the essential self" (p. 203). A fundamental aspect of the essential self during the modern period was being able to hold on to a stable core, or essence. This was the underpinning of James's (1890) hierarchical view of the self and its organization into three interrelated dimensions: the material, social, and spiritual. The notion of a unified and stable community is also inherent in Mead's (1912, 1934) concept of the generalized other and in the concept of the character in McCall and Simmons's (1966) role-identity model.

4.12

Yet from the postmodern perspective, our sense of self is formed by moving from one community to another. In each community, we communicate from the self that is created within the context of that particular relational community.

4.15

Relational Selves on the Move   To relate to this experience, think about how often many of us change our place of residence or place of employment. Each time we move or change jobs, we undergo a process of redefining ourselves. We learn to "repackage" ourselves, so to speak. As Gergen (2000) explains, "At each new location, new patterns of action may be required; dispositions, appetites, and personae all may be acquired and abandoned as conditions suggest or demand" (p. 203).

The 2000 U.S. census determined that 44.3 million people moved from one place to another in the United States during 1999 (Schacter, 2001). This means that just over 1 in 6 Americans relocated in a single year. Americans also change jobs frequently. In today's technological workplace, few people work at the same place or even stay in the same profession for their entire career. Data from the U.S. Department of Labor (2002) indicate that the average tenure of workers in the United States is 3.7 years. Today, the typical career path leads in any number of directions. As noted by Kiplinger (quoted in Moreau, 1990), a person's life of work may involve "not just multi-job but multi*career* work experiences, with individuals routinely holding ten or 12 jobs in as many as four or five careers" (p. xii).

In order to adapt to new relational contexts, the self must be flexible and ready to face whatever is in store. Gergen (2000) calls this quality **plasticity.** And while flexibility has some advantages, it also brings with it the burden of ongoing fluctuation, given the demands of our hectic, everyday lives.

Relational Selves in a Technological Society   Advocates of the relational view also examine the impact of living in a technological society. The earlier view of the self espoused by James (1890) considered individuals living in communities that were homogeneous as well as stable. But James wrote before the advent of today's methods of transportation and communication.

Given the automobile and other methods of transportation, we can live in one community and travel to another to go to work or school. Communication technologies such as the telephone, radio, television, and Internet further undermine the consistency of a single community of meaning. As Gergen (2000) explains:

4.18

plasticity   The ability of the self to adapt to new relational contexts.

A solid sense of self derives from relationships that are coherent and consistent over time. By living in communities where we are known by many people, who also know each other, we each derive a strong sense of "being somebody"—somebody endowed with particular characteristics, capacities, and proclivities. However, the technologies of communication are largely destroying this form of coherent and consistent community. (p. 202)

Instead of having a consistent and coherent view of the world, we have what Gergen calls **polyvocality:** "a condition in which the individual is capable of holding a multiplicity of views, values and sentiments—many of which are implicitly or explicitly conflicting" (p. 203).

In acknowledging the multiplicity of our own views, along with the possibility that others we relate with may also hold a multiplicity of views, we create opportunities for dialogue. In dialogue, each party becomes free to explore feelings, uncertainties, ambiguities, and areas of mutual concern. Polyvocality thus frees us from having to define ourselves as having a single stance or perspective. We can be less rigid in our views and therefore grow in relationship with others.

Even so, there are other costs associated with living in the postmodern world. Because we are constantly inundated with images and information, we fall prey to what Gergen labels *de-authentication.* That is, we risk losing our capacity for creative expression. Along with de-authentication, Gergen laments a condition he calls the *commodification* of the self, especially among public figures, wherein the self becomes a superficial commodity that can be bought by the highest bidder.

VIDEO VIEW

4.6

VIDEO VIEW

4.7

The Construction of Gender   The postmodern perspective has also been applied in contemporary critiques of gender identification and gender roles, which discuss gender as an aspect of the self. In her book *Gender Trouble,* Butler (1990) advances the idea that we construct our sense of being male or female 4.19 as a performance, acting symbolically in ways that are male or female. From this view, gender is less a matter of having an essential identity as a male or a female and more a matter of performing a role. According to Butler, "There is no gender identity behind the expressions of gender; that identity is performatively constituted by the very expressions that are said to be its results" (p. 33). Thus, gender is a socially constructed performance that is crafted symbolically. In other words, what it means when we say that we are a male or a female is that we have learned to perform the role of being male or female. Similarly, in Butler's view, we construct gender-related roles to define ourselves in terms of sexual orientation.

In Butler's view, we acquire the symbolic expressions of gender roles. The rock star Madonna, for instance, is often used to illustrate the idea that we create images of being male and female. Her over-the-top expression of femininity, such as wearing provocative lingerie onstage as costumes, can be interpreted as a parody of the female role. Along with the ultra-feminine aspects of her performance, Madonna extends the parody by taking on stereotypical masculine attitudes such as subjecting male characters in her music videos to being stared at as sex objects.

Implications for Communication: The Relational View of Self

ONLINE JOURNAL

4.16

We Construct Our Relational Selves through Narratives   Even though the relational self has no common core, it does have a story—or many stories—to tell. As explained by Mary Gergen (1997), storytelling provides another means of constructing the relational self. Gergen and Gergen (1986) contend that we make sense of our self by drawing on personal memories in the form of stories.

polyvocality   The ability to hold multiple views, values, and sentiments, many of which may conflict on some level.

By telling stories, we sort out the connections and disconnections of our lives. We make sense of the progression of our lives and understand the relationship between the present and the past. Moreover, our stories have heroes and villains with whom we relate.

Storytelling is an inherently communal action. We tell our stories to audiences—often, to the members of our relational communities. From those relational communities of listeners, we find affirmation for our stories and for their narrative validity.

Storytelling is a central motif in the film *Smoke Signals,* which tells the story of two young Native Americans living on a reservation in Idaho. The character of Thomas, played by Evan Adams, is a visionary who performs the role of shaman, or spiritual advisor. It is through his stories that he makes sense of his own life and that of his friend Victor, portrayed by Adam Beach. The cinematic story of the film, which was created by Sherman Alexie, moves back and forth between the past and the present.

4.5

In the story, Victor struggles with conflicts that have resulted from being abandoned by his father. Thomas provides Victor with stories about the father whom he lost. Upon the death of his father, Victor and Thomas make a journey to Arizona, where Victor's father had moved. Through his father's death and the stories he learns about his father from Thomas and others, Victor is able to heal his old wounds.

4.7

Adapt to New Relational Communities   As we move from one context of communication to another and from one relational community to another, we are challenged to adapt to new circumstances and develop a more open-minded approach to differences. Becoming aware of the differences between ourselves and others recognizes the importance of interdependence, flexibility, and tolerance—all of which are essential for successful adaptation with others.

Kenneth J. Gergen (1992) sees value in how the postmodern world poses a challenge to individualism. In a piece entitled "The Decline and Fall of Personality," published in *Psychology Today,* Gergen observes that the modern view of the essential self, which preceded the current postmodern view, gave too much value to a romantic ideal of individualism. Gergen argues that in the postmodern era, we are experiencing a decline of individualism. This is a movement away from the self-centeredness that is inherent in individualism and toward the appreciation of interdependence of relationships. He concludes:

4.6

> We can move from a self-centered system of beliefs to consciousness of an inseparable relatedness with others. Perhaps then our postmodern selves will contribute to making the globe a better place for living. (p. 5)

Summary

The pragmatic view of the self, represented by James's three-part theory, emphasizes the importance of self-awareness of the material, social, and spiritual dimensions. As communicators, we acquire a sense of self through self-reflection. A self-reflective person gains a realistic sense of self and thus healthy self-esteem. Self-awareness, in James's view, also involves a consciousness of the self that evolves over a lifetime and incorporates qualities of self-seeking, as we perceive and value the changes that occur in our lifetime.

Mead's contribution to the pragmatic view of the self, called symbolic interaction, explains how we form attitudes about ourselves and learn how to relate appropriately with others. According to Mead, we internalize the perspectives of both particular others and the generalized other of society as a whole in forming our sense of self. We take on the views of others as they are expressed in nonverbal and verbal symbols, which articulate the social consciousness of the various relational communities with whom we communicate. The theory of symbolic interaction also equips us with the critical tools we need to decide whether to embrace the attitudes that others communicate to us about ourselves.

The dramatistic view of the self is represented particularly by the contributions of Goffman on self-presentation and of McCall and Simmons on role identity. Both of these perspectives stress the importance of the roles that we perform in the everyday drama of life. Namely, we play our parts as called for in a script and by interacting with an audience. Goffman suggests that the perceptions of the audience are influenced through impression management. McCall and Simmons explain that we play our roles in accordance with an imaginative view of our self that constitutes our role identity. As we play these roles, we also recognize that they are mutually defined; thus, we turn to others for affirmation, support, and legitimation of our roles.

The humanistic view of the self, as represented by the work of Rogers, holds that we gain an awareness of our intrinsic sense of self-worth and live authentically by being faithful to our real self. This involves recognizing and honoring our own process of organismic valuing. The humanistic view also emphasizes interactions with those individuals we turn to for feedback and values the significance of communicating unconditional positive regard. The theory also challenges us to examine how we communicate to discern if the feedback we offer others is expressed as conditional or unconditional positive regard.

The cultural dimensions view examines how the self is formed in terms of the cultural values of individualism and collectivism. Individualistic cultures embrace personal accomplishment and achievement, whereas collectivist cultures perceive accomplishment and achievement as belonging to the group. We thus learn to identify our sense of self with our culture and especially its value system. Given this, differences in values can be observed between cultures and even between groups within a single community. Understanding our own culture, as well as other cultures, also provides insight into how meaning is expressed, especially in recognizing the styles of direct and indirect communication. Having an awareness of cultural differences also helps us understand how to communicate across cultures.

Finally, the relational view suggests that our sense of self is made up of numerous relational selves and that our identity is rooted in our relationships. This view discounts the idea that individual identity is organized around a coherent, essential self but holds instead that we adopt different dimensions of the self as we relate to many people in a fast-changing and complex society. And as we move from one communication context to another, we learn the skills for adapting to different situations. The relational view also identifies the need to communicate collaboratively in a polyvocal world, where perceptions and meanings are complex, ambiguous, and potentially in conflict. We construct our various selves through the communal act of storytelling.

PRACTICE
TEST

References

Baxter, L. A. (1994). A dialogic approach to relationship maintenance. In D. Canary and L. Stafford (eds.), *Communication and relational maintenance* (pp. 233–254). London: Academic Press.

Baxter, L. A., & Montgomery, B. M. (1996). *Relating: Dialogues & dialectics.* New York: Guilford Press.

Burke, K. (1945). *A grammar of motives.* Engelwood, NJ: Prentice-Hall.

Burke, K. (1967). *The philosophy of literary form.* 3rd ed. Berkeley, CA: University of California Press.

Butler, J. (1990). *Gender Trouble: Feminism and the subversion of identity.* London: Routledge.

Campbell, J., & Moyers, B. (1988). *The power of myth.* New York: Doubleday.

Chandler, D. (1998). Personal home pages and the construction of identities on the web. Available online: <www.aber.ac.uk/media/Documents/short/webident.html>. Accessed June 23, 2003.

Fox, K. R., & Corbin, C. B. (1989). The physical self-perception profile: Development and preliminary validation. *Journal of Sport & Exercise Psychology,* 2, 408–430.

Gerbner, G. (1998). Fairness and diversity in television: Update and trends since the 1993 Screen Actors Guild report *Women and Minorities on Television.* Available online: <www.sag.com/special/americanscene.html>. Accessed March 22, 2002.

Gergen, K. J. (1992). The decline and fall of personality. *Psychology Today,* November/December, pp. 58–64.

Gergen, K. J. (2000). The self in the age of information. *Washington Quarterly,* 23, no. 1, 201–208.

Gergen, K. J., & Gergen, M. M. (1986) Narrative form and the construction of psychological theory. In T. S. Sarbin (ed.), *Narrative psychology: The storied nature of human conduct.* New York: Praeger.

Gergen, M. M. (1997). Narratives of the self. In L. P. Hinchman & S. K. Hinchman (eds.), *Memory, identity, community* (pp. 161–184). Albany, NY: State University of New York Press.

Goffman, E. (1959). *The presentation of self in everyday life.* Garden City, NY: Doubleday.

Gudykunst, W. B., & Kim, Y. Y. (1997). *Communication with strangers: An approach to intercultural communication.* 3rd ed. New York: McGraw-Hill.

Hickam, H., Jr. (1998). *Rocket boys: A memoir.* New York: Delacorte Press.

Hofstede, G. (1980). *Culture's consequences: International differences in work-related values.* Newbury Park, CA: Sage.

Homans, G. C. (1958). Human behavior as exchange. *American Journal of Sociology,* 61, 399–402.

James, W. (1890) *the principles of psychology.* Available online: <psychclassics.yorku.ca/James/Principles/index.htm>. Accessed: March 28, 2002.

Lollack, L. (2001). Foreign-born population in the United States. *Current population reports.* Washington, DC: U.S. Census Bureau. Available online: <www.census.gov/population/www/socdemo/foreign.html>. Accessed: March 23, 2002.

Malcolm X. (1992). *The autobiography of Malcolm X.* Alex Haley, cont. New York: Ballantine Books, 1992.

Malcolm X. (1964). Letter from Mecca. Available online: <www.malcolm-x.org/docs/let_mecca.htm>. Accessed June 23, 2003.

Markham, A. N. (1998). *Life online: Researching real experience in virtual space.* Walnut Creek, CA: Alta Mira Press.

McCall, G. J., & Simmons, J. L. (1966). *Identities and interactions: An examination of human associations in everyday life.* New York. Free Press.

Mead, G. H. (1912). The mechanism of social consciousness. *Journal of Philosophy, Psychology and Scientific Methods,* 9, 401–406.

Mead, G. H. (1934). *Mind, self and society.* Chicago: University of Chicago Press.

Moreau, D. (1990). *Take charge of your career: How to profit from a mid-career change.* Washington: Kiplinger Books.

National Election Studies. (2003). Guide to public opinion and electoral behavior. Available online: <www.umich.edu/~nes/nesguide/nesguide.htm>. Accessed July 16, 2003.

Realo, A., & Allik, J. (1999). A cross-cultural study of collectivism: A comparison of American, Estonian, and Russian students. *Journal of Social Psychology,* 139, no. 2, 133–144.

Rebstock, J. S. (2002). "You are there." Unpublished poem.

Rogers, C. R. (1959). A theory of therapy, personality and interpersonal relationships, as developed in the client-centered framework. In S. Koch (ed.), *Psychology: A study of science* (pp. 184–256). New York: McGraw-Hill.

Sannicolas, N. (1997). Erving Goffman, dramaturgy and on-line relationships. *Cybersociology,* 1. Available online: <www.cybersoc.com/magazine/1/is1nikki.html>. Accessed June 23, 2003.

Sanoff, A. P. (1991). Identity through the ages. *U.S. News & World Report,* July 1, 1991, p. 59.

Schacter, J. (2001). Geographic mobility. In *Current population reports.* Washington, DC: U.S. Census Bureau. Available online: <www.census.gov/prod/2001pubs/p20-538.pdf>. Accessed March 23, 2002.

Schmidley, D. (2001). Profile of the foreign-born population in the United States. In *Current population reports: Special studies.* Washington, DC: U.S. Census Bureau. Available online: <www.census.gov/population/www/socdemo/foreign/reports.html>. Accessed March 23, 2002.

Triandis, H. C. (1995). *Individualism and collectivism.* Boulder, CO: Westview.

Triandis, H. C., & Suh, E. M. (2002). Cultural influences on personality. *Annual Review of Psychology,* 133–160.

United States Department of Labor (2002). Employee tenure summary. Washington, DC: U.S. Department of Labor. Available online: <www.bls.gov/news.release/tenure.nr0.htm>. Accessed July 16, 2003.

Interpersonal Communication

Learning Objectives

After reading the module and participating in the activities, you will be able to:

1 Recognize contexts of interpersonal communication and how to adapt to different relationships.

2 Recognize how interpersonal relationships are defined using personal constructs.

3 Understand processes of relational growth and how to seek and share information in order to foster relational growth.

4 Understand the importance of strategies for relational maintenance and develop a positive climate for interpersonal communication.

5 Identify how managing dialectical tensions contributes to successful relationships.

6 Understand interpersonal conflict and how to manage conflict constructively.

7 Understand how relationships end and communicate constructively to mitigate the harms of relational endings and enable you and others to grow.

THROUGHOUT YOUR DAY, you talk to many people. You relate interpersonally from the first moment of the morning, when you have breakfast with a family member or roommate, until you finish off your day with a telephone call to some friends, with whom you are planning a party for the weekend. And in between, you encounter the salesperson in a store who helps you find the right gift to take to the weekend party, chat with your neighbors about an issue in the community, and call or send an instant message from your computer to connect with a member of your family.

During the day, your cell phone rings innumerable times, as other friends and family members check in with you. When you are at work, you also find the time to chat with associates and communicate with clients. At work, you may also attend a formal meeting or take part in an interview or problem-solving discussion. And in the evening, you may have some quality interpersonal time with a loved one—a time to share stories of the day and to affirm the bonds of intimacy and commitment that hold your relationship together.

For many of us, the days are filled with interpersonal encounters. Interpersonal communication occurs in a wide variety of relationships: from fairly impersonal relationships, such as those with acquaintances and co-workers, to relationships that are deeply personal, such as those with family members and long-time friends. In sum, these interpersonal encounters exemplify the experience of being part of a **relational community** on an interpersonal level.

In this module, we focus principally on our more personal, primary relationships and how they grow and deepen. We will concentrate on the importance of communication to the functioning of a family, to the interactions of friends, and to the bonding of romantic partners. We will see how these types of primary relationships evolve. We will also consider how relational partners promote the growth and sustain the well-being of their relationship.

Defining the Context of Interpersonal Communication

LEARNING OBJECTIVE
5.1

We can define interpersonal relationships by their context when we examine three distinctive characteristics of how we relate:

- Interpersonal communication may be personal or impersonal.
- Interpersonal communication may be formal or informal.
- Interpersonal communication may be exclusive or inclusive of larger social networks.

Interpersonal Communication May Be Personal or Impersonal

Our relationships vary in intimacy. One way of thinking about this is to place your different experiences with relationships along a continuum (see Figure 5.1). On one end of the continuum are your most *impersonal* relationships; on the opposite, your most *personal* relationships. As you move along the continuum from your most impersonal

relational community The personal, social, and cultural context of human communication.

As you move along the continuum from your most impersonal to your most personal types of relationships, you will likely see a continually greater level of intimacy and closeness. The level of intimacy and closeness you experience also correlates with the kind of knowledge that you and the other person have of one another.

Source: Based on Miller and Sunnafrank (1982)

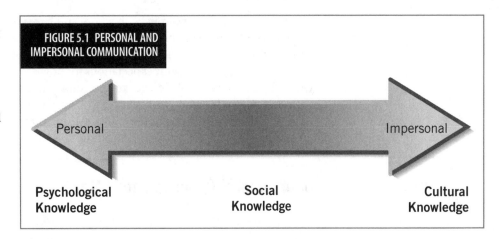

FIGURE 5.1 PERSONAL AND IMPERSONAL COMMUNICATION

Personal — Impersonal

Psychological Knowledge   **Social Knowledge**   **Cultural Knowledge**

to your most personal types of relationships, you will likely see a continually greater level of intimacy and closeness. The level of intimacy and closeness you experience also correlates with the kind of knowledge that you and the other person have of one another (Miller and Sunnafrank, 1982).

On the impersonal end of the continuum, your least personal relationships operate on the basis of **cultural knowledge.** This is the most general level of knowledge that you can have about others. For instance, when you go into a store and interact with a clerk who is helping you find what you want to buy, the chance is rather good that you will not know much about that particular individual. And so you will relate to that person in his or her role as clerk, while you perform the role of customer. In impersonal relationships, interpersonal communicators enact culturally expected **roles** and conform to the norms and expectations that every other member of the culture would subscribe to.

On the opposite end of the continuum are your most personal relationships. These are your closest relationships, in which you and the other person share **psychological knowledge** about one another. These relationships become more personal as a result of the conscious choices that you and another person make to share information about yourselves. Psychological knowledge enables each of you to make useful interpretations of the other and to predict aspects of his or her behavior. In thinking about these types of relationships, consider how well you know a close friend or loved one. You can likely judge how he or she will react to a given situation or circumstance, even predicting what he or she will say. You may know one another and how each of you communicates so well that you have probably developed a private code made up of words and nonverbal expressions that are meaningful only within the context of your personal relationship.

5.1

Moreover, these most personal relationships are unique, even irreplaceable, and thus, the roles that we perform in them are also unique and perhaps rather complicated at times. With a best friend, for instance, you may perform a whole range of roles. You may be fellow students in a class, companions who travel together, and partners in playing a game or enjoying a recreational activity. When one or the other is stressed, you may perform the role of supporter or confidant and try to be helpful.

Some of these different roles have been performed over a long period of time and are part of the continuity of your relational history with one another. Yet, the process of mutually defining your relationship—and its many roles you each perform—is not static. We are continually improvising new roles. In hindsight, you can probably recall some of the turning points in your relationship when new roles were created.

At the midway point of the relationship continuum are other relationships, such as those with casual friends, co-workers you do not know well, and perhaps even more

cultural knowledge   Insights about others based on their membership in a large cultural group. This type of knowledge is often used when relating impersonally to strangers.

roles   Patterns of behavior enacted by an individual within the context of a particular relational community; the expectations for enacting a role are mutually defined by members of a relational community.

psychological knowledge
Personal information about another.

distant members of your family with whom you have fairly little contact. Since you may not know "what makes them tick," as you do your really close friends and loved ones, you are likely to draw more on **sociological knowledge.** In doing so, you might base your expectations for how they will act, as well as how you will perform your role in your relationship with them, on the basis of social factors such as age, gender, and work status. You simply don't know these individuals well enough to have gained psychological knowledge that will set them apart from any or most of the other individuals you encounter in similar social circumstances.

Interpersonal Communication May Be Formal or Informal

Irrespective of how personal they are, our interpersonal relationships also vary in their level of formality. Think about the casual style of communication you fall into with peers and friends, and then contrast it with the style of communication you use with an employer or teacher. Some communication situations call for using more formal types of **speech acts.** Recall from the discussion in Module One how Searle (1969) explains a speech act as a type of utterance that is used in a specific situation in order to accomplish a communicative goal. Interpersonal communicators follow rules as they perform speech acts. Whether we communicate formally or informally, then, will be guided by the rules that govern a particular situation and relationship. Clearly, expectations of formality do not generalize across relationships.

Susan provides an interesting example of the personal yet formal style of interaction that governed her relationship with her old-fashioned grandmother:

I guess you would have to say my grandmother was of the "old school." She thought that I should learn to be a lady. So, I was expected to use a fairly formal style of communication in her presence. At the same time, we were very close to one another. I could share with her many of the things I could not tell anyone else. Grandmother was special, right down to the lace doilies on the sofa and the equally prim and proper way she always dressed.

It is kind of interesting to contrast my grandmother's traditional views with my mother's feminist attitudes. Mom had essentially rejected a lot of my grandmother's ladylike manners as being antifeminist. I guess she did not buy into a lot of Grandmother's regulative rules. Personally, I think I benefited a great deal from both of them. From my mom, I learned how to take care of myself, and from my grandmother, how to adapt to different kinds of situations. I am a more complete woman from gaining the perspectives of each of them.

Rules for using language and nonverbal communication to express ourselves in formal versus informal styles may also differ significantly from one culture to another. Laetitia makes some interesting observations about how the rules she learned living in Africa and France are quite different from the informal ways she has observed as being typical in the United States:

sociological knowledge   Insights about another based upon his or her social grouping.

speech act   An utterance of intent to perform an action that is intended to achieve a specific goal, such as making a promise to do something; organized around an intention that the communicator is trying to achieve and includes a sentence or set of sentences and communicative behaviors that fulfill the requirements of performing the act.

Even though I have lived most of my life in France, I had never felt so out of place, culturally speaking, until I came to the United States. My parents were Africans from the Ivory Coast. Since France colonized the Ivory Coast, a lot of the culture of the Ivory Coast is based on the French culture. Therefore, for a French-speaking person, living in France does not create any cultural shock. Living in the United States is another story. The American culture is a lot more casual than I was used to. There are fewer formalities in everything. The most apparent one is the way people dress. I used to wear a two-piece suit to go to my business school. Here, I can wear a pair of jeans, a T-shirt, and open-toe shoes to school!

The less apparent difference is in the language structure itself and the way people communicate in general. For example, in French, there are two personal pronouns that relate to the word *you* in English: *Tu* is used when talking to relatives and friends or people one is familiar with, and *vous* is used when talking to strangers and people who are higher than one in the hierarchy (that is, until they allow one to refer to them with *tu).*

Interpersonal Communication May Be Exclusive or Inclusive of Larger Social Networks

A third characteristic that can be used to distinguish types of interpersonal communication is the number of people with whom we relate. **Exclusive relationships** are shared when the number of people in them is small. Many of our exclusive relationships are dyadic and thus feature one-to-one interaction, which excludes others. Partners in a romantic relationship, for instance, create a level of intimacy and commitment that is experienced only within the context of that particular relationship. In our exclusive relationships, we are also likely to develop a high level of interdependence.

Consider next how you have formed very exclusive friendships with just a few people. You probably think of them as your best friends. Your interactions with the members of your immediate family are also likely examples of exclusive interpersonal communication. Clearly, these are unique and special bonds that are shared only among particular members of the family. Since an exclusive relationship requires an investment of time and energy, you may also become more selective about with which members to invest yourself. Data from the General Social Survey (GSS) at the University of Michigan (National Opinion Research Center, 1986) found that most people claim they have between two and six close friends. Yet not all of these friendships have the same level of intimacy and commitment. When respondents in the GSS were asked to identify how many people they were likely to communicate significant personal information about themselves, the number went down to one to three friends. And it was with this small set of one to three friends that respondents in the GSS indicated they were more likely to interact frequently by communicating on a daily basis or at least once a week.

At the same time, you may also relate to members of one or more larger **social networks.** Your social networks are somewhat broader groupings, such as circles of friends and various members of your extended family. Your social networks are frequently more distant relationships. Thus, you may not share the same levels of interdependence, intimacy, and commitment with the individuals in these networks that you do with the people with whom you have exclusive relationships. But in terms of number, you are likely to have more relationships with people in social networks than in exclusive relationships.

Figure 5.2 provides a diagram for visualizing the contrast between exclusive relationships and the inclusive aspects of social networks. The smaller diameter of the inner circle of the diagram represents the notion that exclusive relationships are more likely to be few in number and involve higher levels of interdependence, intimacy, and commitment. Inclusive relationships that fall into the wider circle, by contrast, are the social networks that are often characterized by lower levels of interdependence, intimacy, and commitment. You might use this diagram to think about who is in the inner circle among your relationships and who is in the wider circle.

As an illustration, consider how Laverne and Vivien have an exclusive relationship. They live together and have a deep level of intimacy and commitment. At the same time, they relate to a larger social network of friends that get together for social outings. This group of friends, which includes Jaime, Pat, Jean, Leslie, and Hillary, all play on the same

exclusive relationships Relationships marked by one-on-one communication between two people or interactions with few people.

social network Inclusive relationships that are usually larger than a dyad or a few people such as a group of friends or an extended family.

Members of an exclusive primary relationship also interact with others in a more inclusive social network. The boundary between primary relationships and social networks is more or less permeable.

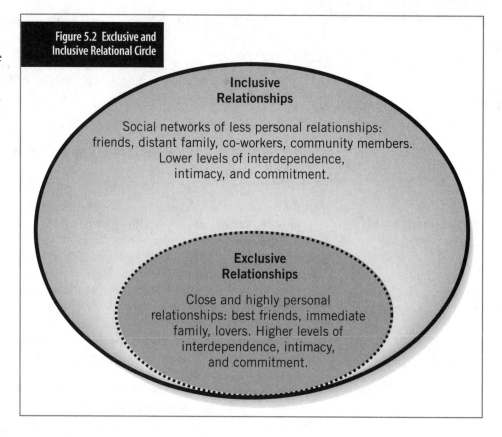

Figure 5.2 Exclusive and Inclusive Relational Circle

Inclusive Relationships

Social networks of less personal relationships: friends, distant family, co-workers, community members. Lower levels of interdependence, intimacy, and commitment.

Exclusive Relationships

Close and highly personal relationships: best friends, immediate family, lovers. Higher levels of interdependence, intimacy, and commitment.

softball team with Laverne and Vivien. The group often socializes by going out for a drink after a game or out to see a movie together. Along with this circle of friends, Laverne and Vivien have other groups of friends that they each know from school and from their workplaces.

ONLINE JOURNAL

5.3

Each of us is likely to belong to several social networks. We may have one social network from a club we belong to, another that we know from attending religious services, and still another from among the people we join to do a recreational activity. Our social networks may also vary in size. As each becomes larger, we will likely establish a hierarchy within the group to distinguish closer relationships from more distant ones.

Implications for Communication: Adapt to Different Communication Contexts and Stay in Touch

ASSESSING YOUR SKILLS

5.1

Adapt the Way That You Communicate to Different Contexts of Interpersonal Communication
Different interpersonal communication contexts call for different ways of relating. To be effective, you need to adjust the way that you communicate with each person in light of where your relationship with him or her falls on the continuum of personal versus impersonal communication.

And since communication situations differ in their levels of formality and exclusivity, a competent interpersonal communicator will see the need to make adjustments when moving from one situation to another and from one person to another. To do so, you must have a mindfulness of what is expected in formal versus informal situations plus a willingness to observe the rules for these different situations. Further, many of your exclusive relationships will require you to communicate in ways that maintain the intimacy of your exclusive bond and express your sense of commitment.

As you move between the inner circle of your exclusive relationships and interact with members of your larger social networks, you also need to make adjustments in how you communicate. Later in this module, we will give greater consideration to the value of sustaining relationships among the members of a social network, which provides people in exclusive relationships with support and affirmation. And we will see that skillful interpersonal communicators deal with the different demands and expectations of their exclusive relationships and those of their larger social networks.

Stay in Touch to Maintain Relationships   In your exclusive and primary relationships, as well as in communicating with your social networks, it is important to find the time and place to stay in contact. Yet how you connect on a regular and consistent basis will also vary from one relationship to another. With one friend, you may have a set time to get together for an activity, while for another, you might make a periodic phone call to touch base and catch up on the latest news. With your intimate relationships and among close family members, the interaction may include your daily routines and rituals as well as the special occasions that you celebrate. While much of your contact will involve a face-to-face encounter, some of it will take the form of writing or communication via electronic media. You may thus write a note or card or go online to keep in touch.

With special reference to online communications, surveys by the Pew Research Center (2003) examine how people communicate interpersonally using the Internet. Their studies observe how young people maintain contact using tools such as online chat and instant messages, while older family members maintain relationships with email. The Pew Internet studies also observe how people use online communications to stay in touch with family members and to maintain ties to social and community groups.

Defining Relationships from Personal Constructs

Regardless of the type of relationship—personal or impersonal, formal or informal, exclusive or wider—the members of a relationship mutually define that relationship. To be sure, the process of defining a relationship is ongoing, one in which relational partners negotiate the meaning of their relationship at different points in its history. We use our **personal constructs** as we define relationships. Kelly (1955) uses a metaphor that compares the way we develop personal constructs to the research method of a scientist working in a laboratory. A scientist develops a theory and then creates a hypothesis to test that theory and to validate its theoretic constructs. Kelly suggests that when we use our personal constructs to make sense of the world around us, we use a similar process, in which we form personal constructs as hypotheses and then test them through experience. We use our constructs to anticipate how we will experience things or relate to others. A similar line of thinking is applied to defining *relational schemata* by Planalp (1985). Relational schemata are constructs that serve as guides for how we act in particular relationships and how we define the nature of a given relationship.

personal construct   A means of assigning meaning to a situation by perceiving how it is similar to a previous situation; enables people to assign meanings to situations and to anticipate events that are part of a history of similarly constituted communication situations.

Friendship

5.1

Consider how you use personal constructs to define what it means to be part of a friendship. For instance, you may have developed a personal construct that defines a *friend* as someone you trust and with whom you can enjoy the following:

■ Sharing personal information about yourself
■ Feeling a sense of loyalty
■ Spending time and enjoying common interests and activities
■ Feeling a sense of supportiveness and encouragement

5.2

Cultural Attitudes toward Friendship   Our personal constructs and relational schemata for defining friendship are affected by the culture in which we live and reflect the cultural values that are identified with being a friend. Popular forms of entertainment across the years have reflected culturally shared values about friendship—from *The Big Chill*, a movie made in the 1980s about a group of college friends approaching middle age who reunite for a short time when one of their group dies, to the long-standing television comedy *Friends*, which portrays the trials and tribulations of six individuals as they grow into careers, marriages, and becoming parents. A national survey of people in the United States (National Opinion Research Center, 1998), found that people are likely to form friendships with those who are perceived as being honest, responsible, fun loving, and intelligent. These four values top the list of attributes that survey respondents ascribed to close friends. The second tier of values include being creative, cultured, and dynamic.

5.4

Nonetheless, you may develop a very unique personal construct that applies to a particular friendship. One friendship may be characterized by powerful bonds of emotional interdependency, while another may be distinguished by a special brand of humor that is uniquely shared.

Family Relationships

How, in similar ways, do you define family relationships and develop expectations about how those relationships will be experienced? In part, you also develop personal constructs for what you think defines a *family* by drawing on cultural assumptions and norms about what a family is supposed to look like and how it is supposed to function. Depending on the definition, a family may be any of several types and serve a range of functions.

Functions of Healthy Family Communication   Experts in family communication, such as Connard and Novick (1996), write about the functions that a healthy family performs. They note that we turn to our family for support and nurturance in order to grow. When our family is healthy, it creates a safe environment that allows each individual in the family to change and to develop his or her potential as a person. Thus, our family nurtures our emotional, intellectual, physical, and moral growth as persons.

Caughlin (2003) identifies a number of factors of effective family communication including openness, while at the same time recognizing boundaries of privacy; maintaining a sense of stability, especially through decision-making, discipline in accordance with rules, and regular routines; shared understanding among family members that is experienced as a kind of positive "mind reading" through which family members can accurately perceive what others think or want; and positive communication marked by affection, support, politeness, and humor.

When a family thrives, so do its members. Interactions among family members affirm self-worth and provide the support that permits each person to become autonomous while also valuing the bonds of affection that connect him or her to the family. As you grow, you learn how to cope with the world outside your family and develop the skills needed to deal with that larger world.

A family is also a legal and economic structure. Membership in a family thus meets individual needs for economic support and legal recognition as well as emotional growth and support. Marital law in the United States and other countries is grounded in protecting property rights as well as providing economic security.

VIDEO
VIEW

5.3

Family Structures   *Family structure,* which defines the roles and form of a family, is also modeled by the culture in which the family lives. In some cultural communities, the ideal family structure may be the two-parent nuclear family, comprised of a mother and father and their children. Yet in other cultural communities, an extended family structure of several generations is more in keeping with the cultural ideal.

WEB
ACTIVITY

5.2

WEB
ACTIVITY

5.3

Data from the U.S. Census Bureau (Fields and Casper, 2001) document a 30-year trend in the United States in which the proportion of families comprised of a married heterosexual couple and their children has declined relative to other family forms. Increasingly, children in the United States may live with parents who are not married. Over the same 30-year period, the number of single-parent families has risen significantly, as has the incidence of three-generation families, in which one or more children reside with their parents and grandparents.

In the period between 1970 and 2000, the number of family households in the United States in which a married heterosexual couple lived *without* children remained about the same relative to the population as a whole. Yet the proportionate number of married heterosexual couples *with* children declined in relation to the increased numbers of single-parent families and three-generation families. Indeed, the cultural stereotype of the American family structure as a "family of four," composed of a married couple and their two children, now represents only 24 percent of the total—down from 40 percent of the households counted in the 1970 census.

Another trend is the increase is the number of gay and lesbian families in the United States. A study by the Human Rights Campaign and the Urban Institute (Smith and Gates, 2001), which drew upon data from the 2000 census, reports 1.2 million people living in gay and lesbian households. This number, the authors note, represents an undercount of the real figure, since gay and lesbian households are not formally identified in the collection of census data. The authors estimate that a more realistic figure, based on other demographic studies, would indicate the number of committed gay or lesbian people residing with partners in the United States as being closer to 3.1 million.

Romantic Relationships

VIDEO
VIEW

5.4

WEB
ACTIVITY

5.4

ONLINE
JOURNAL

5.5

Just as cultural attitudes and demographic factors affect family relationships, so might the perception of what it means to be in a romantic relationship be influenced by cultural attitudes and values about love. For instance, Fehr (1993) has detailed the viewpoint held by many people in the United States that a romantic relationship is characterized by these qualities:

- Trust
- Caring
- Honesty
- Respect
- Friendship

Sternberg's triangular theory of love defines a romantic relationship in terms of three dimensions: intimacy, passion, and commitment. When all three of these dimensions are experienced, partners have developed a consummate love relationship.

Source: Based on Sternberg (1986)

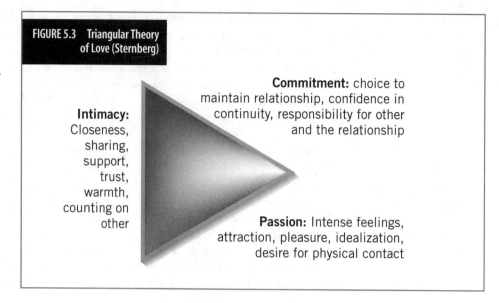

FIGURE 5.3 Triangular Theory of Love (Sternberg)

Intimacy: Closeness, sharing, support, trust, warmth, counting on other

Commitment: choice to maintain relationship, confidence in continuity, responsibility for other and the relationship

Passion: Intense feelings, attraction, pleasure, idealization, desire for physical contact

Triangular Theory of Love In addition to drawing on cultural viewpoints, you might develop your personal constructs for defining *love* by drawing on theoretical definitions. Sternberg's (1986) **triangular theory of love** defines a *romantic relationship* in terms of three dimensions: intimacy, passion, and commitment (see Figure 5.3).

Intimacy is communicated in a relationship as closeness through the sharing of personal information and the development of understanding. It is also experienced with feelings of supportiveness, trust, and warmth and the perception that each person can count on the other in a time of need.

The second dimension of love, *passion*, is marked by intense expressions of feelings, which may be idealizations of the other person. Passionate lovers also express romantic feelings, pleasure, attraction, and the desire for physical contact with one another.

The third aspect of love, *commitment*, is expressed in the decision to maintain a relationship. Commitment is communicated as a result of the expectations and confidence in the continuity and permanence of the relationship. Commitment leads to feelings of responsibility for one another and for the well-being of the relationship. Lovers who are committed to one another view their decision to remain in the relationship as a good one and resolve to stay in the relationship even in the face of difficulty.

When all three of these dimensions—intimacy, passion, and commitment—are experienced, Sternberg (1986) suggests that partners experience a *consummate* love relationship. The consummate love relationship is not the only model, however. Some love relationships, according to Sternberg, may be defined by development of only one or two of the three dimensions.

triangular theory of love Model for defining romantic relationships in key terms of passion, intimacy, and commitment.

Again, as discussed in the consideration of how friendships and family relationships are uniquely constructed, a relationship with a romantic partner will have its own individuality. In a recent line of research, to which we will return later in this module, Sternberg (2000) examines how a romantic couple creates a narrative that tells the story of their unique relationship and how it evolved.

5.3

Implications for Communication:
The Meaning of a Relationship Is Mutually Defined

5.2

Recognize How You Developed Your Personal Constructs for Defining Relationships   Personal constructs differ from one person to another. Each of us has formed our own set of constructs for defining what it means to be in a friendship, to be a member of a family, and to relate with someone romantically on the basis of our own unique life experiences and interactions with our culture. We have each drawn on cultural values about friendship, family norms and structures, and expectations of what constitutes being in a romantic relationship.

Yet even people who come from the same cultural background may still differ in terms of their personal constructs. One party to a friendship may think that the most meaningful aspect of being a friend is to spend time together and do activities together, yet the other party may think that the highest priority in friendship is to have trust and honesty, which is expressed by open dialogue and deep conversation. So, too, lovers may have different personal constructs for what it means to form commitment in the relationship.

These differences may be highlighted when we enter into relationships with people who come from significantly different cultural backgrounds and values. Yvonne discovered that she and her husband had substantial differences in their assumptions about marriage and family. Those differences came to the fore only after they were married and as she became more fully integrated into her husband's extended family. Observe how Yvonne describes her process of adjustment and negotiation:

> When I first met my husband, Jose, who is Mexican American, I really didn't notice that we had many cultural differences. We both liked doing the same things, such as weight lifting/body building, listening to jazz, going salsa dancing, and traveling. It wasn't until he took me to New Mexico to meet his parents that I saw the differences. For one thing, he rarely spoke Spanish to me at home, but that's all he spoke with his parents, brothers, sisters, and friends. Also, he has a really huge family of six brothers, four sisters, and lots of aunts, uncles, and cousins who like to get together regularly to eat and celebrate all those birthdays, weddings, and christenings. I, on the other hand, have one sister who was grown and gone from home by the time I was 10, and we only get together with the extended family every year for a family reunion. It took awhile, but I eventually got over my initial apprehensions and began to look forward to Jose's family celebrations.

Use Meta-Communication to Mutually Define a Relationship   When you consider how people may come to a relationship with different personal constructs, it becomes obvious that arriving at a mutual agreement about a relationship may take some time. Sometimes, we may even need to talk about the differ-

5.2

ences in our constructs as well as how they converge. Mutual understanding of a relationship can be attained by stepping back and engaging in a type of reflective conversation that Watzlawick, Beavin, and Jackson (1967) call **meta-communication.** These authors explain that we use meta-communication "when we no longer use communication to communicate but to communicate *about* communication" (p. 40). Meta-communication is talking about how we communicate with one another and examining the underlying assumptions, values, backgrounds, and motivations for doing so.

meta-communication Communicating about communication. Meta-communication may be used to explore the underlying assumptions, values, background, and motivations for how we communicate.

Many examples can be offered of how meta-communication works. For instance, you may need to tell a friend what you expect to get in your relationship as well as what you want to offer. In a romantic relationship, you may need to explore with your partner what it means to be passionate or intimate. You may also need to explore your expectations about family communication, especially when you enter a relationship with someone whose family of origin differs from your own. Meta-communication can help you recognize your differences and work toward a mutual definition of your relationship.

Arriving at a mutual definition of what a relationship means is an ongoing process. Over time, a relationship develops its own unique qualities that constitute the relational history of the relationship. Next, we will examine some of the ways that we communicate information about ourselves as part of the process of relational growth.

Relational Growth

LEARNING OBJECTIVE 5.3

Relational growth is about change and the deepening of a personal relationship. As you look back at how one of your relationships has grown, you may be able to recall the ways in which the relationship emerged. Your **relational history** includes your perceptions of one another and how you developed your own distinctive ways to communicate in various types of situations. Over time, patterns of behavior are created, which may lead to a strengthening of the relationship or to its decline in the face of difficulties.

Personal and Relational Narratives

Personal stories function as a medium for preserving shared memories and highlighting the changes that occur over the course of a relationship. Those stories reflect how perceptions of one another and the relationship change over time.

Some communication researchers have studied interpersonal relationships by asking people to tell stories about how their relationships developed. Each story chronicles different points as a relationship evolves.

WEB ACTIVITY 5.5

Stories of Relational History   Think about one of your relationships. If you were asked to share a story about it, there might be several you could tell. You might, for instance, have a story about how you and the other person first met and what kinds of initial impressions you had of one another. You might also have a story about how those impressions changed with the nature of the relationship. For some people, the relationship that started out simply as an acquaintanceship grew into a friendship. And for some, a friendship may have become a romantic relationship.

You might also have a story about a relationship in decline, one that experienced significant problems. Even after the relationship ends, the narrative process will continue. Only then, the story will be told from your single point of view, as you try to make sense of how the relationship deteriorated. Thus, at each stage in an evolving relationship, a different chapter of the story can be told.

relational history   The cumulative set of experiences shared by members in a relational community; develops out of the recurring types of communication situations that members repeat as part of their pattern of interaction.

Love Stories   Sternberg (2000) has found that romantic partners develop a theme as part of their story. He hypothesizes that partners in a successful and growing relationship construct substantially similar story lines as they recount the story of their relationship. The account that one member provides is congruent with that of the other and reflects an agreement about the expectations that relational partners have of one another. Each may see the theme of the relationship as one of making sacrifices or of being on a journey, for instance. Partners' stories can also reveal complementary roles that each perceives the other to fulfill, such as prince and princess. The stories with prince and princess characters often cast the lover in idealistic terms, seeing how the other is the perfect partner. When partners in a relationship assume complementary roles, each assumes a distinctly different role that is understood and accepted by the other.

When relationships are in decline, however, the stories sound different. Sternberg describes how he has listened to the stories of two people in the throes of breaking up with one another and heard how they have entirely different accounts of their relationship. They are, he suggests, experiencing very different senses of their relationship.

Recently, the morning television program *Good Morning America* featured the love stories of five couples in a series entitled "Happily Ever After: A Wedding in Times Square" (*Good Morning, America,* 2002). Among the couples who told their stories were Molly and Darren, who talked about how they met when both were enrolled in a school where they were learning how to become clowns. Tad and Jaime, another couple, narrated the tale of how they had known one another most of their lives. Their relationship started as a friendship that began in school. In that phase of their relationship, they had always thought of themselves simply as best buddies and resisted becoming romantically involved, even when others in their network of friends thought they should date. But their story turned out differently. Out of school and on their own, they reunited in a professional context—and from there, the rest was a romantic story. In contrast, Tara and John Paul met on a subway platform and embarked on the classic tale of "love at first sight."

Family Stories Family narratives also develop themes and serve a vital function of binding family members together. Stone (2003) examines how people learn the roles and expectations, the rules and guidelines, for relating to others by hearing stories about their families. The stories from your family of origin go beyond simple recollections of facts and events; they communicate the expectations of how you are supposed to relate to others and form a family of your own. As an example, Stone recalls hearing her own family story of how her grandparents emigrated to the United States from Italy at the start of the twentieth century and how this story shaped her attitudes and values about family life.

In the film *The Joy Luck Club,* which is based on the novel of the same name by Amy Tan, four women who emigrated from China to the United States share with their daughters their powerful family stories as well as their personal narratives. Each narrative reflects the individual struggles of the storyteller and imparts the lessons she learned from her own trials. Moreover, each story has a huge impact on the daughter, who hears it directly from her mother.

Reflect on *your* stories—about friendships, romantic relationships, and family experiences. What kinds of insights can you gain from these stories about how you have learned to communicate interpersonally?

Personal "Getting to Know You" Stories We also use storytelling as a way of sharing information about ourselves. When you first meet someone, you may have a "stock story" that you tell about who you are, along with some very basic information about your background. We may talk about where we come from, what kind of work we do, or what our family is like. Often, our stock story will include only safe topics, so as to create a positive impression with the person we are just meeting. Later, as the relationship deepens, our stories may also become more intimate and we will take greater risks by sharing more personal parts of our life story.

VIDEO VIEW

5.5

5.3

How relationships grow and deepen can also be explained by theories of interpersonal information exchange. In the next section of this module, we will examine two of these theories: Berger and Calabrese's (1975) uncertainty reduction theory and Altman and Taylor's (1987) social penetration model of self-disclosure.

Information Exchange: Uncertainty Reduction

Initial encounters with people can be challenging. We have all probably experienced the apprehension of such meetings. Yet most of our interpersonal relationships begin in this way. In large measure, our apprehension is due to the fact that we don't know enough about the person with whom we are communicating. As a result, we are uncertain of how to act, and we lack the kind of knowledge about the other person that would enable us to predict and explain how and why that person acts as he or she does.

According to **uncertainty reduction theory,** which was developed by Berger and Calabrese (1975), we are likely to seek information about other people as a way of reducing our uncertainty. We do this by employing one or more of three communication strategies:

- *Passive observation,* in which we watch how others act
- *Active information gathering,* in which we find out information from third-party sources
- *Direct interaction,* in which we deal directly with whomever we want to know more about

Uncertainty Reduction Strategies   We can examine how we use these **uncertainty reduction strategies** with a hypothetical example. Suppose that you are at a party. Along with the familiar faces of people you already know from earlier encounters, there are some new faces, as well. Berger and Calabrese (1975) suggest that one strategy you may employ is *passive observation,* in which you make indirect observations of a person you don't know. As you watch him or her, you do a kind of initial sizing up and ascertain your comfort level and willingness to communicate. Remember that you are on the same stage, so it is possible that another person is sizing you up, as well. This may be one of the reasons that in initial encounters, we put so much emphasis on using some of the strategies of **impression management** that we talked about in Module Four.

Another kind of indirect route for reducing your uncertainty might be to use the *active* strategy of *information gathering,* in which you ask other people for information about the person you don't know. You may turn to a friend whom you know has more information about the unknown person than you do. You might ask for his or her insight to help guide you in determining how you can relate to this new person. This is an indirect approach, insofar as you do not directly interact with the person about whom you need to reduce uncertainty.

ONLINE JOURNAL

5.8

The third strategy is *direct interaction.* As you communicate directly with the unknown person, you might make small talk and exchange superficial and nonthreatening information about yourself. This is the tactic of sharing safe background information, such as demographic information, about yourself. You describe where you work and what kinds of personal interests and hobbies you like to pursue. Even the rather mundane chatter you share about the weather or activities like a vacation that you are planning to take become grist for the mill of small talk.

Over the course of time, many of us have developed a set of stock questions and answers that facilitate these initial conversations. The topics of our small talk may seem mundane and inconsequential, but the benefits of these conversations are not. Berger

uncertainty reduction theory
Communicators seek information about others in an effort to predict and control communication. By reducing uncertainty an interpersonal communicator can anticipate how to communicate with others.

uncertainty reduction strategies
Passive strategies involve indirect observations of others. Active strategies may include the indirect approach of asking others information about a party of interest or a direct strategy of asking for information from the person of interest or using small talk to learn information about the other.

impression management   Efforts by a person playing a role to control the way members of the audience perceive him or her.

and Calabrese (1975) suggest that as people do more of this type of verbal interaction, accompanied by nonverbal expressiveness that is comfortable and appropriate to the situation of meeting new acquaintances, uncertainty is reduced. In turn, the information that people gain about others may open the way to more of the kinds of low-level self-disclosures that create meaningful common ground.

It may be especially valuable to use uncertainty reduction strategies when you relate to people who come from a culture that differs from your own. The popular movie *Save the Last Dance* offers an illustration of the uncertainties a person faces when he or she is the outsider in a community. The main character of the story, Sara (played by Julia Stiles), has lived her entire life in a suburban environment and dreams of studying ballet at Julliard after high school. That dream is put on hold, however, when her mother dies and she must move to live with her father in the city. At that point, she enters a dramatically different world. Now attending an urban high school on the south side of Chicago, she must use all three types of uncertainty reduction strategies to adjust to her new life situation, new relationships, and the change in environment. Her adaptations go beyond learning to do the dance steps of hip-hop, rather than ballet. Several scenes of the movie simply show Sara as a passive observer, taking in what she sees around her. Along the way, she develops an attraction to Derek (portrayed by Sean Patrick Thomas). First, she observes him in classes and how he relates to his friends in the school cafeteria and at Steps, the hip-hop club. Later, she turns to a newly found friend, Chenille, to use the active approach of seeking out a third party to learn more about how to relate to her new environment and to find out more information about Derek. Chenille turns out to be an atypical third-party source, as she is Derek's sister. She cools to the idea of Sara's interest in pursuing a deeper relationship with her brother. The most meaningful information that Sara and Derek learn about one another results from their direct interaction as they each talk about themselves and listen to one another's personal stories.

Uncertainty Reduction Outcomes   In the early phases of getting to know someone, our self-disclosures are likely to be reciprocated. We match information so that each person takes turns sharing about himself or herself. Later on, we may not expect that kind of immediate, tit-for-tat, reciprocal disclosure. Indeed, in mature relationships, we may look to others for support and understanding when we disclose information, rather than for immediate matching of self-disclosure. So, when you sit down with your best friend to share how you've experienced a problem, you don't expect him or her to respond right then and there with an account of his or her own problem—that is, unless he or she is attempting to create a sense of empathy on the basis of having been through the same kind of experience.

As we reduce the level of uncertainty we feel about someone by exchanging information in the early stages of a relationship, we may experience greater liking for that person and feelings of being somewhat more intimate. That sense of intimacy will continue to grow through the sharing of deeper levels of self-disclosure.

5.4

Self-Disclosure: Social Penetration

Self-disclosure can be defined as the intentional sharing of personal information about oneself. Disclosure may include sharing both high-risk and low-risk information as well as personal experiences, ideas and attitudes, feelings and values, past facts and life stories, and even future hopes, dreams, ambitions, and goals. In sharing information about yourself, you make choices about what to share and with whom to share it.

self-disclosure   Intentional sharing of personal information about one's self.

Competent communicators use self-disclosure selectively. They make choices about disclosing information judiciously, with awareness of the positive and negative consequences of doing so. They may weigh the impact that disclosing information might have on the growth and well-being of a relationship. In addition, they may consider how learning personal information about themselves may affect another person, especially in light of that person's receptivity and trustworthiness to respond well to what has been disclosed.

Altman and Taylor (1987) developed the **social penetration theory** to describe self-disclosure as the gradual sharing of information about oneself. Drawing on **social exchange theory,** Altman and Taylor sought to explain some of the decisions people make about whether to share information about themselves.

Rewards and Costs of Self-Disclosure

What motivates you to self-disclose? As we have already seen, the kinds of low-level self-disclosures that occur as part of the strategy of uncertainty reduction invite others to reciprocate and share their own information. So, one great payoff of self-disclosing is the reduction of uncertainty and the stress that it creates. And later in a relationship, when a deeper level of self-disclosure occurs, we experience the rewards of having greater intimacy with people we like. We may also self-disclose information in order to gain the help and support of others or to achieve the catharsis that comes from unburdening ourselves from carrying difficult and painful emotional experiences by ourselves. Support, empathy, compassion, and understanding are all powerful rewards that motivate self-disclosure.

At the same time, costs and risks may be incurred as a result of self-disclosure. We may lose face with another or risk a breach of confidence. Sometimes, the cost of disclosure is a burden to the relationship itself, especially when disclosure is associated with demands or expectations that a relational partner does not feel comfortable assuming. In deciding whether to self-disclose, we must weigh these actual and perceived costs against the anticipated rewards.

Disclosure of Breadth and Depth

Altman and Taylor (1987) describe the process of self-disclosure as **social penetration**. By this, they mean that self-disclosing and learning about others constitute the process of penetrating deeper into the selves of those people—and enabling others to penetrate ourselves and gain a deeper understanding of us. This process of penetration is a gradual one, in which each communicator reveals layers of personal depth.

 As a way of visualizing this process, Altman and Taylor use the metaphor of an onion and its layers of rings. Disclosure begins on the outer layer and proceeds to the core of the onion. These authors also suggest that there are two levels of disclosure (see Figure 5.4). The first level is called the **breadth** dimension. This is the skin of the onion and its most outer layers. In terms of self-disclosure, this layer is largely made up of superficial information about ourselves that we commonly share with a number of different people. On this superficial level, there is a great deal of information that will likely cost little to disclose. This peripheral information will likely be exchanged early in a relationship. Moreover, Altman and Taylor observe that when we share superficial information—that is, from the breadth dimension of ourselves—the process of penetration is fairly quick.

Later, in a relationship, communicators gradually share **depth** of information. Again, using the onion metaphor, these are the inner layers and the core of the onion. Information at the depth level is more significant and more central to who we are. Thus, sharing information from our depth may incur greater risk taking. The information from this dimension of self is typically known by and held in confidence by only a few people. Sometimes, it includes very strong feelings, beliefs, and concerns. It may also include secrets, regrets or hurtful experiences, and painful memories. Information from

---

social penetration theory A model of self-disclosure that examines how relationships develop through the gradual sharing of information.

social exchange theory The theory of behavior that examines how individuals are motivated by efforts to maximize rewards and minimize costs.

social penetration Gradual process of sharing information through self-disclosure that enables another to penetrate to the point of developing a deep understanding of another.

breadth Self-disclosures that include sharing of superficial information about oneself on a broad range of subject areas.

depth Self-disclosures that encompass sharing of personally significant information about oneself.

Altman and Taylor describe the process of self-disclosure as social penetration. As a way of visualizing this process, they use the metaphor of an onion and its layers of rings. Disclosure begins on the outer layer and proceeds to the core of the onion.

Source: Based on Altman and Taylor (1987)

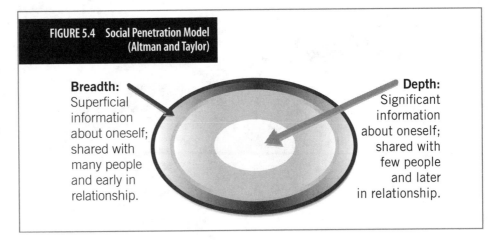

FIGURE 5.4 Social Penetration Model (Altman and Taylor)

Breadth: Superficial information about oneself; shared with many people and early in relationship.

Depth: Significant information about oneself; shared with few people and later in relationship.

the depth dimension, which is more private and significant, will likely be exchanged later in a relationship.

Disclosure and Relational Development   When Altman and Taylor (1987) introduced their model, they hypothesized that self-disclosure and relational development followed a linear path. According to this view of the theory, relationships grow as communicators become more willing to self-disclose information. Relationships may also go through a process of depenetration, as partners stop sharing information. This view of relational development and self-disclosure was also incorporated into models by communication theorists, especially in DeVito's (1986) stages of relational development (see Figure 5.5) and Knapp's (1984) relational stages model (which is also sometimes referred to as the "staircase" model of relational development). Both of these models conceptualize relational growth in terms of the process of sharing information as relationships develop and withholding information as relationships decline.

 5.6

 5.8

Disclosure as a Dialectical Process   In more recent work on the model, Brown, Werner, and Altman (1996) have explained **self-disclosure as a dialectical process.** From this perspective relationships don't always follow a straight line from distance to closeness but rather go back and forth between the two. Periods of social penetration may be followed by periods of depenetration. We may move forward in a relationship, becoming closer, but then pull back before becoming closer again. This dialectical view reflects a kind of inner struggle that also arises in the tension between our desire to reveal information about ourselves and our tendency to want to conceal. It also recognizes that alongside the values of disclosing information, there are good reasons in some situations and relationships for not revealing information.

In the next section of this module, we will examine this concept of dialectical tensions further. Before we go ahead, however, we will consider one more aspect about self-disclosure: how it is interpreted from a relational point of view.

self-disclosure as a dialectical process   Sharing of information alternates between direct sharing and pulling back from disclosure.

 5.10

Interpreting Self-Disclosure as a Significant Relational Event   When self-disclosure is considered from a relational perspective, the actual sharing of information may not be as important as how the process of sharing information is perceived by the listener. Relate this distinction to the contrast made in Module One in comparing the transmission view of communication with the relational view of communication.

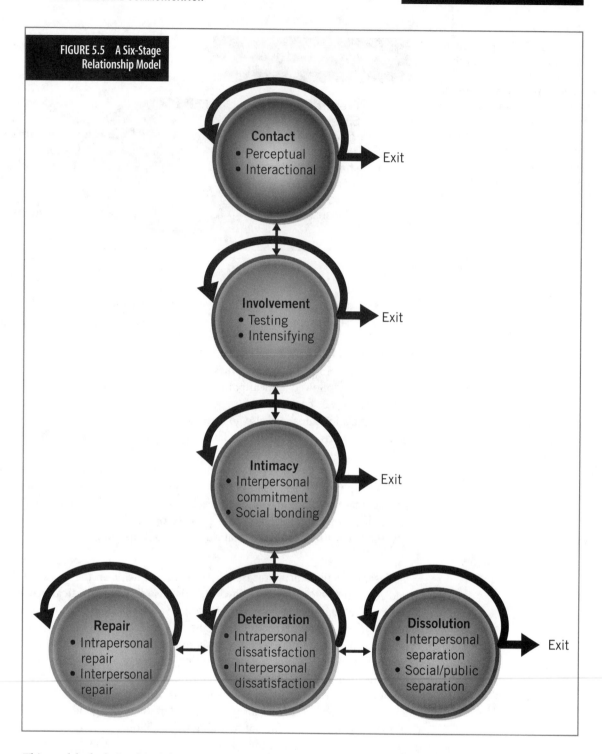

FIGURE 5.5   A Six-Stage Relationship Model

This model of relationships is best viewed as a tool for talking about relationships rather than a specific map that indicates how you move from one relationship position to another.

Source: Used with permission from Joseph A. DeVito, *Human Communication: The Basic Course,* 9th Edition. Allyn & Bacon, 2003.

The **transmission view of communication** examines how information is exchanged between communicators. With reference to self-disclosure, this is a matter of recognizing what kind of content has been communicated. Suppose, for instance, that in the course of their relationship, Laverne decided to share with Vivien stories about a sexual experience that Laverne had had prior to meeting Vivien. From the perspective of the transmission view of communication, Vivien would know more about Laverne's past. This information would further contribute to the kind of psychological knowledge that Vivien possesses about Laverne. Vivien would thus be able to make better predictions about Laverne and how Laverne feels about things.

If we looked at the same self-disclosure using the **relational view of communication,** we would examine how Vivien interprets the significance of Laverne's decision to share information about the earlier sexual experience. In that regard, Vivien might perceive that Laverne thinks their relationship is very important or that Laverne really trusts Vivien to be willing to make such a significant disclosure.

Perhaps you have had a similar experience, in which it wasn't just the content of what your friend or loved one disclosed that brought you closer, but the implicit message about the relationship that was communicated through the act of disclosure. You may have thought, "Wow, we are so close that we can communicate really meaningfully with one another!" It's also possible that you may have wondered why he or she had previously concealed that information. "Hasn't this person trusted me or felt comfortable enough in our relationship?" you may think to yourself.

RAPID REVIEW

5.4

Reflecting from his perspective as a gay man, John observes that he faces a quandary in deciding when and with whom to disclose that he is gay. Moreover, it's clear that sharing information about one's sexual orientation and relational status is a matter of breadth for most heterosexuals but an issue of disclosing depth for him:

> Most straight people that I know don't hesitate to announce to the world if they are married or dating someone. Many of the other teachers at my school have photos of their husbands and kids on their desks that anyone can see. For them, sexual orientation is one of the "outer layers of the onion" for self-disclosure.
>
> I don't think it is the same for a lot of gay people. I have to gauge carefully whether to tell someone that I am gay or whether to talk about my partner. That is a matter of disclosing from my depth when you consider the kinds of risks that are involved and the vastly different comfort levels of potential listeners.
>
> Sharing what most people consider to be basic facts of life becomes a struggle. I have to weigh the costs against the benefits. There is the fear of being rejected or retaliated against professionally if I am open. On the other hand, if I am not totally honest or open, there is the personal cost of not being authentic or of appearing two-dimensional to friends or co-workers who never hear the day-to-day details of my life or hear them only in guarded or sanitized versions.

transmission view of communication A theory of communication for describing, explaining, and evaluating how information is conveyed or exchanged between communicators.

relational view of communication A theory of communication that focuses on how relational communities are created and how they provide a context for members of a community to share meaning with one another.

Implications for Communication: Seek and Share Information in Order to Foster Relational Growth

Weigh Costs and Rewards and Take Risks to Get to Know Others   Telling our stories, seeking information about others by using the strategies of uncertainty reduction, and self-disclosing breadth and depth of information about ourselves all involve making choices. We must decide whom to entrust with our stories. And that means we have to take risks to get to know people better so that our relationships can grow.

5.3

An initial step in developing a relationship is lowering your anxiety about talking with someone you don't know well. Berger and Calabrese's (1975) research suggests that reducing uncertainty paves the way for reducing apprehension. As we gain information about another person by using the passive strategy of observing or the direct strategy of asking others about him or her, we lessen some of our apprehension. And then, when we interact directly with the person, we learn even more. Effective communicators may even hone their skills at the kind of small talk that is effective in learning information about others. In this regard, having a "stock story" is a helpful strategy.

5.11

As a relationship grows beyond an initial stage, we can also broaden the range of information that we share with one another. Further growth will occur when we make appropriate self-disclosures and share depth of information about one another. But along with the rewards of relational growth, self-disclosure involves risks, as well. Thus, it is important to think through what makes self-disclosure effective. Consider questions like these:

5.6

- Does the potential cost of a self-disclosure outweigh the potential benefit?
- Do both parties feel comfortable with the depth of information that is being shared?
- Have we arrived at a point of trust and intimacy that fits the level of disclosure?
- Is this the right time or place to share a personal disclosure?
- Does the sharing of information communicate relational messages?

Beyond the sharing of information, relationships continue to grow and thrive as we create patterns of communication that provide relational maintenance.

Relational Maintenance

The basic concerns of *relational maintenance* are to identify healthy and constructive patterns of interpersonal growth and to avert problems in a relationship. Relational well-being is also facilitated by creating a favorable interpersonal communication climate.

Relational Stability and Well-Being

As illustrated in Figure 5.6, Stafford and Canary (1991) identify five strategies of relational maintenance that serve as predictors of relational satisfaction, commitment, mutual control, and liking:

- Showing positiveness
- Demonstrating openness
- Providing reassurance
- Integrating into social networks
- Sharing tasks and responsibilities

showing positiveness A strategy of relational maintenance that involves developing a positive attitude, optimism, and willingness to work constructively on resolution of relational growth or conflicts.

According to Stafford and Canary, **showing positiveness** involves expressing the favorable attitudes that communicators have of one another. We communicate a positive attitude in everyday interaction by being polite and showing courtesy. We also express positiveness in dealing with conflicts, especially by taking a cooperative and optimistic approach to dealing with our problems as they arise. This involves being able to recognize and acknowledge problems and being willing to work on constructive and positive responses to problems.

Stafford and Canary identify five strategies of relational maintenance that serve as predictors of relational satisfaction, commitment, mutual control, and liking.

Source: Based on Stafford and Canary (1991)

FIGURE 5.6 *Five Strategies of Relational Maintenance (Stafford and Canary)*

Strategies
- Showing positiveness
- Demonstrating openness
- Providing reassurances
- Integrating into social networking
- Sharing tasks and responsibilities

Demonstrating openness, Stafford and Canary explain, relates to the depth of self-disclosure. Openness is also communicated by sharing feelings about the relationship. Parties who are open are not reluctant to share with one another how meaningful the relationship is or to declare their affection for one another.

People in open relationships are able to express their wants and needs freely. They also feel free to communicate their willingness to satisfy one another's wants and needs. Statements of wants and needs in open relationships are made as simple descriptions or requests. Open relationships also provide the latitude of acceptance that allows one partner to freely choose to decline or respond favorably to the other's wants and needs.

Providing reassurance involves the demonstration of commitment and loyalty to the relationship. Stafford and Canary (1991) observe that we communicate reassurance by verbalizing our continued commitment as well as by following through to do the things that demonstrate it. We do this by investing time, energy, and self in the relationship. Reassurance is also coupled with the strategies of positiveness and openness. For instance, you may have friends who tell you that you are a meaningful person in their lives. Lovers may develop ways of showing one another how much they cherish each other. In these relationships and in our family communications, we may symbolize our pledges of closeness, loyalty, and commitment verbally and nonverbally. Even something as simple as remembering a birthday or doing a special favor may constitute a reassurance in the relationship.

Integrating into social networks happens when members of a primary relationship, who have an exclusive relationship with one another, are connected to a larger social circle. Members of a couple can draw on this larger circle for affirmation, support, and recognition of their relationship. These larger social networks may also legitimatize a primary relationship by recognizing and affirming it.

Sometimes, the members of an exclusive relationship are not supported or integrated into their social network. This is a recurring theme in literature, as portrayed in the conflict between a romantic couple and its social network. Examples include Shakespeare's play *Romeo and Juliet,* in which the young lovers are committed to one another in defiance of their extended families, and the movie *Save the Last Dance,* in which Sara and Derek face resistance from their friends and disapproval from Derek's sister Chenile, who cannot accept them as an interracial couple.

Tension can also arise within an exclusive relationship when the partners find themselves at odds with one another about their social network. This happens, especially, when couples face the competing demands of maintaining the exclusiveness of a primary relationship and satisfying the requirements for interacting with a larger social network. The conflict that comes from this type of competition is well illustrated in the

demonstrating openness A strategy of relational maintenance that emphasizes self-disclosure and sharing needs and wants in a relationship as well as feelings about the relationship.

providing reassurances A strategy of relational maintenance that involves expressing commitment and loyalty to the relationship and making investments of time, energy, and oneself in the relationship.

integrating into social networks A strategy of relational maintenance that is experienced when members of a relationship draw upon a larger relational community for support, affirmation, and recognition.

award-winning television comedy *Everybody Loves Raymond.* In it, Deborah, who is married to Raymond, often finds herself in conflict with Marie, her mother-in-law. This means that Raymond is often caught in the middle, looking for ways to appease both his wife and his mother. We will explore this type of tension later in the discussion of relational dialectics.

Sharing tasks and responsibilities, the final strategy offered by Stafford and Canary, includes the handling of day-to-day household tasks for relational partners who live together. Matters as mundane as shopping for groceries and picking up around the house can be issues of relational maintenance. The sharing of responsibilities also relates to the concept of interdependence in a relationship, as partners count on one another to carry an equal burden. Sharing tasks and responsibilities leads to a sense of mutuality in a relationship.

5.12

Taken together, these five strategies of showing positiveness, demonstrating openness, providing reassurance, integrating into social networks, and sharing tasks and responsibilities constitute a pattern of ongoing, everyday interaction that contributes to the stability and well-being of a relationship. When one or more of these strategies are missing in a substantial and consistent manner from a relationship, it will likely show real signs of distress.

Destabilized Relationships in Distress

Four Horsemen of the Apocalypse   Gottman (1994) uses the very descriptive metaphor of the "four horsemen of the Apocalypse" to examine the four signs of a **destabilized relationship.** When these four signs are experienced as a recurring pattern of interaction and dominate the communication between relational members, they signify that a relationship is in deep distress—even on the point of ending. As shown in Figure 5.7, these are the four signs of a destabilized relationship:

- *Criticizing and complaining* about the other
- *Showing hostility and contempt,* which may be expressed overtly in verbal interchanges or through nonverbal responses
- *Responding defensively* to the negative patterns of communication
- *"Stonewalling,"* or the avoidance of problems and resistance to working to solve them, sometimes even refusing to speak about relational difficulties and their underlying sources

sharing tasks and responsibilities
A strategy of relational maintenance that fosters interdependence and equality in a relationship by cooperative management of day-to-day tasks and responsibilities.

destabilized relationships Distressed relationships that are characterized by patterns of criticism and complaining, hostility and contempt, defensiveness and the avoidance of relational problems, which is termed *stonewalling.*

Like the strategies recommended by Stafford and Canary (1991) for ensuring the stability and well-being of a relationship, the destabilizing signs that Gottman has identified occur in a consistent and enduring manner.

Patterns of Negative Communication   Gottman's further studies on marital communication highlight how patterns of negative communication serve as predictors of divorce. In a study that followed married couples over the course of 14 years, Gottman and Levenson (2002) identified two patterns of negative communication that emerged as the principal predictors of divorce. The first is a pattern of *negative volatility,* which they also describe as the pattern of *attack and defend.* The second pattern is a more subdued style of *emotional inexpressiveness,* in which couples avoid dealing directly with one another or with relating their feelings. In discussing the use of therapy to help repair problematic marriages, Gottman and Levenson recommend that couples replace a "climate of criticism" with a "climate of appreciation."

5.9

Gottman uses the very descriptive metaphor of the "four horsemen of the Apocalypse" to examine the four signs of a destabilized relationship. When these four signs are experienced as a recurring pattern of interaction and dominate the communication between relational members, they signify that a relationship is in deep distress—even on the point of ending.

Source: Based on Gottman (1994)

FIGURE 5.7   Four Horsemen of the Apocalypse

Signs of a Destabilized Relationship

- Criticizing and complaining about the other
- Showing hostility and contempt, which may be expressed overtly in verbal interchanges or through nonverbal responses
- Responding defensively to the negative patterns of communication
- "Stonewalling," or the avoidance of problems and resistance to working to solve them, sometimes even refusing to speak about relational difficulties and their underlying sources

Defensive and Supportive Communication Climates

5.7

Gibb's (1999) model of **defensive communication,** which was initially developed to analyze the dynamics of small-group interaction, can also be applied to examine the stability and well-being of interpersonal relationships. Gibb observes that people feel defensive when they perceive that they are under attack. In circumstances similar to what Gottman refers to as negative criticism and contemptuous attitudes that produce defensive reactions, a person who is defensive devotes a significant amount of personal energy to self-protection. When defensive responses arise in interpersonal communications, it is the relationship itself that becomes defensive. Defensive behavior from one party in a relationship evokes defensive behavior on the part of the other. Moreover, this dynamic cycle of defensiveness can intensify.

Gibb elaborates six patterns of behavior in a relationship that evoke defensive reactions and contribute to the cycle of defensiveness:

- *Evaluation:* When we perceive that someone is judging us
- *Control:* When we perceive that someone is attempting to change us or impose on us a solution for a problem
- *Strategy:* When we perceive that someone is trying to manipulate us or to conceal or disguise his or her true motives
- *Neutrality:* When we perceive that someone is indifferent to our feelings and unconcerned about our welfare
- *Superiority:* When we perceive that someone assumes that he or she has a higher status or worth than we do or acts in a unilateral manner that shuts out feedback
- *Certainty:* When we perceive that someone holds an unyielding and dogmatic position that is not open to dialogue

defensive communication climate Patterns of communication that undermine the stability and well-being of an interpersonal relationship when interactions involve evaluation, control, strategy, neutrality, superiority, and certainty.

Describe Instead of Evaluate   Instead of communicating with patterns of behavior that arouse defensiveness, like those just listed, Gibb suggests using a corresponding set of

Gibb's model of defensive communication identifies six patterns of behavior in a relationship that evoke defensive reactions and contribute to the cycle of defensiveness. Instead of communicating with these patterns of behavior, Gibb suggests using a corresponding set of supportive communication behaviors.

Source: Based on Gibb (1999)

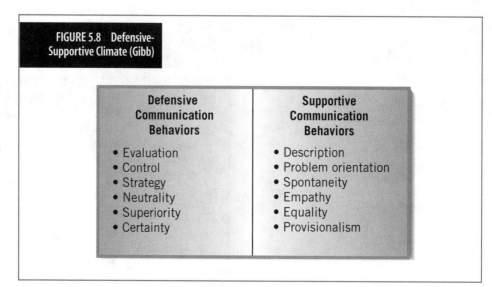

FIGURE 5.8 Defensive-Supportive Climate (Gibb)

Defensive Communication Behaviors	Supportive Communication Behaviors
• Evaluation	• Description
• Control	• Problem orientation
• Strategy	• Spontaneity
• Neutrality	• Empathy
• Superiority	• Equality
• Certainty	• Provisionalism

supportive communication

Patterns of communication that enhance the stability and well-being of an interpersonal relationship when interactions involve description rather than evaluation, a problem-orientation instead of control, being spontaneous rather than being strategic, empathy rather than neutrality, equality instead of superiority, and provisionalism rather than certainty.

supportive communication behaviors (see Figure 5.8). For instance, rather than *evaluate* another person, we might be more effective if we *describe* a concern. Suppose, as an illustration, that Vivien and Laverne live together. Suppose further that Vivien is irritated by one of Laverne's personal habits—say, leaving dirty dishes in the sink. In place of calling Laverne a slob, an evaluative behavior, Vivien could describe how or why the unwashed dirty dishes create a problem. But it would be Vivien's problem, not Laverne's.

Use Problem Orientation Instead of Control   Vivien has a tendency to bark orders such as: "Put your dirty dishes in the dishwasher as soon as you finish eating!" This is an example of a control behavior that does not give Laverne very much of a voice in deciding what to do. Instead of *control*, Vivien might use what Gibb calls a *problem orientation*. Vivien might seek input from Laverne by asking "What do you think is a good way to take care of the dishes?" This opens up a range of choices and shares decision making. By using a problem orientation, control is shared and each has a voice.

Be Spontaneous Instead of Strategic   Spontaneous responses to problems disclose true feelings and motives. Being spontaneous also means refraining from trying to manipulate others. Suppose that the real reason behind Vivien's concern for neatness is insecurity, which is based in the fear that other friends or family members will see the dirty dishes and think that it is Vivien rather than Laverne who is the slob. But, rather than acknowledging those true fears Vivien would prefer to manipulate Laverne into feeling shame. Consider how the interaction would be much less defensive if Vivien decided to make an honest disclosure by saying: "I get uptight about dirty dishes in the sink. I am afraid that someone else is going to see the mess and think I made it. What if my mother suddenly showed up at the door? She would think I was a slob."

In being spontaneous and making this admission, Vivien has taken a big risk. Laverne should also respond by being supportive. Sometimes, the best way to be supportive is simply to say "I understand." For this response to be effective, however, it needs to be genuine.

There are many situations like this one in which the best course of action is to explore the real source of our own or another's fears. Laverne could simply say "Tell me more about this" and then indicate a willingness to lend a supportive ear. By being a supportive listener, Laverne could help Vivien respond less defensively.

Respond with Empathy Instead of Neutrality

Gibb (1999) suggests that when we respond to others with *empathy,* we signal that we acknowledge and accept their feelings. When we respond with *neutrality,* on the other hand, we signal that we dismiss or are indifferent to their feelings. By showing empathy, we demonstrate a sense of concern for them and for our relationship with them. If Vivien were to follow the suggestions discussed thus far for using supportive communication behaviors—that is, to describe the problem and explore all of the feelings associated with it—Laverne might be inclined to empathize with those feelings.

When we respond to situations with supportive communication behaviors, such as demonstrating empathy, we can create a cycle of supportiveness, rather than defensiveness. Supportive behavior from one party in a relationship can evoke the same behavior on the part of the other.

Regard One Another with Equality Instead of Superiority

A supportive communication climate is also engendered when we resist the tendency to claim or assert *superiority.* Instead of taking the upper hand in the relationship, we should strive for *equality.* Gibb (1999) draws the connection between treating another person as an equal by expressing mutual trust and demonstrating genuine openness to his or her views. Being willing to listen to another person's ideas is a part of the supportive behavior of being problem oriented.

Returning again to the hypothetical example, Vivien should resist the temptation to claim that the tidier person is the superior person. Defensive responses are interactive. Gibb observes that when we feel we are being evaluated, we will sometimes lash out in response. So, Laverne should also refrain from judging Vivien as being overly concerned with or even ridiculous about the matter of neatness.

Be Provisional Instead of Certain

The final type of supportive behavior identified by Gibb (1999) involves speaking *provisionally* instead of with absolute *certainty.* Provisional speech demonstrates open-mindedness and flexibility, a willingness to entertain ideas other than your own. Along that line, being provisional demonstrates a respect for other people's opinions and thus for them, as well.

Again, we can apply this idea of communicating provisionally to the relationship between Laverne and Vivien. When Vivien is falling prey to the tendency toward certainty, for instance, Laverne hears phrases such as: "You must clean up those dirty dishes, right now!" The words "must" and "now" and the issue of a command to Laverne are examples of certainty. But how would the dynamic of their relationship change if Vivien qualified the statement by phrasing it this way? "When you get a chance, I would like it if you cleaned up the dishes."

At other times, beyond the example given here between Laverne and Vivien, we may trap ourselves into certainty when we resist hearing arguments or facts that would cause us to reassess a position we hold. This is a hallmark of a dogmatic thinking that goes with the attitude of certainty. To respond by being provisional rather than with certainty would call us to be open to examining our own views and assumptions.

When the practice of provisionally stating your views is joined with the other supportive behaviors—that is, describing issues and concerns, using a problem orientation to explore alternatives, stating feelings and disclosing motives in a genuine and spontaneous manner, conveying empathy, and expressing a sense of equality—you will create a supportive climate of communication.

Implications for Communication: Recognize and Change Patterns of Communication for Effective Relational Maintenance

Become Aware of Patterns of Communication That Contribute to Stability and Well-Being
Maintaining the stability and well-being of a relationship requires that you practice a kind of mindfulness. With that, you gain an awareness of how you communicate with a partner and what impact each of your behavior has on the overall climate of communication. Sometimes, having that mindfulness is a matter of stepping back from the relationship to see the patterns and how they recur. But keep in mind that *patterns* of communication are not actions performed unilaterally by one of the people in a relationship. Patterns of communication are created and performed in tandem by both partners in a relationship. Over time, the patterns are repeated with great frequency.

Gottman and Levenson (2000) claim that they can best see patterns of communication by making videotapes of married couples having arguments. By counting the frequency of negative communication, they can predict with better than 90 percent accuracy if couples will fail in their marriages. Their study has found that the most crucial predictor is the frequency of negative communication strategies relative to positive communication strategies. When the ratio of negative to positive communication falls to 4 to 1 (with the dominant pattern being instances of negative communication such as criticism, contempt, defensive responses, or efforts at stonewalling to positive and few instances of supportive communication behavior), a relationship is in deep trouble.

Pearson (1991) identifies another attribute of successful romantic relationships, which she calls *positive distortion*. Pearson's studies of successful relationships found that a critical factor explaining the endurance of some relationships is the way that partners looked for the positive qualities of the other. Somewhat like the adage of seeing a glass half full rather than half empty, we can focus more of our attention on our partner's positive qualities rather than overemphasizing the negative. That sometimes requires that we let go of negative feelings in place of harboring them; and in some circumstances we might actually practice a kind of benign blindness that allows us to overlook negative qualities.

VIDEO VIEW

5.8

ASSESSING YOUR SKILLS

5.4

Change Patterns of Communication to Affirm and Support One Another   Ideally, people in a relationship strive to create a positive climate, one that is supportive and open. Effective interpersonal communicators also maintain the stability of their relationships by providing reassurance to their partners that they are involved and committed to their relationships. By sharing tasks and responsibilities, partners know that they can count on one another and build a sense of interdependence and equality. Support for the relationship comes both from within the relationship and from the social networks outside the relationship. Secure and stable relationships are not without tension, however. To explore this idea, we turn next to the theory of relational dialectics and examine how successful communicators are able to manage dialectical tensions.

RAPID REVIEW

5.5

Managing Dialectical Tensions

LEARNING OBJECTIVE

5.5

dialectical approach to communication A model of communication that examines how opposing goods or values create a dynamic tension.

The **dialectical approach to communication** examines the tension between two desirable goals or values. When two contradictory "goods" are in dialectical tension with one another, you may want both of them. For instance, you may feel a contradiction between liking the companionship that comes from being with other people but still need some time to be by yourself. Or you may enjoy the comfort of being in a predictable and stable relationship, in which the rules are crystal clear, yet want to

Studies by Baxter identify three major types of contradictions in interpersonal relationships. Dialectical tensions are likely to occur over these issues.

Source: Based on Baxter (1994)

FIGURE 5.9 Relational Dialectics (Baxter)

Major Contradictions in Interpersonal Relationships

Integration and Separation

Stability and Change

Expression and Privacy

"break out of the box" from time to time and do something zany and unpredictable. Finally, you might feel the value of sharing information while simultaneously recognizing that a particular disclosure is better left unsaid. In each of these kinds of situations, you feel tension between conflicting "goods."

Studies by Baxter (1994) identify three major types of contradictions in interpersonal relationships (see Figure 5.9). Dialectical tensions are likely to occur over these issues:

- Integration and separation
- Stability and change
- Expression and privacy

Internal Tensions within a Relationship

Baxter (1994) observes that **internal dialectical tensions** are experienced directly by people within a relationship, such as a dyad or a few people who have an exclusive relationship. Opposing wants and needs create internal contradictions in relational members (see Figure 5.10). However, Baxter describes these tensions as being inherent to

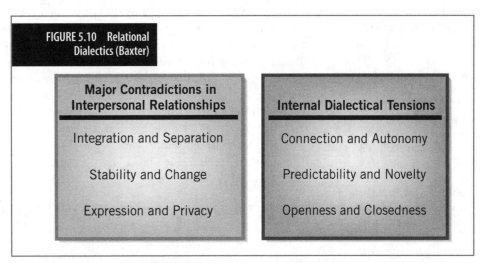

FIGURE 5.10 Relational Dialectics (Baxter)

Major Contradictions in Interpersonal Relationships	**Internal Dialectical Tensions**
Integration and Separation	Connection and Autonomy
Stability and Change	Predictability and Novelty
Expression and Privacy	Openness and Closedness

internal dialectical tensions
Dialectical oppositions felt directly by the primary partners in a relationship. Internal dialectics include the oppositions of autonomy and connection, novelty and predictability, and openness and closedness.

Baxter observes that internal dialectical tensions are experienced directly by people within a relationship, such as a dyad or a few people who have an exclusive relationship. Opposing wants and needs create internal contradictions in relational members. However, these tensions are inherent to relationships and necessary for intimacy.

Source: Based on Baxter (1994)

relationships and necessary for intimacy. This last thought bears repeating: Internal dialectical tensions can actually bring the people in a relationship together when they are managed well.

Within a relationship, the tension of *integration and separation* is experienced as need for **connection** when we recognize the value of togetherness and closeness along with the need for **autonomy**, which manifests itself in independence. Maintaining both of these opposites contributes to the well-being of the relationship.

The dialectic of *stability and change* is experienced within a relationship by having **predictability** in order to achieve a sense of stability, which enables us to predict how the other will act and shape expectations about how we are supposed to act while at the same time having **novelty** as part of the value of change so that a relationship does not get stuck in a rut.

The dialectic of *expression and privacy* is experienced with the value of **openness** when partners disclose information while at the same time, they appreciate the importance of **closedness** and recognize that sometimes it is better to choose not to disclose.

A humorous illustration of these internal dialectical tensions can be seen in the recent film *My Big Fat Greek Wedding* in terms of how the main character, Toula Portokalos (played by Nia Vardalos), relates to her extremely ethnic, large, and close-knit family. That family, headed by Toula's father, Gus (with decidedly subtle input from her mother, Marie), holds firmly onto their Greek identity and celebrates everything in the Greek manner. Toula's decisions to break away from that identity and experience life outside the Greek community—including most importantly, a romantic relationship with a man who is not Greek—create a variety of dialectical tensions for her.

Internal Dialectic of Integration and Separation: Connection and Autonomy   Some of us may be able to relate to tensions such as those experienced by Toula. In the film, she works for her family in their restaurant yet desires to go to college and have her own career. For her, it is not simply a question of wanting to have either a close connection with her family *or* being independent of them. Rather, she recognizes that *both* are desirable. Thus, dialectical tensions are not questions of *either/or* but of *both/and*. To manage the tension, we look for ways to satisfy both needs or desires.

Internal Dialectic of Stability and Change: Predictability and Novelty   Baxter (1994) observes that the dialectic of stability and change is often about how we experience a sense of continuity as well as moments of discontinuity. Predictable relationships provide continuity and a sense of security that comes from following a routine. As *My Big Fat Greek Wedding* opens, Toula is being driven to the family restaurant at the crack of dawn by her father, Gus (who is played by Michael Constantine). This daily opening of the restaurant is so tightly scripted that Toula and Gus can almost do it in their sleep. Toula's life seems to be predictable, too. She is expected to marry a man from a Greek family and continue the family identity. But she eventually realizes that she wants a different life. Along with an education and career, Toula wants to marry Ian Miller (played by John Corbett), who is not Greek. This part of the story illustrates the third dialectic of openness and closedness.

5.13   **Internal Dialectic of Expression and Privacy: Openness and Closedness**   The dialectical tension surrounding being open and being closed goes beyond simply deciding whether to self-disclose information or how much to share about your self. Self-disclosure is a dialogue that encompasses being open *to* another (by acknowledging and accepting what another person discloses) as well as being open *with* another (by sharing self-disclosures about your self). When we are open to someone else, we indicate our willingness to listen to them and to their feelings, and demonstrate responsiveness, understanding, and empathy. In *My Big Fat Greek Wedding*, Toula decides initially not to be open with her family about the fact that she

---

connection and autonomy An internal dialectic of a relationship where the contradictory values of togetherness and closeness are in tension with the values of independence.

predictability and novelty An internal dialectic of a relationship in which the values of regular routine and the ability to anticipate the behavior of another are in tension with the values of being spontaneous and appreciating new experiences.

openness and closedness An internal dialectic in a relationship in which the values of sharing information through self-disclosure is in tension with the value of withholding information.

FIGURE 5.11 Relational Dialectics (Baxter)		
Major Contradictions in Interpersonal Relationships	**Internal Dialectical Tensions**	**External Dialectical Tensions**
Integration and Separation	Connection and Autonomy	Inclusion and Seclusion
Stability and Change	Predictability and Novelty	Conventionality and Uniqueness
Expression and Privacy	Openness and Closedness	Revelation and Concealment

Despite the many tensions that can exist within a relationship, at times, the tension lies outside the relationship—namely, with the way that members of a primary relationship relate to the larger relational community, or their social networks. Baxter refers to these as external dialectical tensions. Just as with internal dialectical tensions, external tensions represent ongoing opposition between desirable "goods" from each pole of the contradiction.

Source: Based on Baxter (1994)

is dating a person who is not Greek. Perhaps, she senses that her parents are not likely to be open to her disclosures.

Baxter and Montgomery (1996) suggest that when we enter into a dialogue of being open with and to one another, we create the opportunity to construct new relational selves. This process of creating new selves is like going on a journey of shared discovery and redefinition of one another as well as of ourselves. As Baxter and Montgomery state the matter: "Relationships become 'close' and 'personal' to us because they celebrate the ongoing creation of ourselves with those who have been most crucial in inviting our potential" (p. 151). And so when Toula's parents do eventually learn of her involvement with Ian and even become open to the idea that she will marry him, it creates the opportunity for all to grow and acquire new selves.

External Dialectical Tensions in Relationships with Social Networks

Despite the many tensions that can exist within a relationship, at times, the tension lies outside the relationship—namely, with the way that members of a primary relationship relate to the larger relational community, or their social networks. Baxter (1994) refers to these as **external dialectical tensions** (see Figure 5.11).

Think of the types of tensions that you experience. For instance, you and one of your friends might experience conflict in relating to a larger circle of friends. The members of your family might experience tension in observing how you relate to your larger community, such as your neighborhood. With your partner in a romantic relationship, you might find yourselves in opposition to your respective extended families. And in the workplace, the specific team that you work with might experience conflict with the larger organizational structure of your company.

Just as with internal dialectical tensions, external tensions represent ongoing opposition between desirable "goods" from each pole of the contradiction. It is wonderful to relate to these larger social networks; we turn to them for support and growth. Yet relating to the members of our broader social networks can pose problems, as well.

external dialectical tensions
Dialectical oppositions felt directly by the primary partners in a relationship as they relate to a larger social network. External dialectics include the oppositions between inclusion and seclusion, conventionality and uniqueness, and revelation and concealment.

External Dialectic of Integration and Separation: Inclusion and Seclusion   External dialectics manifest themselves as tensions between members of a particular relationship and how they relate to their larger relational communities. If we were to extend this analysis to the film *My Big Fat Greek Wedding,* we would examine how Toula and her boyfriend, Ian, form a primary relationship. External dialectical tensions arise when they decide to relate as a couple, rather than as individuals, to their respective families of origin.

The external dialectic of integration and separation is experienced as desire for **inclusion** in a larger relational community while at the same time having a sense of separation. Baxter's term for the separation from social networks is **seclusion.** Toula and Ian thus desire inclusion into their respective families of origin while at the same time they recognize the need for a measure of seclusion. If you are in a committed relationship, you may be able to relate to Toula and Ian. Like them, you may want to be embraced by your extended families, but have time away from them as well. If you have seen the film *My Big Fat Greek Family*, you will recall that Toula's family is a very large extended family. The numerous Portakalos family gatherings include not only Toula's immediate family of parents, a brother and a sister, but nieces and nephews, first cousins, aunts and uncles. Toula and Ian want to be included in the family, yet at the same time they need their own time away from it.

The dialectic of integration and separation—whether manifested as the internal expression of autonomy and connection or as the external expression of inclusion and seclusion—might be thought of metaphorically as building a bridge while also creating a boundary. We build bridges to provide ourselves with connection and inclusion, yet we need boundaries to ensure that we have autonomy and seclusion.

External Dialectic of Stability and Change: Conventionality and Uniqueness   Baxter (1994) observes that individuals in a relationship may behave in a conventional manner in order to be accepted by their larger relational communities. By acceding to norms and conventions that reproduce the behavior of the larger community, couples achieve recognition and legitimacy for their relationship. Yet at the same time, having too much **conventionality** undermines the sense of **uniqueness** that a relationship needs for the sake of its own integrity. Baxter describes the need for being conventional and unique at the same time:

> In complying with such conventions [of their larger relational communities], a pair constructs a public identity for their relationship that is familiar and easily legitimated by others. On the other hand, however, a highly conventionalized relationship denies the parties a sense of their pair uniqueness, a quality which is essential for intimacy. (p. 240)

Like the characters of Toula and Ian in the film *My Big Fat Greek Wedding*, you may follow the norms of your extended family or community, abiding by the rules and playing the roles they set forth. However, you also probably realize the need to guard against losing uniqueness and getting stuck in a rut of conformity.

External Dialectic of Expression and Privacy: Revelation and Concealment   Another concern for members of a primary relationship is the dialectic of **revelation and concealment,** or deciding what kinds of information to share about their relationship to the people in their larger social networks. How members of an exclusive relationship decide this question will also affect the public identity they construct. This is a parallel to how individuals use candor and discretion to choose what to share with relational partners.

As noted earlier in examining Stafford and Canary's (1991) model of relational maintenance, openness is a vital element for the health and well-being of a relationship. The

inclusion and seclusion   An external dialectic between the values of being integrated into a larger social network and maintaining separateness.

conventionality and uniqueness   An external dialectic in which tension arises around being accepted and conforming to the conventions of a larger social network and having a sense of unique identity.

revelation and concealment   An external dialectic in which tension arises over the value of sharing of information that is otherwise held in confidence within a relationship with parties outside the relationship or of not sharing the information.

5.14

theory of relational dialectics also recognizes the value of being open yet points out that certain types of information need to be withheld—either in the communications between the parties in an exclusive relationship or in their interactions with those outside the relationship who comprise their social networks.

Baxter (1994) observes that intimate relationships are often bound by a norm of confidentiality to keep certain kinds of information private and within the relationship. The expectation of privacy and confidentiality can be seen rather clearly in romantic relationships. At the same time, partners may have several motivations for revealing information to their larger circle of friends and perhaps their extended families. Baxter comments on several motivations in favor of revelation. The first motive is to gain emotional or even material support from others. In addition, a couple may choose to share for cathartic reasons and to celebrate the relationship with those in their social networks. The third reason stems from the perception that disclosing information about the relationship is expected and required.

5.5

Implications for Communication: Use Strategies for Managing Dialectical Tensions

Recognize the Value of Both Sides of a Dialectical Contradiction   Experiencing dialectical tensions is not harmful to a relationship. In fact, it can be a valuable experience, provided we don't get stuck in the kind of *either/or* thinking that implies that we must always emphasize one pole of the dialectic over the other. Moreover, as long as we talk about the tensions and maintain flexibility in relating to others, dialectical tensions can be managed.

Strive for Dynamic Equilibrium   Baxter (1994) points out that when we experience the pulls of opposing tensions, we may comfortably manage them by alternating back and forth between them. Much like alternating the weight on either side of a teeter-totter, we move back and forth from one pole to the other. This is the concept of **dynamic equilibrium,** which Baxter defines as the "ongoing motion between two dialectical poles" (p. 296). When we are able to move back and forth between poles in this manner, our relationships do not get stuck in one position.

Thus, in a healthy relationship, there are times to be together, emphasizing the value of connection, as well as times to pull away and be apart, stressing autonomy and independence. We may act in very predictable ways for a while, fulfilling one another's expectations and conforming to the conventions of our larger social networks, but then break out of our regular patterns by doing something spontaneous and unique. Likewise, we may alternate between times of deep self-disclosure and periods of retreat and withdrawal.

Recognize the Turning Points in a Relationship   While we often make slow, gradual shifts in our relationships between the opposing poles of dialectical contradictions, we sometimes also create patterns of interaction in which particular poles are dominant. For instance, a close and exclusive relationship may

5.8

be characterized by high levels of connection, predictability, and openness. A move away from these qualities to autonomy, novelty, and closedness will likely be a temporary one and soon followed by a cycling back to the usual, dominant pole.

However, members of a relationship sometimes make sudden and dramatic shifts. These are *turning points* in a relationship. At some turning points, the movement is so significant that we change our interpretation of the relationship, redefining what it is and what place it has in our lives. When this occurs, the shift to the other side marks the

dynamic equilibrium   The ongoing motion between poles of a relational dialectic.

change to a new dominant pole. Thus, a turning point may signal a shift toward partners' growth and greater closeness in the relationship or a shift away from one another and toward greater distance, sometimes indicating problems in the relationship.

Acknowledge When Dialectical Tensions Become Matters of Serious Conflict Most of the time, dialectical tensions can be managed fairly easily. We regularly make small adjustments as part of the give-and-take of relating. At other times, or turning points, dramatic shifts occur and may be welcomed as signals of growth. At still other times, however, the tensions may also indicate serious conflicts, especially when relational partners become polarized, each stuck at one end of the dialectic. When this happens, tension turns to antagonistic conflict.

In explaining the concept of *antagonistic conflict,* Baxter (1994) uses the metaphor of geological fault lines. Think of the issues that underlie a personal conflict as being similar to the geographic plates underneath a continent, which continually move and rub up against one another. Sometimes, the tension reaches an extreme and erupts as an earthquake. It is then that the opposing values of the dialectic become a matter of antagonistic conflict and require relational repair, rather than simple management.

5.6

Managing Conflict

5.6

Conflict is inevitable and unavoidable in any mature and meaningful relationship. In fact, it is probably even beneficial for sustaining meaningful communication and deepening bonds in personal relationships. The key to success in this regard is having the skills to manage conflict constructively, and to take the steps needed to repair relational problems.

Defining Conflict

UIDEO VIEW

5.9

Wilmot and Hocker (2001) define **interpersonal conflict** as "expressed struggle between at least two interdependent parties who perceive incompatible goals, scarce resources, and interference from others in achieving their goals" (p. 41). To illustrate this definition, let's return to Laverne and Vivien, this time engaged in an interpersonal conflict over budgeting. How to spend money triggers their conflict, for each has rather different and apparently incompatible priorities for how and where their money should be spent. This is a fairly common issue for people who are financially interdependent.

As revealed in the dialogue that follows, Laverne and Vivien see their shared pool of money as a scarce resource. In particular, their goals and intentions about spending money collide when Laverne wants to buy a new computer and Vivien wants to save money for a vacation:

> **Laverne:** I have had it with this computer! It's way too slow! We have to buy a new one that's faster. This thing is a piece of junk!
>
> **Vivien:** No way! We don't have the money for that.
>
> **Laverne:** That's nonsense! We've got a bundle of money in our savings account.
>
> **Vivien:** We can't spend a huge amount of money from our savings on something stupid like a new computer for you. We need to keep saving that money for our vacation next year. Remember, we are planning to go to Australia in December, and that's going to set us back a lot.

THINK ABOUT THIS

5.9

interpersonal conflict Expressed struggle between at least two interdependent parties who perceive incompatible goals, scarce resources, and interference from others in achieving their goals.

Laverne: Look, computers are really cheap right now. We could easily put the cost of a new computer on our credit card and then pay it off in a few months. That way, we'd still have enough money to pay for the trip.

Vivien: No way! We finally got our credit card balance paid off. From now on, we are going to pay in full every month rather than carry a balance.

Laverne: You get so agitated and uptight over paying interest charges! It's just a few dollars a month!

Vivien: Who's agitated? *You* are the one who gets uptight if it takes a few minutes to download a stupid piece of music! And if I am concerned about money, it's because *you* always overspend every month.

Laverne: Forget it! I will go borrow the money from my dad.

Vivien: But then we will owe money to your dad! He's not just going to give us the money without expecting us to pay it back. When are you going to get it into that thick head of yours that you always have to pay for things eventually!

Laverne: Stop lecturing me! I know I can repay a loan to my dad, and then we won't have to rack up any interest charges. *That's* what you keep worrying about!

Vivien: What I keep worrying about is that you are not responsible when it comes to money!

Laverne: Forget it! I'm sorry I even brought it up! Get out of here! I am listening to my music.

Conflict is seldom simple. Along with what is at stake as the content issue, or what the conflict is about, there are additional layers involving each party's **perception** of the conflict and of each other. Ironically, the content issue is what gets a lot of attention when we argue, but the perceptual issues are there, nonetheless. Wilmot and Hocker (2001) observe that the basis for understanding any conflict situation is to recognize the importance of those perceptions. When we are in a struggle with someone, we may perceive that each of us has different goals or that the scarce resources for which we are competing are limited so much so that one person's gain will be the other's loss. In this sense, if Laverne prevails and buys the new computer, Vivien will perceive the situation as losing the argument.   And if Vivien prevails, Laverne will see it as a loss to be stuck with the old computer. Vivien and Laverne see each other as standing in the way of what they want.

Conflict and the "Blame Game" Moreover, as Wilmot and Hocker explain, we also sometimes perceive that our opponent in the conflict is willfully trying to prevent us from attaining our goal. Our perceptions during a conflict then come down to seeing the other person as being to blame. And so we play the **"blame game."** Blaming is very much at the heart of Laverne and Vivien's "battle of the budget." Along with the content issue about how to spend money (whether to go into debt, draw from savings, etc.), Vivien and Laverne have hostile perceptions and feelings toward one another as each blames the other as being at fault for the conflict. So, Vivien thinks that Laverne is incapable of managing money, and Laverne perceives Vivien as being uptight.

Stone, Patton, and Heen (1999) have done research about conflict as part of the Harvard Negotiations Project and observe in their book *Difficult Conversations* what happens when we see another person as being at fault for a conflict. Namely, our emotional responses intensify and we typically lash out, accusing the other of being selfish, irrational, naïve, and controlling. That seems to be exactly what Vivien and Laverne have done. Vivien likely thinks that Laverne is selfish for wanting a bigger and faster computer, and Laverne probably regards Vivien's apprehension about debt as an irrational worry. Vivien, in turn, may think that Laverne is naïve about managing money, and each seems to be trying to control the other.

Playing the "blame game" makes us blind to the other things going on in a conflict situation. We see *our* side of the conflict with great clarity, often asserting that our view

perception Subjective process of constructing meaning. Individuals receive information through the process of sensation and selective attention and then assign meaning by organizing and interpreting the experiences they perceive.

blame game A dimension in an interpersonal conflict that goes beyond the content issue to accuse the other for being at fault or in the wrong in the conflict. Common strategies for the blame game include labeling the other as selfish, irrational, naïve, or controlling.

makes complete sense, but we fail to see the perspective of the other person and how it may also make sense. According to Stone, Patton, and Heen (1999), "We don't see ourselves as the problem because, in fact, we aren't. What's often hard to see is that what the other person is saying also makes sense" (p. 28). Our biggest blind spot, moreover, may be that we can't see how we are also responsible for the conflict situation. Instead, we fall into the trap of arguing over who is right and who is wrong.

In order to get beyond the deadlock over who is right, individuals in a conflict need to listen to one another's perspectives. That may entail recognizing the ways in which *both* individuals are right. Moreover, to be able to truly understand another person's perspective, we need to adopt an attitude that Stone, Patton, and Heen call the **"And Stance."** When we listen to one another's perspectives with this attitude in mind, we are willing to acknowledge the validity of both perspectives. As the authors explain:

> The And Stance gives you a place from which to assert the full strength of your views and feelings without having to diminish the views and feelings of someone else. Likewise, you don't need to give up anything to hear how someone else feels or sees things differently. Because you both have different information or different interpretations, both stories can make sense at the same time. . . . Sometimes people have honest disagreements, but even so, the most useful question is not "Who's right?" but "now that we understand each other, what's a good way to manage this problem?" (p. 40)

Understanding a conflict fully also requires an understanding of our motivations and how they affect the way we respond to conflict situations.

Conflict and Motive

5.10

Paul and Paul (1994)—a married couple who collaborated in developing a model for analyzing conflict in their book *Do I Have to Give Up Me to Be Loved By You?*—identify two common motivations that influence how we respond to conflict:

- The *path of protection* is motivated by the need to defend ourselves.
- The *path of evolution* is motivated by the intent to explore the conflict so that we can understand our selves and the other person.

  Let's consider each individually.

The Path of Self-Protection   Conflict situations worsen when we follow the path of **self-protection,** which happens when we become defensive and close ourselves off from our partner. Paul and Paul identify three different strategies that we may use to protect ourselves in a conflict situation:

- We protect ourselves with an *indifferent stance* by withdrawing or passively resisting our partner. We express indifference by tuning the other out or by making ourselves busy.

5.11

- We protect ourselves with the *controlling stance* by trying to change the other. Making the partner feel wrong in the conflict often does this. Tactics such as shame and guilt may also be used to force the partner's compliance.
- We protect ourselves with the *compliant stance* when we give in out of fear of rejection and disapproval. This may also be a fear of conflict that, itself, motivates us to avoid conflict by giving in.

The Path of Evolution   As much as we may feel the need to protect ourselves, there is a better alternative, according to Paul and Paul (1994). That is the more vulnerable path of

And Stance   A response to a conflict situation that avoids blaming the other for a conflict or perceiving the conflict from one's own point of view, alone.

self-protection   A response in a conflict that is motivated by the need to defend oneself. It may include adopting a stance of indifference, control, or compliance.

evolution through exploration, which is taken when we try to understand the conflict. Paul and Paul describe this path as the intent to learn. In doing so, we must set aside our defenses and take the risks involved in learning about ourselves and our partner. Doing so further entails the need to explore our own feelings and understand the feelings of our partner. Taking this path is difficult because it requires that we confront fear, pain, sadness, frustration, and possibly even elements of shame and guilt. Nonetheless, the reward is considerable, as the path leads to compassion toward ourselves and our partner.

Paul and Paul observe that when we seek to understand ourselves and each other, we assume responsibility for our feelings, our behaviors, and for the consequences of our behaviors on the relationship. Ideally, this happens as a process of mutual discovery, in which partners are willing to experience together the transitory pain of facing themselves and accepting the idea that each has good reasons for taking his or her stance in the conflict.

In our hypothetical situation between Vivien and Laverne, the path of exploration might lead Laverne to grant that Vivien has a good reason for not wanting to dip into their savings to buy a faster computer. And perhaps Vivien's explorations would uncover deeper reasons for feeling insecure about money and insisting on managing it so tightly. So, too, the discussion might bring about the deeper mutual realization that Laverne's reason for wanting to buy a new computer is not nearly as much about speed and efficiency as it is about wanting to have some autonomy in spending money and disliking being lectured to about how to manage the finances, among other things.

Confronting Conflict Instead of Avoiding It   Paul and Paul (1994), as well as the members of the Harvard Negotiation Project, offer insights about how important it is to get to the heart of a conflict situation and communicate in a cooperative manner. Too often, however, we respond to conflict by trying to avoid it or by using aggressive behaviors that serve to divert attention or to shut down communication. Yet Paul and Paul observe that when we take the self-protective route of becoming indifferent or trying to tune out the conflict, or when we give in too easily and become compliant in the face of opposition, the conflict doesn't go away. In fact, it may even get worse. Taking the more aggressive response of controlling the conflict situation can also make matters worse. At that point, conflict becomes truly destructive.

Destructive Conflict: Aggression and Passive Aggression

Johnson and Johnson (2003) observe that destructive conflict leads to deep personal loss, sadness, and grief, perhaps even heightened anxiety or depression. Regrettably, such conflict can also culminate in violence that is inflicted psychologically or physically.

Destructively waged conflict can be overt and expressed with stinging verbal accusations, recriminations, shouting, and "in your face" power plays. On the other hand, it can be quite subtle and expressed through more insidious means such as the "silent treatment," which may take the form of sarcasm, demeaning facial responses, attitudes of seeming indifference, complete avoidance of communication, or failing to acknowledge feelings and issues of conflict. Be assured, these more subdued forms of conflict can be just as destructive as the more overt ones—if not more so!

A particularly destructive form of conflict is characterized by what psychologists label **passive-aggressive behavior,** which is essentially acting one way while feeling another. In an interpersonal relationship, for instance, a partner may demonstrate passive-aggressive behavior by being sweet and cooperative yet also displaying veiled expressions of negativity and resistance. Your passive-aggressive friend will promise to meet you at a certain time but then show up late.

5.12

evolution through exploration
A response to conflict that involves understanding it. This entails examining oneself, the conflict, and the other.

passive-aggressive behavior
A response to conflict that communicates a double message that appears to be positive and cooperative, along with veiled expressions of negativity and aggression.

ASSESSING YOUR SKILLS

5.6

Your passive-aggressive lover will agree to help you with a task but sulk while doing it. A family member who is passive-aggressive will put on a polite and pleasant face while seething with anger inside.

In each of these cases, when you ask the individual about his or her seeming indifference to you and the issue at hand, he or she will protest so loudly that you will start to question yourself for ever doubting his or her commitment in the first place.

Implications for Communication: Waging Conflict Constructively

ONLINE JOURNAL

5.15

Given the consequences of handling conflict badly, why wouldn't anyone want to deal with it constructively? For many of us, the problem lies in the difficulty of *facing* conflict. By learning strategies for dealing with conflict, we can help remedy this problem. Consider these five strategies for confronting and managing a conflict successfully:

- Understand your emotions as you confront the conflict.
- Understand the conflict situation as well as yourself and the other person.
- Find common ground.
- Brainstorm possible solutions.
- Choose a solution that both of you like and then follow it.

Understand Your Emotions as You Confront the Conflict   The first step in confronting a conflict constructively is to understand your feelings. Sometimes, it's important to ask not only "What am I feeling?" but "Why am I feeling this way?" It may also be important to look realistically at the level of emotional energy that you are feeling and decide whether the present is the right time to communicate with your partner about the conflict. Sometimes, it is more constructive to step back and cool off before discussing a conflict.

By stepping back to cool off, you are not avoiding the conflict situation. Rather, you are trying to manage your emotional responses so that they don't get in the way of effective communication. You are also wise to step back to discern if your emotional response to the situation is on the same level of seriousness and intensity as the gravity of the situation—not more and not less. You've probably had the experience of "flying off the handle" when your emotional response was too great. By contrast, sometimes you may need to step back from a conflict in order to explore your feelings more deeply. Getting in touch with the full range of your feelings is especially important if you are the sort of person who tends to underplay or suppress your feelings. Exploring and understanding deep-level emotions may sometimes constitute the largest step toward effectively resolving a conflict.

Understand the Conflict Situation as Well as Yourself and the Other Person   The next step is to explore the conflict situation. Since conflict is a matter of perception, the partners in a conflict should examine what is at stake and talk openly about the issues. In doing so, they must recognize that each of them may have a different perception of what is at stake, and those perceptions may be at odds. In taking a page from Gibb's (1999) model of supportive communication, you need to describe what is at stake for you and avoid the tendency to want to evaluate or play the "blame game." This is when it is also important to listen deeply and adopt the attitude of the "And Stance," which allows you to see that you and your partner may both be right.

Don't rush to a solution. It is very important to take a lot of time in the exploration, and it takes patience and perseverance to stay with it. Again, you may need to back away and take a time-out from the discussion to do some personal self-examination and confirm what you are feeling. It also takes time to understand on a deep level how the other person really feels. When you take a time-out from the discussion, it may also be beneficial to you and the other person to state explicitly that you want some time to ponder the matter. Without such a declaration, your silence might be interpreted as withdrawal, or worse, as the passive-aggressive behavior of using the "silent treatment." That is not what a time-out is about. It is a matter of stepping back so that you can gain perspective on your feelings, fully intent on engaging the other person at a later time.

Find Common Ground   The third step in resolving a conflict is to discover areas of common ground. You might ask questions like these:

- What do we both want?
- What are the positive benefits for both of us that can be achieved through resolving the conflict?
- What are the values that we share?
- How can we each contribute to resolving the conflict?

As you and your partner answer these questions, you will be working toward a mutual outcome. Again, draw on Gibb's model of supportive communication and recognize that each party in the conflict is entitled to an equal say.

Brainstorm Possible Solutions   *Brainstorming* is a way of thinking creatively, in which you and your partner try to come up with a number of possible solutions to the conflict. You will be more creative in your brainstorming if you adopt a couple of simple rules:

- Emphasize quantity. The more solutions, the better.
- Don't judge or dismiss any solution out of hand, and don't toss out any ideas out until all of them have been explored. Sometimes, a seemingly odd or impractical idea will actually work.
- Build on one another's ideas as you go.

Choose a Solution That You Both Like and Then Follow It   Once you've brainstormed possible solutions for addressing the conflict, the next step is to choose the one that is best for both of you and then follow it. This is sometimes referred to as a *win/win approach* to conflict resolution because the solution that is ultimately chosen may enable each party in the conflict to achieve his or her goals. Many times, creative brainstorming will hit on a solution that gets parties beyond the kind of *either/or* thinking that assumes their goals are completely incompatible.

Carrying out the solution means that you have to commit to put this theory into practice. Moreover, you must be fully committed to the agreed upon solution. This may be a good time to take stock of your feelings once again. Ask yourself: Am I comfortable with this outcome? Does it feel equitable and fair?

When you are able to manage conflict constructively, your relationships become healthier and more whole. And from that new ground, you may be able to look back at a conflict situation and be grateful for the opportunity that it provided for the growth and deepening of the relationship.

5.16   5.7

Ending Relationships

In 1878, when the curtain closed on the initial performance of Henrik Ibsen's play *A Doll's House,* an outraged audience roared its disapproval, rather than applauding the show. The play, about a troubled marriage, ended with the slamming of a door. Nora, the main character in the story, had decided to leave her husband, Torvald.

LEARNING OBJECTIVE
5.7

For the audience, the abrupt end to the marriage between Nora and Torvald was unsettling, but that was what Ibsen intended. He had crafted the play to force the audience to confront the troubling thought that some relationships should end. Nora had come to the realization that her marriage to Torvald was fundamentally unhealthy. And even after Torvald conceded to make drastic changes in his behavior, Nora saw that the relationship was irrevocably broken. She saw that Torvald's good intentions simply would not address the core issues. Rather, it was time for her to leave.

Relational Dissolution

5.17

Relationships Fail Like Nora, many of us have faced the quandary of having to decide whether to remain in a relationship or move beyond it. These are not normally decisions that are made on a whim or out of capricious motives. We may have made significant efforts to deal with the relational problems and to repair them. Yet the sad fact remains that some relationships are not meant to be.

When *A Doll's House* is performed well (as it was in the film version starring Claire Bloom and Anthony Hopkins), it becomes clear to the audience that the source of the relational problems did not lie individually with Torvald or with Nora, but with the way that they related to one another. Similarly, Duck (1987) contends that rather than looking for individual failures to account for the end of a relationship, we should examine the relationship itself. We should ask, "'What is it about a particular *relationship* that ends up being problematic?' rather than, 'what is it about the partners, isolated from that relationship, that account for their difficulties?'" (p. 284).

Phases of Relational Dissolution Duck (1982) traces the progression of relational dissolution through a series of phases:

- A *breakdown phase* occurs when one or both of the partners recognize that there is a serious problem in the relationship.
- An *intrapsychic phase* follows. This is an internalization of the problems as a brooding over the difficulties. Individuals may also complain to members of their social network.
- A *dyadic phase* involves confronting the partner. Sometimes the dyadic phase results in repair and meaningful resolution of the problem.
- If efforts to repair the problem fail, parties turn to their social network in the *social phase*. At this phase, the decision to end the relationship has usually been made by one or both parties and thus the social phase is aimed at seeking the support of the social network.
- A "*grave-dressing*" *phase* is aimed at bringing closure. At this point, the parties do things to get over the relationship and formulate a public account that explains the reasons for the ending.

5.7

Implications for Communication: Ending a Relationship Constructively

Even though it is painful and regrettable, the ending to a relationship can be accomplished in a way that enables each party to grow and to maintain per-

5.11

sonal dignity. To do so requires that we communicate constructively during the phases of dissolution.

Try Hard before Conceding to Dissolution Just as it is usually unwise to force a quick solution to a conflict, it is usually unwise to end a relationship without taking the time to deal with all of its issues. People in the throes of ending a relationship should give themselves time to sort things out and explore all of their options. In some circumstances, it will be valuable to bring in a third party, such as a counselor or a therapist, to facilitate a deep discussion of the feelings and issues. The intent here is to get help from someone who is impartial. This is different from what occurs during Duck's social phase, when the motivation for turning to friends or family is to gain support, often with the expectation or even the demand that people take sides in the conflict.

Take Mutual Responsibility for the Outcomes of Dissolution When individuals are not able to resolve relational issues, even after taking the time to deal with them constructively, it is time to own up to the fact that an ending is inevitable. But responsibilities don't end there, especially when others are affected by the dissolution.

There can be severe consequences for others when a primary relationship ends. In the case of friends or lovers, other friends and family members who make up the couple's social networks may be torn by their breakup, too. When a married couple or unmarried committed partners end a relationship, there may be significant economic and legal issues to resolve. Children clearly suffer the consequences of divorce, emotionally as well materially. Divorcing parents have the responsibility to mitigate those consequences for their children.

In the case of a divorce, the children deserve the ongoing presence of and support from both of their parents. The costs of divorce can be lessened when divorcing parents commit to working with one another to ensure the following:

- Children should receive the financial support that they need.
- Children should be allowed meaningful and ongoing opportunities to communicate with both of their parents. For this to be achieved, divorcing parents need to refrain from undermining their child's affections or positive images of one another.
- Children should not be used in efforts by divorcing parents to punish each other.
- Children should be given opportunities to explore their feelings about divorce and loss in a supportive environment. Exploration can also help children understand that they are not at fault when their parents divorce.

Learn and Grow from Relational Dissolution Any relationship can end in a moment of hope—namely, that we will learn more about ourselves and about relationships. The play *A Doll's House* ends on such a note when Nora observes that she and Torvald both have much to learn about themselves.

5.12

Duck (1987) refers to the "postmortem" that can occur in the "grave-dressing" phase of relational dissolution. This is the time for reflecting on the communication patterns that led to the end. And while we may feel confident about ending the relationship and declare resolutely that we never want to see

5.8

that person again, we will go on to relate to other people. From this respect, doing the postmortem and trying to understand how and why a relationship failed can yield insights that we can bring to other relationships and hopefully avoid falling into the same negative patterns all over again.

Summary

We enter into a wide range of types of interpersonal communication situations and contexts. The contextual definition of interpersonal communication allows us to see how some of our relationships are more personal than others. In addition, we communicate interpersonally in contexts that may call for formal or informal styles of interacting. Some of our relationships are exclusive and characterized by interdependence, intimacy, and commitment. Other of our relationships comprise broader relational communities that are inclusive of social networks.

We can also see that each interpersonal relationship is unique and defined in light of our own personal constructs. We define what it means to be part of a friendship, to be committed to a romantic relationship, or to participate in a family relationship. Our constructs influence how we perceive the meanings of different types of relationships and establish expectations of how to communicate within them.

Each relationship has its own story, as does each individual who participates in the relationship. Each story reflects the growth and well-being of a relationship. The sharing of information between interpersonal communicators facilitates growth. We use uncertainty reduction strategies to gain information about others in order to reduce our level of apprehension. And as a relationship grows, we take the risk to self-disclose deeper levels of information about ourselves.

A mature relationship also requires ongoing maintenance in order to ensure its stability and to create a supportive climate of communication that is conducive to further growth and well-being. In this regard, communicators are particularly effective when they can recognize the patterns of communication that contribute to stability and supportiveness.

Communicators can also sustain the well-being of their relationships by managing the tensions that arise from various relational dialectics. This includes managing internal tensions as they occur within an exclusive relationship, and dealing with external tensions, which arise when members of a primary relationship interact with broader social networks.

Since conflict is a normal and natural part of any relationship, success in interpersonal relationships depends on being able to manage conflict constructively. This entails recognizing how a conflict is a matter of perception and being willing to communicate with a relational partner in understanding a conflict. In doing so, successful communicators confront conflict, explore the personal dimensions of the conflict, and work collaboratively to arrive at a mutual understanding and solution.

Successful communicators also manage the endings of relationships, finding ways for each person to grow and maintain integrity in the face of relational dissolution. Responsible interpersonal communicators take time to fully explore the decision to end a relationship and then act responsibly to achieve the outcomes of the dissolution.

PRACTICE
TEST

References

Altman, I., & Taylor, D. (1987). Communication in interpersonal relationships: Social penetration theory. In M. E. Roloff and G. R. Miller (eds.), *Interpersonal processes: New directions in communication research* (pp. 257–277). Newbury Park, CA: Sage.

Baxter, L. A. (1994). A dialogic approach to relationship maintenance. In D. Canary and L. Stafford (eds.), *Communication and relational maintenance* (pp. 233–254). London: Academic Press.

Baxter L. A., & Montgomery, B. M. (1996). *Relating: Dialogues & dialectics.* New York: Guilford Press.

Berger, C. R., & Calabrese, R. I. (1975). Some explorations in initial interaction and beyond: Toward a developmental theory of interpersonal communication. *Human Communication Research,* 1, 99–112.

Brown, B. B., Werner, C. M., & Altman, I. (1996). Choicepoints for dialecticians: A dialectical/transactional perspective on close relationships. In L. Baxter & B. Montgomery (eds.), *Dialectical approaches to studying personal relationships* (pp. 137–154). Hillsdale, NJ: Erlbaum.

Connard, C., & Novick, R. (1996). *The ecology of the family: A background paper for a family-centered approach to education and social service delivery.* Northwest Regional Educational Laboratory: <www.nwrel.org/cfc/publications/ecology2.html>. Accessed April 29, 2003.

Caughlin, J. P. (2003). Family communication standards: What counts as excellent family communication and how are such standards associated with family satisfaction? *Human Communication Research,* 29, 5–40.

DeVito, J. A. (1986). *The communication handbook.* New York: Harper and Row.

Duck, S. W. (1982). Dissolving personal relationships. In S. W. Duck (ed.), *Personal relationships,* vol. 4. London: Academic Press.

Duck, S. W. (1987). How to lose friends without influencing people. In M. E. Roloff and G. R. Miller (Eds.), *Interpersonal processes: New directions in communication research* (pp. 277–298). Newbury Park, CA: Sage.

Fehr, B. (1993). How do I love thee? Let me consult my prototype. In S. W. Duck (ed.), *Understanding relationship processes, 1: Individuals in relationships* (pp. 87–122). Newbury Park, CA: Sage.

Fields, J., and Casper, L. M. (2001). America's family and living arrangements: March 2000. *Current Population Reports,* P20-537. Washington, DC: U.S. Census Bureau.

Gibb, J. (1999). Defensive communication. In J. Stewart (ed.), *Bridges not walls.* 7th ed. (pp. 442–448). Boston: McGraw-Hill.

Good Morning, America. (2002). "A Wedding in Times Square," television program broadcast April 26, 2002. Available online: <more.abcnews.go.com/sections/GMA/GoodMorning America/GMA020416Sandy_and_junius_wedding_couple.html>. Accessed May 1, 2003.

Gottman, J. M. (1994). *Why marriages succeed or fail.* New York: Simon and Schuster.

Gottman, J. M., & Levenson, R. W. (2002). A two-factor model for predicting when a couple will divorce: Exploratory analysis using 14-year data. *Family Processes* 41, no. 1, 83–96.

Homans, G. C. (1958). Human behavior as exchange. *American Journal of Sociology,* 61, 399–402.

Johnson, D. W., & Johnson, F. P. (2003). *Joining together.* Boston: Allyn & Bacon.

Kelly, G. A. (1955). *The psychology of personal constructs.* New York: W. W. Norton.

Knapp, M. (1984). *Interpersonal communication and human relationships.* Boston: Allyn & Bacon.

Miller, G. R., & Sunnafrank, M. J. (1982). *All is for one but one is not for all: A conceptual perspective of interpersonal communication.* In F. E. X. Dance (ed.), *Human communication theory* (pp. 220–242). New York: Harper and Row.

National Opinion Research Center (1998). *General social survey: Friendship.* Available online: <www.icpsr.umich.edu/GSS/rnd1998/merged/indx-sub/friends.htm>. Accessed July 22, 2002.

Paul, J., & Paul, M. (1994). *Do I have to give up me to be loved by you?* Center City, MN: Hazelden Foundation.

Pearson, J. C. (1991). *Lasting love: What keeps couples together.* Dubuque, IA: Brown & Benchmark Publishers.

Pew Research Center. (2003). *Pew Internet and American life research reports.* Available online: <www.pewinternet.org/reports/index.asp>. Accessed January 26, 2003.

Planalp, S. (1985). Relational schemata: A test of alternative forms of relational knowledge as guides to communication. *Human Communication Research*, 12, 3–29.

Searle, J. R. (1969). *Speech-acts: An essay in the philosophy of language.* London: Cambridge University Press.

Smith, D. M., & Gates, G. J. (2001). *Gay and lesbian families in the United States: Same-sex unmarried partner households.* Available online: <www.hrc.org/familynet/chapter.asp?article=341>. Accessed May 1, 2003.

Stafford, L., & Canary, D. J. (1991). Maintenance strategies and romantic relationships type, gender, and relational characteristics. *Journal of Social and Personal Relationships*, 8, 217–242.

Sternberg, R. J. (1986). A triangular theory of love. *Psychological Bulletin*, 102, 331–345.

Sternberg, R. J. (2000). What's your love story? *Psychology Today*, 33, July 1, 2000, pp. 52–60.

Stone, E. (2003). Family ground rules. In K. M. Galvin and P. J. Cooper (eds.), *Making connections: Readings in relational communication.* 3rd ed. (pp. 70–79). Los Angeles: Roxbury Press.

Stone, D., Patton, B., and Heen, S. (1999). *Difficult conversations: How to discuss what matters most.* New York: Penguin Books.

Watzlawick, P., Beavin, J. H., and Jackson, D. D. (1967). *Pragmatics of human communication: A study of interactional patterns, pathologies, and paradoxes.* New York: W. W. Norton.

Wilmot, W. W., & Hocker, J. L. (2001). *Interpersonal conflict.* 6th ed. New York: McGraw-Hill.

Professional Communication

Learning Objectives

After reading the module and participating in the activities, you will be able to:

1 Understand types of interviews and how to prepare for them as an interviewer and an interviewee.

2 Understand the structure of a small group and its place within a larger organizational system.

3 Understand how groups strive for equilibrium by resolving tensions between conflicting values.

4 Understand the models of leadership.

5 Understand how a problem-solving group develops an agenda and functions in a private or public setting.

www.ablongman.com/doyle

VIDEO VIEW

YOUR WELL-DEVELOPED interpersonal communication skills, along with your subject-area expertise, helped you land your first professional position. And once you were on the job, you learned that in addition to working by yourself and collaborating with a co-worker, you would be part of a work team. Your team holds regular staff meetings to discuss changes in company policies and to troubleshoot problems as they arise. Along with this long-term, intact team, you have been assigned to work on a wide range of task forces that deal with particular issues and problems that come up from time to time. Your organization has also entered the global marketplace, and you've found it especially challenging (albeit rewarding) to participate in virtual teams that communicate by way of the Internet and bring together professional colleagues from around the globe.

As you have risen in the ranks of the company, you've taken on your share of group leadership roles. When called upon, you have been ready to oversee complicated projects and help coordinate a wide range of work groups. To do so has required a lot of coordination of roles and integration of viewpoints from many people.

Indeed, the work that you and your various groups have done has been so successful that you've needed to hire new staff as the company has grown. Another sign of the great work you've done is that you have been called upon to attend professional seminars and to make presentations about your company and its products.

On the whole, you have found your job very satisfying. It is gratifying that most of what you do throughout the day involves interpersonal communication, and you are an expert interpersonal communicator.

The contemporary workplace demands such communicators. O'Neill (1997) has concluded from reviewing a number of studies about workforce development that communication competencies—such as effective interpersonal relating, collaborating in groups, listening, and being able to speak and write effectively—are required for success in a vast majority of job situations and thus critical to professional success.

In a similar vein, a study sponsored by the U.S. Department of Labor (1992) came to this conclusion: "Tomorrow's worker will have to listen and speak well enough to explain schedules and procedures, communicate with customers, work in teams, understand customer concerns, . . . probe for hidden meanings, teach others, and solve problems" (p. 16).

This module focuses on communicating in the workplace. The primary aim is to explore how we can use interpersonal communication skills to participate effectively in various types of interviews and other contemporary work situations, such as small-group interactions, leadership roles, problem-solving discussions, and group presentations. We will begin by examining interviewing.

ASSESSING YOUR SKILLS

6.1

Interviewing

LEARNING OBJECTIVE

6.1

An **interview** is a specialized type of interpersonal communication that is organized around a specific goal, such as getting information for a newspaper story or applying for a job. An interview usually involves just two people, although in some situations, several people may participate as a group.

We can also define an *interview* in terms of two other qualities: It is organized according to a specific structure, involving a series of questions and answers, and it is usually conducted in a more formal manner than is the case with most interpersonal interactions.

Types of Interviews

Again, an interview has a predefined goal that is usually clear to each of the participants. While there are many different types of interviews, we will highlight four main types:

- Information sharing
- Persuading
- Helping and counseling
- Employment-related, such as job seeking, appraisal, and exit interviews

As you will see from the discussions that follow, however, an interview can sometimes have more than one goal.

Information-Sharing Interviews   You might do an **information-sharing interview** if you need to learn about a topic that you are going to speak or write about. Public speakers include in their speeches what they've learned from interviews with experts, and writers gather information for essays and stories by interviewing subjects and witnesses. A consumer may ask questions of a salesperson to learn more about a product or service, and a job seeker may do informational interviewing to learn about a prospective career.

6.1

We are probably most familiar with the information-sharing interviews that we see on television or hear on the radio. Think about the early morning network programs that bring in authors to talk about their newly published books and medical experts to go over the findings of the latest research studies. Television and radio programs also feature interviews with public officials and political analysts, who discuss current events. There is also a genre of television programs offered during prime time hours that feature interviews, such as *20/20* or *48 Hours.* Popular late-night entertainment programs, including *The Tonight Show with Jay Leno* and *The Late Show with David Letterman,* are built around interviews with celebrities.

Sometimes, information-sharing interviews are conducted to disseminate information to a mass audience. For instance, in October of 2001, when the news was reported about the discovery of anthrax in government and media office buildings, Americans became concerned about the safety of the mail service. In response, authorities from the U.S. Postal Service and other government agencies appeared in televised interviews to discuss the effects of anthrax and ways to be protected against exposure. Some of these interviews also featured scientific experts who hoped to use their expertise to help quell people's fears.

Moreover, a secondary goal of some of these interviews about anthrax was to persuade people that they were safe and that the situation was under control. Interviews of authority figures, such as the Secretary of the Department of Health and Human Services, helped achieve this purpose.

Persuasive Interviews   A **persuasive interview** involves one party advocating a position or urging others to do something. For instance, the interchange between a salesperson and a customer involves persuasion. Also consider the example of news programs in which advocates for particular causes and

VIDEO VIEW

6.1

interview   A specialized type of interpersonal communication that is organized around a specific goal; usually involves two people but can include several people participating as a group.

information-sharing interview   An interview that has the goal of obtaining or presenting information; for instance, an interview with an expert or a witness.

persuasive interview   An interview in which one party is advocating a position or urging the other party to do something; for example, an interview on a news program.

6.2

political platforms are interviewed to explain and defend their views. Many such programs interview advocates on opposing sides of a controversy, pitting them against one another in a sometimes heated discussion. For instance, you will see brief interchanges of this type on morning news programs such as the *Today* show on NBC or *Good Morning America* on ABC. Somewhat deeper discussions of opposing sides can be heard in the evenings during the *News Hour with Jim Lehrer,* which is broadcast on PBS stations.

Sometimes, an interview that's intended to be persuasive falls short of making its point. Pop music star Michael Jackson was interviewed as part of a documentary about his life and asked about having undergone numerous plastic surgery procedures to alter his face. Jackson commented to the filmmaker that he had had plastic surgery only twice to correct problems with his nose. Jackson claimed that these surgeries were necessary to enable him to breathe easier and to help him hit particular high-pitched notes when he sang. Despite Jackson's claims, not everyone was persuaded. In fact, a plastic surgeon who was interviewed on the ABC program *Prime Time* discounted Jackson's claims.

6.3

Helping and Counseling Interviews   Health care professionals, therapists, social workers, teachers, and clergy may use **helping/counseling interviews,** which usually focus on problems and assist people in dealing with them. Barbara, who is a professional nurse practitioner, describes the kinds of interviewing she does as she visits patients in their homes:

> When I first see a patient, I do a rather thorough interview to get the sense of their overall health history. Then, with each later visit to my patients, I use a fairly informal style of interviewing. I need to check up on them to determine their current health status and simply see how they are coming. Sometimes, that also involves gathering information from family members or caregivers in the home. I also need to see how they are coming with their meds and other procedures we have prescribed. It is very important in some cases to make sure that the patient and the caregiver really understand how and when to provide the treatment that has been recommended. Sometimes, I need to reinforce for them the importance of following through on the treatment and motivate the patient and caregiver to do the appropriate follow through.

Helping interviews, as shown by these examples from Barbara's work, may involve aspects of informational and persuasive interviewing, too.

Helpers also differ in how direct or indirect they are in offering assistance and guidance. While the prescription of a medication or the counseling of a patient to change a behavior is very direct, a therapist may provide guidance in a less direct manner. Many therapists use a non-directive and suggestive style, asking questions that are geared toward helping the individual discover for himself or herself how to change behavior.

The film *Antwone Fisher,* which starred Denzel Washington as Dr. Jerome Davenport, depicts the development of a relationship between Davenport, a psychiatrist in the U.S. Navy, and one of his patients, a young sailor named Antwone Fisher, who is played by Derek Luke. In the movie, which is based on the life experiences of its author, Fisher faces expulsion from the navy because of incidents of violent behavior. As we watch the movie, we see how years of pent-up anger are brought to the surface and analyzed as Davenport counsels Fisher and attempts to get him to change his ways. For Fisher, who was raised in an abusive foster care home, the core issue of his counseling was his need to locate his family of origin and come to grips with reasons he was placed in foster care. One of the most dramatic scenes in the film is his experience of finding his family.

Employment Interviews   In the workplace there are a range of types of **employment interviews.** The type that's most common and perhaps most important to many people is the **job-seeking interview.**

helping/counseling interview An interview that focuses on problems and assists someone in dealing with them; for instance, an interview with a therapist, teacher, or clergy member.

employment interview An interview conducted in the workplace for a work-related purpose; for instance, a job-seeking interview, appraisal, or exit interview.

job-seeking interview An interview conducted for hiring purposes; also called a selection interview.

In a job interview, which is sometimes called a *selection interview,* each party is making a choice. For the employer, there is the choice of whom to hire, and for the prospective hiree, there is the choice of deciding whether to take the position if it's offered. Job-seeking interviews also involve information sharing on the parts of the interviewer and the interviewee and a fair amount of persuasion, as each person tries to sell the other on what a good match could be struck upon hiring.

We will devote more attention later in this section to how job interviews are conducted. But for now, we will look at several other types of interviews conducted in the work environment. Namely, some interviews are conducted to assess employees' performance at various stages of employment.

An **appraisal interview** is often done as part of the evaluation of a worker's job performance. It usually provides feedback to the employee about his or her performance and offers an opportunity to ask questions or explore concerns. An appraisal interview may contain elements of counseling or helping if the supervisor conducting the interview uses it as a way of offering guidance or coaching. And given that the interview might also include discussion and negotiation of a worker's salary, it may also be a persuasive interview. There are also times when an appraisal interview takes on the quality of being a *disciplinary* interview, especially if problems in a worker's performance need to be assessed. Such a disciplinary interview may also be a kind of fact-finding interview, and often an opportunity for the employee to present his or her perspective on the perceived problems.

An **exit interview** may be done to gain feedback when an employee is leaving the workplace. When employees leave a job, they may be able to provide useful information about reasons for quitting or offer suggestions about how the company or the product it creates can be improved. Exit interviews also allow managers and workers to provide closure to their work experience.

Exit interviews do serve a useful purpose, according to a recent study reported in *Personnel Today.* A survey conducted by the Chartered Institute of Personnel and Development (2002) found that 45 percent of the companies that conducted exit interviews used that information to change their personnel policies. According to the study, feedback from departing employees is used to revise pay and benefit options, change working conditions, and adjust working hours for continuing employees.

6.1

The Interview as a Type of Interpersonal Communication

An interview can be considered a form of interpersonal communication because it typically involves two people interacting with one another. And like other types of interpersonal interactions, an interview has several distinct features:

- It involves communicators who perform the roles of interviewer and interviewee.
- It has a formal structure and procedure.

Roles of Communicators   When we compare an interview to a conversation, there are some differences in how the parties relate; namely, in an interview, each participant has a more clearly designated role to perform than is usually the case in a conversation. As noted earlier, most interviews are conducted between two people and those people play specific roles: One person, the **interviewer,** asks most of the questions and assumes the greater portion of the responsibility for controlling the exchange. The second person is the **interviewee,** and his or her principal purpose is to respond to the questions. An interviewee may also ask a few questions, and in some situations, like a job-seeking interview, he or she may even plan to ask some questions at the end of the interview.

appraisal interview   An interview in which an employee's job performance is evaluated; provides feedback to the employee and offers an opportunity for him or her to ask questions or explore concerns.

exit interview   An interview conducted with an employee who is leaving his or her position; provides feedback about his or her work and brings closure to the work experience.

interviewer   The person who conducts the interview by organizing the structure, asking the questions, and generally controlling the exchange.

interviewee   The person whose primary purpose is to respond to the questions asked of him or her; generally follows the lead of the interviewer.

Even when an interview involves more than two people, as is the case in a *group-centered interview,* there is still a fairly clear delineation of the roles of interviewer and interviewee. You might, for instance, participate in a job-seeking interview conducted by a panel of interviewers. Also consider the case of a counseling interview, in which one therapist may deal with more than one client, such as a couple or a family.

Advertisers and marketing specialists conduct group interviews when they use the format of a **focus group.** The people in a focus group are brought together to offer their perceptions of a product or a concept—say, a new type of toothbrush. Participants are selected so that they represent a random sample of the larger audience to whom a product or advertising campaign is targeted. A moderator asks a sequence of questions about the product or concept and tries to stimulate discussion among the group members. The moderator is supposed to observe and monitor the group but not guide it toward any particular opinion.

Interviews presented on the radio and television also sometimes use a group format with multiple interviewers or multiple interviewees. Devotees of the popular television program *Survivor* often tuned in the next morning to the *CBS Early Show* to catch the debriefing of the previous night's show. The interviewee was the contestant who had been voted off the night before. The entire group of *Early Show* hosts conducted this weekly debriefing.

You are also likely to see a group interview format when news agencies report the views of a group of people. For instance, presidential debates are often followed by a group discussion, in which a news anchor asks a panel of voters who they think won the debate. The group interview is often structured to resemble a focus group.

Formal Structure and Procedure　　Some interview situations allow for informality, such as an information interview with someone you know well, perhaps a relative or neighbor. But most interviews are conducted in a formal setting and follow a highly structured procedure.

The formality level may be particularly pronounced for job-seeking interviews, especially in "white collar" professional work environments. In any event, interviewees may be expected to dress and act in ways that fit the level of formality of a particular profession. Most interviews presented on the radio and television news programs are also conducted in a fairly formal manner. Thus, it is common for the reporter or anchorperson conducting an interview to be formally dressed. And, the interviewee will often act and dress with a level of formality that is in keeping with the norms of whatever profession he or she represents.

Contrast the formality of an interview with that of an everyday conversation. A conversation has an easy flow and a seemingly unstructured quality in the sense that there is a give-and-take of ideas and comments. An interview, by contrast, is organized with a structure that typically includes these three parts or stages:

1. The *opening,* in which the goal of the interview is stated and the participants make initial contact and establish rapport.
2. The *business,* in which the basic questions are asked and answered.
3. The *closing,* in which the participants discuss what follow-up will be needed and then end the meeting.

An interview is also formal in the sense that the agenda of questions and topics is usually planned in advance. Since those questions and the answers provided to them make up the business part of the interview, we will now examine common types of questions asked in an interview.

focus group　A group of individuals brought together to offer their perceptions of a product or a concept; participants are selected so that they represent a random sample of the larger audience to whom a product or advertising campaign is targeted.

6.2

Types of Questions

Interviewers commonly ask these types of questions:

- Open and closed questions
- Fact and opinion-centered questions
- Direct and hypothetical questions
- Primary and follow-up questions

Any interview, irrespective of its goal, may include a combination of these types of questions. To illustrate how they differ, we will focus on how they are used in a job-seeking interview.

6.4

Open and Closed Questions   Whether a question is open or closed has to do with how much latitude the interviewer grants the interviewee in answering. **Open questions** afford the interviewee a wide range of options for responding. For instance, in a job interview a very open question would be:

> **Interviewer:**   What are some of your work experiences, and how do they qualify you for our position?

In a job-seeking interview, open questions can be beneficial to both parties. For instance, they give the prospective employee a lot of freedom in providing information about himself or herself. This gives the employer an opportunity for a greater breadth of information. Moreover, in some types of job situations, the employer can assess how well the job applicant can organize ideas and communicate a clear and direct answer.

Closed questions address narrow areas of concern and provide little or no latitude of response. They are meant to elicit specific information in a time-efficient manner. For instance, in hiring someone to work as a web designer, an interviewer might ask a closed question such as this:

> **Interviewer:**   Which web-authoring tools have you used in your prior work experiences?

This very specific question directs the prospective employee to focus more narrowly on the web-authoring tools he or she has used in other jobs.

Fact and Opinion-Centered Questions   **Fact questions** seek specific factual details and examples or ask about trends and patterns of information. As such, questions focused on facts can be open or closed. A factual question that is phrased as an open question might be something like this:

> **Interviewer:**   What kinds of training in web design have you completed?

Sometimes, it's useful to ask a fact question about the job seeker's résumé or to get feedback about something that has already been said. A fact question of this type would be phrased like this:

> **Interviewer:**   Can you elaborate more on some of the things you learned in the web design workshops that you list on your résumé?

open questions   Questions that afford the interviewee a wide range of options for responding.

closed questions   Questions that address narrow areas of concern and provide little or no latitude of response.

fact questions   Questions that seek specific factual details and examples or ask about trends and patterns of information; can be open or closed.

An example of a closed question to get at facts might be something like this:

Interviewer: Did you manage databases in addition to web authoring, in your previous work experiences?

In contrast to fact questions, **opinion-centered questions** ask for judgments. For example, as a job applicant, you would need to make an evaluation if the employer asked you a question such as this:

Interviewer: Which web-authoring tools do you like the best?

Another opinion-centered question could be worded like this:

Interviewer: How comfortable are you in making presentations to clients to explain a web design?

Each of these questions asks the interviewee to offer an opinion or make a judgment.

Direct and Hypothetical Questions   **Direct questions** are worded so that the expected focus for the answer is explicitly stated. The examples used in the previous section are all illustrations of direct questions. As the interviewee, you will know that the questions are about work experiences, training, and web authoring.

Hypothetical questions are stated in a more indirect manner than direct questions. In a job-seeking interview, the interviewer might ask you to imagine yourself in a hypothetical situation and then explain how you would respond to it. Hypothetical questions are "What if?" questions.

As an example, suppose again that an interviewee is seeking a job as a web designer. The interviewer might describe a problem and ask the interviewee how he or she would go about solving it. For example, the employer might want to determine if the prospective job seeker was attuned to issues of copyright law and likely to use good judgment when presented with an unclear situation. A *direct question* on this matter would ask the interviewee for specific information about copyright law:

Interviewer: What kinds of permission are needed in order to reproduce a copyrighted image for use in a web design without paying for duplication rights?

A hypothetical question on a copyright issue might be phrased something like this:

Interviewer: Suppose that you are working with a client who wants some specific graphic images incorporated into a web design. The client tells you that she will be providing the digital images. When you see the pictures, however, you realize that they appeared in a recent news magazine. How would you deal with this situation?

This question is intended to draw on more than content knowledge. By asking the question indirectly in the form of a hypothetical situation, the interviewer also learns about the interviewee's problem-solving skills in dealing with a copyright problem. The interviewer would also find out additional factors about the prospective employee's skills for dealing with clients.

Consider how an interviewer could assess the strengths of an interviewee who answered the hypothetical question about copyright infringement in this way:

opinion-centered questions
Questions that ask for judgments.

direct questions   Questions that are intended to evoke answers that are explicitly stated.

hypothetical questions
Questions that are intended to evoke less direct and more thoughtful answers. These are often phrased as imaginary situations.

Interviewer: I would probably share my concern about the photos with my supervisor, and then we would have to decide how to talk through the situation with the client. If my supervisor wanted me to handle the matter, I would probably call the client on the phone to sort out any possible issues of copyright infringement. In a phone call, I could sense whether the client was fully aware of the issues of copyright law and the need to get permission or pay for rights to duplicate the photos as part of the design.

VIDEO VIEW

6.2

Primary and Follow-Up Questions   **Primary questions** are asked by the interviewer to introduce topics to the interviewee. These questions are typically planned out carefully and thus used to structure or organize the interview. Primary questions provide transitions to new subjects and stages of the interview—for instance, signaling that it's time for the interviewee to ask questions of the interviewer or perhaps that the interview is coming to a close.

THINK ABOUT THIS

6.1

Along with primary questions, an interviewer may ask **follow-up questions** that seek additional information or clarification. Follow-up questions prompt the interviewee to expand on what he or she has already shared about a topic. Most of the time, follow-up questions arise within the course of an interview when the interviewer wants more details than the primary question elicited or when a previous answer seems ambiguous or contradictory.

THINK ABOUT THIS

6.2

RAPID REVIEW

6.3

Strategies for Answering Questions

Effective communication during an interview is vital for success in a job-seeking interview. A survey of large corporations (Peterson, 1997) found that 90 percent of interviewers rated oral communication skills as essential for success. Among the specific skills the survey highlighted were being able to communicate clear and relevant responses to questions, to use appropriate grammar, and to respond to feedback.

Grice's Conversational Maxims   Grice (1975), an expert on using language in various types of interpersonal communication situations, offers guidelines for developing the kinds of interviewing competencies just described. His model of **conversational maxims** identifies four benchmarks that are essential for successful communication:

- *Quantity:* The amount of information shared
- *Quality:* The truthfulness of information
- *Relation:* The relevance of information
- *Manner:* The clarity and organization of information

The **maxim of quantity** concerns the amount of information that a communicator shares. When applied to participating in an interview, it means finding the right balance between saying too little and saying too much. Grice suggests providing as much information as is required in a given circumstance.

Sometimes, you will be most effective by listening carefully to a question, assessing what is being asked, and answering with just that much information. If you are asked about your formal educational experience, that should be the focus of your response. Your answer should include details about where you went to school and what kinds of courses you took that pertain to the position for which you're being interviewed. It will be a matter of judgment on your part as to how much detail to provide in answering this or any other question.

primary questions   Questions that introduce topics; typically planned out carefully and thus used to structure or organize the interview.

follow-up questions   Questions that seek additional information or clarification; prompt the interviewee to expand on what he or she has already shared about a topic.

conversational maxims   From Grice's model, which identifies four benchmarks essential to successfully coordinating communication; the benchmarks are quantity, quality, relation, and manner.

maxim of quantity   Concerns the amount of information that a communicator shares; in an interview, means finding the right balance between saying too little and saying too much.

Another guiding principle in answering interview questions is to make a complete response to the question as it was asked. Listen carefully to the type of question that is asked to discern how much detail to share. Thus, an open question will likely call for a more extensive response than a closed question, which seeks a narrowly focused response.

The amount of information you provide may also be governed by the amount of time available. If it seems that little time is available for the interview, less may be expected of you in terms of providing detailed answers. Pay attention to the nonverbal feedback being communicated by the interviewer. Look for signals that indicate that you've provided a satisfactory depth of response or that you might be talking too much.

The **maxim of quality** has to do with making ethical responses to questions. When answering a question, an interviewee needs to know the facts and state them accurately. You must be sincere and truthful in order to maintain credibility. The requirement of being truthful is absolutely essential for a job-seeking interview. If you fabricate information, you might be taken out of the running for a position or lose the job after you've been hired.

The issue of credibility is explored in the recent film *Catch Me If You Can*, in which Leonardo DiCaprio plays the role of Frank Abagnale, Jr. Based on a true story, Abagnale pretends at various times to be an airline pilot, a physician, and a lawyer. In one job interview in which he is seeking the position of director of the emergency ward in a hospital, he claims to have graduated from a prestigious medical school. No one checks on his credentials or background, and he gets the job.

When you interview for a job, you should expect that a competent interviewer will check your credentials and background. Also realize that even small acts of deceit, such as telling partial truths, can have damaging consequences. So, for instance, if you are asked to describe your educational preparation for a position, it's out of bounds not only to make up a degree but also to shade the truth by making up courses or grades.

Let's return to our hypothetical interview for the position as a web designer. Suppose you are asked if you have ever taken a course in web design. In fact, you have not taken a full-fledged course, but you did attend a professional demonstration done by a salesperson of a web-authoring product and you've picked up a lot on your own. No matter how qualified you think you are, it would be inappropriate to embellish your experience by saying you've taken a course. But it would be perfectly appropriate to say something like this:

Interviewer: While in college, I became interested in web authoring when I attended a sales presentation on how to use Dream Weaver. That experience motivated me to learn more about various web-authoring tools on my own. And when I was experimenting with a number of different tools, I found that I could apply many of the principles that I learned in my graphics design classes to web design, too.

maxim of quality Concerns making ethical responses to questions; an interviewee must be sincere and truthful in order to maintain credibility.

maxim of relation Concerns the relevance of the information shared; interviewees should not digress to talk about things that don't fit the focus of the dialogue.

Grice's third aspect of effective communication, the **maxim of relation,** has to do with the relevance of the information shared. Communicators violate the maxim of relation when they digress to talk about things that don't fit the focus of the dialogue. In other words, what you say in an interview should be on point and clearly related to the matter at hand. Don't get off track by sharing information that is extraneous.

You may sense a bit of overlap in thinking about the maxim of relation and the maxim of quantity. Both address how much information is shared. Where they differ is that the maxim of *quantity* has to do with how much detail a communicator provides—that is, how many examples are used and how broadly or narrowly a topic is covered. The maxim of *relation* has to do with relevance—whether the examples and the level of detail are pertinent to the topic at hand.

6.3

6.4

6.5

6.6

Think of it this way: If you were asked in an interview to describe what in your formal educational experience has prepared you to be a web designer, the maxim of *quantity* would govern whether you shared the short or the long version of the story. The maxim of *relation* would govern whether you confined your answer to your educational experiences, not other aspects of your experiences, as well. So, if you answered the question about your formal educational experience by proclaiming how excited you are about the profession of web design or if you went off on a tangent about what kinds of projects you would most like to create, you would violate the maxim of relation—however short or long your response.

The final aspect of effective communication is to abide by the **maxim of manner.** According to Grice, this means using the correct style for a given type of dialogue. It's important in an interview, for instance, to speak clearly and to organize your ideas so that the interviewer can follow them easily.

Clarity is enhanced by word choice; thus, it's usually best to avoid obscure terms. For instance, in a job-seeking interview, you should not use slang or jargon that does not have a broad application to the specific job you are applying for. You will also enhance your clarity if you think about ways that words can be ambiguous. Finally, consider how to organize your ideas so that you will be as clear as possible. Effective job seekers hone their verbal skills by doing research before a job interview and then thinking through possible responses to the questions they might be asked.

6.1

The maxim of manner also applies to nonverbal communication. It's important to follow appropriate norms for such nonverbal behaviors as tone of voice, eye contact, and gestures. Also consider how you use nonverbal communication to provide feedback to the interviewer. Some experts in job-seeking interviews even coach job applicants in the value of making a firm business handshake when first greeting the interviewer and dressing the part for the interview.

6.4

Implications for Communication: Learn Effective Interviewing Skills

Interviewing requires preparation by both the interviewer and the interviewee, and the preparation needed by each party will vary, depending on the type of interview. Since interviews are organized around different types of goals, the interviewer and the interviewee should assess what kinds of outcomes are expected.

Prepare to Conduct the Interview

- Assess the reason for the interview.
- Gather information.
- Invite and schedule the interviewee, and plan the logistics of the interview, as needed.
- Prepare questions.

After identifying the reason for the interview, the interviewer may need to gather additional information. If you are conducting an information-sharing interview, you may need to do a substantial amount of research from other sources before talking with the expert you plan to interview for more information. Your background research should also guide the kinds of questions that you prepare.

When the interviewer is doing a counseling interview or a job appraisal or exit interview, he or she can prepare by reviewing the interviewee's records prior to the interview. By thinking through the issues that may arise during one of these kinds of

maxim of manner Concerns using the correct style for a given type of dialogue; in an interview, it's important to speak clearly and to organize your ideas.

interviews, the interviewer can also plan the best way to structure the interview and determine the sequence of questions to ask.

There may also be some logistical matters, such as scheduling the time for the interview and arranging for the space where the interview will occur. At times, information-sharing interviews are tape recorded. You should get the interviewee's written permission before making any type of recording. In part, that is a matter of courtesy. But it may also involve legal questions of privacy rights.

There are also important guidelines to follow if you are conducting a job interview to be certain that the questions you plan to ask satisfy legal requirements. You will need, therefore, to be familiar with federal, state, and local guidelines for what constitutes an illegal question. In general, it is *inappropriate* to ask questions that do not have direct bearing on a prospective employee's professional background or job qualifications. This pertains particularly to certain issues of personal privacy such as his or her age, gender-related concerns, family status, racial or ethnic background, sexual orientation, religious affiliation, health status, or history of disabilities.

6.5

Prepare to Be Interviewed

- Anticipate the types of questions that may be asked.
- Gather and organize information.
- Decide how to present yourself.

6.2

For the interviewee, the amount and kind of preparation will also vary with the type of interview. Regardless, prior to the interview, you should anticipate the types of questions that will be asked and rehearse how to respond to them. You can do this on your own or in a practice run-through by role playing with a friend. Some interview situations are more stressful than others, so it is wise to practice in advance.

As you plan for a job-seeking interview, it is vital to do research about the company and the particular type of job that you've applied for. Sometimes, a particular position will require that you organize documents or work samples in a portfolio. An applicant for a position such as web designer, for instance, will most likely need to present examples of earlier design projects. You may also need to provide documents that substantiate your formal records, such as an academic transcript or a certificate of specialized training. Some positions require documentation of prior work experience and matters such as citizenship. What you need to gather will vary from one field to another. For this reason, it's a good idea to make a phone call in advance of the interview to see whether you need to bring along specific items of information. After an interview has been conducted, it is also appropriate to write a brief letter to thank the person with whom you interviewed. This may also be another opportunity to highlight a few of the things that you spoke about during the interview. If you were the interviewer, say, for researching a topic for a speech or for learning about career choices, it would also be appropriate to thank the person who gave you the interview.

6.6

Finally, since most job interviews are more formal than day-to-day interactions, it is important to think about how to dress. The best rule is to fit the norms of the profession and the kind of job for which you are applying.

In sum, interviewing occurs in a special context of interpersonal communication and can be distinguished from other types of interpersonal encounters by the way that it is organized. Interviewers and interviewees use a question-and-answer format to achieve one or more of several communicative goals. We turn next to another specialized type of communication that is used in professional contexts: small-group communication.

6.2

6.5

Small-Group Communication

6.2

In Module One, we observed that a distinguishing feature of small-group communication is the pursuit of a common goal by the group's members. In this module, we will develop the idea further by elaborating on some of the ways that groups are structured.

We will use a systems view, based on **general systems theory,** to explain how people interact with one another in various small-group and organizational contexts. Although our primary focus will be on the small group, the general systems model will enable us to observe how many work-related small groups are parts of larger organizational structures, such as corporations and government agencies. In particular, we will look at the following aspects of professional communication:

6.7

- Small groups are organized to achieve shared goals.
- Many small groups are parts of larger organizational systems.
- Small groups, as well larger organizations, use a wide range of channels of communication.

Purposes for Organizing Small Groups

6.3

Several kinds of small groups can be identified according to the purpose for which they are formed. **Task groups** are organized for a variety of reasons—for instance, to solve problems and make decisions or to complete a specific project or job. **Social groups** form for personal reasons, such as for socialization or to pursue individual growth intellectually, spiritually, or emotionally. In this module, with its emphasis on professional communication, we will give primary attention to the kinds of group interactions that take place in the workplace.

Short-Term Task Forces   In the workplace, groups have tasks to perform, products to create, and jobs to accomplish. Sometimes, a group is formed for the sole purpose of completing a specific task. A **task force** that is assigned to work on a particular product or to study a particular issue may exist only as long as it takes to complete the task.

In the communication class in which you are presently enrolled, you may, for instance, be asked to participate in a group project that involves doing a specific task. Suppose that you and a group of classmates have been assigned a topic dealing with a contemporary social problem or to propose a solution to a problem on your campus. You have been asked to research this problem and do a formal presentation to the rest of your class. Your work would represent the effort of a short-term task force that is similar to types of task forces found in the workplace. Once you have completed your presentation, your group would cease to exist. On the other hand, if you were part of a study group in your class that met throughout the semester and worked together on a wide range of types of tasks, say, studying for exams, doing peer editing of written work for the class, preparing group discussions and group performances in class, and helping one another prepare speeches, you would be an *intact work group.*

6.4

Intact Work Groups   Sometimes, the same group of people will work together for an extended period of time and accomplish many different tasks. Such a long-term group is called an **intact work group.** You may have been part of a group like this at some point. Consider how long you and your work colleagues have been together and how many different tasks you've completed.

6.6

general systems theory   A theory that explains how the components of a system interact with one another in ways that enable the system as a whole to maintain equilibrium and to adapt to its environment; explains how work-related small groups are parts of larger organizational structures.

task group   A small group that's formed for a specific purpose; may be formed to solve problems and make decisions or to complete a specific project or job.

social group   A group that's formed for personal reasons; may be formed for socialization or to pursue individual growth intellectually, spiritually, or emotionally.

task force   A group that's formed to work on a particular product or to study a particular issue; may exist only as long as it takes to complete the task.

intact work group   A group that's formed to work together for an extended period of time and to accomplish many different tasks.

Yet that is not the only model for organizing work groups. At other times, group membership may be more fluid. A new member might be brought in to work on a particular task. Alternately, a fairly stable and intact group of fellow staff members may be assigned to work in different teams on different projects. On Mondays, you might find yourself in a meeting to work on project X alongside Carlos, Juanita, Mary, Lakeisha, and Bill. And on Wednesdays, you might work in a different group comprised of Juanita, Carlos, Tyrone, Murray, and Kim to work on project Y.

Place in the Larger Organizational System

If you are a salaried employee working for a business firm in the United States, there is an 84 percent chance, according to data from the most recent U.S. census (U.S. Census Bureau, 2002b), that you work for an organization that has 20 or more employees. About 17 percent of U.S. employees work for an organization with a payroll of between 20 and 99 workers, and almost 57 million, or nearly half, of all workers in the United States work for a company with 500 or more employees.

Workers in the public sector are also likely to belong to large organizational systems. Of the more than 15 million state and local government workers, most are employed in large organizations—for example, schools, hospitals, health care agencies, and other public services such as police departments, highway crews, and fire departments (U.S. Department of Commerce, 2002). Similarly recent data indicate that the federal government employs about 3 million civilian workers, most of whom belong to large executive agencies (U.S. Census Bureau, 2002a). Finally, the four major branches of the U.S. armed forces have a total of 1.4 million active-duty members (U.S. Department of Defense, 2002).

In sum, no matter what field you go into or whether you work in the private or public sector, you will likely interact with many co-workers on a regular basis.

Corporate Culture   The large institutions for which people work in the private and public sectors create the organizational contexts within which members of small groups work together. Each organization develops its own **corporate culture,** which in turn affects the nature of small-group interaction.

Like other types of cultural groups, members of a corporate culture align with the views and vision of their culture. The corporate culture of an organization is usually articulated in its mission statement, policies, and manuals. The organization's values and traditions are also communicated through its stories and rituals. Likewise, the organization's norms and practices reflect the values of its corporate culture.

6.8

6.5

Corporate Culture and Hierarchies   Corporate culture also establishes structures and hierarchies of power and status, which affect the procedures and methods of decision making as members of small groups work together. We may thus speak of "lines of authority" or how to communicate "through proper channels." Organizational charts trace these lines of authority and reveal how information flows among the various parts of an organization.

Channels of Communication Used

Contemporary organizations and the small groups within them use many different channels of communication to communicate both formally and informally. Along with formal written types of communication, such as letters, memoranda, and reports, there

corporate culture   The larger organizational context within which members of a small group work; members align with the views and vision of their culture, as articulated in its mission statement, policies, and manuals.

are many oral channels of communication—some formal, such as speeches and presentations, and some informal, such as phone calls. Interactions also take place using a variety of electronic channels of communication in the digital workplace.

Traditional Channels of Communication and the Digital Workplace A study published by the National Telecommunications and Information Association (2002), an agency of the U.S. Department of Commerce, describes the growth of the contemporary *digital workplace* and its increased use of computer-based communication over the last 10 years. The study reports that 56.7 percent of American workers today use a computer as part of their job. These data include workers who do manual labor as well as workers who do administrative and professional types of work.

The figure rises to 80 percent when considering only those who work in managerial and professional specialty areas and to 70 percent when considering workers in technical, sales, and administrative support jobs. Computer use may include things such as word processing and manipulating data. The most popular use of the computer at work is using the Internet to send e-mail. Two-thirds of those who work in managerial positions use e-mail.

Traditional Work Groups versus Virtual Work Groups The growth of the digital workplace has clearly affected how workers interact in small groups. Watson-Manheim and Belanger (2002) describe the **virtual work team,** whose members do a substantial amount of their interaction through electronic channels of communication.

In contrast to traditional work groups, who may meet formally around a conference table or informally when they drop in at one another's offices, virtual work groups rely on a host of communication technologies for their interaction. Those technologies may include e-mail and voice mail, voice or desktop video conferencing, pagers and cellular phones, personal digital assistants, online chat or instant messaging, and asynchronous discussion boards.

Thus, while members of the traditional work team generally interact through face-to-face meetings in the same physical location, the members of the virtual work team are often physically separated from one another—maybe even working on opposite sides of the globe. Technologies such as video conferencing and instant messaging may be used to allow members to communicate at the same time, which is **synchronous communication.**

Some groups may meet exclusively in virtual space, while others may schedule face-to-face communications along with virtual meetings. Watson-Manheim and Belanger observe that groups may also be temporally separated. So, electronically mediated communication may be **asynchronous communication** if all of the members of a group are interacting at different times, as with a bulletin board.

Groups of all kinds can use special types of software and **group decision support systems (GDSS)** to deal with certain communication issues. A GDSS is a computer-mediated type of interaction that allows members to brainstorm ideas and discuss issues in a fairly anonymous manner. Here is how it typically works: Each member of a group sits at a separate computer and enters ideas that are then organized by a software program. In theory, the authors of the various ideas that are contributed are not identified. The software can also combine ideas and tabulate responses made by contributors, which are commonly displayed for all to see. Wilkinson (1989) observes that "because everyone must participate, must push their button, the tools encourage teamwork. . . . This in turn helps ensure participants will buy into the decisions made at the meeting" (p. 50).

 A study by Aiken, Vanjami, and Krosp (1995) found that work groups can shorten meetings by as much as 50 percent by using GDSS hardware and software. Why such an increase in productivity? This study points to the fact

6.6

virtual work team A group whose members do a substantial amount of their interaction through electronic channels of communication.

synchronous communication Communication in the here and now; occurs when the source and receiver are communicating without a significant delay between their sending and receiving of a message.

asynchronous communication Occurs when there is a lapse of time between when the sender transmits a message and when the receiver decodes it and provides feedback.

group decision support systems (GDSS) A computer-mediated type of interaction that allows members to brainstorm ideas and discuss issues in a fairly anonymous manner.

that there is little or no social interaction among group members. However, other studies have found inconsistent results from GDSS technologies, especially if the facilitator is unfamiliar with the topic. Others have questioned whether the system truly is anonymous, especially when members can infer the identities of participants from the context of what their fellow members write.

Because virtual teams can include people who are widely disbursed, they allow even the smallest of organizations to tap into a worldwide pool of human resources. A company can support a virtual team that is truly international without making huge expenditures for travel or relocation of employees. Yet as Kiser (1999) notes, differences in language and cultural understanding arise, providing new obstacles to confront.

6.3

6.9

There are other problems with electronic communications that are unique to the virtual workspace. Watson-Manheim and Belanger (2002) observe that the range of choices for electronic communication can be complex. In addition, the interpersonal dimensions of messages can be misunderstood because of the lack of nonverbal communication. And as workers rely more and more on communicating with e-mail, there is the additional problem of managing the volume of these messages.

Perhaps the most significant challenge, as reported by Geber (1995), is that members of virtual work teams may feel isolated from one another, since they have few or no opportunities for face-to-face contact. Some virtual teams compensate for this lack of day-to-day contact by having occasional meetings. Doing so seems sufficient for developing the kinds of interpersonal bonding and trust that are necessary for groups to work well together. Geber observes that face-to-face contact is important even when it is purely social rather than work oriented. The work can be done online; the time spent together should be for team building and play.

6.4

Implications for Communication:
Understand the Principles of General Systems Theory

Small groups are often components of larger systems and thus corporate cultures. Small-group communication is often more effective when the system as a whole operates in accordance with the principles of interdependence and by becoming open and adaptive to its environment.

6.7

Effectiveness Is Enhanced by Becoming Interdependent   The principle of **interdependence** is one of the core concepts of general systems theory. Sometimes referred to as the principle of *holism,* the idea is that the members of a group need to pull together to accomplish a task in a cooperative and collaborative manner. This means that they need to agree about shared goals and how to achieve them. Small-group communication is effective only when group members can coordinate their efforts and work interdependently to achieve shared goals.

The principle of holism has sometimes been expressed as the idea that the whole is greater than the sum of its parts, which is the concept of **nonsummativity.** In terms of the workplace, the various departments of a company and the members of the small groups who work in an interdependent fashion represent the concept of nonsummativity. That is, when they pull together, they can accomplish more than any single organizational unit or individual might achieve by himself or herself.

In his discussion of holism and nonsummativity, Fisher (1982) observed that a "system is the 'all' of a thing" (p. 198). He explained further that "the parts of a system are less important than the connectedness of the parts." Given this, in some cases, the

interdependence   Describes how the members of a group need to pull together to accomplish a task in a cooperative and collaborative manner; one of the core concepts of general systems theory; sometimes referred to as the principle of holism.

nonsummativity   Describes how the whole is greater than the sum of its parts; a restatement of the principle of holism.

whole might work out to be *less* than the sum of its parts. This is the reason that a dysfunctional group that does not get its act together, for instance, is likely to achieve less than individuals might accomplish working by themselves.

An Open System Will Be Able to Adapt to Its Environment   The immediate environment for many work groups is the larger organizational structure of which they are a part. A single work group will be effective when its members and leaders maintain open lines of communication with the other parts of the organizational structure.

Fisher (1982) observes that the hallmark of an *open system* is its capacity for the exchange of information. When a system is open, its boundaries are permeable. Members are able to exchange information between levels of the hierarchy and between small groups. Moreover, since the contemporary organization uses a wide variety of formal and informal channels of communication, effectiveness requires that the members of small groups be able to use all available channels well.

The value of information exchange also applies to how open the organization is to seeking and receiving information from *outside* the corporation or small group. Information exchange is a two-way process: An effective organization seeks information from outside and communicates with its public outside, as well.

In the final segment of this module, we will examine one of the venues that groups use for communicating outside their boundaries by considering the preparation of public group presentations. But first, we will explore another aspect of effective group communication: the concept of equilibrium.

6.3

RAPID REVIEW

6.7

Group Communication and Equilibrium

LEARNING OBJECTIVE

6.3

For the last 50 years, social psychologists and communication scholars have developed a body of theory that examines how a group strives to achieve a sense of **equilibrium.** Translated literally from Latin, the word *equilibrium* means "equal and in balance." A group experiences equilibrium when its members are able to resolve tension between competing values.

Burns (1978) notes in his book *Leadership* that equilibrium "rests on a structure of give and take" (p. 290). Among the tensions that a group strives to keep in balance are the following:

- Task cohesion and social cohesion
- Task-centered roles and social-centered roles
- Group goals and individual goals
- Cooperation and competition

Task Cohesion and Social Cohesion

You have probably experienced the tension that comes from trying to be productive and social at the same time. Consider the last time that you worked with fellow classmates to complete a class project, such as a group research presentation. While you worked on the project, you may have spent a lot of your shared time comparing notes from your research and planning how to do the presentation or write the report. At the same time, you may also have enjoyed the company of the group as you socialized with one another. It was fun to relate to others by getting to know them and forming casual friendships. Exchanging light banter and making small talk about your lives outside the group were probably welcome diversions to the task at hand. Yet at the same time, you

equilibrium   Translated literally from Latin, means "equal and in balance"; occurs when a group's members are able to resolve tension between competing values.

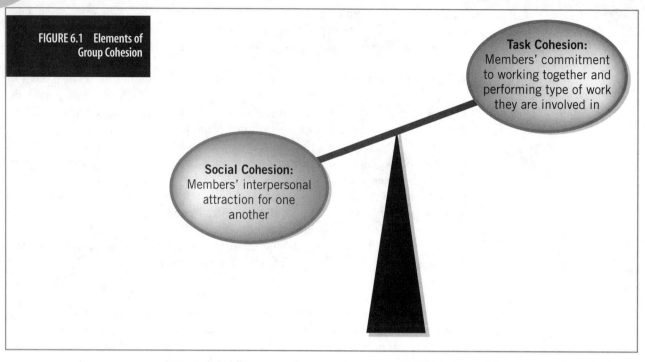

FIGURE 6.1   Elements of Group Cohesion

Task Cohesion: Members' commitment to working together and performing type of work they are involved in

Social Cohesion: Members' interpersonal attraction for one another

The balance that comes from working on a task and relating socially creates group cohesion.

were accomplishing a specific task. In doing so, you experienced equilibrium between being productive and being social.

The balance that comes from working at a high level of productivity on a task and relating socially creates a sense of **group cohesion:** an attraction that members feel toward the group and its task and the intensity with which they value their affiliation. Group cohesion has two components (see Figure 6.1):

■   **Task cohesion** reflects how much members are committed to working together and to performing the type of work that they are involved in.
■   **Social cohesion** reflects how much members are interpersonally attracted to one another.

6.8

In group theory, there is interplay between these two elements of group cohesion. When there is a high level of task cohesion, members work well together as a team and mostly value the work they are doing. This contributes to their motivation and enthusiasm for doing the job. When there is a high level of social cohesion, members get a sense of relational satisfaction from their working together.

6.9

That was the finding of a study by Anderson, Martin, and Riddle (2001), who identified how group relational satisfaction is comprised of a set of positive attitudes about participating in a group. A high level of group member satisfaction is reflected in attitudes of cooperation and willingness to collaborate. When members feel relational satisfaction in the group, they experience feelings of affection, involvement, liking, belonging, freedom to communicate, friendship, and trust. Cooperation and commitment are also reflected in positive work-related attitudes such as looking forward to group meetings, wanting to spend time with other group members, and feeling that one's absence from the group will matter to others. Relational satisfaction is developed over the life history of a given group's interaction.

group cohesion   An attraction that members feel toward the group and its task and the intensity with which they value their affiliation; dimensions include task cohesion and social cohesion.

task cohesion   Reflects how much members are committed to working together and to performing the type of work that they are involved in.

social cohesion   Reflects how much members are interpersonally attracted to one another and feel a sense of relational satisfaction and group unity.

Anderson et al. also found that the feedback that group members give one another influences relational satisfaction and thus the level of cohesion that members experience:

> Feedback serves a necessary and instrumental function in groups. During the group process, members encourage participation, offer support, and even challenge each other's ideas and contributions. This type of participatory climate establishes that members are free to speak up. (p. 228)

Over a period of time, as you work with the other members of the group, you may develop friendships. The classic television program *The Mary Tyler Moore Show,* which first aired in the late 1970s and has been replayed in syndication many seasons since, illustrates how a long-term, intact group can achieve task and social cohesion. The storyline of the program portrayed members of a local 6:00 P.M. news team and how they worked together to plan the nightly news. At the same time, the program presented the development of close personal relationships among the group's members.

Viewers of *The Mary Tyler Moore Show* may recall that the program ended with the disbanding of the fictional group, which was brought about when the senior management of the television station decided that a new team was needed to enhance ratings. All of the members of the show's staff were fired except for Ted Baxter, the bumbling anchorman. The "group hug" in the show's final episode portrayed the ending of the personal relationships among the characters as well as the conclusion of their work together. If you recall the humor of the group hug, it demonstrated the level of social cohesion among the members of the group. They did not want to let go of one another, even to get the box of tissues that they needed to dry their eyes. So, arm in arm, they moved in concert, still embracing, to lift the box of tissues from Mary's desk.

Whatever the nature of the group—whether a task force with a single job to do or a long-term, intact group with many assignments—its members need to relate interpersonally to achieve equilibrium between productivity and sociability. When members have little time or inclination to relate to one another socially and develop personal rapport, the group may lose a sense of equilibrium. Alternately, a group may be out of balance when the time and energy spent socializing interferes with the group's productivity.

Task-Centered and Social-Centered Roles

Group **roles** are patterns of behavior. Earlier, we looked at roles in the context of the development of a person's self-concept and in various types of interpersonal relationships. We saw how the roles that people perform reflect various aspects of their identity and role performances vary from one relationship to another. Similarly, within groups, members perform specific patterns of behavior that comprise their roles.

The work environment provides a good illustration of how members of a group often perform particular and unique *task-centered roles.* Sometimes, a job title sums up the person's role. Drawing again from *The Mary Tyler Moore Show,* the job title of Mary Richards (Moore's character) was assistant to the producer. She worked for Mr. Grant, the producer (played by Ed Asner). Murray Slaughter (played by Gavin McLeod) was the writer for the news program, and Ted Baxter (played by Ted Knight) was the news anchor. All of these individuals had particular task roles to perform in accordance with their job descriptions.

Some work groups require that role performances be highly specialized. This is also particularly the case in work environments that involve the use of technology for which special skills and training are needed. The recent television drama *CSI* and its spinoff *CSI Miami* illustrate the highly specialized roles involved today in criminal

role patterns of behavior performed by individuals in a relationship; roles are mutually defined by members of a relational community or cultural group.

investigations. A visit to a hospital will also illustrate the highly complex set of roles found in that workplace.

Task-Centered Roles   Group members also perform a range of **task-centered roles** in a group discussion, and sometimes role performances overlap so that more than one person is performing the same role. As you can see on the list that follows (which is based on the model by Benne and Sheats, 1948), here are some examples of these task-centered roles that enable members of a group to collaborate in solving problems or making decisions:

- *Initiator/contributor:* Gets the discussion started and generates new ideas.
- *Information seeker:* Asks for information about the task at hand.
- *Opinion seeker:* Asks for input from group members about their position on subjects under discussion.
- *Information giver:* Offers facts and generalization to the group.
- *Opinion giver:* States his or her position about a group issue.
- *Elaborator:* Explains ideas within the group, builds on others' ideas, and offers examples to clarify ideas.
- *Coordinator:* Shows the relationships between ideas.
- *Orienter:* Shifts the direction of the group's discussion.
- *Evaluator/critic:* Measures the group's actions against some objective standard; may also serve as a "devil's advocate" when the group needs critical feedback.
- *Energizer:* Stimulates the group to a higher level of activity.
- *Procedural technician:* Performs logistical functions for the group.
- *Recorder:* Keeps a record of the group's actions.

6.10   A particular person may perform one of these task-centered roles uniquely. For instance, someone who helps keep the group on track as a kind of moderator will likely assume the role of *coordinator.* This person may also be the *initiator/contributor* in getting the group going on a new task or the *orienter,* especially if the group is following a preplanned agenda. (We will devote a section later in this module to how a group leader or the whole group can preplan an agenda for a problem-solving discussion.) Another person may serve as the group *recorder* and take charge of documenting the group's actions.

At the same time, there are some task-centered roles from the Benne and Sheats inventory that are likely to be performed by several or even all members of the group. A discussion group, for instance, may profit by having everyone in the group contribute ideas. Thus, the roles of *information giver* and *opinion giver* may very well be assumed by everyone in the group.

The list of roles from Benne and Sheats covers a lot of tasks that are common to many types of task-centered groups, but it is not intended to be complete. A particular group may require additional roles, depending on its task. Suppose, for instance, that you are part of a task force that is going to solve a problem and then present its findings to an audience. Your group might decide to use a PowerPoint presentation as part of communicating information to its audience. One or two persons in your group might be designated as presentation coordinators and charged with pulling everyone's ideas together and designing the PowerPoint presentation.

Social-Centered Roles   In addition to performing task-centered roles, groups also benefit by performing **social-centered roles,** which contribute to the social cohesion of the group. As such, these roles are sometimes referred to as *group-maintenance roles,* since they function to maintain the interpersonal harmony of the group.

Another way of distinguishing social-centered roles is to liken them to the relational maintenance strategies that we studied in Module Five. When group members

task-centered roles   Specific roles performed by group members that enable them to work together to solve problems and make decisions.

social-centered roles   Specific roles that contribute to the social cohesion of the group; sometimes referred to as group-maintenance roles, as they function to maintain the interpersonal harmony of the group.

create patterns of positive and supportive communication and manage tensions and conflict, they are performing social roles. For example, Benne and Sheats (1948) suggest the following social-centered roles:

- *Encourager:* Offers praise and positive reinforcement for the ideas of others.
- *Harmonizer:* Mediates differences among group members.
- *Compromiser:* Finds common ground and works toward solutions that are supported by all group members.
- *Gatekeeper/expediter:* Keeps communication channels open and gets nonparticipators to take a more active role.
- *Standard setter:* Suggests standards for the group to achieve; may also suggest or enforce group norms.
- *Group observer:* Keeps records of group activities and uses this information to offer feedback to the group.
- *Follower:* Goes along with the group and accepts its ideas.

6.10

To illustrate these social roles in practice, think of a time when you were part of a task force or participated in a problem-solving discussion group. Recall how certain members of your group were good at easing group tensions. In doing so, they played the role of *harmonizer* or *compromiser*. Someone playing the *gatekeeper/expediter* role may have initiated the forming of relationships by having members introduce themselves and share a few personal tidbits. Some members may have been *encouragers* in building up the group by offering praise and support. A *standard setter* may have modeled constructive interpersonal behaviors, such as effective listening.

As your group progressed in its work, members probably experienced some conflicts. As we saw in our study of interpersonal relationships, conflict is inevitable in meaningful relationships. Moreover, when a group is working together to solve a problem or make a decision, it is very constructive to examine the different sides of a question. Conflict is managed successfully when one or more group members perform the role of *harmonizer* or *compromiser*.

Group Goals   Group goals are met through the collective efforts of members as they complete their designated tasks and relate to one another in ways that maintain satisfying interpersonal relationships. Burns (1978) made this observation about groups that successfully meet common goals:

> Small group members talk with one another, laugh with one another, offer and receive advice, provide cues to one another, give and receive help, or, less typically, disagree and show antagonism. The more familiarity, the more interaction—and vice versa. A powerful factor is a sense of mutual obligation and a need for reciprocity. (p. 290)

Thus, for a group to be successful in achieving its goals, its members must perform task-centered and social-centered roles effectively. Members must also maintain a sense of equilibrium, achieving an appropriate balance between these two types of roles.

Self-Centered Roles   Benne and Sheats (1948) also observed how some members of groups perform dysfunctional roles that impede a group's progress. These are identified as **self-centered roles:**

- *Aggressor:* Attacks other group members, deflates the status of others, and engages in other aggressive behaviors.
- *Blocker:* Resists movement by the group.
- *Recognition seeker:* Calls attention to himself or herself; a group clown, for instance, may use inappropriate humor.
- *Self-confessor:* Seeks to disclose nongroup-related feelings and opinions.

self-centered roles   Dysfunctional roles performed by group members that impede the group's progress.

6.8

- *Dominator:* Asserts control by manipulating other group members.
- *Help seeker:* Tries to gain the sympathy of the group.
- *Special-interest pleader:* Uses stereotypes to assert his or her own prejudices.
- *Withdrawer:* Often misses group interactions or otherwise fails to participate.

Individuals who play self-centered roles create strain within a group. As the next section suggests, these roles may be enacted when the needs of an individual are thwarted.

Group Goals and Individual Goals

The third area in which members of a group need to strike a balance is between group goals and individual goals. To achieve group goals requires adherence to group norms, such that each member submits to the values and practices of the group. And to achieve individual goals requires satisfying the individual needs of the group's members.

6.12

Norms as Standards of Behavior   Groups establish mutual obligation and reciprocity by developing **norms:** patterns of behavior that all or most members of a group are expected to perform. The norms of a group reflect the shared attitudes and values of the group's members. We learn norms through our interactions with larger relational communities, such as the social groups in which we participate. A professional work environment, for instance, likely has an identifiable corporate culture that reflects the vision and values of the organization.

6.5

Sometimes, the norms of a group are explicitly stated as *rules.* Upon being hired, an employee might be issued a manual that spells out these rules. At other times, however, rules and the norms behind them are not directly stated. Even so, everyone in the group is expected to meet certain standards of behavior.

Since the norms of a group specify how its members are expected to perform, they can sometimes be reduced to "should" statements:

- Everyone should contribute to the discussion.
- Everyone should be an attentive and respectful listener.
- Everyone should come to work and to group meetings on time.
- Everyone should dress in a professional manner.
- Everyone should communicate with clients in a professional and respectful manner.

Whether norms are explicitly stated as rules or implicitly understood by all, they exert a powerful force of conformity on the members of a group.

Successful groups find equilibrium between satisfying the shared goals of the group and the individual goals of its members. Again, this is a matter of give and take.

Interpersonal Needs   As individuals, we all come to group situations with our own needs and expectations. These needs and expectations can be met along with the shared needs and expectations of the group to develop norms for productivity and for interpersonal harmony.

Schutz (1966), an expert on small-group dynamics, outlines three particular **interpersonal needs** that group members bring to their interactions. Each person, according to Schutz, has these three needs:

- *Inclusion:* The need to belong, or to experience social acceptance from others and relate on a social level in a group. May occur when others make us feel welcome and recognize our contributions to the group.
- *Control:* The need for order and power in a group. May occur when we feel that the group's efforts are organized and that we have a voice in controlling the

norms   Patterns of behavior that all or most members of a group are expected to perform; reflect the shared attitudes and values of the group's members; sometimes explicitly stated as rules.

interpersonal needs   The needs and expectations that individual group members bring to the group; basic needs are inclusion, control, and affection.

FIGURE 6.2
Interpersonal Needs

Inclusion: Belonging		
Oversocial	Social	Undersocial

Control: Order and power		
Autocrat	Democrat	Abdicrat

Affection: Being liked and respected		
Overpersonal	Personal	Underpersonal

High Need	Moderate & Normal	Low Need

Interpersonal needs for expressing and receiving inclusion, control, and affection vary from one person to another. These needs can be expressed along a continuum.

Source: Based on Schutz, 1966.

group's outcomes and shaping its decisions. We may exercise a need for control by serving as a group leader or feeling that we have influence over others.

- *Affection:* The need to be liked and respected by others in the group. May be met through personal sharing and by being supported and affirmed. In some groups, we may experience affection in the form of close bonds of friendship and collegiality.

Schutz observes that individuals differ from one another in terms of how much they need to express and receive inclusion, control, and affection. For instance, some of us may have particular needs to feel included, whereas others may have a stronger need for order and control. Finally, people vary in how much affection they want to express and receive from others.

6.6

As Figure 6.2 indicates, some people have high needs in one or more of these three areas, and others have low needs. Extremely high and low needs fall outside the normal range and may explain why individuals violate group norms. For instance, a person who is extremely high in the need for affection might go overboard in personal self-disclosure, whereas a person whose need for inclusion is very low may not choose to participate in the group's activities. An individual's needs might be seen as falling along a continuum. In the middle are the normal needs for inclusion, control, and affection that most people bring to a group. On the outer extremes are those needs that fall outside a normal range.

Schutz's theory of interpersonal needs can serve as a useful tool for understanding your own motives in a group and for seeing how other members of a group relate to each other. As you reflect on your own needs, you might see how you contribute to the overall group effort as well as meet your own needs. This will help you gain meaningful insight about why others in the group differ from you.

Meeting Needs as a Transaction   Burns (1978) observes that it is normal for conflict to occur when the needs of the group as a whole differ from the needs of individuals—or for that matter, when individuals differ in what they expect to get from one another. Burns also observes that group communication is a *transaction*, or a type of exchange that occurs between parties. Sometimes, the exchange is a matter of giving up your individual needs in favor of the group's needs; at other times, the exchange involves the group giving up its needs in order to accommodate your particular needs.

Thus, transactional communication among group members involves give and take. Later in this module, we will look further at Burns's ideas of transaction as a facet of leadership.

Cooperation and Competition: Conformity and Dissension

Most groups experience an ongoing tension between cooperation and competition. Members cooperate with one another to arrive at a shared understanding of the group's goals and the tasks necessary to achieve them. Cooperation is also experienced as members comply with the norms and rules of the group and acknowledge and accommodate one another's different needs and interests. A high level of cooperation is essential for effective group performance.

At the same time, however, a group also benefits from competition. Competition within a group is a valuable and indeed a necessary element, especially for groups that have to solve problems or make and implement decisions. Having a contest of ideas will ensure that the group is effective in its tasks of critical thinking. At other times, competition comes from outside the group. In the face of outside opposition or the perception of being in a contest with another group, members often pull together and intensify their joint efforts.

Conformity   Conformity has some benefits, since it tends to increase the attractiveness of the group and thus enhance social and task cohesion. Conformity to group norms also brings the benefits of predictability and accountability.

In their book *Conformity,* Kiesler and Kiesler (1970) summarize some of the research done by social scientists about group conformity. They suggest that members are more likely to conform to the goals of a group and commit to working on the group's task when they feel they have a voice in developing the group's goals. That is, when group members have the power to make decisions, establish procedures, and form group policies, they are more likely to cooperate with one another.

In addition, members of a group are more likely to be committed to the group's goals when they have a clear understanding of them and see them as relevant to their own interests. Conformity also increases when members see the group's goals as realistic and attainable, rather than too difficult to accomplish.

Individuals are also likely to conform to others in the group, according to Kiesler and Kiesler, if doing so brings individual benefits. For example, conforming to the will of the group can win status for an individual or enable him or her to satisfy individual needs, such as being liked and appreciated. Negatively, some individuals conform to the group out of fear, particularly the fear of being perceived as incorrect.

Many groups go to great lengths to ensure that their members are in conformity. When providing positive rewards is not effective, negative responses and sanctions may be communicated to bring nonconformists into line. In cases when breaches of the group's norms or violations of its rules are considered severe, the offending member may even be threatened with expulsion from the group.

VIDEO
VIEW

6.7

Groupthink   While conformity among group members is generally valuable, too much conformity can be a curse. Janis (1989) explains how some groups engage in **groupthink,** which results in bad decision making. This occurs when, in a rush to conformity, the prevailing majority of a group does not listen to alternative points of view. In addition, the majority gives too much credence to the opinions of members with higher status while dismissing the perspectives of minority members and those with lower status. When groups that are plagued by groupthink place too much pressure on dissenters in the hope of silencing them, they lose these individuals' valuable ideas and insights.

6.7

In medieval debates, the disputants sometimes appointed one debater to be the so-called *devil's advocate,* whose role was to challenge the argument just for the sake of argument. Putting someone in this role provides an effective corrective against the problem of groupthink. A group should encourage its members to express opposing points of view so that all the information it needs is available and so that all possible options are put on the table. To avoid groupthink, a group must be able to engage in healthy, idea-centered conflict that encourages critical thinking.

Janis developed the model of groupthink after studying political policymaking groups, including the group of advisors to President John F. Kennedy. Shortly after Kennedy assumed office in 1960, he and his foreign policy advisors approved an ill-fated plan by the Central Intelligence Agency (CIA) to invade Cuba. That operation, which was called the Bay of Pigs invasion, was a failure.

6.8

As a result of their failure in planning the Bay of Pigs invasion, members of the Kennedy administration instituted new decision-making procedures that took into account the problems of groupthink. According to Robert McNamara (2002), who was the secretary of defense under Kennedy, these new procedures called for intensive debate of options and deliberate effort to weigh all possible options, rather than rush to a decision.

In McNamara's view, the new procedures proved effective when the Kennedy administration faced its next major foreign policy crisis: the Cuban missile crisis, which occurred when Soviet-made intercontinental ballistic missiles that could reach the United States were discovered on Cuban soil in 1962. The events of this crisis were dramatized in a film entitled *Thirteen Days.* Even though the film exercises some poetic license in its portrayal of characters, it is essentially faithful to McNamara's description of how the ExComm, Kennedy's group of foreign policy advisors, developed a successful plan to blockade Cuba.

Before coming to that solution, however, the group of Kennedy advisors weighed a number of different options. On one end of the scale, they could do nothing at all. Yet, another, far more extreme, choice was to launch a first strike invasion of the Cuban mainland. The ExComm also explored different viewpoints about the nature of the crisis that the United States was facing. Some viewed the presence of missiles in Cuba as a genuine threat to the security of the United States and thought that Soviet Union might use Cuban bases to attack the United States. Others saw the problem as a diplomatic issue. That is, the Soviet Union was placing the missiles in Cuba in order to gain diplomatic concessions from the United States. Still a third camp within the Kennedy administration saw the situation from the perspective of American domestic politics. As noted by Pious (2001) this group perceived that if the administration did not make a dramatic move to remove the missiles from Cuba, it would be accused by Republicans of allowing the Soviet Union to intimidate the United States.

As another illustration, Cohan (2002) describes the corporate scandal involving Enron as a more recent case of groupthink. According to Cohan, the executives leading

groupthink   Occurs when, in a rush to conformity, the prevailing majority of a group does not listen to alternative points of view and exercise critical thinking; results in bad decision making.

the company made bad investment decisions when they insulated themselves from adverse information about the company's holdings and the value of its stock and then withheld information from shareholders, including their employees. Overall, the failure to use critical thinking, which means examining all the available information, is at the core of groupthink.

Social Cohesion and Groupthink   Studies by Bernthal and Insko (1993) disclose that a group's level of cohesiveness, especially its measure of social cohesion, also contributes to groupthink. We can think of this in another way: The overemphasis on social cohesion (without a counterbalancing emphasis on task cohesion) may undermine a group's efforts at encouraging the idea-centered conflict that's needed for effective critical thinking. Bernthal and Insko observe that groups that have a high level of task cohesion relative to social cohesion are less likely to become mired in groupthink if they focus on analytical decision making.

This is the kind of balance that the Kennedy ExComm group used successfully in addressing the Cuban missile crisis and that the Enron executives seemingly failed to use. Bernthal and Insko offer this explanation:

> Social-emotional groups, however, even when the group's task is clearly outlined, will tend to focus on maintaining the social aspects of the group. Although they [highly social groups] may have a high drive to accomplish the task, their initial social-emotional orientation will interfere with any task-related activities that may produce conflict between members. (p. 71)

This explanation seems to support the adage that people "Go along to get along," especially when getting along is what takes priority in the value system of the group. In contrast, groups that balance task cohesion along with social cohesion will develop norms for the application of critical thinking and avoid the trap of groupthink.

The Abilene Paradox: Another Problem of Conformity   While groupthink arises when group members suppress critical thinking in the face of pressures to conform with one another, another problem of conformity is what Harvey (1988) calls the Abilene Paradox. It occurs when group members fail to state their real positions. So, a situation arises where the other group members make assumptions—often wrong assumptions—about what they *think* is the consensus firmly held by others. But, in fact, there is no strong measure of support at all. The whole perception of a group consensus rests on false assumptions.

As a metaphor for consensus that is rooted in false assumptions, Harvey tells the story of an imaginary family living in Texas. One member of the family acts on the assumption that everyone else in the family wants to drive to Abilene to have dinner at a restaurant. Next, other members of the family chime in their support for the plan because they each think everyone else in the family—other than them—wants to go to Abilene. In reality, nobody wants to drive to Abilene for dinner! They don't learn that absolutely no one is really in agreement with the idea until they get back from the long trip and the dinner and share their real feelings that nobody wanted to go in the first place.

Lacking the full input from each of the other members of the group can produce such a false consensus. To guard against it, individual group members need to clearly state their views. Assumptions need to be checked. And a group leader should create the climate in which members feel free to state honestly and fully what they think.

Implications for Communication: Achieve Equilibrium in a Group

Equilibrium is a matter of finding the right balance, so in order to achieve it, group members must communicate with an attitude of give and take. Some specific ways to enhance group communication include the following:

- Assess how the group is moving toward disequilibrium.
- Change ineffective patterns of group communication.

Assess How the Group Is Moving Toward Disequilibrium   Each member of the group should be mindful of how the group is communicating as a whole. As you participate in a group, take stock of the tensions that arise and realize when the group is moving toward **disequilibrium:** how the group is losing a sense of balance. Try to open your eyes to the functioning of the entire group, rather than thinking only about your place or role in it.

You may, for instance, note how the group is doing a lot of work but is not very cohesive on a social level—in other words, "all work and no play." Since cohesiveness is comprised of two elements—task cohesion and social cohesion—something may need to be done to lighten the work-heavy group and enhance its interpersonal climate. Conversely, the group that has tilted the balance too far in the direction of being social may need to increase its focus on getting work done and decrease the interpersonal aspects.

Also take inventory of the various roles that members of your group perform, including the roles that you perform. Again, some give and take is needed for a group to achieve the proper balance in the performance of task-centered and social-centered roles. As you examine how various roles are performed, you might also determine whether certain members are performing self-centered roles that prevent the group from working well.

You can gain a similar awareness by examining the norms and rules that your group is following. Keep in mind that many norms are invisible, so to speak, until we take a moment to think consciously about them. Once you have identified the norms of the group, think about how those norms facilitate effectiveness. This assessment will also disclose how the various members of your group (you included) are motivated by interpersonal needs for inclusion, control, and affection.

As you make such an inventory, you may recognize some of the values of cooperation and conformity that are helpful for achieving the group's goals. At the same time, you may see ways in which your group is ineffective because of excessive pressures toward conformity.

Change Ineffective Patterns of Group Communication   Your responsibility for the group extends beyond observation. You also ought to make changes that will bring the group back into balance. There are two valuable ways that you can communicate with other group members and change ineffective patterns of group communication: You can talk about what you see as the problem, and you can change your own behavior when you see yourself as a contributor to group ineffectiveness.

On the first matter, use **meta-communication** to discuss the ways that your group is experiencing imbalance. Recall from our module on interpersonal relationships that meta-communication is talking about how we communicate. As defined by Watzlawick, Beavin, and Jackson (1967), episodes of meta-communication occur "when we no longer use communication to communicate but to communicate about communication" (p. 40).

As a group member who engages in meta-communication, you are performing the vital role of *evaluator/critic.* This is not always an easy role to perform, for you may face

---

disequilibrium   Being out of balance; occurs when components of a system are not experiencing equilibrium such as when a group's members are not able to resolve tension between competing values.

meta-communication   Communicating about communication; may be used to explore the underlying assumptions, values, background, and motivations for how we communicate.

strong forces of opposition. Ironically, a group that is out of balance sometimes prefers to stay dysfunctional and unproductive. In playing the part of evaluator/critic, you may find it valuable to provide members with support and understanding as you describe the problem as you see it. Your efforts at meta-communication may very well engender constructive changes for the group.

Another vital group role that you can perform is what Benne and Sheats (1948) call the *standard setter*. This is the person who uses meta-communication to articulate how group members should develop a norm for more productive interaction. Alternately, the standard setter may remind members when one of the group's norms or rules is not being followed.

Sometimes, groups invite help from outside their membership. A trained facilitator can help identify problems in a group's patterns of communication and guide individual members in making the changes needed to bring the group back to a state of equilibrium.

While meta-communication is an overt form of talking about patterns of communication in order to change them, you can also bring a group back into balance by using a more covert approach: that is, by simply changing the way you communicate in the group. Examining group behavior from a general systems perspective points out that every member of the group can have an impact on the group as a whole.

Recall the principle of interdependence (or holism), which states that each individual in the group affects the whole. This notion is aptly explained using the metaphor of dancing. Suppose that you are dancing with a partner. The tempo of the music is slow and so your movements are slow, as well. But then, the tempo picks up. The slow dance has been jazzed up. As you change your movements to adjust to the music, so will your dance partner.

As a responsible group member, you can change how the group as a whole communicates by taking the initiative to change yourself. That may mean making a simple statement like "I am going to get to work on Project X" at a time when everyone else is deeply involved in making small talk. Or it may mean asserting yourself to take on a social role or task role that needs to be performed. You may make a significant change when you sacrifice one of your own needs for the needs of the group or give acknowledgement and encouragement to another member who is making accommodations for the group.

Sometimes, one person can—and must—stand up to an entire group that has become overly conformist and may be rushing toward a bad decision as a result of groupthink or the type of false consensus described as the *Abilene Paradox*. Simply changing your own pattern of compliance, raising questions, and asserting yourself in the role of devil's advocate can bring a group back into balance. The classic film *Twelve Angry Men*, which starred Henry Fonda, dramatically portrays such a scenario. The film is shot almost entirely inside the jury room as members of the jury deliberate a murder case. Most members of the jury are playing self-centered roles, and it is rushing toward a guilty verdict without having examined all of the evidence of the case in a critical fashion. The film depicts how one person can turn around a dysfunctional group by earning the respect of others and by encouraging them to become effective critical thinkers and responsible jurors. The film also offers a good illustration of leadership.

6.4

RAPID REVIEW

6.9

Leadership

leadership Comprises those behaviors that guide a group toward accomplishing its goals.

LEARNING OBJECTIVE

6.4

Leadership is another important factor in the success of small groups and organizations. It can be thought of as comprising those behaviors that guide a group toward accomplishing its goals. Leadership can be understood in terms of three theories or models:

- *Leadership as influence:* How particular members use a style of leadership to guide the group to accomplish its goals.
- *Emergent leadership:* How particular members are perceived by others in the group as fulfilling leadership functions.
- *Relational leadership:* How particular members relate to followers as transactional and transformational leaders.

6.11

Leadership as Influence

The theory that effective leadership is rooted in influence can be illustrated by considering the classical styles of leadership defined by White and Lippit (1953). While their focus was the study of small-group behavior, White and Lippit borrowed their terminology from the study of politics and described these different styles of influence:

- *Authoritarian leadership* exerts a high level of control over group decisions. The leader may maintain a significant amount of distance from his or her followers. In the most extreme form, decisions are made by a single person and imposed upon the group.
- *Democratic leadership* emphasizes participation by the whole group in shared decision making. Democratic leaders interact with followers and energize members to become involved in the group's activities.
- *Laissez-faire leadership* emphasizes individual decision making by delegating responsibilities and power to members of the group, who act in an autonomous manner. This more relaxed style of leadership allows individuals to work independent of one another.

6.13

This classical model of leadership styles might be a useful tool for helping you see how leadership affects the way that decisions are made. Consider these questions: Which style of leadership is best? When you think of yourself in a leadership role, which style would you most likely use? Which would you prefer in someone who is leading you? Many times, these questions can be answered by considering the task to be performed and the level of expertise of group members.

Authoritarian Leadership **Authoritarian leadership** is most effective when decisions have to be made quickly. Likewise, it will likely work well when group members are relatively inexperienced and need a substantial amount of direction from a leader. In other words, authoritarian leaders are effective in situations that require that someone take charge.

Democratic Leadership **Democratic leadership** takes much more time and interaction with members. After all, the goal of democratic decision making is to hear from everyone and then reach agreement about which of the various perspectives to follow. This style of leadership is particularly useful when a task is complex and the exchange of differing points of view will give everyone a better understanding of it. Since members of the group will each have had their say in the decision, they will likely feel a greater sense of commitment to and responsibility for the group's effort.

Laissez-Faire Leadership There are also situations in which **laissez-faire leadership** works best. For instance, when the task the group must complete does not require a great deal of interaction, members can successfully do their parts on their own. You may wonder whether this is leadership at all. Indeed, some people refer to laissez-faire leadership as *nonleadership.*

authoritarian leadership A style of leadership that is characterized by a high degree of control and influence on the part of a leader.

democratic leadership A style of leadership that emphasizes participation by all members of a group in shared decision making and control.

laissez-faire leadership A style of leadership that delegates responsibilities and enables individual members to make decisions and work autonomously.

Consultation and coordination are needed for laissez-faire leadership to work. If the members of the group are self-motivated and follow through on doing their parts, some general coordination may be all that is needed. On the other hand, if individual members fail to take responsibility, laissez-faire leadership can result in a sense of drift.

Emergent Leadership

The theory of **emergent leadership,** which was developed by Bormann (1969), holds that certain members of the group will be perceived as performing important leadership functions. Many times, this will be a member of the group who has earned the role of leader by gaining the support of followers.

Emergent Leadership in Leaderless Groups   Bormann's studies of leadership were conducted with *leaderless groups,* or groups that are formed without anyone being designated to head them. What happens in these groups is that members gradually vie with one another to assume leadership functions. When the group begins, any of its members could assume the leadership role. But as time goes on, the group eliminates some of its members from contention based on their initial group behaviors. (See Figure 6.3.)

Key factors involved in being eliminated include the perception that someone is not capable of leading the group (perhaps because of timid behavior or lack of involvement and commitment to the group) or that he or she is overly dogmatic and inflexible (as in the case of someone who is too forceful and aggressive). Some members may decline to assume leadership functions, perhaps even declaring themselves unwilling or unable to do so.

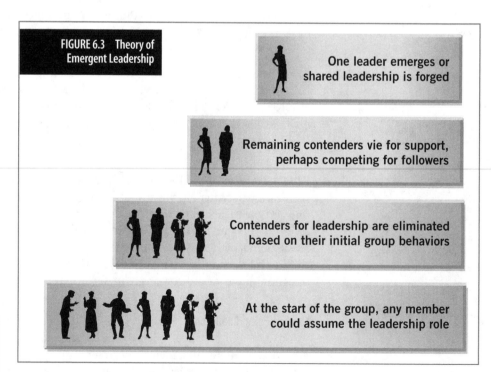

FIGURE 6.3   Theory of Emergent Leadership

One leader emerges or shared leadership is forged

Remaining contenders vie for support, perhaps competing for followers

Contenders for leadership are eliminated based on their initial group behaviors

At the start of the group, any member could assume the leadership role

emergent leadership   The theory that certain members of the group will be perceived as performing important leadership functions and therefore be accorded leadership status.

Certain members of the group will be perceived as having leadership qualities.
Source: Based on Bormann, 1969.

As members of the group continue to work together, a leadership struggle may develop, in which the leading contenders of the group compete for followers. A leader is *chosen* when most members of the group agree implicitly or explicitly that a particular person should guide them. Bormann explains that this often occurs when members see a particular person as contributing valuable leadership assets to the group.

While many groups are headed by a single member, there are situations in which more than one leader may emerge. In these cases, leadership is done collaboratively.

6.14

Emergent Leadership and Designated Leaders   The theory of emergent leadership suggests that leaders perform in certain ways that make people want to be led by them. But what happens when someone is designated as a leader (especially when authority was vested by sources outside the group) and may not have the full support of followers?

Perhaps you have been in a situation in which a designated leader, such as a work supervisor who holds authority to lead by virtue of his or her job title, was not effective and thus the members of the group did not look to him or her for leadership. In such a situation, the members of the group might look among themselves for real leadership.

What counts most in the theory of emergent leadership is not the title someone holds but how the members of the group perceive him or her as having the authority to lead the group.

Relational Leadership

The third theory of leadership is based on how leaders form a relationship with their followers. Burns (1978) defines *leadership* as "leaders inducing followers to act for certain goals that represent the values and the motivations—the wants and needs, the aspirations and expectations—of both leaders and followers" (p. 19).

There are two ways in which leaders and their followers relate to one another: via *transactional leadership* and via *transformational leadership*. The two can be differentiated in terms of the kinds of motivation that leaders use as they relate to followers.

Transactional Leadership   According to Burns, **transactional leadership** involves an exchange between leaders and followers—a give and take. The followers give their support to the leader and work productively for the good of 6.8 the group. In return, the leader offers rewards and encouragement to insure that followers continue to participate in the group. When the followers fail to contribute, the exchange may involve punishment that is enforced by the leader. Effective transactional leaders recognize the needs and interests of their followers and attempt to satisfy those needs. Transactional leaders may also use negative sanctions or threaten to withhold their efforts to meet followers' needs as forms of negative motivation.

You may be able to relate to this type of leadership from your own work experiences. Some companies and managers use systems of rewards and punishments to motivate workers. Again, it is a matter of exchange: If you perform well, you will get rewards, such as a pay raise or a bonus. If you are a responsible and effective team member, you will get high marks on your performance appraisal. If you don't perform well, however, you will suffer the consequences, perhaps ultimately losing your job.

The "bottom line" of transactional leadership is that it appeals to the self-interests of all parties. The leader gets what he or she wants in terms of the followers' performance, and the followers gain rewards and avoid punishment.

Transformational Leadership   According to Burns (1978), **transformational leadership** involves a higher level of motivation than self-interest. It "occurs when one or more

transactional leadership   A form of relational leadership that involves an exchange between leaders and followers—a give and take.

transformational leadership   A form of relational leadership that involves a higher level of motivation than self-interest; leaders and followers engage one another so as to raise levels of morality and motivation.

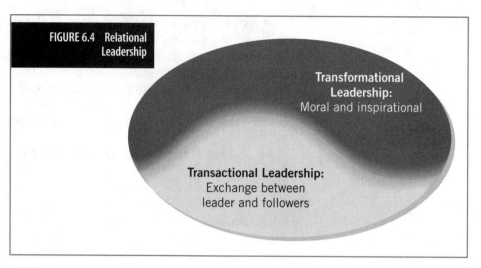

FIGURE 6.4 Relational Leadership

Transformational Leadership:
Moral and inspirational

Transactional Leadership:
Exchange between
leader and followers

Effective relational leadership is often a matter of combining elements of both transformational and transactional leadership. The two are not opposites but rather complementary forms.

Source: Based on Burns, 1978.

persons engage with others in such a way that leaders and followers raise one another to higher levels of morality and motivation" (p. 20).

In studying leadership in the political arena, Burns has observed how transformational leaders are often charismatic persons who are able to create a noble and heroic vision. Such leaders appeal to the core values of their followers. Many effective transformational leaders call upon followers to make sacrifices and transcend their own self-centered motivations.

VIDEO VIEW

6.9

Combining Transactional and Transformational Leadership   Effective relational leadership is often a matter of combining elements of both transactional and transformational leadership. Indeed, these two aspects of relational leadership are not opposites but complementary forms that can be used together (see Figure 6.4).

To illustrate this concept, Burns has identified a number of great political leaders. A historic example of someone who led in both the transactional and transformational manners was Franklin D. Roosevelt, who served as president from 1933 to 1945 and led the United States throughout the Great Depression and World War II. Roosevelt, according to Burns, was a skillful politician who knew how to employ the give and take of transactional leadership to make the kinds of political deals that were needed to enact the policies and programs that he wanted. At the same time, Roosevelt was a transformational leader who offered his fellow Americans a compelling vision of the nation's future.

While Burns has focused principally on political leadership, Bass (1985) has done extensive research on how the concepts of relational leadership apply in organizational and small-group communication contexts. Like Burns, Bass emphasizes the way that effective leadership combines aspects of transactional and transformational relationships. Namely, leadership of a small group may be transactional when it involves an exchange and transformational when it involves motivating others to a higher vision.

THINK ABOUT THIS

6.9

Anybody Can Lead   Before leaving this topic, it must be said that *anyone* in a group can and should exercise leadership in many situations. It's very easy to sit back and let others take control. Individuals who take this approach not only avoid the work and responsibility of leadership but also have the satisfaction of being able to blame someone else for the group's problems. Transformational leadership is exercised from the bottom of groups as well as from the top. Everyone has the opportunity to be a leader.

Thembi Scott (2002), a student from the University of Maryland, described this concept very eloquently when she appeared before a committee of the House of Representatives on April 11, 2002. Scott, along with several other student interns who participated in the James McGregor Burns Academy of Leadership, traveled to South Africa during the summer of 2001. Scott went to learn about apartheid and the work of Nelson Mandela. She described her experience as follows:

6.12

> Prior to even learning about the study abroad trip sponsored by the Academy of Leadership here at the University of Maryland, I had digested the autobiography of Nelson Mandela (*Long Walk to Freedom*) as if it were an adventure novel or better yet a how-to manual for societal revolution. You can imagine my awe when I found myself standing on Robben Island, the former location of the prison where many of the freedom fighters who had struggled against apartheid were imprisoned. Suddenly, the very scenes I had only previously read about came alive in three-dimensions.

Scott learned that many people—not just the people at the top—in the anti-apartheid movement had exercised transformational leadership. From her encounters with a less well-known freedom fighter named Maggie and others who had "the gumption to make a difference, to make a change," Scott gained a new understanding of leadership. As she explained to members of the congressional committee:

> I began to understand that leadership is more than fancy titles or positions; it is whenever we make a choice to make change, no matter where we are or what our station in life. Our decision to change our present reality is our first step into our role as "Leader." This struck me as such an epiphany because I realized that I myself can commit to making a difference just as surely as Maggie, in fact, I have very little excuse not to—I do not face such great odds or consequences for my actions as she. I can make changes, in big and little ways. In fact, many of the things I do already I am realizing would fall under this expanded definition of leadership. This experience made me realize that in my own ways, I too am a leader.

Implications for Communication: Learn Effective Leadership

Effective leadership is vital to successful small groups as well as larger organizations. You can enhance your effectiveness in three ways:

- Recognize different styles of leadership.
- Be ready to assume a leadership role.
- Combine the facets of transactional and transformational leadership.

Recognize Different Styles of Leadership Leadership is not a "one size fits all" matter. The classical styles of leadership as influence—authoritarian, democratic, and laissez-faire—are best suited to different kinds of situations. As you communicate in a group or when you assert a leadership role, you can decide what kind of leadership will be most effective.

When circumstances call for a quick decision or the group needs a great deal of direction, it may be wise to use an authoritarian style. On the other hand, if individual group members group are capable of working on their own and need a minimal amount of coordination and guidance, a laissez-faire style will work well. When the group will benefit by soliciting input from each member and hearing diverse points of view, a democratic style of leadership will likely be the best approach.

Your mindfulness as a group member or group leader should help you to see when a less effective style of leadership is being followed. If strong-armed direction by an authoritarian leader means that good ideas aren't being heard, try to change the direction of the group. That will involve playing the role of group critic or devil's advocate to identify the problem and suggest a change. You may have to take the risk to stand up to others who are not serving your group well. If a group is taking too long to deliberate a matter that could better be handled by a single decision maker, you may need to speak up and point out that democratic leadership is slowing the group down. If your group is going adrift for lack of guidance from a laissez-faire leader, you may need to ask for more direction or more group input for decision making.

Be Ready to Assume a Leadership Role   You may need to take on a leadership role yourself. This is often the case in leaderless groups for which leaders have not been designated or appointed from outside the group and in the circumstances in which designated leaders are not performing their roles well. Some of the specific leadership behaviors that you can perform are as follows:

- Take responsibility for leadership in your group, rather than allowing the group to fail.
- Give the group guidance on its task.
- Organize group efforts.
- Encourage others to participate so that they will offer ideas and contribute to the collective critical thinking of the group.
- Facilitate conflict resolution in a group.
- Build social cohesion in a group by encouraging appropriate personal sharing, creating a positive interpersonal climate, and satisfying the interpersonal needs of members.

By demonstrating these qualities of leadership, you will likely emerge as a leader in your group.

Combine the Facets of Transactional and Transformational Leadership   Being an effective leader involves creating a relationship with your followers. Thus, effective leaders are able to combine facets of transactional and transformational leadership. As you lead from any position within a group, use some of the qualities of relational leadership.

In creating a checklist for effectiveness, Alimo-Metcalfe and Alban-Metcalfe (2001) list these factors of transformational leadership that encompass transactional aspects:

6.10

- *Shows genuine concern for others:* Takes an interest in group members' well-being and is concerned with developing their strengths.
- *Demonstrates political sensitivity and skills:* Understands the political dynamics of leading and works with members to achieve results.
- *Is decisive, determined, and confident:* Is decisive when required; is prepared to make difficult decisions; is confident in own abilities and resilient to setbacks.
- *Demonstrates integrity, trustworthiness, honesty, and openness:* Makes it easy for others to admit mistakes and to develop trust; guides decision making based on moral and ethical principles.
- *Empowers others and develops their potential:* Trusts members to take stands on important issues and make decisions; delegates effectively and empowers members to use their potential.
- *Networks and promotes:* Develops a wide network of links to the external environment and promotes the achievements of the organization; effectively communicates the vision of the organization to the community.

- *Is accessible and approachable:* Is accessible to staff at all levels; keeps in touch using face-to-face communication.
- *Clarifies boundaries and involves others in decisions:* Defines boundaries of responsibility and involves others when making decisions; keeps people informed of what is going on.
- *Encourages critical and strategic thinking:* Encourages others to question traditional approaches to tasks and to think of entirely new solutions to problems; encourages strategic rather than short-term thinking.

ASSESSING
YOUR SKILLS
6.5

ONLINE
JOURNAL
6.15

Leaders also assume the vital function of guiding public discussions. The next section will examine some of the techniques that members of a small group can use in problem-solving discussions.

THINK
ABOUT THIS
6.10

Techniques for Problem-Solving Discussions

LEARNING
OBJECTIVE
6.5

Brilhart (1986) defines a **problem-solving group** as one that "discusses for the sake of devising a course of action to solve a problem" (p. 4). In this final section of the module, we will examine how to organize a problem-solving discussion. Sometimes, a group holds a private discussion to solve a problem, while other times, the discussion is carried on for the benefit of an audience.

A problem-solving discussion may be organized in one of two ways:

- By developing a problem-solving agenda
- By organizing a public discussion format

Developing a Problem-Solving Agenda

For most of the last 100 years, academic approaches to group problem solving have drawn on the work of John Dewey, the pragmatist philosopher who developed the stages of reflective thinking in his seminal book *How We Think* (1910). Dewey proposed that thought processes follow a logical series of steps.

WEB
ACTIVITY
6.13

Dewey's method focused principally on how individuals solve problems. However, communication theorists have applied his method to group discussions of problems. An example of this is Brilhart's (1986) **general procedural model for problem solving,** which comprises a series of five steps that are based on Dewey's steps for individual reflective thinking (see Figure 6.5):

1. Problem description and analysis
2. Generation and elaboration of possible solutions
3. Evaluation of possible solutions
4. Solution decision
5. Planning for implementation

This model can be followed by a group leader or by group members who want to create a five-step agenda for holding a discussion. A **problem-solving agenda** is a sequence of topics that is followed as the group members interact to solve a problem. The topics are often phrased as questions, which is the approach we will use in the following sections.

Step 1: What Is the Nature of the Problem Facing Us?   During step 1, group members attempt to understand the problem they are collectively trying to solve. This often involves asking how the problem affects the group and perhaps others, as well. Note that

problem-solving group   A group formed to discuss a problem or issue for the purpose of resolving it.

general procedural model for problem solving   A five-step method of systematically solving a problem; entails (1) problem description and analysis; (2) generation and elaboration of possible solutions; (3) evaluation of possible solutions; (4) solution decision; and (5) planning for implementation.

problem-solving agenda   A sequence of topics that is followed to organize a discussion; often phrased as questions; organized in a logical sequence for group reflective thinking.

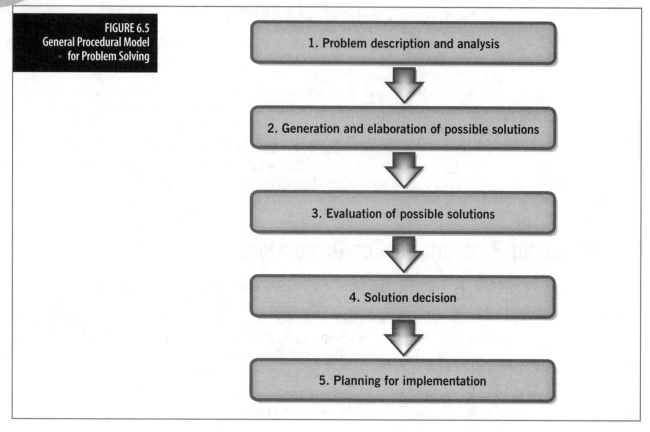

FIGURE 6.5
General Procedural Model for Problem Solving

1. Problem description and analysis

2. Generation and elaboration of possible solutions

3. Evaluation of possible solutions

4. Solution decision

5. Planning for implementation

This model can be followed by a group leader or by group members who want to create a five-step agenda for holding a discussion.

Source: Brilhart, 1986.

at this early stage in the process, it is premature to talk about possible solutions. Instead, Brilhart (1986) suggests that a number of other questions should be answered first:

■ What is unsatisfactory at present?
■ What does the problem mean to us?
■ Who is affected by the problem?
■ What are the contributing causes of the problem?
■ In general, what is the desired outcome?

Note that an *outcome* is not a specific concrete solution to the problem but rather a more general goal related to some aspect of the problem. In fact, depending on the complexity of the problem, it may have several desired outcomes (perhaps related to budget, safety, scheduling, and so on).

To illustrate this step, let's consider an example: Suppose that you are part of a group in a communication class that wants to tackle the problem of a lack of parking places on campus. There is a common joke among students that when you buy a parking permit, it is really more like a *hunting permit* to seek a parking space. There is no guarantee of being able to find a space.

6.11

If you and your group jumped immediately to the solution phase of the discussion, you might suggest that the trustees of your school should simply provide more parking spaces by creating a new lot or building a parking garage. These might seem obvious outcomes of the discussion, but how do you know they are the only possible outcomes or even reasonable outcomes? Before proposing a solution, you need to study the problem for a while.

Your questions for this first step of the discussion might be a series of primary and secondary questions that include topics such as the following:

1. What is the current availability of parking spaces on campus?
2. How does the parking problem affect students?
   - Does the parking shortage affect safety?
   - Does the parking shortage undermine the educational mission of the college?
3. Which groups of students are most affected by the difficulty of finding a parking space?
   - Is availability affected by time of the day?
   - Is the problem greater in certain areas of the campus?
   - Are certain groups of students more likely to be affected by the parking shortage (for instance, students who are physically challenged, who are older, who are commuters, etc.)?
4. Why is there a shortage of parking spaces?
5. What are the desired outcomes?
   - How can safety be improved?
   - How can conditions be improved for those groups of students most affected by the shortage?
   - How can the school's resources best be used?

Generating a list of questions like this can be especially valuable for doing research about a problem. In solving the parking shortage, your group may need to check public records and interview officials on campus to learn more about what's behind the shortage. You can then bring that information back to the group for a private discussion or share it with members of an audience if you are doing a public discussion.

Step 2: What Can Be Done to Solve the Problem?   Brilhart (1986) suggests that in step 2, the group should think about the entire range of possible solutions. This is the time to be creative! To get the ideas flowing, brainstorm answers to questions like these:

1. How could we create more parking spaces?
2. How could we make better use of existing parking spaces?
3. How else could students get to campus other than by driving their own cars?

Again, the group needs to resist the idea of settling on a particular solution. The goal is to be as creative as possible and come up with a number of alternatives for solving the problem. In this step, you are generating ideas, but **not** critically assessing them. The reason for withholding critical scrutiny at this point in the process is that you do not want to inhibit any members of the group from expressing their ideas. The time for a critical examination will come later in the problem-solving process.

Step 3: What Are the Relative Pros and Cons of the Possible Solutions?   Now, says Brilhart (1986), you should begin to weigh the choices and critically examine each. To do that systematically, you need to determine what criteria to use in evaluating all of the possible solutions. That is, you need to measure each solution against the same standards.

For the parking space problem, your criteria might include items like these:

1. What are the positive outcomes of each solution?
2. What are the negative outcomes of each solution?
3. What are the practical limitations of each solution?
4. What groups or individuals will need to accept the solution?

When conducting a group discussion, this is a good time to narrow down the choices by eliminating the ones that don't satisfy the criteria. But this should be done systematically and deliberately. Spend some time weighing each of the options and make sure that everyone gets a voice and votes about the relative pros and cons of the various options.

Step 4: What Seems to Be the Best Solution That Everyone Can Support?   Brilhart's (1986) fourth step is a continuation of the third step in that it involves finalizing the decision. Before moving ahead, it's vital that everyone in the group is on board with the decision.

For some groups and for some problems, this is a relatively easy matter. Even so, it's important to be on guard against groupthink. Perhaps it would be useful to have one or more devil's advocates in the group. In deciding how to solve the shortage of parking spaces, they could ask questions like these:

1.   Have we fully weighed all of the options?
2.   Are there any negative consequences that we haven't examined?
3.   Do we need to develop a compromise solution that dissenting members of the group can agree on?

Step 5: How Can We Implement Our Solution?   The final step is the implementation of the decision (Brilhart, 1986). It involves working out the practical details and monitoring whether the problem has been solved once the solution has been put in place. Two main questions can be asked here:

1.   Who should do what, when, where, and how in order to put our solution into practice?
2.   How will we judge whether our solution has been effective?

In the parking space example, implementing the solution might involve first writing a report to those who are in a position of authority to act on your recommendation. With their support, you could then proceed with the details of your plan. Judging whether your solution has been effective will take some time and observation. Specifically, you will need to determine whether the issues that led to discovery of the problem have been eliminated or at least improved.

6.12

Brilhart's (1986) general procedural model for problem solving is intended to be a flexible instrument. That is, a group leader or group members can adapt the five steps for approaching different kinds of problems.

6.11

Organizing a Public Discussion Format

6.10

public discussion format   A structure for discussing a problem or issue in the presence of an audience; may be a panel discussion, a symposium, and/or a forum.

A final consideration for a group that will hold its discussion before an audience is to decide on a **public discussion format.** There are three types of formats:

■   A *panel discussion* is often organized using the questions of the problem-solving agenda and involves the give and take of dialogue. A moderator asks the questions on the agenda, and group members respond in a somewhat conversational manner.

■   A *symposium* is an organized sequence of somewhat formal speeches that are presented by group members and focus on particular aspects of the topic. A symposium is effective in presenting different perspectives on a single issue.

■   A *forum* is a question-and-answer session in which the audience members express their concerns about an issue. It usually occurs after the group has made its initial presentation. A forum may be used in conjunction with a panel or a symposium.

Holding a public discussion is an effective way for an organization or small group to communicate with an audience. You have likely observed or participated in discussions such as this. For instance, the members of a city council or campus leadership group might hold a public meeting to assess a problem and develop a solution. That meeting might start out with some kind of presentation to the audience, such as a symposium, and then move to a public forum, in which audience members can make statements or ask questions.

The format of a panel discussion or a symposium can also be adapted to contexts other than problem-solving discussion groups. For instance, news programs such as *Wall Street Week in Review* and *Washington Week in Review,* which are broadcast on PBS, bring together experts who commonly sit around a table to share their respective viewpoints about current events and issues. In addition, professional societies often use the symposium format for researchers to present their findings at meetings and conventions.

Implications for Communication: Use Effective Problem-Solving Techniques

Use an Orderly Method of Problem Solving   Presenting a public discussion should not be done haphazardly. Doing so requires a systematic effort by the group's organizer or in some cases by all of the group's members to plan an orderly method for conducting the discussion. The key is *plan.* There are some practical considerations, as well:

- Plan in advance so the discussion will be systematic.
- Outline an agenda of questions such as Brilhart's general procedural model for problem solving.
- Make sure the agenda for discussion is thorough and that ample time is given for reflective thinking.
- Provide members of the group with the agenda well in advance of the discussion.

Choose the Format That's Appropriate for a Private or a Public Discussion   If you are in charge of organizing a public discussion, you will need to do some special planning. To plan a public panel discussion, symposium, or forum, address the following:

- Invite members to participate, and ensure that different points of view will be considered.
- Plan the progression of topics. For a panel discussion, that entails using an agenda of questions. For a symposium, determine the most logical order for the presentations. For a forum, determine what sort of presentation should precede the question-and-answer session.
- Arrange the physical space for the discussion. Consider what furniture arrangement will facilitate interaction among members of a panel, how to set up a speaker's rostrum for participants in a symposium, or how to ensure that the audience members in a forum can hear and be heard.
- Assign one person to serve as the moderator. In a panel discussion, the moderator should introduce the members of the panel, ask the questions on the group's agenda, and facilitate the interaction of group members. At the conclusion of a panel, the moderator may also provide a summary and thank the participants. For a symposium, the moderator's job is to introduce each participant before he or she is going to speak. The moderator for a symposium may also provide a summary at the end. The moderator of a forum will field questions from the audience and perhaps direct them to specific participants.

ASSESSING
YOUR SKILLS
6.6

✔
RAPID
REVIEW
6.12

Summary

Interpersonal communication in a professional and public context requires competence in a variety of communication skills. One such skill is interviewing. Planning for an interview should be based on the predetermined goal of the interview, whether information sharing, persuading, counseling and helping others, or dealing with employment matters such as job seeking or evaluating performance. The interviewer's tasks include developing a set of questions, reviewing materials relevant to the interview or the person being interviewed, and conducting the interview. The interviewee should also prepare by anticipating questions and doing research, especially when interviewing for a job.

In the contemporary workplace, a worker is likely to be part of a large public or private organization. The larger organizational culture serves as the context for small-group communication. Organizational and small-group communication may occur as face-to-face interaction or through virtual interaction with the help of communication technologies.

In the workplace, small groups are typically task oriented. Groups whose tasks are completed in a short period of time may be temporary, whereas groups with long-term projects may develop a long history of interacting. In either case, members of small groups develop a degree of interdependence as they work together and operate as part of an open system that is responsive to its environment.

As systems, groups also seek equilibrium. Successful groups deal with the tensions between being productive and being social; between playing task-centered roles and social-centered roles; between satisfying group goals and individual goals; and between developing conformity and encouraging dissent. Too much conformity can lead the group to making poor decisions as the result of groupthink.

Leadership is also vital to the successful functioning of groups and organizations. One theory of leadership suggests that it is a form of influence that may be exercised in several different ways: as authoritarian, democratic, or laissez-faire. The theory of emergent leadership proposes that members of groups perceive particular individuals as possessing leadership qualities. Leaders of organizations and small groups also form relationships with followers that involve transactional and transformational aspects.

Finally, the effectiveness of small groups whose aim is to solve problems is enhanced when they use a systematic procedure for problem solving. Some problem-solving groups benefit from developing a structured agenda that guides members to make a systematic assessment of problems and solutions. A group may also present its discussion to an audience by using a panel discussion, a symposium, or a forum.

PRACTICE
TEST

References

Aiken, M., Vanjami, M., & Krosp, J. (1995). Group decision support systems. *Review of Business,* 16, no. 3, 38–43.

Alimo-Metcalfe, B. A., & Alban-Metcalfe, R. J. (2001). The development of a new transformational leadership questionnaire. *Journal of Occupational and Organizational Psychology,* 74, 1–26.

Anderson, C. M., Martin, M. M., & Riddle, B. L. (2001). Small group relational satisfaction scale: Development, reliability and validity. *Communication Studies,* 52, no. 3, 220–234.

Bass, B. M. (1985). *Leadership and performance beyond expectations.* New York: Free Press.

Benne, K. D., & Sheats, P. (1948). Functional roles of group members. *Journal of Social Issues,* 4, no. 2, 41–49.

Bernthal, P. R., & Insko, C. A. (1993) Cohesiveness without groupthink: The interactive effects of social and task cohesion. *Group & Organization Management,* 18, no. 1, 66–88.

Bormann, E. G. (1969). *Discussion and group methods: Theory and practice.* New York: Harper and Row.

Brilhart, J. K. (1986). *Effective group discussion.* 5th ed. Dubuque, IA: William C. Brown.

Burns, J. M. (1978). *Leadership.* New York: Harper and Row.

Carron, A. V., Widmeyer, W. N., & Brawley, L. R. (1985). The development of an instrument to assess cohesion in sport teams: The group environment questionnaire. *Journal of Sport Psychology,* 7, 244–266.

Chartered Institute of Personnel and Development. (2002, December 10). Exit interviews set stage for policy reforms. *Personnel Today,* p. 51.

Cohan, J. A. (2002, October 15). "I didn't know" and "I was only doing my job": Has corporate governance careened out of control? A case study of Enron's information myopia. *Journal of Business Ethics,* 40, no. 3, 275–300.

Dewey, J. (1910). *How we think.* Boston: D. C. Heath.

Fisher, B. A. (1982). The pragmatic perspective of human communication: A view from systems theory. In F. Dance (ed.), *Human communication theory* (pp. 192–219). New York: Harper Collins.

Geber, B. (1995). Virtual teams. *Training,* 32, no. 4, 36–41.

Grice, H. P. (1975). Logic and conversation. In P. Cole (ed.), *Syntax and semantics, Vol.3: Speech acts* (pp. 41–58). New York: Academic Press.

Harvey, J. B. (1988). *The Abilene paradox and other meditations on management.* San Francisco: Jossey-Bass Publishers.

Janis, I. L. (1989). *Crucial decisions.* New York: The Free Press.

Kiesler, C. A., & Kiesler, S. (1970). *Conformity.* Reading, MA: Addison-Wesley Publishing Company.

Kiser, K. (1999). Working on world time. *Training,* 36, no. 3, 28–35.

McNamara, R. S. (2002, November). Fifty years after 13 days. *Arms Control Today,* 32, no. 9, 4–9.

National Telecommunications and Information Administration. (2002). *A nation online: How Americans are expanding their use of the Internet.* Available online: <www.ntia.doc.gov/ntia-home/dn/html/toc.htm>. Accessed August 18, 2003.

O'Neil, H. F., Jr. (1997). *Workforce readiness: Competencies and assessment.* Mahwah, NJ: Lawrence Erlbaum Associates.

Peterson, M. S. (1997). Personnel interviewers' perceptions of the importance and adequacy of applicants' communication skills. *Communication Education,* 46, 287–291.

Pious, R. M. (2001). The Cuban missile crisis and the limits of crisis management. *Political Science Quarterly,* 116, no. 1, 81–106.

Sawyer, K., & Smith, R. J. (2003, March 1). NASA's culture of certainty debate was muffled on risks to shuttle. *Washington Post,* p. A–1. Available online: <www.washingtonpost.com/wp-dyn/articles/A23858-2003Mar1.html>. Accessed August 18, 2003.

Searle, J. R. (1969). *Speech-acts: An essay in the philosophy of language.* London: Cambridge University Press.

Schutz, W. C. (1966). *The interpersonal underworld.* Palo Alto, CA: Science and Behavior Books.

Scott, T. (2002). *On life and leadership in South Africa.* Testimony delivered April 10 before the U.S. House of Representatives. Available online: <www.academy.umd.edu/education/student_showcase/SouthAfrica/SA2001/index_event.htm>. Accessed August 15, 2003.

U.S. Census Bureau. (2002a). *Federal government civilian employment.* Available online: <www.census.gov/govs/apes/00fedfun.txt>. Accessed August 18, 2003.

U.S. Census Bureau. (2002b). *Statistics of U.S. businesses.* Available online: <www.census.gov/csd/susb/susb2.htm#go00>. Accessed August 18, 2003.

U.S. Department of Commerce. (2002). *State and local governments employ more than 15 million.* Available online: <www.census.gov/Press-Release/www/2002/cb02-88.html>. Accessed August 18, 2003.

U.S. Department of Defense. (2002). *Military personnel statistics.* Available online: <www.dior.whs.mil/mmid/military/miltop.htm>. Accessed August 18, 2003.

U.S. Department of Labor. (1992). What work requires of schools: A SCANS report for America 2000. *Economic Development Review,* 10, 16–19. Available online: <wdr.doleta.gov/SCANS/whatwork/whatwork.html>. Accessed August 18, 2003.

Watson-Manheim, M. B., & Belanger, F. (2002). Exploring communication-based work processes in virtual work environments. In *Proceedings of the Hawaii International Conference on Systems Sciences.* Available online: <www.computer.org/proceedings/hicss/1435/volume8/14350272babs.htm>. Accessed August 18, 2003.

Watzlawick, P., Beavin, J. H., & Jackson, D. D. (1967). *The pragmatics of human communication: A study of interactional patterns, pathologies, and paradoxes.* New York: W. W. Norton.

White, R. K., & Lippit, R. (1953). Leader Behavior and Member Reaction in Three "Social Climates." In D. Cartwright & A. Zander (eds.), *Group Dynamics: Research and Theory.* Evanston: Row, Peterson.

Wilkinson, S. (1989, February 6). Decision-support tool streamlines meetings: A laptop takes on the ultimate target; unproductive meetings. *PC Week,* pp. 49–50.

Public
Speaking

Learning
Objectives

*After reading the module
and participating in the
activities, you will be able to:*

1 Understand the value of learning how to be a public speaker.

2 Understand the general goals of speaking and be able to use
strategies for identifying topics for presentations.

3 Understand the demographic and psychological methods of
audience analysis.

4 Understand the factors that comprise the speaking situation and
how to adapt your speech so that it meets the demands and
expectations of a situation.

5 Develop research skills for gathering information and organizing
ideas for a presentation.

6 Be able to create an effective structure for a presentation.

7 Be able to choose and implement a style of presentation for
performing a speech.

VIDEO VIEW

LEARNING OBJECTIVE

7.1

YOU MAY HAVE MANY OPPORTUNITIES to be a speaker or listener in public dialogues. In your workplace, you may be called on to present your ideas to co-workers or to an audience outside your company. In community and academic organizations, you may want to participate by expressing your views or sharing information. And as a student, you may be required to present a speech in which you report information or make an argument.

Sometimes, there are special occasions that we participate in to mark the rites of passage of our lives. We make toasts to congratulate the happy couple at a wedding or a commitment ceremony. We mark milestones in our lives and those around us with parties to welcome new births, to celebrate birthdays, and to honor anniversaries. We experience losses and participate in rites of grieving. On any of these occasions we participate with others who are assembled as public communicators.

In virtually any arena of public life—from corporations to religious institutions to community organizations—public speaking is a critical form of exercising leadership. By learning the principles of public speaking presented in this module, you will be able to prepare yourself to speak confidently to audiences and to be a responsive and critical audience member.

rhetoric The academic study of public speaking; theories of rhetoric emphasize the philosophical and ethical foundations of speech making and provide grounds for the critical analysis of public discourse.

deliberative speaking Speaking that involves discussion and debate of matters of policy, as in a legislative assembly.

Public Speaking and Society

forensic speaking Speaking that occurs in courts of law for determining issues of justice.

epideictic speaking Speaking that addresses the particular concerns of audiences on special occasions, often celebrating shared values and giving voice to shared feelings.

relational view of communication A theory of communication that focuses on how relational communities are created and how they provide a context for members of a community to share meaning with one another.

relational community The personal, social, or cultural context in which communicators interact with one another.

Rhetoric is the academic study of public speaking. From the start of formal and systematic education in rhetorical theory over 2,500 years ago, many societies have valued the contributions of public speakers. Rhetorical education has been the training ground for preparing citizens to participate fully in democracy, for deliberating policy in the public forum, and for debating matters of justice in the courts.

Traditional theories of rhetoric establish three types of public speaking: **deliberative speaking,** which involves discussion and debate of matters of policy; **forensic speaking,** which occurs in courts of law for determining issues of justice; and **epideictic speaking,** which addresses the particular concerns of audiences on special occasions, often celebrating shared values and giving voice to shared feelings.

Today, the focus in studying public speaking could also be called *public dialogue.* As we observed in Module One in discussing the **relational view of communication,** the interaction between a speaker and his or her audience takes place within the context of a **relational community.** Our focus on public speaking as a form of dialogue also reflects the concept that communication is an interactive process, in which both parties (the audience members as well as the speaker) collaborate to construct meaning. Regardless of the speaker's specific goal, he or she is intent on relating to an audience.

WEB ACTIVITY

7.1

In this module, you will learn how to plan a speech, following a "recipe" for public speaking. Knowing this recipe will also help you become a discerning and critical audi-

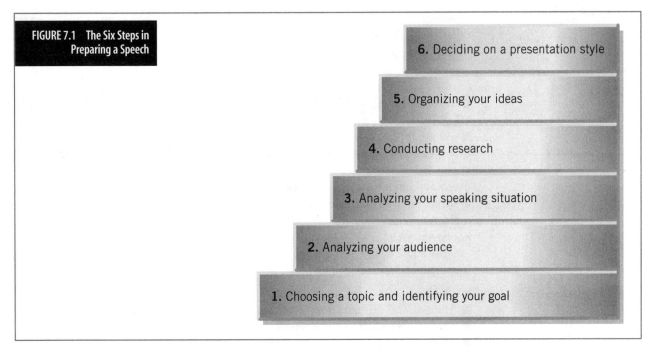

FIGURE 7.1   The Six Steps in Preparing a Speech

6. Deciding on a presentation style

5. Organizing your ideas

4. Conducting research

3. Analyzing your speaking situation

2. Analyzing your audience

1. Choosing a topic and identifying your goal

Following this "recipe" for preparing a speech will make the task a manageable one.

ence member. When you become an experienced chef, you not only know how to prepare food yourself but you also learn to savor a meal prepared by others. Public speaking, like good cooking, is an art. The artistic speaker, like the expert chef, will use a tried-and-true recipe as the basis for preparing an endless variety of new creations.

The public speaking "recipe" that we will follow in this module includes these six steps (see Figure 7.1):

1. Choosing a topic and identifying the goal of your speech
2. Analyzing your audience so that you can adapt your ideas to your listeners
3. Analyzing your speaking situation in order to develop a plan for your speech
4. Conducting research to develop the content of your speech
5. Organizing your ideas and developing an outline to structure your presentation
6. Deciding on a presentation style to relate with your audience

7.1

Choosing a Topic and Identifying the Goal of Your Speech

7.2

7.1

7.2

Imagine that you have just learned that you have to give a speech. At work, perhaps, your supervisor has asked you to attend a conference and make a presentation about the product that your team has been working on for the last year. Or maybe in one of the classes that you are taking, your instructor requires everyone to do a presentation in front of the class.

In many speaking situations, the choice of what to talk about will be made for you—for instance, the topic of a presentation at a conference. Your challenge in those situations is to limit the focus, or the range of the topic. In many other speaking situations—in your classes, for example—you will likely choose your own topic, or at least select from among a range of possibilities.

Brainstorming Possible Topics

If you are in the position of having to choose your own topic, you may wonder: What do I have to say? What will my audience be interested in hearing about? In answering these questions, think about starting points that you can use to develop topic ideas, especially for a classroom speech. Engage in a bit of brainstorming to generate a list of possibilities before you settle on a final topic. You might also talk with members of your audience or with a friend who knows you well.

7.1

7.3

Use some of the following as starting points for generating creative ideas (see Figure 7.2):

- Your personal experiences
- Professional expertise from your work or major field of study
- Your hobbies and special interests
- Current events
- Controversial political or social issues
- Your cultural and relational communities
- Your personal or political philosophy of life
- Your concerns about personal growth and well-being

For instance, Azadeh, whose niece was diagnosed with childhood leukemia, decided to draw on that personal experience as a starting point for her speech. She recognized that most of her audience knew little about childhood leukemia and thus chose to present an informative speech to explain the illness.

You may also draw on your professional expertise. Frederick, who works for an Internet service provider, became concerned about the problem of unsolicited e-mail messages, called *spam*, in the workplace. Brian, a firefighter, drew on his professional

Brainstorm to generate a list of possibilities before you settle on a final topic. Also talk with members of your audience or with a friend who knows you well.

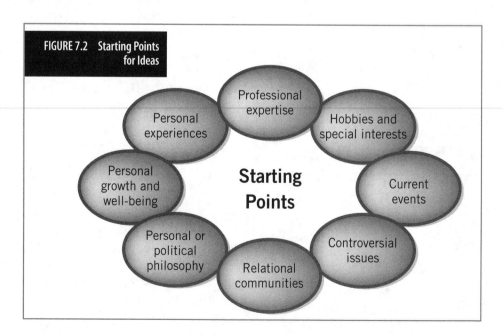

FIGURE 7.2   Starting Points for Ideas

expertise to urge members of his audience to install devices that monitor carbon monoxide levels in their homes. Melanie, a special education major, spoke about assistive technologies that help people who are physically challenged.

Hobbies and personal interests are another area to consider. That's what Sue did when she decided to talk about the history of NASCAR and what Dang did in choosing break dancing as his subject.

Current events can also pique your interest in a subject. Tammy decided to talk about the risks of using ephedra, an herbal dietary supplement that is sometimes taken by athletes to enhance performance and to lose weight. She became interested in this topic when she heard about a baseball player who had died, apparently as a result of taking ephedra in combination with diet pills.

Sometimes, current events and trends reflect ongoing controversies. A. J. chose the subject of cloning and stem cell research and decided to argue that a total ban on cloning would be undesirable because of some of the benefits of research connected with cloned cells.

Controversial topics often center on political and social questions about which people have intense feelings. For instance, the October 2002 sniper shootings in and near Washington, DC, raised questions about the death penalty for Shannon. She wondered whether the death penalty was appropriate for one of the defendants in that case, who was a juvenile. Doan Thao chose as her topic the rights of gay and lesbian couples and asked whether they should receive the same societal benefits accorded to married heterosexual couples.

Your cultural community and the various relational communities you belong to can also provide starting points. An Nguyet, who immigrated to the United States from Vietnam, decided to explain some of the beliefs of Caodaism, a Vietnamese religion that emerged in the twentieth century. Rasheen, whose cultural community favors arranged marriages, decided to explain how marriages are contracted in her native country. Both of these speeches also reflected the speakers' personal philosophies of life.

7.2

A host of possibilities can be found with topics related to personal growth and well-being. Sonja presented a speech about the value of sleep and the problems associated with getting too little or too much sleep. Kim focused on economic well-being and urged members of her audience to consider a systematic program of saving for retirement—beginning as early as one's late teens or early twenties. Janet talked about the kinds of preventive maintenance that a homeowner can do to prevent water damage after a snowstorm. Matt combined his expertise as a professional trainer and his concern for physical well-being by talking about the three elements basic to a well-rounded exercise program.

Clarifying Your Speaking Goal

After you have generated some broad ideas about a possible topic for your speech, the next step is to determine the goal of your speech. There are three primary types of goals for speaking:

- *Persuasive speaking* aims to advocate a position or move the audience to change their behavior.
- *Informative speaking* aims to enhance the audience's understanding.
- *Entertainment speaking* aims to evoke a pleasurable and aesthetic response from the audience.

In a given speaking situation, you may attempt to achieve any one of these goals or all three together, although you will usually have a primary goal that you are striving to

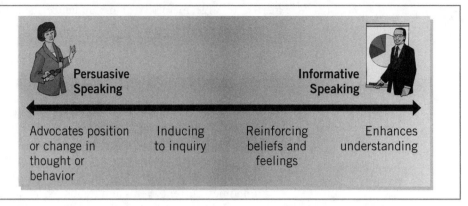

FIGURE 7.3   The Persuasive/Informative Continuum

Rather than drawing a categorical distinction between persuasive and informative speaking, it is more useful to think of them as opposing ends of a continuum of purposes or goals.

Source: Based on Wilson and Arnold, 1964.

accomplish. If you are taking a communication class, you may be assigned a particular goal for your speech.

Assigned types of speeches often have labels. For instance, you might be assigned to present a *how-to* or *demonstration speech,* in which you show your listeners how to do something. In that situation, your primary goal would be to *inform* your listeners. For another assignment, you might be asked to deliver a *persuasive speech,* in which you develop an argument on a certain issue or make the case for a particular solution to a problem.

Whenever you urge your audience to change what they believe or how they act, your primary goal is to persuade them. And to achieve that goal, you also need to provide your audience with information as to why they should be persuaded. Building an argument requires a clear exposition of the evidence that supports the argument.

Rather than drawing a categorical distinction between persuasive and informative speaking, it may be more useful to think of them as opposing ends of a continuum of purposes or goals (see Figure 7.3). That way, we can define a speech as being *primarily* persuasive or *mostly* informative while allowing elements of both. How close a speech is to either end of the persuasive/informative continuum is often revealed by how explicitly the speaker states the goal of his or her speech. And depending on where the speaker's goal falls along the continuum, audience members will be asked to respond differently.

Persuasive Speaking

Persuasive speaking involves a clear call for action, in that the speaker is asking audience members to change their mind and do what he or she is advocating. If you are in the audience for such a speech, you will have to decide whether you agree or disagree with the speaker. And in making that judgment, you will have to determine whether the speaker has provided you with good reasons for change.

Wilson and Arnold (1964), in their contemporary classic on public speaking, *Public Speaking as a Liberal Art,* have identified three key qualities of effective persuasion: desirability, justification, and motivation (see Figure 7.4).

persuasive speaking   Speaking in which the primary aim is to advocate a position or move the audience to change their behavior.

Desirability   In a persuasive speech, the speaker asserts a judgment, stating either implicitly or explicitly that something is good or bad or better or worse.

FIGURE 7.4 Qualities of Effective Persuasive Speaking	**Desirability** • A judgment that something is good or bad, better or worse	**Justification** • Based on self-interest • Based on reasoning and evidence • Based on source credibility	**Motivation** • Appeals to individual needs and drives

In deciding whether to be persuaded, the audience must determine whether the speaker has provided good reasons for them to change.

Source: Wilson and Arnold, 1964.

This judgment points to the **desirability** of the object or idea. When a speech includes "any material that affirms or denies the desirability of something, [it] forces speakers and listeners into the realm of persuasion" (p. 165).

For instance, in Carlos's speech to his communication class about the dangers of talking on a hand-held cell phone while driving, he urged his audience to use a hands-free phone if they had to make a phone call while driving. By stressing the safety issue, he convinced his audience that talking on a hands-free cell phone was more desirable than using a hand-held phone. He also argued in his speech that the most desirable choice was not to talk on the phone while driving at all, if possible.

Justification   A critical audience member will also ascertain whether a persuasive speaker has provided a valid **justification** for asking him or her to change. The speaker can justify the position he or she presents on three levels:

- A *personal interest justification* shows audience members how a change affects them and addresses their main concerns.
- A *rational justification* rests on the basis of evidence and reasoning and provides audience members with a logical reason for change.
- A *source justification* establishes that the speaker is authoritative and thus shows the audience that he or she is a legitimate advocate for change.

So, put yourself in the audience that Carlos spoke to about cell phones. In light of the personal interest justification, you might ask "What's in it for me?" or "How does this relate to my concerns?" Petty and Cacioppo (1986) have developed the *elaboration likelihood model of persuasion* to explain how listeners are more likely to focus their attention on the content of a speaker's message if they perceive that what the speaker is advocating relates to their own experiences and concerns. When a speaker can win the audience's attention in this way, they are more likely to be convinced by the persuasive proof presented in a speech, according to Petty and Cacioppo.

As an illustration, consider how Carlos generated personal interest justification: He cited statistics of how many people use hand-held cell phones in their cars and how many were likely to have some sort of accident as a result. Speaking bluntly to his audience, he said, "If you use a hand-held cell phone when you drive, your level of distraction is about the same as someone who is drunk."

The second level of justification, rational justification, is achieved when a speaker presents convincing arguments that are supported by evidence and reasoning (Wilson & Arnold, 1964). As just noted, Carlos gave his audience statistics about the prevalence of cell phone use by drivers as well as the car accidents that result from such use.

desirability   A quality of effective persuasive speaking that is achieved when the speaker asserts a judgment, stating either implicitly or explicitly that something is good or bad or better or worse.

justification   A quality of effective persuasive speaking that is achieved when the speaker provides the audience with a valid reason for change; may be based on self-interest, reasoning and evidence, or authority.

Finally, an audience is more likely to be persuaded when they perceive the speaker is someone who speaks with authority. This is source justification. We will explore this concept in more depth later with special reference to the topic of source *credibility.* But for now, let's continue with our example about Carlos.

Carlos came across as being very credible, primarily because he was well prepared. He did a good job researching his topic and so was able to demonstrate that he was knowledgeable and well informed. But perhaps his most convincing effort was achieved through a strategy of motivation.

Motivation   The third quality of effective public speaking cited by Wilson and Arnold (1964) is **motivation,** which addresses the needs and drives of the audience. By appealing to an audience's core emotions, a speaker can move them to embrace change.

In his book on *Rhetoric,* Aristotle referred to appeals to an audience's feelings as persuasion based in *pathos.* An effective speaker could arouse the basic passions, such as fear, hatred, love, contempt, magnanimity, generosity, and hope. Contemporary approaches to motivation also emphasize the psychological goals and motives of listeners.

Carlos provided motivation for his audience to stop using their hand-held cell phones by emphasizing how they should be concerned about their physical safety and well-being. This provided emotional support for his position and further established his credibility as someone who cared about the welfare of his listeners.

Informative Speaking

On the opposite end of the continuum from persuasive speaking is **informative speaking.** As Wilson and Arnold (1964) explain, in informative speeches, "speakers are fully satisfied if their hearers understand what is said" (p. 164).

The information shared in a speech should clarify and amplify the audience's understanding of the subject, building on whatever earlier understanding audience members may have. For the audience, the test of understanding can be measured with three standards (see Figure 7.5):

- *Accuracy:* How truthful the information is in terms of specific details and proportion
- *Completeness:* How comprehensively the speaker has covered the subject to achieve his or her specific goal
- *Unity:* How information is presented so that it is "intelligible as a whole, not as a mere miscellany of items" (p. 165)

To achieve this last standard, the speaker must organize the material so that the audience can see the connections among ideas and understand the coherence of the presentation.

When these three standards are met, audience members will respond along these lines:

- "Yes, now I understand."
- "I know more about this subject now than I did before."
- "I see how this makes sense and have a better idea of the 'big picture.'"

When Anna, a nurse, first discussed with her classmates the idea of giving an informative speech about automatic external defibrillation (AED) in their speech class, most had little or no knowledge of the subject. In fact, several asked, "What on earth are you talking about?" But by the end of her speech, Anna had clearly explained what AED is and how it is used to shock a person's heart back to a normal rhythm.

Sue's speech about NASCAR traced its history from the 1940s, when it began as a race on the beach in Daytona, to today, demonstrating how the sport has grown to

motivation   A quality of effective persuasive speaking that is achieved by addressing the needs and drives of the audience.

informative speaking   Speaking in which the primary aim is to enhance the audience's understanding.

| FIGURE 7.5 Qualities of Effective Informative Speaking | **Accuracy** Truthfulness in terms of specific details and proportions | **Completeness** Comprehensiveness of coverage in light of speaker's goal | **Unity** Presentation as intelligible whole |

The information shared in a speech should clarify and amplify the audience's understanding of the subject, building on whatever earlier understanding they may have.

Source: Wilson and Arnold, 1964.

become a multibillion-dollar business. Her speech clearly gave the audience the "big picture," in that she covered the history and development of the sport.

Between Persuasive and Informative Speaking

In the middle of the continuum, between informative and persuasive speaking, are two types of speeches that combine the goals of both. These include the speech for *inducing inquiry* about a problem and the speech for *reinforcing audience beliefs and feelings.*

Inducing Inquiry When a speaker explains a problem and then urges his or her audience to help solve it, he or she is **inducing inquiry,** or engaging them to get involved. Such a speech combines elements of persuasive and informative speeches.

A speech that induces inquiry differs from a straightforward persuasive speech because it does not advocate a specific solution. Rather, it persuades the audience that something needs to be done and offers justification for some course of action. It falls short, however, of telling the audience exactly what to do. The speaker may go so far as to outline the possible solutions in an effort to engage the audience in collaborating to find a best solution. In doing that, the inducement to inquiry speech recognizes that a great deal of discussion is needed to settle the matter at hand.

Griffin (2003) describes a similar goal when she writes about the *invitational speech,* for which the goal is to create an invitational environment. According to Griffin, that is "an environment in which understanding, respecting and appreciating the range of positions possible on an issue, even if those positions are quite different from the speaker's own, is the highest priority" (p. 375).

The information-sharing aspect of the inducement to inquiry speech involves the careful laying out of evidence about a problem. Moreover, by making the audience aware of a problem and its severity, the speaker also motivates them to accept the idea that something has to be done about it.

Wilson and Arnold (1964) observe that when inducement to inquiry is the speaker's primary goal, he or she may find it helpful to use a pattern of reflective think-ing—one that's comparable to that used by members of small groups to do problem solving. (The final step of selecting and acting on a solution is left to the audience, how-ever). Following that pattern, the speech would follow this sequence (see Figure 7.6):

- Share information about a problem and analyze its underlying causes and sources.
- Motivate members of the audience to be concerned about the problem.

inducing inquiry A type of speech in which the speaker explains a problem and then urges his or her audience to help solve it; combines elements of persuasive and informative speaking.

**FIGURE 7.6   Steps for a
Speech to Induce Inquiry**

1. Share information
about a problem and
analyze its underlying
causes and sources.

2. Motivate members
of the audience to be
concerned about
the problem.

3. Generate possible
solutions.

4. Urge the audience
to develop a solution
and participate in
an ongoing dialogue
about it.

When inducement to inquiry is the speaker's primary goal, he or she may find it helpful to use a pattern of reflective thinking.

Source: Based on Wilson and Arnold, 1964.

- Generate possible solutions.
- Urge the audience to develop a solution and participate in an ongoing dialogue about it

Sometimes, the speaker simply doesn't know what would be the best solution to a problem. In that case, inducing the audience to engage in dialogue about the problem will help him or her. The outcome for the audience is to agree to participate in sorting out the solutions because they now have a better understanding of the problem.

A speech that intends to induce inquiry is also effective when members of a group are polarized in terms of what course of action to pursue. A polarized group is a paralyzed group in the sense that it cannot follow the course of one side without severely alienating the other side.

Part of the speaker's intent in this circumstance is to move opposing sides to a point at which dialogue can occur. This may involve getting opponents to find some common ground, such as agreeing about the nature of the problem. The speaker can also help the opposing sides recognize that a compromised solution is preferable to no solution or to seeing their opponent's solution be put in place. As explained by Foss and Griffin (1995), the goal of this type of invitational rhetoric is to work collaboratively toward "understanding as a means to create a relationship rooted in equality, immanent value, and self-determination" (p. 5).

reinforcing beliefs and feelings   A type of speech in which the speaker intends to intensify or amplify the audience's current position; combines elements of persuasive and informative speaking.

Reinforcing Beliefs and Feelings   Another type of speech in which the goal includes both the persuasive aspect of advocacy and the informative aspect of enhancing understanding is one in which the speaker wants to **reinforce beliefs and feelings** that the audience already holds. Unlike the typical persuasive speech, the primary goal here is not to have the audience alter their beliefs or develop a new position but to intensify their current position. And in terms of presenting an informative speech, the speaker must provide the kinds of evidence that will amplify and enhance what the audience already believes.

7.2

Given the purpose of this type of speech, the outcome for the audience is to feel affirmed and bolstered. Members may also develop a deeper commitment for their position and perhaps take further steps to act on what they believe.

Wilson and Arnold (1964) observe that many speeches presented at ceremonies and other special occasions are intended to reinforce beliefs and feelings. For instance, when a graduation speaker extols the virtues of education, he or she reinforces values about the desirability of learning that are already held by those who are celebrating the event. And when a speaker at a funeral presents a eulogy, offering praise and appreciation for the person who has died, he or she rarely has to insist that the deceased person will be missed or that his or her accomplishments were worthy. The members of the audience know that already.

VIDEO VIEW

7.1

Speeches to reinforce often emphasize values and the feelings associated with those values. Thus, the words and actions of the speaker can embody profound feelings and stir strong emotions in audience members. For instance, in Module One, we viewed a video of President Ronald Reagan eulogizing the members of the *Challenger* crew, who died in the first space shuttle explosion in 1986. Long after the event we may still be able to feel some of the depth of emotion that the president and his audience shared. A more recent occasion for grief and remembrance was the tragedy of 9/11. Three days after the 9/11 tragedy, President George W. Bush spoke at the Washington National Cathedral, observing a Day of Prayer and Remembrance. His speech, like Reagan's, was a response to the sorrow and anger that many felt as well as a tribute to those who died during the events of 9/11.

VIDEO VIEW

7.2

It follows that speeches to reinforce beliefs and feelings foster a sense of cohesion among group members. Wilson and Arnold point out that such speeches build the relational community, encourage commitment to it, and cement the bonds that unite its members. In 1963, when the Reverend Martin Luther King, Jr., addressed the audience assembled at the Lincoln Memorial, where the March on Washington had culminated, he presented the inspiring "I Have a Dream" speech. In the final portion of his speech, King endeavored to foster people's commitment to the civil rights cause.

Speeches to reinforce beliefs and feelings are meaningful not only for social movements, like that led by King, but also for organizations and relational communities of any size—even for a society as a whole. As Wilson and Arnold point out:

> Through such speaking [to reinforce beliefs and feelings] organizations are unified and kept faithful to their goals, religious congregations are sustained in their faiths, and social and political virtues such as civic pride and mutual respect are maintained as active forces. Indeed, the bonds that give cohesion to all our social groupings are the chief subject matters of society's most important reinforcing communication. And it could be added that without reinforcement through public speeches and other media of communication, social bonds would begin to atrophy and any society would begin to drift toward anarchism. (pp. 174–175)

Interestingly, Wilson and Arnold's observation about the role of public speaking and communication in building relational communities and affirming the cohesion of social groups presaged the latter-day concept of social capital that gained popularity in the writings of Putnam (2000), author of *Bowling Alone.*

Entertainment Speeches

speech to entertain Speaking in which the primary aim is to evoke a pleasurable and aesthetic response from the audience; may be a secondary goal of an informative or persuasive speech.

The **speech to entertain** represents a third type of public speaking opportunity. The primary goal of such a speech is not to advocate a position or induce change, nor is it to enhance the audience's understanding of a subject, although either of these outcomes could be a secondary goal of the speech. Rather, the primary goal of the speech to entertain is to provide pleasure.

Wilson and Arnold (1964) suggest that the distinguishing feature of a speech to entertain is the manner in which the subject of the speech is presented. The presenter of this type of speech must be able to create and maintain a high level of attention that will carry the audience along. Moreover, if the only goal of the speech is to amuse, what the speaker says may be less important than how the speech is presented.

Even when there is a persuasive goal or information to be shared, advocacy and creating understanding take second place to entertainment. Showmanship comes first, and content and serious purpose second. In fact, watching a skillful speaker use creative language and skillful aspects of delivery in presenting a speech to entertain is quite a show.

Incorporating Entertainment into Persuasive and Informative Speeches   The speaker whose primary goal is to persuade or to inform his or her audience may incorporate entertainment into the speech in order to develop and maintain the audience's attention. Winans (1917), one of the early figures in the study of communication, saw the development and maintenance of attention as vital to effective persuasive and informative speaking.

Implications for Communication: Determine Your Goal

Public speaking requires preparation and clarifying the goal of giving a speech. This involves three interrelated tasks:

- Determine your goal or goals for speaking.
- Recognize that the outcome for each goal will differ.
- Formulate your primary and secondary goals for a speech.

Next, we will turn to the second step in the public speaking process: analyzing your audience.

Analyzing Your Audience

In defining *rhetoric*, Bryant (1974, pp. 211–212) says that it is an art of "adjusting ideas to people and people to ideas." This is not a matter of "complete accommodation," or "tell[ing] people what they want to hear." Neither is it the notion that "ideas speak for themselves." Rather, the speaker must find some middle ground, in which he or she determines the best way to relate ideas to listeners so that they will understand them. An effective speaker, then, seeks to understand the viewpoints of his or her audience, or listeners, in order to tailor the speech so that it will achieve its intended goals.

Not all audiences are the same, which means a speaker must learn about the particular audience for his or her presentation. There are two types of audience analyses:

- **Demographic analysis** takes into account the social groups that audience members belong to.
- **Psychological analysis** profiles the attitudes, beliefs, and values of the audience as well as the emotional response they will likely have to a subject.

demographic analysis   An assessment of the social groups that audience members belong to—for example, age, sex, cultural and racial/ethnic background, education, and so on.

psychological analysis   An assessment of the attitudes, beliefs, and values of the audience as well as the emotional response they will likely have to a subject.

The listeners in every audience bring to a speaking situation their social and cultural backgrounds.

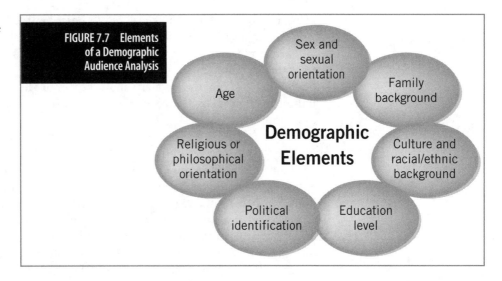

FIGURE 7.7 Elements of a Demographic Audience Analysis

Demographic Audience Analysis

Depending on who makes up your audience, you will need to tailor your topic so that they will be as receptive to it as possible. Think about the metaphor of a "tailor" for a minute. A tailor has to measure the person for whom the garment is being made before cutting the cloth and actually doing any sewing in order to ensure that the garment will fit. Likewise, a speaker should prepare by seeking the right style and content to fit his or her particular audience.

The listeners in every audience bring to a speaking situation their social and cultural backgrounds. In thinking about your audience, consider some of the following audience demographics (see Figure 7.7):

- Age
- Sex, sexual orientation, and family background
- Culture and racial/ethnic background
- Education level
- Political identification
- Religious or philosophical orientation
- Any other meaningful group membership

Age When Kim was preparing for her speech advocating the importance of saving early for retirement, she recognized that the members of her audience would be from different age groups. She decided to tailor the speech to those different groups by outlining kinds of savings plans that audience members could adopt based on their age and how many years they had to save for retirement. Sue also considered the age of her audience in preparing her speech about the history of NASCAR. She decided that she would need to explain some events in more detail for younger members of her audience who didn't live through the 1950s and 1960s, as she did.

Sex, Sexual Orientation, and Family Background While it is important to avoid overgeneralizing about the differences in attitudes and experiences between men and women, there may be some differences. Political commentators have identified the concept of a *gender gap* to describe the difference between men's and women's stands on some social and political issues.

Men and women may also have different levels of interest in certain topics. When Gary was planning to talk about Title IX—a federal law requiring that equal resources be allocated to women's and men's sports at the college level—he took into account the importance of gender. He recognized that men and women might respond differently to his topic.

When Doan Thao was planning her speech in favor of extending marital benefits to gay and lesbian couples through the adoption of domestic partnership legislation, she realized that she didn't know how many people in her audience would define themselves as being gay or lesbian. She knew of only one member of the group who had identified himself as being gay, and she decided to ask his permission to identify him during her speech and to use him as an example of someone who had been denied equal protection of the law. At the same time, she wanted to make the point that he was probably not the only gay or lesbian person in the audience—in other words, that this issue affected others around them. When the man agreed to being identified in this way, Doan Thao felt she would be able to able to make a personal connection with the audience.

You should also consider the kind of family background that members of your audience bring to the speaking situation. For instance, after Nichola chose to speak in favor of legislation that limits no-fault divorce, she decided that it was important to know how many members of her audience had come from divorced families and had been married and divorced themselves.

Similarly, when Yvonne was planning her presentation on the therapeutic benefits of owning pets, she decided it was important to find out how many members of her audience had owned or currently owned pets. Moreover, since an important focus of her speech was on the benefits of pet ownership for older individuals, who are more likely to be housebound, she sought information about whether members of her audience came from families with senior members.

Culture and Racial/Ethnic Background

Our cultural background, including the racial or ethnic group to which we belong, affects many of our attitudes and beliefs. We learn these attitudes and beliefs as we adopt the customs and norms of our culture. An effective speaker strives to be sensitive to and respectful of differences in cultural values.

Of particular concern is the need to guard against **ethnocentrism,** or the attitude that the value system, beliefs, and practices of one's own culture are superior to those of others. The ethnocentric person uses his or her own cultural value system as a standard for judging others, which is clearly a form of prejudice.

When Rasheen was preparing her speech about arranged marriages, she thought about the stereotyped views that some members of her audience might have about this practice. To address this possibility, she decided to begin her speech with an explicit plea for members of the audience to be open minded. She also decided to ask them to adopt the viewpoint that there is no single global standard for determining how marriages should be contracted.

Education

The educational level of your audience will also be a consideration in how you tailor your speech. Sometimes, you will know the general educational level of your audience—for example, in a professional or classroom setting. But in other situations, you may have little to go on in analyzing this audience characteristic. Then, you might consider what is the educational level of the average person in a community. You can then expect that in some communities, a high school level of education is the baseline. In other places it might be typical for many members of the community to have attended college.

VIDEO VIEW

7.3

ethnocentrism The attitude that the value system, beliefs, and practices of one's own culture are superior to those of others and thus can be used as a standard for judging others.

Attention to educational level might also involve an inquiry about whether members of your audience have specialized types of training and education. For instance, when Anna planned her speech on automatic external defibrillation (AED), she took into account that only one other member of her audience was likely to have had the kind of specialized training she had received as a nurse. Thus, Anna recognized the need to define some of the more technical terms she planned to use in her speech. At the same time, she determined that since she was giving her speech to a college class, most of the audience would have had a biology class at some previous point. With that in mind, she assumed that most people in her audience would know some basic facts about the workings of the human heart.

Political Identification   Membership in a political organization may also affect some of the opinions that a person holds. Along with determining whether members of your audience are likely to be affiliated with a particular party, you can discern general ideological perspectives about whether audience members tend to identify with a liberal or conservative point of view.

Political identification also relates to audience members' level of political involvement or apathy. In general, if many members of your audience are largely apathetic about political topics, you may need to spend more time in your speech establishing the personal interest justification.

Bill acknowledged the problem of political apathy as he planned a speech urging his audience of fellow college students to participate in upcoming elections. A survey of his classmates revealed that relatively few of them actually voted. This finding corresponded to the findings of national surveys, which have found that younger Americans are less likely to vote than older Americans. Given this, Bill decided to focus a substantial portion of his speech on developing the self-interest justification by providing concrete details about how the results of the upcoming elections would directly affect his audience.

Religious or Philosophical Orientation   One's religious background or philosophical orientation embodies a set of beliefs, opinions, and values in much the same manner as one's cultural, racial/ethnic, and political identifications.
This means that in planning a speech, a speaker is wise to honor the diversity
of views that may exist within an audience. Sometimes, a topic can be specifically tailored to consider the range of viewpoints that audience members hold on religious and political matters.

As part of her preparation for a class speech about Caodaism, An Nguyet surveyed her audience and asked each person to identify his or her own religious affiliation. The survey revealed that most of her listeners thought of themselves as being religious and belonged to some type of church. Of special pertinence to the topic, An Nguyet wanted to know which religious groups her audience members identified with, since Caodaism is a synthesis of many world religions, including Christianity, Islam, Buddhism, Confucianism, Hinduism, Geniism, and Taoism.

Finding Common Ground   Most of the points covered so far about the demographics of an audience concern ways to adapt a speech topic so that it can be tailored to a specific audience. In part, we want to find out what is distinctive about the background of our particular group of listeners. At the same time, we also can use a demographic analysis to find common ground with our audience. This is a matter of recognizing the similarities between our experiences and those of the various members of the audience. For instance, in the "I Have a Dream" speech, Martin Luther King, Jr. spoke eloquently of the shared experiences of his immediate audience, emphasizing how all were part of a common struggle against racial injustice.

Burke (1950) uses the term *identification* to explain how a speaker creates a connection with his or her audience. Burke observes how the common ground that we share with our listeners can also be expressed by invoking symbols that we share with one another. Burke describes the use of common symbols as the basis for identification in rather broad terms. "You persuade [another person] only insofar as you talk his [or her] language, by speech, gesture, tonality, order, image, attitude, idea, *identifying* your ways with his [or hers]" (p. 20).

7.5

At times, a speaker will create identification with an audience by literally speaking the same language as members of the audience. For instance, English-speaking politicians in the United States may switch to do a portion of a campaign speech in another language, say, Spanish, if they are addressing a community of Spanish speakers. When American presidents go overseas, they sometimes also use phrases from the language of the country that they are visiting. In 1963, at the height of the Cold War when tensions were high between the United States and the Soviet Union, President John F. Kennedy made a historic trip to Germany and visited the Berlin Wall. As a result of tensions between the United States and the Soviets, Berlin continued to be separated into two zones, a West Berlin that had a democratic government that was friendly with the United States and its allies, and East Berlin, which was part of East Germany, a communist country that was part of the Soviet bloc. Speaking to an audience of citizens of West Berlin, and presumably within earshot of those on the other side of the wall in East Berlin, Kennedy wanted to express his identification with the people of Berlin on both sides of the wall. So, he used the German phrase "Ich bin ein Berliner" with the intention of saying I am a citizen of Berlin, also. His German phrasing and syntax, however, missed the mark. Kennedy actually referred to himself as a jelly-filled pastry. Nonetheless, his efforts probably did create identification with the audience as reflected in the wild and enthusiastic response his listeners gave him—especially for those in West Berlin to whom he spoke about democratic values.

In sum, demographic audience analysis helps a speaker recognize where the audience members are coming from in terms of their memberships in various types of social groups. With this information, the speaker can target the audience and tailor what he or she has to say so that it will appeal directly to those individuals. At the same time, it is important to be on guard against overgeneralizing about group members. To do so is to rely on stereotypes.

7.6

As noted earlier, demographic analysis is just one way to gain information about the audience. The second way is to conduct a psychological analysis.

Psychological Audience Analysis

To be responsive to the unique audience that will gather for your speech, you need to take into account how people are predisposed on a psychological level to respond to you and your topic. You want to get a composite picture of the audience—one that takes into account the range of perspectives as well as the typical perspective. That is the goal of psychological audience analysis.

Psychological audience assessment is premised on the idea that a person's attitudes, beliefs, and values create the frame of reference that he or she brings to any situation. A psychological study of audience members will thus consider factors such as these:

- *Attitudes,* which are predispositions to respond favorably or unfavorably to a topic
- *Beliefs,* which are positions or standards that are held to be valid and truthful
- *Values,* which represent a hierarchy of deeply seated attitudes that are commonly rooted in core beliefs and usually establish the intrinsic worth of something
- *Emotional responses and motivations,* which include basic emotional states and drives or needs that motivate behavior

An assessment of these qualities is especially pertinent to the speaker whose goal is persuasion.

Appealing to Attitudes   An analysis of **attitudes** can be useful for determining whether an audience is likely to agree or disagree with the position that a speaker is advocating. By understanding audience members' attitudes, a speaker can recognize points of resistance and plan on how to address them in his or her speech. Such an analysis is also useful for determining which attitudes to reinforce.

For instance, when Jahn was planning his speech to discourage audience members from buying exotic animals (such as lizards, iguanas, and snakes) from commercial pet stores, he realized he needed to know how the audience felt about the topic. Upon surveying his class, he found out that some members held negative attitudes toward particular exotic animals, so there was no need to persuade them not to buy those animals. Other members had positive attitudes toward owning a lizard or a snake, at least in theory. None of Jahn's prospective audience members actually owned an exotic pet, but a significant number of them thought they would like to. Many who held positive attitudes toward buying exotic pets also believed that the amount of care required by these animals was about the same as that for taking care of a dog or a cat. And almost everyone agreed with the value statement that "Pets deserve to be protected and cared for."

Appealing to Beliefs   Much of Jahn's purpose was to persuade his listeners that exotic animals are frequently neglected because their owners do not understand the special requirements for caring for them. To be effective in making this point, Jahn would have to address the audience's **beliefs:** positions or standards that people hold as valid and truthful.

Contrary to the assumptions of many in Jahn's audience, exotic animals require much more care than other domesticated pets. But Jahn wouldn't have known about this misconception without his audience analysis. Having that bit of information about audience members was vital in helping Jahn plan an effective persuasive speech.

Earlier, we used the metaphor of a tailor as a way of thinking about the value of audience analysis. Another useful metaphor is that audience analysis is like target shooting. There are specific facets of your audience's attitudes, beliefs, and values that you want to hit. Jahn's audience analysis enabled him to recognize that his audience's beliefs had to be challenged before he could make his case. Thus, he planned on spending a significant amount of time in his speech talking about the great commitment required for taking care of exotic pets. His planning paid off: He hit the "bull's eye" with the speech.

Many theorists in rhetoric have observed an interrelationships among people's attitudes, beliefs, and values and that behavior is greatly influenced by attitudes, beliefs, and values. A useful tool for understanding the connections among these elements is the *Pyramid of Persuasion* that was created by Grice and Skinner (2003). As you look at Figure 7.8, note how *behavior* is placed at the top. Then, as you move down through the pyramid, you find attitudes, beliefs, and values. Values, positioned at the bottom, are the very broad foundation of all these other elements.

By looking at where on the pyramid each of these elements is placed, we can also understand how flexible people likely are in these areas. For instance, audience members will likely be more open to changing behavior and attitudes, the top two levels of the pyramid, than they will be to changing beliefs and values, the bottom two levels. This is because beliefs and values, which form the base of the pyramid, are central to how a person defines himself or herself. Conversely, a speaker can reinforce audience members' beliefs and values as a strategy of persuasion.

attitude   A predisposition to respond favorably or unfavorably to a topic.

belief   A position or standard that is held to be valid and truthful.

This is a useful tool for understanding the connections among people's attitudes, beliefs, values, and behaviors.

Source: Grice and Skinner, 2003.

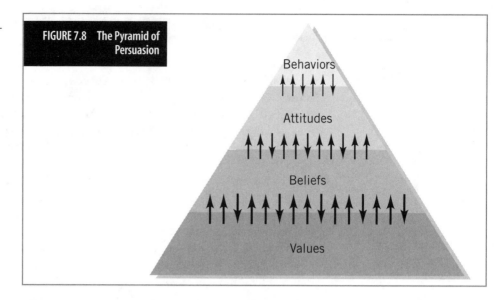

FIGURE 7.8   The Pyramid of Persuasion

Appealing to Values   To see the pyramid of persuasion in action, consider how Doan Thao presented her speech advocating domestic partnerships for gay and lesbian couples. From her audience analysis, she discovered that about half of her audience favored her position and that half were largely opposed. Only a few audience members took the middle ground of being uncertain. Yet her survey of her audience also found a nearly universal endorsement of certain core values and beliefs, such as freedom and equality and believing that loving relationships should be honored.

Realizing that **values** are deeply held attitudes that reflect audience members' core beliefs and judgments about the intrinsic worth of things, Doan Thao designed a persuasive strategy to affirm the audience's ideas about freedom, equality, and honoring relationships. From there, she posed a challenge to the members of her audience who held negative attitudes toward domestic partnerships. She argued that if her listeners truly valued freedom and equality and thought that loving relationships deserved to be honored, they should favor domestic partnerships for gay and lesbian couples.

As a strategy of persuasion, Doan Thao employed the *cognitive dissonance theory* that was introduced by Fetsinger (1957). According to this theory, people strive for a sense of consistency between their underlying values and beliefs and their outward behaviors and attitudes and thus develop behaviors and attitudes that are consistent with those core values and beliefs. Fetsinger also suggests that when there is a mismatch between our outward behaviors and attitudes (at the top half of the Grice and Skinner pyramid) and our core beliefs and values (at the bottom half), we will change our attitudes and behaviors in order to achieve consistency. Inconsistency, according to Fetsinger, creates the feeling of cognitive dissonance. People find it uncomfortable to experience dissonance and thus are motivated to change in order to bring about relief.

Appealing to Needs   Persuasive speakers may also analyze the psychological needs most important to their audience. Appealing to psychological needs can provide motivation for change, especially because fundamental psychological needs are closely associated with core values. Sheldon, Elliott, Kim, and Kasser (2001) outline 10 fundamental needs and explain how each is related to our deeply seated values:

7.5

- *Autonomy:* Feeling like you can make your own choices without an excessive amount of pressure from others
- *Competence:* Feeling capable and able to do things well

value   A deeply seated attitude that is commonly rooted in a core belief and usually establishes the intrinsic worth of something.

- *Belonging:* Feeling that others care about you and that you are connected to people
- *Self-actualization:* Feeling that you are living up to your capabilities and potential and growing in a meaningful way
- *Security:* Feeling safe and having a sense of control over things
- *Money:* Feeling that you have the money to buy what you want and can possess high-quality things
- *Influence:* Feeling that you are liked and respected and that others acknowledge your views
- *Physical well-being:* Feeling healthy and in good physical shape
- *Self-esteem:* Feeling that you are as good as anybody else
- *Pleasure:* Feeling enjoyment from pleasurable experiences that are interesting and stimulating

Psychological Analysis for Informative Topics   Psychological audience analysis is important for informative as well as persuasive speaking, since the audience's attitudes, beliefs, and values toward a topic, as well as their psychological needs, will affect their interest level. In general, the higher the level of interest that the audience has in the topic, the greater their motivation to fully participate in a speech.

Implications for Communication: Adapt Your Speech to Reach Your Audience

You've chosen a topic for your speech that interests you, but that's no guarantee that your audience will share your enthusiasm. Likewise, you may have very strong feelings about the problem you are solving, but it may not touch your audience in the same way. In planning your speech, you must ask: How interested will my listeners be in my topic? As you assess your audience's level of interest, consider some of the following points:

ASSESSING YOUR SKILLS

7.2

- Relate to the experiences of your audience. By doing a demographic analysis, you can discover common ground among your listeners and between you and your listeners.
- Adapt to the psychological views of your listeners. Take into account the positive or negative emotional response that audience members might have to your topic in accordance with their attitudes, beliefs, values, and needs.

Analyzing Your Speaking Situation

LEARNING OBJECTIVE

7.4

Along with making an assessment of the audience, a successful speaker will also assess the situation in which his or her speech will be presented. The importance of considering the situation is summed up in this quote from Zarefsky (1999): "Unlike great dramatic or literary works, which speak to the ages, the principal test of a good speech is whether it responds most effectively to the needs of the situation in which it is given" (p. 8).

Scholars in public speaking credit Bitzer (1968) for developing a simple model to describe the speaking situation, or the **rhetorical situation.** Others, including Vatz (1973) and Zarefsky, have added to Bitzer's model, especially in considering how the speaker plays an active role in shaping the situation.

The concept of rhetorical situation can also be discerned from Aristotle's *Rhetoric,* the first systematic account of strategies for the public speaker. According to Aristotle, rhetoric is the "faculty of discovering in the particular case what are the available means of persuasion" (Cooper, 1960, p. 7). We can apply Aristotle's ideas to a given speaking situation by asking the following questions:

rhetorical situation   The speaking situation; includes the audience, the occasion, exigencies and constraints, and the speaker's credibility.

- What should I say to respond appropriately to this occasion?
- What kinds of information and what arguments are available to achieve my speaking goal?
- Should my speech be intended principally as a persuasive speech or as an informative speech?
- Does the situation call for adopting a middle ground between a persuasive and informative speech, such that the audience will be induced to seek a solution or that their beliefs and attitudes will be reinforced?

In addressing these questions, the speaker needs to take into account the components of the speaking situation along with the audience. We have already considered the importance of demographic and psychological audience analyses. In addition, we will examine three other aspects of the speaking situation:

1. *The occasion:* The setting and scene for a speech; may also pertain to audience member's purpose and motivation in being present for a speech.
2. *The exigence and constraints:* The demands, expectations, and perhaps burden placed on the speaker
3. *The speaker's credibility:* The audience's favorable or unfavorable disposition toward the speaker

Assessing the Occasion

In assessing the occasion for a speech, you are assessing the circumstances for the event. Namely, where does the speech take place? What is the situation or the scene for the speech? Why is the audience present? And quite bluntly, do they want to be?

The answers to these questions will guide the development of your speech as you ascertain what you need to do to motivate your audience to pay attention to what you have to say. Sometimes, members of the audience make a conscious choice to attend a speaking event; that in itself is a positive motivation. Other times, audience members are present purely out of obligation.

ONLINE JOURNAL

7.5

Consider this breakdown of types of audiences (see Figure 7.9):

- *Voluntary audience:* The listeners choose to attend and are thus highly motivated to listen and become involved.
- *Captive audience:* The listeners are obliged or required to attend and may need to be won over.
- *Pedestrian audience:* The listeners simply happen to be at the location of the speech, and it will require significant effort to get and maintain their attention and involvement. For instance, shoppers at a mall who pass by a product being promoted or attendees at a convention who walk by the booths set up by companies or organizations to represent a product or group.
- *Dispersed audience:* The listeners are not in a single location but rather in their own homes or at their own computers (for example, the audience of a mass-mediated speech).

Assessing the Exigence and Constraints

The **exigence** a speaker confronts, as defined by Bitzer (1968) in his rhetorical situation model, is a demand, burden, or expectation inherent in the situation. In some cases, the type of speaking occasion stipulates the demand a speaker must fulfill.

For instance, the U.S. Constitution requires the president to present an occasional message to Congress describing the "state of the union." As this constitutional provision

exigence A demand, burden, or expectation inherent in the speaking situation.

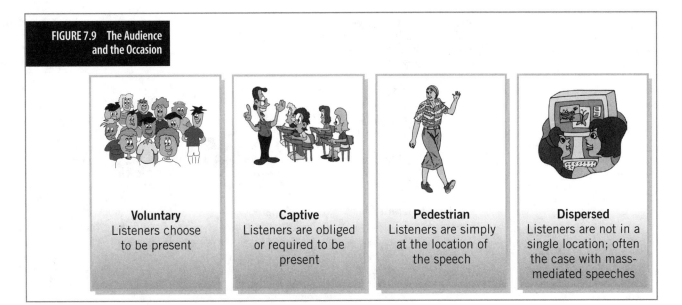

FIGURE 7.9   The Audience and the Occasion

Voluntary
Listeners choose to be present

Captive
Listeners are obliged or required to be present

Pedestrian
Listeners are simply at the location of the speech

Dispersed
Listeners are not in a single location; often the case with mass-mediated speeches

Knowing why your audience is in attendance is important to planning what you need to do to motivate them to pay attention to what you have to say.

has been interpreted through historical practice, the president is expected to present an annual speech about the nation's political state of affairs. This speech, traditionally delivered early in the year, focuses on the most pertinent domestic and international concerns.

7.8

On a smaller scale, in a basic speech course, you might be required to present a persuasive speech. Inherent to such a speech is the expectation that you will talk about a meaningful social issue and provide convincing reasons and evidence to support your position.

Other times, the exigence is an urgent need that must be met. For instance, in the heat of a political campaign, when a candidate's credibility has been seriously questioned, a disclosure must be made to repair the damage. Or when a group faces a crisis, they will turn to their leader to seek guidance or a solution.

The **constraints** of a rhetorical situation are the limitations placed on a speaker. For instance, certain topics might be inappropriate on a given occasion or for a particular audience. A speaker might also need to conform to particular rules of etiquette inherent in a situation. In addition, there are important practical constraints, such as the amount of time available. This will obviously limit how broadly or narrowly the speaker can focus his or her topic.

Audience predispositions can also place constraints on the speaker. His or her choice of content, for instance, might be limited upon considering audience members' attitudes, beliefs, and values. Similarly, the occasion establishes limitations. A style of speaking that is entirely appropriate in a court of law would likely be out of place in informal types of speaking situations. Likewise, what is appropriate for delivering a eulogy at a funeral or memorial would be highly specific to the occasion, but out of line at another type of occasion.

Finally, the medium of communication may also impose constraints. For instance, a speaker on the radio lacks visual contact with his or her audience, and a speech on television is tailored to meet the time constraints of that medium.

constraints   The limitations placed on a speaker in a given speaking situation.

The perception that members of an audience have of a speaker will affect their response to him or her.

FIGURE 7.10   Factors Involved in Speaker Credibility

Competence
Expertise and knowledge

Character and trustworthiness
Moral virtues, such as reliability, consistency, fairness, and open-mindedness

Goodwill
Audience rapport, based on common experiences and interests

Assessing Speaker Credibility

Speaker **credibility** is the perception that members of an audience have of a speaker and that affects their response to him or her. For persuasive speakers, high credibility creates source justification.

Audience members judge a speaker's credibility in terms of three factors: competence, character and trustworthiness, and goodwill (see Figure 7.10).

Competence   **Competence,** the first aspect of credibility, comprises the speaker's expertise and knowledge. A competent speaker is knowledgeable about his or her topic and has the education, professional expertise, personal experience, or research to support his or her position. A speaker creates the perception of competence by demonstrating a depth of knowledge about a topic and sometimes by explaining how he or she knows it. You might, for instance, describe how you got interested in a topic you speak about on the basis of your experience with it or your specialized training in that field.

The burden of creating competence may be influenced by the topic and how much the audience is predisposed to agree or disagree with the speaker. In general, the greater the degree of resistance from the audience, the more the speaker will need to provide credible evidence and expertise.

In addition, the perception that the speaker is confident about what he or she knows contributes to perceptions of competence, and this is often communicated through a smooth and dynamic delivery. Unfortunately, some highly knowledgeable speakers will undermine their competence and thus their credibility by giving a talk using uninspired or poorly prepared delivery. They will thus sabotage their credibility—even though they may know a great deal about the subject.

Character and Trustworthiness   The perceptions of **character and trustworthiness** are value judgments that audience members make about a speaker's moral virtues. A speaker creates a sense of character by stressing how he or she embodies personal values that are meaningful to the audience. In addition, a speaker earns the audience's trust by demonstrating that he or she has acted and spoken in a reliable and consistent manner. Presenting oneself as being fair and open minded also creates trustworthiness.

credibility   The perception that members of an audience have of a speaker and that affects their response to him or her.

competence   An aspect of credibility that addresses the speaker's expertise and knowledge.

character and trustworthiness   Aspects of credibility about which audience members judge the speaker's moral virtues.

Again, the nature of the topic may affect the speaker's ability to create perceptions of character and trustworthiness, especially if the topic is a controversial issue that is value laden or highly emotional. For instance, intensely debated topics that touch on strong religious and political beliefs may require the speaker to make a special effort to build credibility.

Since topics like these may involve matters of intense disagreement, audiences sometimes become polarized, holding fixed positions on opposite sides. Polarization, in turn, may lead to a sense of dogmatic certainty, in which some audience members feel that they are morally correct and that others are morally wrong.

Goodwill   **Goodwill,** another factor of credibility, is linked with building rapport with the audience. A speaker achieves goodwill by demonstrating that he or she has common experiences and interests with the audience and is concerned for their well-being. Sometimes, listeners feel a greater sense of rapport with a speaker on the basis of shared demographic factors and the perception that they hold similar values.

A speaker's language choices can further enhance the development of goodwill. By using terms of self-identification with the audience and personal pronouns that emphasize common bonds, a speaker can engender a greater sense of rapport and immediacy with the audience.

7.6

In sum, credibility is important whether your speaking goal is to share information or to persuade. To achieve the goal of informative speaking, the speaker needs to instill in the audience the sense that he or she is truthful and trustworthy. By establishing that you are competent to talk about your subject, you can give greater credence to the information you share in your speech.

Implications for Communication:
Fit Your Speech to the Situation

Your assessment of the situation—which encompasses taking into account the audience, the occasion, the exigence and constraints, and the speaker's role (your credibility) in shaping the situation—will guide you later in developing your speech.

7.7

Remember these important principles as you assess the situation for a speech:

- Adapt your speech so that it responds to the occasion.
- Recognize the uniqueness of each rhetorical situation and its particular exigencies and constraints.
- Develop your credibility in order to be more effective.

7.3

The information you have gathered thus far will be put to use in researching your topic, which is the next step in the speech preparation process. As you conduct your research, the materials you discover may also motivate you to reassess your topic, your focus, and even your particular goal.

7.3

Conducting Research

goodwill   An aspect of credibility that is linked with the speaker's building rapport and developing a relationship with the audience.

Researching your speech will be much simplified if you break the task into these steps (see Figure 7.11):

- Develop research questions.
- Create a research plan that will enable you to find a variety of types of evidence about your topic.

Researching your speech will be much simplified if you break the task into these four steps.

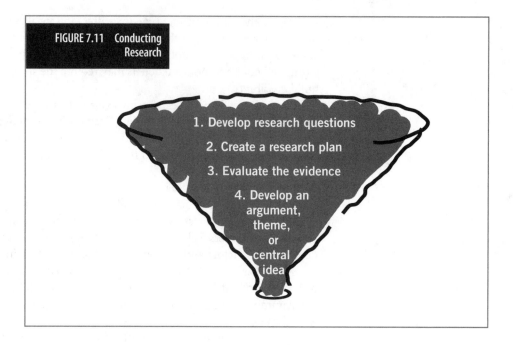

FIGURE 7.11 Conducting Research

1. Develop research questions
2. Create a research plan
3. Evaluate the evidence
4. Develop an argument, theme, or central idea

■ Evaluate the evidence that you have found.
■ Reformulate your research question as the central idea of your speech and develop the main theme or argument for your presentation.

Develop Research Questions

Why ask **research questions?** Doing so prompts you to conduct a deeper exploration of your topic, going beyond what you already know or already think and looking at all aspects. In fact, to begin, you should have several research questions—several directions in which to explore. And depending on what you find out in conducting research—in terms of both quantity and quality of information—you will ultimately focus on one question, or one specific aspect of your topic.

If you are intent on *informing* your audience, your initial research questions will guide you in discovering what you still don't know about the topic. What you find out by looking into these undiscovered aspects of your topic might shed new light on the plan for your speech and help you zero in on a single question. If your aim is to *persuade*, pursuing several research questions will help you explore alternative points of view. Doing so will require that you keep an open mind during the research phase, even changing your point of view given the weight of the evidence that you find. You should deliberately look for evidence that disproves what you already think as well as evidence that proves your point.

Indeed, no matter what your goal for speaking, it is dangerous to start out with an unalterable viewpoint and do research merely to prove what you already think or know. If your goal is to inform, you will miss out on the latest developments in the field and other theories and approaches to the same topic. If your goal is to persuade, you will overlook the facts that give those on the other side of the argument the stronger case.

In his *Rhetoric,* Aristotle describes the practical benefit of researching both sides of the same issue. When you know what both sides think, you can respond to the opposing side more effectively because you know it thoroughly. As Aristotle explains:

research questions Questions that prompt deep exploration of your topic, going beyond what you already know or already think and looking at all aspects.

We should be able to argue on either side of a question; not with a view to putting both sides into practice—we must not advocate evil—but in order that no aspect of the case may escape us, and that if our opponent makes unfair use of the arguments, we may be able in turn to refute them. (Cooper, 1960, p. 6)

As we explore the different sides of a question, it is also important to sort out the kinds of questions one may ask in different types of speaking situations. At the start of this module, we observed that classical rhetoricians, following Aristotle, distinguished various types of situations: deliberative, forensic, and epideictic.

Classical theories of rhetoric frame rhetorical situations for the speaker (and the audience) in terms of three types of **classical questions.** For the deliberative speaker, whose task is to explain what course of action should be followed, the issue centers on a *question of policy:* What is the best course of action to pursue? For the forensic speaker pursuing a case in court, a *question of fact* is the primary focus: How do the facts of the case support a verdict? For the epideictic speaker delivering a special occasion speech, it is a *question of value:* Is the subject good or bad, desirable or undesirable? A fourth type sometimes identified is a *question of definition:* What does this mean, or how should it be named?

Classical Questions   We can take this discussion a level deeper by seeing how each of these types of questions raises a host of other related questions that research should address:

- *Question of policy:* What are the various policy options for responding to a problem or concern? What has been tried before? Which of these solutions to the problem were successful? What possible courses of action have not been tried? What is the best course of action to follow given the possibilities? Which course of action will likely be most effective in solving the problem? Which course of action is most desirable? Which course of action can be implemented practically? Which course of action will result in more benefits than costs?
- *Question of fact:* What evidence exists to prove and to disprove what I believe about my topic? Which factual claims related to my topic have the greatest probability of being truthful and verifiable? Is the evidence that supports factual claims about my topic internally consistent and coherent?
- *Question of value:* What about my idea is praiseworthy, and what about it is faulty? What are the good qualities of my topic? What are the bad qualities? How does what's good about my topic compare with what's good about other topics?
- *Question of definition:* What general or specialized definition do I need to use to understand my topic? Which definition provides the most valid and comprehensive way of describing or distinguishing my topic?

classical questions   A category of research questions that frame research in terms of the type of speaking occasion: (1) a *question of policy* asks what course of action to pursue; (2) a *question of fact* asks what facts support the case at hand; and (3) a *question of value* asks whether the subject is good or bad, desirable or undesirable. (A fourth type sometimes identified is a *question of definition,* which asks what something means or how it should be named.)

Although each of these four types of classical questions can be developed by itself for a particular topic and in a given speaking situation, you will likely be able to use a combination of question types together, depending on your subject. Consider how Shannon addressed all four types of questions in doing the research for her speech on whether the juvenile defendant in the Washington, DC, sniper case should be tried as an adult and sentenced to death if found guilty. She explained:

On one level, I approached the research for my topic as a question of policy. Where should Lee Malvo [the juvenile defendant] be tried? The deliberations had centered on whether it should be in Maryland or the District of Columbia, jurisdictions in which a minor cannot be tried with the death penalty, or in Virginia, which does have a death penalty statute that can be applied to a juvenile.

   Then, from there, I looked at this as a question of definition. What does it mean to say that someone is an *adult* as opposed to being legally defined as a *juvenile?* That raised another question for me: Why do we make a distinction between adults and juveniles?

On the matter of questions of fact, I began to wonder whether Lee Malvo was operating as an independent person. Was Muhammad, the co-defendant in the case and the older man, manipulating him? Was Malvo fully responsible as an adult? I also soon recognized that I could not answer some of these questions and that they would probably be developed in the trial.

So, I turned to look at this as a question of value: Will it be fair and just to apply the death penalty if Lee Malvo is found guilty of the sniper murders?

Other topics will lend themselves to focusing on just one or two types of analyses. As an example of a more narrowly focused set of research questions, Tammy, the student who spoke about the possible hazards of using the herbal supplement ephedra, confined her research to questions of fact: What are the chemical properties of ephedra? What are the chemical elements of various dietary supplements that produce lethal results when combined with ephedra? Moreover, since Tammy was using for illustration the case of Steve Bechler, the pitcher for the Baltimore Orioles whose death may have been associated with using ephedra, she researched the details of his case. She asked whether the Bechler case was an isolated example or if ephedra use was a more frequent problem among professional athletes. This led her to look for statistics that would provide a bigger picture of the problem. And from this research, Tammy learned that members of the medical community and the U.S. Food and Drug Administration were concerned about problems with ephedra use. She then looked into that body of scientific research. In sum, most of Tammy's research involved a kind of scientific inquiry. Yet many scientific questions also address matters of value.

For instance, when A. J. began his exploration of the matter of cloning from human stem cells, he focused mainly on scientific issues. His initial plan for the speech was simply to talk about how cloning is done from stem cells and how those cells are used for medical research. His initial plan was to do a speech to inform. A. J. realized, however, that he was also dealing with a question of value: What are the benefits of human cloning, especially for making advances in medical research? At the same time, he wanted to explore the undesirable aspects of cloning, so he looked into how human cloning might be abused. This exploration led him to realize that some of those who oppose cloning and stem cell research frame the issue as a question of definition: Do human stem cells constitute human life or potential human life? And in pursuing this line of thought, A. J. learned about efforts to enforce a total ban on stem cell research efforts and the introduction of legislation called the Human Cloning Prohibition Act of 2003.

What A. J. learned about his topic in conducting research caused him to change the goal of his speech. What started out as a speech to inform his audience about stem cell research and medical applications changed to a speech with a persuasive message, advocating the need for ongoing stem cell research. With this new purpose, A. J. decided to appeal to his listeners to write letters or send e-mail messages to their congressional representatives, asking them to oppose the bill that called for a ban on stem cell research.

Exploratory Questions   Reading about Shannon and Tammy and A. J. may make you wonder about their research efforts, as it sounds as though they each went off in many different directions. In fact, they did—and you will, too! The goal of researching your topic is to explore, and that process may take you along paths you had not even considered before.

You may also be saying to yourself "I've found way too much information to use in my speech!" That's not a problem but a benefit. When you have discovered many different angles for your topic, you will have a wide range of options from which to choose the best approach for your speech. Much of the information that you found in your research may not end up being used in your speech, but it is all nonetheless valuable in terms of helping you find the best approach.

You might draw on the experience of movie makers. When they film a scene, they use several cameras and shoot from different angles of vision. A lot of that footage ends up on the cutting room floor. It is the director's careful editing of the images available to him or her that makes a good movie. The same is true for good speech making. Remember what Aristotle said: Rhetoric is the art of discovering the *available* means of persuasion.

Journalistic Questions   Another way to frame the research for your speech is to use **journalistic questions:** broad questions that encourage you to explore different aspects of your topic. The journalist asks: Who? What? When? Where? Why? and How? Thus, journalistic questions are valuable for making sure your research is comprehensive.

Janet used journalistic questions to research how to protect your house from being flooded when a large accumulation of snow is melting. She began with her own experience of having eight inches of water flood the ground floor of her house and asked: Why was my house flooded? Where does water seep into my foundation? How many people have this problem? What needs to be done? When should maintenance be done to prevent the problem? Who can do this preventive maintenance—a professional person or a homeowner? How much does it cost for materials and labor? After researching the answers to these questions, Janet had more information than she could use. She decided to focus mainly on the answers to two questions: what needs to be done to prevent flooding and how a homeowner can take four simple steps as preventive maintenance.

Gary used journalistic questions to do the research for his speech on the implementation of Title IX in intercollegiate sports. He asked: How has the implementation of Title IX affected participation in men's and women's sports programs? Who have been the winners and the losers as a result of Title IX? The answers to these questions led to the development of his central persuasive speech question: Why should Title IX be continued?

7.8

Create a Research Plan

Along with developing research questions, you need to develop a research plan. Specifically, you need to decide what kinds of information to incorporate into your speech and where you can locate different kinds of evidence.

Kinds of Evidence   **Evidence** is the supporting material you use to prove a point or to amplify one of your ideas. So again, the goal of your speech—whether to inform or to persuade—is relevant here.

Proof is essential if you are trying to be persuasive and establish a rational justification for the audience to accept the main argument of your speech. Proof provides the reasonable basis upon which the audience can agree with you. Proof is also expressed in the form of your credibility—particularly your competence in terms of what you know about the topic—which provides source justification for the audience.

When your goal is to inform or to reinforce the beliefs and feelings of the audience, evidence serves the function of **amplification.** The notion that evidence amplifies an idea invites a metaphor to the way that a sound system amplifies the voice of a speaker. Just as a sound system enables the audience to hear the speaker's voice more clearly and perhaps more fully in its richness, amplifying an idea with evidence allows the audience to comprehend it more fully and clearly. This metaphor communicates a caution, as well: Just as an amplification system can electronically alter the sound of a voice, information that is inaccurate or otherwise invalid can distort an idea and discredit a speaker.

journalistic questions   Broad questions that frame research by encouraging the speaker to explore different aspects of his or her topic: Who? What? When? Where? Why? and How?

evidence   The supporting material a speaker uses to prove a point or to amplify one of his or her ideas.

proof   Evidence that provides the reasonable basis upon which the audience can agree with the speaker; essential when trying to persuade.

amplification   Evidence that informs or reinforces the beliefs and feelings of the audience.

So, what types of evidence should you use in your speech? Not surprisingly, it depends on the basic elements of your speaking situation:

- What is your experience with and expertise on the topic?
- Who is the audience?
- What is the speaking occasion?

Your experience and expertise establish your credibility to speak about the topic. We all have a body of personal knowledge that's made up of all of our experiences; this knowledge can be the starting point for a speech. If you can qualify yourself as an expert in the minds of the audience your credibility will go a long way to justify their agreement with you. The evidence you use from outside your own direct experience will simply amplify the points you are making. If the audience does not perceive your expertise, you will need to use evidence to prove your points.

The audience will also dictate how much and what types of evidence to use. As a general rule, you should use more evidence if the audience is skeptical about your topic or questions your credibility. Audience members will be skeptical about your topic when they disagree with you or can't make up their minds about where they stand. The same is true of your credibility: The audience may be more skeptical about you and your credibility if they are uncertain about the topic or disagree with your position.

Persuading a skeptical audience will thus likely require more external forms of evidence, or sources outside the experience of the speaker. In his *Rhetoric,* Aristotle distinguishes between *internal* and *external* sources of evidence. He calls internal sources *artistic proof* and external sources *inartistic proof.* Internal sources of evidence come from the resources of the speaker; they include his or her credibility, feelings, and logical inferences. External sources, which come from outside the experience of the speaker, include various forms of tangible evidence.

In contemporary rhetorical practice, there are four basic forms of evidence:

7.7

- **Expert testimony** comprises quotes from people or organizations that the audience recognizes as having the authority to offer credible commentary on the topic.
- **Quantitative evidence** takes the form of statistics or probabilities based on statistics.
- **Examples** are concrete illustrations, often expressed as narratives or as case studies. Examples may be actual or literary. An *actual* example is a real-life illustration, such as a historical incident or case study. A *literary* example is a fictional illustration from a novel, movie, or television show.
- **Objects and presentation aids** include charts, diagrams, pictures, and drawings as well as sound and video clips. You may use presentation aids in traditional formats, such as posters and pictures, or in a multimedia format, such as a slide presentation from a laptop computer.

The occasion for your speech may also motivate your choice of evidence. For instance, a lawyer presenting a case in a courtroom will probably need to meet different expectations than you will as a student speaking in a classroom. Even as a student speaker, you may need to satisfy a different standard of evidence in your public speaking class than in your sociology class. In the sociology class, for instance, you may be expected to draw on the expert testimony of particular sources who have published their ideas in sociology journals.

Research Strategies   The next step is to do the legwork involved in finding the information that you need. The library is the traditional location of much of the material that you will incorporate into your speech. It is a good idea to tour your campus library and learn about the host of types of information available there.

Along with library research, you will also likely draw on electronic sources of information. Your campus library can also provide many of these electronic sources, which can often be accessed from remote locations such as your home or workplace.

expert testimony   A form of evidence that comprises quotes from people or organizations that the audience recognizes as having the authority to offer credible commentary on the topic.

quantitative evidence   A form of evidence that comprises statistics and probabilities based on statistics.

examples   A form of evidence that comprises illustrations, whether actual or literary; often expressed as narratives or as case studies.

objects and presentation aids   A form of evidence that comprises concrete objects, charts, diagrams, pictures, and drawings, as well as sound and video clips.

Evaluate the Evidence

7.8

As you are looking for research materials, consider using the 5 R's for evaluating the usefulness of evidence:

1. *Relevance:* Is the evidence directly related to the topic at hand? Does the evidence offer support or amplification for research questions that you are asking?
2. *Recency:* Is the evidence the most up-to-date information for the topic? (Naturally, this may depend on the subject field and how quickly new knowledge is discovered in that field.)
3. *Reliability:* Can the source of the evidence be trusted? Is the source unbiased? Did the person or group that developed the evidence use reliable research methods?
4. *Recognition:* Is the source of evidence familiar enough that the audience will find it credible? If not, what information is needed to establish the reliability and integrity of the evidence and its source?
5. *Rules of evidence pertinent to a discipline or situation:* Is the speaking situation governed by special rules of evidence? (For instance, the mathematical evidence used in a chemistry class will differ from the legal evidence used in a courtroom or the literary evidence used in an English classroom.)

Types of Sources   Among the types of sources that are physically housed in a library, accessed online, or available by making personal contact with sources of information are the following:

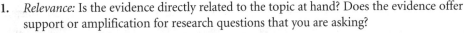

7.9

- Books
- Reference works
- Periodicals (including newspapers, magazines, and journals)
- Government documents
- Electronic media
- Special interest groups
- Online sources
- Personal interviews

Books   Look to books for an in-depth coverage of ideas. As you read about your topic, make a list of some of the authors who have written about it and the terms that are used to discuss it. (Chances are, you will see many of the same names and terms used across several sources.) Then use these names and terms to search for more sources in your library's catalog. Many libraries have banks of computer terminals that you can use to do a search of the library's catalog, and many libraries also enable you to search the online catalog by way of the web. When you go to the library, find out how you can use the catalog.

Take notes as you are doing research with a book. To begin, write down the author of the book, its title, and when, where, and by whom the book was published. Be sure to record all of this information accurately, as you will need it later for citing your sources, especially in a printed bibliography (which you may be expected to turn in for a classroom speech). Regardless, you will also need this source information to properly credit the person or organization from which you learned the information. As you are presenting your speech, you will want to name the author and how he or she is especially qualified to write on your topic.

Failing to give proper credit to your sources—not only books but other sources, as well—undermines your credibility and opens you to the charge of plagiarism. **Plagiarism** is a form of academic dishonesty, in which one person presents another person's ideas as his or her own (that is, without acknowledging the original source). Grice and Skinner (2003), who wrote a chapter on the ethics of public speaking in their book

plagiarism   A form of academic dishonesty, in which one person presents another person's ideas as his or her own without acknowledging the original source.

Mastering Public Speaking, provide this definition: "The word *plagiarize* comes from the Latin meaning, 'to kidnap,' so in a sense, a plagiarist is a kidnapper of the ideas and words of another" (p. 33, italics added).

Some cases of plagiarism are clear cut and intentional, according to Grice and Skinner. For instance, if you copy something straight out of a book and read it word for word in delivering your speech, you have committed deliberate plagiarism. However, you can quote an expert if you give him or her credit for the information—for instance, "According to . . . ." You must also credit the source when you paraphrase or summarize what he or she has said or written. Failing to provide credit in either of these instances may be an oversight but it is plagiarism nonetheless.

The problem of plagiarism does not end just with copying someone's words or taking someone's ideas. You are also plagiarizing if you present the organization of someone's ideas as being your own without giving them credit or if you use illustrations or other graphics without indicating where they came from or who created them. And again, the rules for citing sources apply to all of the types of evidence that you may use in your speech, which we will explore next.

Reference Works   Dictionaries, encyclopedias, and almanacs are all reference works, which typically provide general information that's intended for a general audience. In fact, some speakers may find it useful to start by reading reference works, just to get an overview of a subject and the current state of knowledge about it.

You have probably used dictionaries over the years, and it's likely these were general dictionaries. For instance, the *American Heritage Dictionary* and *Webster's Collegiate Dictionary* are both general dictionaries. Sometimes, you will benefit by using a specialized dictionary. Many academic disciplines and professional fields have such dictionaries, which define so-called *terms of art* by providing meanings that are unique to that discipline or field. For legal topics, you might consult a dictionary such as *Black's Law Dictionary.* When you present evidence from a specialized dictionary, you may also need to translate the terms of art into everyday language so that your listeners will understand you.

An encyclopedia, a second type of reference work, provides a good overview of a subject. Similar to dictionaries, there are general encyclopedias, such as the *Encyclopaedia Britannica,* as well as specialized encyclopedias, such as the *Astronomy Encyclopedia.* For topics in law enforcement and criminal justice, you can use the *Encyclopedia of Crime and Punishment,* and for specialized issues in communication, check out the *Encyclopedia of Communication and Information.* You can probably find a special encyclopedia about your area of interest. Use the online catalog of your library to search for this and other reference works by using key terms related to your subject.

Almanacs are a third type of reference work. Sometimes called "fact books," they are organized like encyclopedias and cover a wide range of topics. Also like dictionaries and encyclopedias, almanacs can be intended for general or specialized fields and audiences. Since almanacs are usually published on an annual basis, they are good sources of recent information, particularly statistical information.

Periodicals   Newspapers, magazines, and journals are all examples of periodicals: publications that are printed on a periodic basis. For instance, newspapers are commonly published daily, magazines are usually issued once a week or once a month, and journals are typically published on a monthly, quarterly, or even annual basis.

Most of us are familiar with the newspapers and magazines that have a wide distribution, such as the *New York Times* and *Newsweek.* Intended for a general readership, these types of periodicals are usually written at a basic reading level and provide basic coverage of topics. To address the narrower concerns of a specific topic, there are specialized periodicals, or *journals.* A professional journal is published for a relatively small segment of experts in a given subject area, such as professionals who do research in autoimmune diseases or early child development.

As you gain experience in your chosen professional field, you will likely learn to read its journals. In reading specialized journal articles, it is often helpful to begin by reading the *abstract,* or the overview of the article, which can usually be found on the first page. Then, skip to the *summary* or *conclusion* at the end of the article, where the authors explain the findings of their study. The middle part of the article is also important. This is the *methodology* section, which presents the details of the research that was done. By reading it, you can determine whether the researchers took the right steps to ensure the reliability and validity of their research findings.

Most periodicals are *indexed,* which means you can find articles about specific topics by looking up those topics. By using the index of subjects provided by major newspapers, you can search through issues of the paper for stories that they have published on your topic. Another useful source is ProQuest, which indexes many newspapers throughout the country. Magazine and journal articles are also indexed. One useful source that you may be familiar with is the *Readers' Guide to Periodical Literature.* There are also other specialized indexes that identify articles from discipline-specific journals, such as the social sciences or literature.

Many periodicals are also available online and provide opportunities to search for content via computer. The organizations that publish online periodicals may require that you register with them before being able to access their information, and they may charge a small amount of money for retrieving articles from their archives.

Government Sources   The U.S. government is one of the largest publishers in the world and is thus a rich mine for finding information about a variety of topics. The various branches of the federal government—executive, legislative, and judicial—issue documents in print and electronic forms. You can order hard copies of documents from the Government Printing Office, which is an arm of the U.S. Congress. Learn more about the Government Printing Office by going online to <www.gpo.gov/>.

Also, don't overlook state and local government sources. Agencies at the state and local levels are particularly valuable sources of information about issues affecting the people in these regions. For instance, the state will be able to provide materials about a new gun possession law, and the city or county will have information about a local pollution issue.

Electronic Media   Radio and television broadcasts, along with online databases, are all electronic media. Broadcast programs that feature speeches and interviews of public officials and subject-matter authorities offer opportunities for you to collect expert testimony about your subject. You can also find such information online by using the web pages of news agencies. If your topic entails doing recent historic research, Vanderbilt University provides a summary of news programs dating back to 1968 <tvnews.vanderbilt.edu/>.

Electronic databases archive materials such as newspaper stories and journal articles that were originally or simultaneously published as print sources.

Special Interest Groups   Organizations and professional associations who have a stake in providing research and policy statements on specific topics are known as *special interest groups.* Such an organization likely has a particular political agenda and represents a specific ideological perspective. Given this, the depth and integrity of their research should be carefully evaluated to determine its credibility. It is often useful, nonetheless, to contact these organizations.

Online Sources   Throughout this class, we have drawn on a wide range of online sources, including web pages, chat rooms, and bulletin boards. Virtually every topic and every organization has some sort of presence on the Internet.

You can greatly facilitate online research by using *search engines*. As shown in Figure 7.12, there are various types of search engines. Most look for key words in online

FIGURE 7.12   Types of Search Engines

Type	Description	Examples
1st Generation	• Non-evaluative, do not evaluate results in terms of content or authority. • Return results ranked by relevancy alone [number of times the term(s) entered appear, usually on the first paragraph of the site]	AltaVista (www.altavista.com/) Excite (www.excite.com) HotBot (www.HotBot.com) Infoseek (guide.infoseek.com) Ixquick Metasearch (ixquick.com) Lycos (www.lycos.com)
2nd Generation	• More creative in displaying results. • Results are ordered by characteristics such as: concept, document type, website, popularity, etc., rather than relevancy.	Ask Jeeves (www.aj.com/) Direct Hit (www.directhit.com/) Google! (www.google.com/) HotLinks (www.hotlinks.com/) Simplifind (www.simpli.com/) SurfWax (www.surfwax.com/) Also see Meta-Search engines below. Evaluative Search Engines About.Com (www.about.com) WebCrawler (www.webcrawler.com)
Commercial Portals	• Provide additional features such as: customized news, stock quotations, weather reports, shopping, etc. • They want to be used as "one stop" web guide. • They profit from prominent advertisements and fees charged to featured sites.	GONetwork (www.go.com/) Google Web Directory (directory.google.com/) LookSmart (www.looksmart.com/) My Starting Point (www.stpt.com/) Open Directory Project (dmoz.org/) NetNow (www.inetnow.com) Yahoo! (www.yahoo.com/)
Meta-Search Engines *Integrated Result*	• Display results for search engines in one list. • Duplicates are removed. • Only portions of results from each engine are returned.	Beaucoup.com (www.beaucoup.com/) Highway 61 (www.highway61.com) Cyber411 (www.cyber411.com/) Mamma (www.mamma.com/) MetaCrawler (www.metacrawler.com/) Vivisimo (www.vivisimo.com) Northern Light (www.nlsearch.com/) SurfWax (www.surfwax.com)
Meta-Search Engines *Non-Integrated Results*	• Comprehensive search. • Displays results from each search engine in separate results sets. • Duplicates remain. • You must sift through all the sites.	Dogpile (www.dogpile.com) Global Federated Search (jin.dis.vt.edu/fedsearch/) GoHip (www.gohip.com) Searchalot (www.searchalot.com) 1Blink (www.1blink.com) ProFusion (www.profusion.com/)

You can greatly facilitate your research online by using search engines.

Source: Doyle and Barr, 2003.

FIGURE 7.13   Types of Arguments

Argument from sign	**Argument from causality**	**Argument from analogy**	**Argument from generalization**
• Connects observable signs with certain phenomena	• Connects effect with certain set of causes	• Involves comparing two things	• Connects conclusion and specific cases • Deduction versus induction

An argument is a conclusion that you draw on the basis of a sufficient amount of evidence. It is developed using any of several common patterns of reasoning.

---

documents. Some also help narrow the search so that you can find the web sites most relevant to your topic. Still other search engines provide evaluations of web pages.

Like any evidence, the information that you find online must be evaluated to ensure its accuracy and reliability. Given how quickly material can be put on and taken off the Internet, it's especially important to consider the information and its source with a healthy dose of skepticism. Doyle and Barr (2003) provide five criteria that are especially pertinent to evaluating web pages:

- *Accuracy:* How reliable is the information?
- *Authority:* Who is the author, and what are his or her credentials?
- *Objectivity:* Does the site present a balanced point of view?
- *Coverage:* Is the information comprehensive enough for your needs?
- *Currency:* Is the site up-to-date?

7.4

Develop an Argument

Researching your speech will provide you with the information you need to form and test arguments for your speech. An *argument* is a conclusion that you draw on the basis of a sufficient amount of evidence. It is developed using any of several common patterns of reasoning. An effective speaker can guide the audience to see the connections between evidence and the conclusion the speaker is developing by using one of four types of arguments (see Figure 7.13):

- Argument from sign
- Argument from causality
- Argument from analogy
- Argument from generalization

Arguments from Signs   An **argument from sign** claims that an observable or measurable indicator, or sign, is associated with a certain phenomenon. Signs are often physical and observable, such as the physical symptoms of an illness. For instance, Heather used sign argument to identify the symptoms of various kinds of skin cancers in her speech about problems of exposure to the sun. Others are measured numerically, such as economic statistics. For instance, economists will speak of "leading indicators" that identify significant aspects of the economic situation.

argument from sign   A claim that an observable or measurable indicator, or sign, is associated with a certain phenomenon.

In his speech on Body Image Disturbance, Heath Rainbolt described two kinds of eating disorders—bulimia and anorexia nervosa—as signs of a psychological problem called *body image disturbance.* He argued that the physical signs of these eating disorders are the outward manifestations of an underlying psychological problem. To make that claim, he first described eating disorders, including his own experiences with them, and then argued that the underlying problem is body image disturbance.

Arguments from Causality

An **argument from causality** claims that there is a logical connection between an effect and a certain set of causes. Such causal arguments demonstrate that one or more causes are necessary and sufficient to produce a given effect. As a way of organizing ideas in a speech, some speakers begin by describing a problem or a condition and then documenting how the problem is caused by one or several factors.

Heath Rainbolt also developed a causal argument in his speech when he made the claim that body image disturbance is caused when people adopt the social ideals of what a perfect body is supposed to look like. These social ideals, Rainbolt said, are expressed in the images of the perfect body that are communicated by mass media outlets. This then, in his view, is the root cause of body image disturbance.

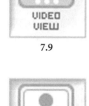

7.9

7.10

Arguments from Analogy

An **argument from analogy** involves comparing two things. An analogy is, in fact, a metaphor, which asks us to see that one thing is substantially similar to something else, or a kind of parallel situation. The speaker who uses an analogy guides his or her audience to see how two situations are similar, such that what is true of one case can reasonably be claimed for another.

For instance, the First Amendment of the U.S. Constitution provides the right of free speech among other rights of expression, such as the rights of assembly and petition. This is not, however, a totally unfettered right. There are some limits. A large body of case law and legal precedent has been developed to interpret the First Amendment and stipulate the kinds of situations in which speech is permitted and limited. Much of this case law deals with aspects of political expression. The case of *Texas v. Johnson,* for instance, raised the question of whether the state of Texas could punish a person for burning the American flag during a political protest rally. In the case of *Texas v. Johnson,* the U.S. Supreme Court ruled that when Gary Lee Johnson burned the flag in 1984, his action was similar to other forms of political dissent that are protected under the Constitution—even if some members of his audience regarded the flag burning as a deeply offensive act.

The process of arguing by analogy can also be used to show how two things are dissimilar. What is true of one case is not always true for another. For instance, the case of *Roth v. United States,* which the U.S. Supreme Court heard in 1954, distinguished between certain aspects of pornography and other types of constitutionally protected free speech. Justice William Brennan, who wrote the majority decision in the *Roth* case, argued that obscenity does not enjoy the same protections as other types of speech:

> All ideas having even the slightest redeeming social importance—unorthodox ideas, controversial ideas, even ideas hateful to the prevailing climate of opinion—have the full protection of the guaranties [of the First Amendment], unless excludable because they encroach upon the limited area of more important interests; but implicit in the history of the First Amendment is the rejection of obscenity as utterly without redeeming social importance. (pp. 484–485)

argument from causality A claim that there is a logical connection between one or more effects and one or more causes that produces the effect(s) that are claimed.

argument from analogy A claim that involves comparing two things and showing that one is substantially similar to the other.

So, in other words, Justice Brennan was saying that certain forms of so-called obscene or pornographic speech are not the same as political expression protected by the First Amendment, unless it can be demonstrated that they have redeeming social importance that would be found in serious literary works, artistic productions, political statements, or writings with scientific value.

7.11

Arguments from Generalizations   An **argument from generalization** claims a logical connection between one or more examples and a general conclusion. Such an argument commonly takes one of two forms: induction and deduction.

Induction involves drawing a general conclusion after examining a number of specific cases. In the *Rhetoric*, Aristotle refers to inductive reasoning as argument by example and states that the speaker's goal is to "derive a general law from a number of like instances" (Cooper, 1960, p. 10). The order of presentation for induction calls for citing specific examples and then drawing a generalized conclusion about what is common among all of them.

Historians sometimes use the inductive method. For instance, historian Doris Kearns Goodwin, who studies the American presidency, among other things, developed an inductive argument about the anguish that American presidents experience as they make the decision to commit troops to war. Speaking on NBC's *The Today Show* on the day that President George W. Bush issued an ultimatum that threatened war against Iraq in 2003, Goodwin recounted the anguish that Presidents Franklin D. Roosevelt and Lyndon B. Johnson faced during their presidencies as they ordered troops into harm's way. She concluded with a generalization that presidential angst accompanies the decision making involved in going to war and that Bush, like his predecessors, would likely experience the same anguish.

In some ways, an inductive argument is like an analogy. While an analogy involves a comparison among a relatively limited set of related examples, an inductive argument draws on a large host of examples. Therein lies the power of an inductive argument: It is based on many instances.

When too few examples are used as the basis for making a generalized claim, the result is a *hasty generalization*. Sometimes, this result can be attributed to a time constraint inherent in the speaking situation, as was perhaps the circumstance facing Goodwin when she appeared on *The Today Show* and was

7.12

permitted only a matter of seconds to make her argument. Because both the time that you have to develop your argument and the number of the examples that you can use to draw a generalization will almost always be limited, it is very important to establish the connection among your examples and show that your generalized conclusion indeed follows from them. You will also make your point more successfully if the examples selected for your argument are highly representative of a larger body of examples, not random and incidental cases.

Deduction, the second type of argument from generalization, is the opposite of induction. As such, it involves beginning with a general conclusion and providing specific cases to develop and structure an argument. Deductive reasoning is also called *syllogistic reasoning* because it involves using the three-part structure of a syllogism. A syllogism begins with a generalization, which is called the *major premise.* For instance, the classic syllogism begins with the major premise *All men are mortal.* This generalization creates a category and makes a claim about an attribute that is common to the category as a whole—to all men. The second part of the argument, the *minor premise,* cites a particular example that is representative of the category referred to in the major premise. So, in the classical syllogism, the second premise is *Socrates is a man.* The third part of a syllogism is the *conclusion,* which must flow logically from the major and the minor premises. In our example, *Socrates is mortal.*

As part of her presentation to the House Judiciary Committee that met in 1974 to deliberate whether to impeach President Nixon, Congressional Representative Barbara Jordan offered several deductive arguments to make a case for impeachment. For instance, one of her arguments began with the general premise articulated by James Madison, one of the principal authors of the Constitution, who said: "A President is impeachable if he attempts to subvert the Constitution." From there, Jordan moves to state the minor premise of her argument by citing a number of specific situations of Nixon's efforts to

argument from generalization
A claim that suggests a logical connection between an example and a general conclusion.

induction   A type of argument from generalization that involves drawing a general conclusion after examining a number of specific cases.

deduction   A type of argument from generalization that involves beginning with a general conclusion and providing specific cases to support it; also called *syllogistic reasoning.*

subvert the Constitution: ". . . the President has counseled his aides to commit perjury, willfully disregarded the secrecy of grand jury proceedings, concealed surreptitious entry, attempted to compromise a federal judge while publicly displaying his cooperation with the process of criminal justice." This leads to the conclusion of her argument: therefore, Nixon should be impeached.

7.5

Implications for Communication: Conduct Effective Research

Researching your speech topic is a process of discovery. Your goal is not simply to find evidence to prove what you already think or know as much as to find out new ideas and gather the evidence needed to support them in developing your speech. You might even be challenged to reconsider what you thought before you began your research or to expand your view of your topic in order to see it in much greater depth.

7.7

As you move along in the research process, you will refine what you think about your subject. And in the final phases, you will narrow your focus even further as you develop the central idea for your speech.

Four cardinal principles sum up effective research

7.11

■ Adopt an exploratory stance.
■ Be systematic in conducting research.
■ Explore a range of sources and types of evidence.
■ Critically evaluate your evidence.

7.4

Organizing Your Ideas

With your research completed, your goal determined, and with the specific purpose of your speech in mind, the fifth step in the speech-making process is organizing your presentation. Another way of looking at organization is to think in terms of organizing yourself and providing a structure for your audience to follow the progression of your speech. That structure will help them understand your evidence, point by point, as you lead them through your argument. Thus, when you are organizing yourself for speaking, you are not creating a thing called a *speech* as much as a relationship with your audience. You want to invite them to go along with you, one step at a time.

7.6

A well-developed speech has four parts (see Figure 7.14). If we approach communication from the *relational view,* which emphasizes how communication is a collaborative process between audience and speaker, we can think of each part as a collaborative interaction:

1. The *introduction* engages the audience by gaining their attention and establishing their relationship with the speaker.
2. The *partition* focuses the audience's attention on the central idea and goal of the speech and previews its main points.
3. The *body* develops each main point and demonstrates to the audience how it supports the central idea of the speech.
4. The *conclusion* provides a summary as well as a sense of closure by restating the central idea and main points and by offering a dramatic finish.

FIGURE 7.14 Parts of a Well-Developed Speech

I. Introduction
   A. Engages audience by gaining attention
   B. Engages audience by establishing relationship with speaker
II. Partition
   A. Focuses audience's attention on central idea/goal
   B. Previews main points
III. Body
   A. Develops first main point
      1. Provides support
      2. Provides support
   B. Develops second main point
      1. Provides support
      2. Provides support
   C. Develops third main point
      1. Provides support
      2. Provides support
IV. Conclusion
   A. Restates central idea
   B. Restates main points
   C. Offers dramatic finish

Each part of a speech can be thought of as a collaborative interaction between the speaker and audience.

Part 1: The Introduction

Speaking is a process of relating. Given that, the **introduction** of your speech is your initial interaction with your audience. In the introduction, you want to get their attention and then create a connection with them that lays the groundwork for introducing your central idea (see Figure 7.15). But before you get to that idea, take your time. First, provide a fully developed introduction.

Some speakers err by starting out prematurely. Think about the speeches you've listened to that began with something like "My topic is about . . ." or "Today, I want to tell

Think of the introduction of your speech as your initial interaction with your audience. Use it to gain their attention and build rapport with them.

introduction The first part of a speech; engages the audience by gaining their attention and establishing their relationship with the speaker.

FIGURE 7.15 The Introduction

Gain the audience's attention
   ✔ Questions
   ✔ Thought-provoking quotation of statistic
   ✔ Concrete example
   ✔ Humor
   ✔ References to occasion or audience

Build rapport
   ✔ Relate to credibility
   ✔ Create motivation

you about . . . ." These phrases belong to the second part of the speech: the partition. Don't get ahead of yourself. First things first: Establish a connection with your audience and gain their attention so as to pave the way for the second step.

7.8

Gaining Attention   You can use a number of strategies to gain the attention of your audience. For instance, you might begin by asking them questions that elicit an overt or silent response, or you might use a thought-provoking quotation or statistic. Some speakers begin by citing a concrete example. A detailed example is especially useful for getting attention because it paints a verbal picture to engage the audience's imagination. Speakers may also use examples or images that evoke feelings to create a sense of identification and empathy. If you have skill at using humor, a tasteful and appropriate joke can be a good way to start. And in some speeches that address the issues and concerns of a special occasion, it may be appropriate to gain attention by referring to the occasion and the reason the audience is present.

A creative speaker can also combine several of these attention-getting strategies, as Janet did in her speech about how to protect your house from being flooded when a heavy snowfall is melting. She referred to concrete examples in describing the personal belongings that were destroyed when her own home was flooded. She even placed some of these damaged objects, including books and photographs, on a table in front of the room. Then Janet asked the audience if they had similar types of cherished items at home that they would hate to lose, not only getting their attention but getting them to identify and empathize with her, as well.

There are also some things you should *not* say at the start of your speech. For example, there is no need to tell your audience how much difficulty you had coming up with a topic or to apologize for what you perceive to be the shortcomings of your speech. If you have a cold, there is no need to tell the audience you have a congested head or a sore throat; they can probably see and hear that for themselves. Finally, don't come right out and state the topic or goal of your speech, since that's done in part two, the partition. Instead, start with a strong attention getter. Make your audience want to listen to you.

Whichever attention-getting strategy or strategies you use, your goal is to gain your audience's attention right from the start. As you deliver your introduction, it's also important to use a significant amount of eye contact with your audience—in keeping with the norms of your relational community for using eye gaze. This will further enable you to establish rapport from the beginning of your speech.

7.12

7.9

Building Rapport   Building rapport is related to developing credibility. When you establish your credibility to speak about your topic, you motivate your audience to be receptive to your central idea and the main points of your speech. How much effort you make to building credibility and motivating your audience to listen should be determined by your audience analysis. Consider how receptive they will likely be to you and your ideas when you prepare your introduction.

partition   The second part of a speech; focuses the audience's attention on the central idea and purpose of the speech and provides an overview of its main points.

central idea   A single sentence stated in the partition to synthesize each of the main points of a speech; the thesis sentence.

Part 2: The Partition

The second part of your speech, the **partition,** is where you state your central idea and goal and introduce your *main points.* You might think of your **central idea** as one single sentence that crystallizes everything you want to say in your speech. Sometimes, this is also referred to as the thesis of a speech. Each of the main points that you develop stems from the central idea.

While the purpose of the introduction is to gain attention and develop rapport with your audience, the purpose of the partition is to focus the audience's attention on your central idea and preview the main points you plan to present in support of that idea. In some speaking situations, it may also be valuable to further motivate listeners to stay attuned to you and your topic by demonstrating how your subject is relevant to their own needs and self-interests. Overall, the partition is vitally important for laying a foundation for the rest of your speech. Let's examine its elements in more detail.

The Central Idea and Goal   To reiterate, use your introduction to gain the audience's attention and build rapport with them. Then, state your central idea forcefully in the partition of your speech. Don't get ahead of yourself by stating your central idea too soon.

To make sure they deliver their central idea with appropriate force and timing, some speakers pause at the end of the introduction. Using pauses is a great way to punctuate the separate parts of your speech. Or you can use a transitional phrase to move from your introduction to your partition. Common transitional phrases include "This leads me to my speaking goal . . ." and "Today, I want to convince you that . . . ." Another suitable transition is "After you hear my speech today, I want you to understand that . . . ."

You may be skeptical about why it's important to state your central idea and reveal your goal now, during the partition, without also offering the necessary proof for the audience to accept them. You may be thinking, "I don't want to tell my audience what my central idea is right up front because they might reject it before even hearing the rest of my speech, where I tell them my main points and evidence." Is this a valid concern?

Research on this subject by O'Keefe (1998) has found that speakers are usually more persuasive when they explicitly state their argument and then later go into detail about their sources of evidence. In other words, the more clearly you lay out the structure of your speech for your audience, the more clearly they will understand your argument. And that, in turn, leads to your being more, not less, persuasive. In addition, O'Keefe suggests that by providing more explicit details of an argument and its elements, a speaker will be perceived as more credible by his or her listeners.

Preview of Main Points   In addition to stating your central idea and goal in the partition, you should also do a preview of the main points that you will cover in the body of your speech when you develop the central idea and fulfill the goal. Think of it using a "roadmap" metaphor: Your preview provides your listeners with a mental roadmap of the highlights of your speech, showing them the general route you're going to take.

Think carefully about how many main points you can successfully develop in your speech. Of course, that will depend a great deal on the nature of your topic and the kinds and amount of evidence you gathered and selected in conducting research. The speaking occasion and audience are also important considerations here. In most cases, however, you want to have a limited number of main points. In a 10-minute speech, for instance, you can successfully develop three or four main points in support of your main idea.

For instance, in her speech on home maintenance to protect against flooding, Janet developed four main points. During the partition of her speech, she stated this central idea: "With a few easy steps of maintenance, you can save yourself from the aggravation of having your home flooded when snow melts." From there, she continued by outlining the four steps, previewing them without actually explaining how to do each one. She said, by way of a forecast:

> Today, I want to tell you first about the importance of first sealing the foundation with caulking materials. A second easy step is to make sure that water is being diverted from the foundation with proper placement of downspouts. The third step is to make sure the gutters and downspouts are kept clear. And the fourth step, which may be especially

important when there is an excessive snowfall—like the one we had last month—is to get out a shovel and move large snow accumulations away from your house.

Speakers who integrate presentation aids into their speech, such as a flipchart or a series of PowerPoint slides, will sometimes use a bulleted list of main points for this forecasting part of the partition.

As mentioned earlier, it's sometimes effective to use the partition step of the speech to emphasize how the topic relates to the audience. This is especially true for persuasive speeches. When you establish for listeners how the topic connects with them, you provide further justification for them to be persuaded: special interest justification.

Once you have completed the partition of your speech, your audience will have a clear sense of where you are headed. Moreover, by hearing your central idea and goal, audience members will know what kind of response you expect of them. After hearing the introduction and partition of a speech intended primarily to persuade, for example, audience members will know that they are expected to make a choice and either agree or disagree with the speaker. And the speaker whose goal is to share information will communicate through his or her introduction and partition that audience members are expected simply to understand that information.

VIDEO VIEW

7.13

Again, the partition of your speech is where you create the foundation. You will elaborate on each of your main points in the body of your speech. This process of establishing a foundation and then building on it can be compared to the discussion of Gernsbacher's (1997) *structure-building framework theory,* which we explored in Module Three. Gernsbacher suggests that listeners receive and comprehend information by building cognitive structures. In terms of speech making, when you use the partition to lay the groundwork for the rest of your speech—stating the central idea and goal and previewing the main points—your listeners are able to create cognitive structures early on that serve as the foundation for understanding you.

Remember, structure building is *collaborative.* The speaker provides the blueprint to help the audience see the coherence of the speech. The speaker then guides the audience through the steps of adding information onto the foundation and showing the connections among ideas.

The process of building the structure will also be enhanced by the way that you organize the main points of your speech. As noted above, each of those main points stems from the central idea of the speech. The speaker's task is to organize information into a meaningful pattern in the body of the presentation so the audience members can understand it given the foundation of previous information.

Part 3: The Body

Next, it's time to prepare the **body** of your speech, where the main points outlined in the partition are developed. You can use any of several patterns of arrangement to structure the body, depending on your specific goal and how you have phrased your central idea.

> **body** The third part and essential core of a speech; develops each main point and demonstrates to the audience how it supports the central idea of the speech.
>
> **patterns of arrangement** Organizational plans or structures that guide the audience to follow the progression of the speech.

ONLINE JOURNAL

7.11

Patterns of arrangement are organizational plans or structures that guide the audience to follow the progression of the main points of your speech. Here are some of the most common patterns (see Figure 7.16):

- *Logical order:* Develops a sequence of arguments that justify the central idea and goal.
- *Problem-solving order:* Analyzes a problem and advocates a way of responding to it.
- *Motivational order:* Develops a sequence of motives for understanding information or adopting a course of action.
- *Groupings order:* Explains a topic as a set of subtopics, develops a chronology, creates a spatial map of ideas, or ranks ideas in ascending or descending order.

FIGURE 7.16 Common Patterns of Arrangement

Logical order	Problem-solving order	Motivational order	Groupings order
• Develops a sequence of arguments that justify the central idea and goal	• Analyzes a problem • Advocates a way of responding to it	• Develops a sequence of motives for understanding information or adopting a course of action	• Explains a topic as a set of subtopics • Develops a chronology • Creates a spatial map of ideas • Ranks ideas in ascending or descending order

FIGURE 7.16 Common Patterns of Arrangement

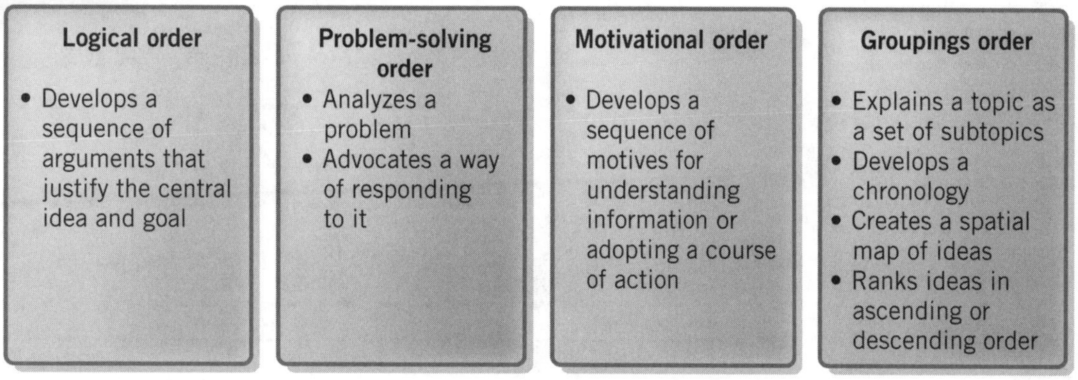

Use one of these organizational plans or structures to guide your audience in following the progression of your speech.

Logical Order   A **logical order** guides the audience through the reasoning process that justifies the speaker's central idea and goal. When the goal is to persuade, the speaker may also engage audience members in constructing the logical connections between the evidence and claims and the link between the main points and the central idea and goal.

When a speaker uses a logical order of arrangement, he or she may develop one or several arguments as main points to justify the central idea. In his speech about body image disturbance, for instance, Heath Rainbolt developed two different main points. The first main point was an argument to explain anorexia and bulimia as symptoms of body image disturbance. The second main point was a causal claim that body image disturbance results from embracing false ideals of what one is supposed to look like.

The body of the speech may also have just one main point to make a single argument. For instance, a single effect might be explained by outlining a series of causes. The logical development of a speech about that topic would be to establish the order of causes, from one to the next. The argument would be that these causes, in succession, led to the observed effect or that a number of different causes interacted with one another to produce the effect.

Problem-Solving Order   In using a **problem-solving order,** the speaker explains a problem and its causes and then advocates the best course of action for solving it. A problem-solving speech may also engage the audience by urging them to do something to solve the problem or think about possible solutions, as is the case with a speech in which the goal is to induce further inquiry.

Figure 7.17 depicts a common sequence for developing the body of a problem-solving speech. Notice how a speaker might first focus on the problem by describing it and its significance. In some ways, this part of the speech is a combination of informing and persuading the audience to understand and acknowledge the significance of the problem. From there, the speaker examines the underlying causes of the problem and then explains a course of action that should be followed. This involves making the case as to why this particular solution is more desirable than other possible solutions. In the final part, the speaker urges audience members to take action. This may entail motivating the audience to do something directly to solve the problem, such as change their

logical order   A pattern of arrangement in which a sequence of arguments is developed that justify the speaker's central idea and purpose.

problem-solving order   A pattern of arrangement in which a problem is analyzed and a way of responding to it is advocated.

In using this pattern of arrangement, the speaker explains a problem and its causes and then advocates the best course of action for solving it. He or she may also engage the audience by urging them to do something to solve the problem or think about possible solutions.

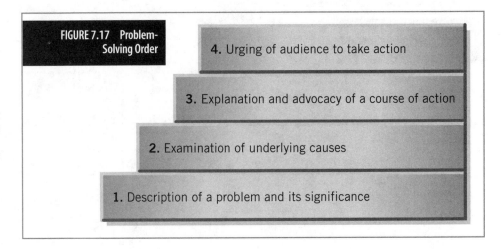

FIGURE 7.17 Problem-Solving Order

4. Urging of audience to take action

3. Explanation and advocacy of a course of action

2. Examination of underlying causes

1. Description of a problem and its significance

own behavior, or to take an indirect course of action, such as persuade others with decision-making authority to act.

A variation on the problem-solving order is used for speeches in which the speaker's primary goal is *inducement to inquiry*. Recall that in this type of speech, the speaker invites the audience to become involved in the process of problem solving. The speaker, whose purpose is to induce inquiry, will begin with an explanation of a problem and why it is significant and then explore the causes of the problem. But the next steps will be to provide an overview of possible solutions and then to call for action by *inviting the audience* to participate in the process of problem solving. Remember, the speaker who is inducing inquiry does not advocate a preferred solution to the problem.

The **method of residues** is another variation of the problem-solving speech. In this pattern, the speaker first outlines several solutions to a problem. Then, he or she explains why each of the proposed solutions, except the last solution, is not satisfactory. Finally, he or she provides reasons for adopting that last solution. Another way of thinking of the method of residues is to describe it as a process of elimination. You probably do this in everyday situations in which you eliminate all of your options but one, and then follow through with the last option.

Motivational Order　Alan H. Monroe developed the *Monroe Motivated Sequence* in the 1920s. His book *Principles of Public Speaking* is one of the long-standing guides for teaching public speaking. It is now in its fifteenth edition. German and Gronbeck, coauthors who succeeded Monroe (and Ehninger), wrote the most recent edition (German, Gronbeck, Ehninger, and Monroe, 2004). As described by Wilson and Arnold (1964):

> [The] motivated sequence, more than any other [pattern of arrangement,] is psychologically planned to lead your audience's thinking naturally and easily from a vague interest in your subject to a definite acceptance of the attitude or action you are advocating. Each step in the sequence is built on the preceding steps. (p. 219)

The basic format of the **motivated sequence** is outlined in Figure 7.18. The five steps are as follows:

1. The *attention step* is part of the introduction. It is emphasized in this sequence in order to arouse audience awareness to a situation. A strong attention step is especially important if your audience analysis has revealed that your listeners are not interested in your topic or do not see how it has a vital link to their experience.

method of residues　A variation of the problem-solving order in which several possible solutions are identified and then eliminated until only the predetermined desirable solution remains.

motivational order　A pattern of arrangement in which a sequence of motives is developed for understanding information or adopting a course of action; the five steps include attention, need, satisfaction, visualization, and action.

FIGURE 7.18
Motivational Order

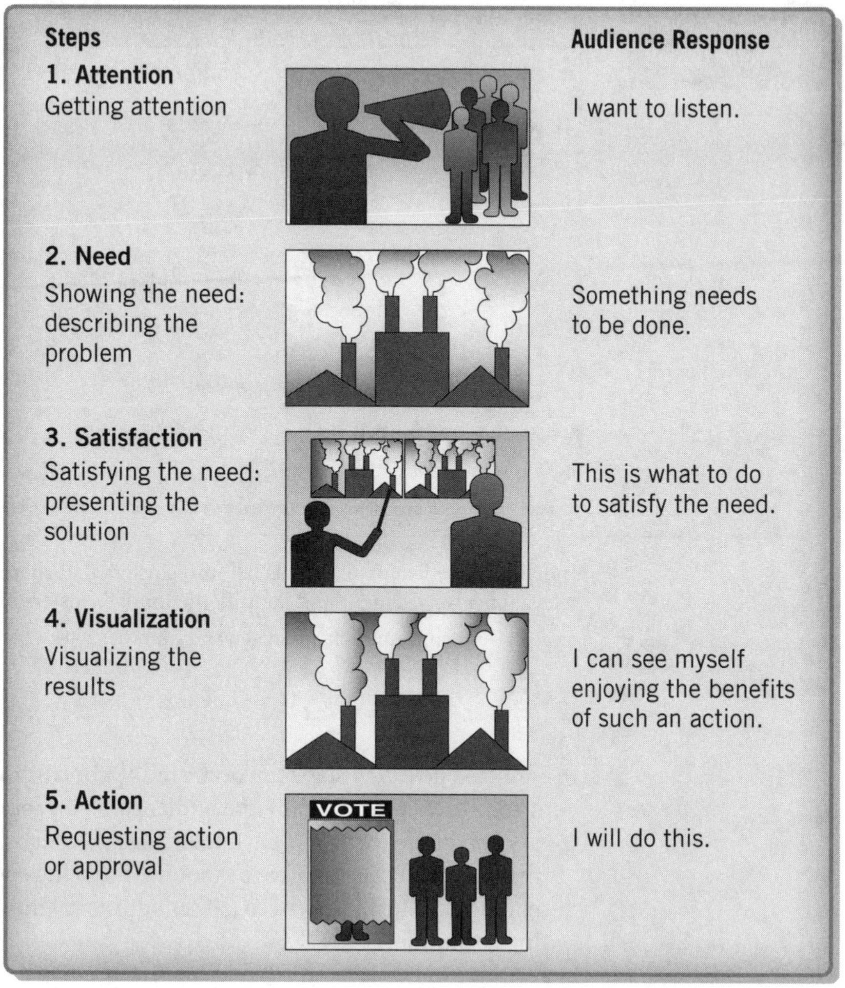

Monroe's motivated sequence identifies the five steps involved in persuading an audience to your attitude or action.

Source: German, Gronbeck, Ehninger, and Monroe, 2004.

2. The *need step* focuses the audience's attention on how one of their basic psychological needs, wants, or interests is not currently being met. This step may be used in a problem-solving speech to explain how the problem is the frustration of a basic need. In an informative speech, the need step establishes audience members' need to know more about the subject, especially how the information will help them.

3. The *satisfaction step* provides the means for meeting audience members' unmet needs. For a problem-solving speech, this would involve presenting the proposed solution. For an informative speech, this would mean presenting a detailed body of information that the audience needs to know.

4. The *visualization step* engages the audience in using their imagination to envision how the solution or information provided in the satisfaction step will solve the unmet need identified in the need step. For a problem-solving speech, this may involve having the audience visualize how the proposed solution will resolve the problem or proving to them that the problem will worsen if the proposed solution is not implemented.

FIGURE 7.19
Motive Clusters

Affiliation	Achievement	Power
Companionship	Acquisition/saving	Aggression
Conformity	Success/display	Authority/dominance
Deference/dependence	Prestige	Defense
Sympathy/generosity	Pride	Fear
Loyalty	Adventure/change	Autonomy/independence
Tradition	Perseverance	
Reverence/worship	Creativity	
Sexual attraction	Curiosity	
	Personal enjoyment	

Individual motivational appeals fall into clusters that share a common theme. Think of a current television advertisement and identify the motive clusters in it.

Source: German, Gronbeck, Ehninger, and Monroe, 2004.

5. The *action step* may occur in the conclusion of the speech as the speaker makes a specific call to action by the audience. In a problem-solving speech, the speaker may ask the audience to do particular things, which he or she will outline in a concrete manner. In an informative or inquiry-inducing speech, the speaker may urge the audience to take further steps to gather additional information or to take part in formulating a solution.

Advertisements provide compelling illustrations of the different types of motivational appeals. For instance, many ads provide a kind of fictional dramatization that grabs our attention and then imply or state how one of our basic needs is not being fulfilled. This is sometimes described as *creating a need*. When Monroe developed his model in the 1920s, he drew on his observations of how radio advertisements constructed needs. In a more recent version of his work (German et al., 2004), the **motive clusters** from the original model have been categorized to form three motive clusters: affiliation, achievement, and power (see Figure 7.19).

7.9

Once the advertiser has planted the need, or listeners have been convinced that one of their motivational needs is not being met, the next step is to claim that buying the product being promoted will satisfy that unmet need. The visualization step depicts the happy product buyer, whose need has now been fulfilled, and the action step provides the details about how much the product costs and where and when to buy it.

Some speeches and advertisements shorten the motivational sequence, usually including just the first three steps of attention, need, and satisfaction. Wilson and Arnold (1964) suggest that this is particularly pertinent for informative speeches, in which there may not be a follow-up action.

Groupings Order: Topical, Chronological, Spatial, Ascending, and Descending   The fourth approach to organizing the body of your speech is simply a matter of creating groupings of interconnected ideas. You can use any of these **groupings orders** to help your audience see the relationships among the main points of your speech:

motive clusters   Affiliation, achievement, and power.

groupings order   A pattern of arrangement in which a topic is explained as a set of subtopics, developed as a chronology, depicted as a spatial map, or analyzed as a set of ideas in ascending or descending order.

- *Topical order:* Examines a topic as a set of interrelated subtopics, or parts of the whole.
- *Chronological order:* Develops a timeline or presents the sequence of steps in a process.
- *Spatial order:* Creates a visual map of ideas.
- *Descending or ascending order:* Ranks ideas by familiarity or order of importance.

Let's consider each of these types of groupings individually.

Dividing the topic into several subtopics can develop a **topical order.** Use the analogy of a "pie" to visualize how you might cut your topic into wedges, or subtopics, in order to explain it. Typically, a speaker identifies three or four different parts of the whole and talks about each in turn. Each part is explained using the evidence that supports or amplifies it.

For instance, An Nguyet's speech about Caodaism discussed four different yet interconnected core principles that the followers of this faith believe in. As she spoke about each principle, she also observed how it was based on the traditions of one of the major world religions from which Caodaism was derived.

A **chronological order** develops a timeline, organizing events according to the order in which they happened. This organization is useful for narrating a story or talking about historical developments. When Sue spoke about NASCAR, for instance, she covered three phases in the history of the sport.

A chronological method of arrangement is also useful for discussing the steps or phases in a process, especially when one builds on or follows directly from another. For instance, Cassidy outlined stages of maturation based on Erik Erikson's theory of development. She focused on the four adult stages of development and noted that at each stage, an individual must deal with different psychological challenges before moving in a healthy manner to the next stage. Many procedures can also best be explained as a sequence of steps that must be completed in an appropriate order. So-called how-to speeches typically use a chronological order.

A **spatial order** is used to map ideas, or show the physical relationship among them. Sometimes, a speaker may literally use a map to distinguish the parts of his or her topic. For instance, Labov's (1996) map of regional dialects of English shows distinctive patterns of speech for the communities of people residing in certain geographic areas. Someone presenting a speech on regional speech patterns would do well to follow Labov's map in organizing his or her ideas.

Another example of mapping is illustrated with the "Great Pop vs. Soda Controversy" web page created by McConchie (2002). It provides an online survey, which viewers can complete to register their preference for naming a carbonated beverage. After the viewer votes, he or she can see a color-coded map that sorts out regional differences in preferences. This map would provide a logical organizational tool for developing a speech about this topic.

In describing the three facets of a well-rounded exercise program, Matt used a spatial order in a creative way, rather than a topical method of organization. Since he is a professional trainer, he was able to take photographs of the various rooms at the gym where he works. He then used the photos to create a PowerPoint slide show. As Matt moved through the parts of his speech, he showed slides of the various rooms where each of the three major types of physical activities is performed. He started in the weight-training room, discussing the types of weights and electronic weight-resistance machines that are used for strength training. From there, Matt took his audience to the aerobics room, where he once again identified types of equipment and described the values of aerobic exercise. His final stop dealt with the third component of an exercise program: stretching. While showing photos of people doing various types of exercises, he explained the benefits of stretching.

topical order A variation of the groupings pattern of arrangement in which a topic is examined as a set of interrelated subtopics, or parts of the whole.

chronological order A variation of the groupings pattern of arrangement in which a topic is examined by developing a timeline or presenting the sequence of steps in a process.

spatial order A variation of the groupings pattern of arrangement in which a topic is examined by creating a visual map of ideas.

A **descending or ascending order** is used to rank a series of ideas by order of familiarity or importance. A *descending order* moves from most to least familiar or important. For instance, someone presenting an informative speech might begin by discussing the idea that the audience is most familiar with and then progressively discuss less and less familiar ideas. A persuasive speaker might use a descending order to rank the possible solutions for a problem, starting with the most effective solution and then going through the list of less effective solutions.

An *ascending order* proceeds from least to most familiar or important. As such, it's an effective way to build up to the best solution or the most common reason. An informative speaker, for example, might begin by presenting lesser known details about his or her subject and build up to more common and significant points. A persuasive speaker can develop his or her case by leading the audience through a series of minor arguments to the final main argument. In sum, using an ascending order provides a strong finish to a speech.

Whether the speaker's plan is to use a descending or an ascending order, it's important that he or she provide suitable transitions between ideas. Using transition words and phrases—such as *next* and *another, first* and *final*—help the audience keep track of the progression of ideas.

Part 4: The Conclusion

The final part of the speech, the **conclusion,** is a relatively brief step but vital nonetheless. It has two main functions: to restate your central idea and main points and to end with a sense of dramatic finality.

The **restatement** of your central idea and main points is important for reinforcing the message of your speech. To do so, you want to rephrase your central idea in a creative way and repeat the three or four main points that you developed in the body of your speech. As an example, Matt ended his speech on a three-part exercise program with this restatement:

> Well, we're at the end of the tour of our gym. On it, I have tried to emphasize that all three parts of an integrated exercise program—weight training to build muscle mass, aerobics to get your heart thumping, and stretching to enhance your flexibility—are important. It isn't enough just to yank a few barbells or jog on a treadmill. Both of those need to be done, but don't forget to include those smooth, slow, stretching exercises, too.

7.12

A **statement of dramatic finality** provides closure to your speech. This is another opportunity to use your creativity. Some speakers will end with a flourish by asking a challenging question or making a bold and dramatic statement. A quotation or a vivid illustration can also be a creative way of leaving a lasting impression at the end. A quotation or the refrain from a popular saying or song can also be used to create finality.

In this final part of Matt's speech, he showed a PowerPoint slide of a group of happy exercisers, talking with one another in the juice bar of the gym. His speech ended with these words:

> And after you've hit the showers, make a final stop in the juice bar, where you can join friends and celebrate the hard work you've done. I'm looking forward to seeing you at the gym soon.

descending or ascending order
A variation of the groupings pattern of arrangement in which a topic is examined by ranking ideas by familiarity or order of importance.

conclusion   The fourth and final part of a speech; provides a summary as well as sense of closure by restating the central idea and main points and by offering a dramatic finish.

restatement   A summary statement made during the conclusion to repeat and reinforce the main ideas and central idea.

statement of dramatic finality
The last line in the conclusion that is intended to give closure to the speech.

7.14

Implications for Communication: Outline Your Ideas

When you organize your speech, you are basically organizing yourself and providing your audience with a structure to follow as they listen to your speech. To be most effective, keep in mind three main principles for organizing your ideas:

7.10

- *Create a sequence.* Decide on a sequence for your ideas that will make sense to your audience. Each part of the sequence should build on the previous one, such that you lead your audience through your argument.
- *Create an outline.* Document your sequence by creating an outline. Doing so will provide you with a plan to follow in delivering your speech and keep you and your audience on track.
- *Use the four parts of a speech.* Make sure your speech includes these four essential parts: an introduction to gain the audience's attention; a partition to focus them on your central idea and goal and to preview your main points; a body to develop your main points; and a conclusion to restate your central idea and main points and to provide a sense of dramatic closure.

7.5

7.6

Deciding on a Presentation Style

It might be useful for you to consider everything you have done up until now—selecting a subject, analyzing the audience and situation, formulating goals, conducting research, and organizing your ideas—as the conceptualization of a performance. For indeed, the **delivery** of a speech is a performance. It involves using both verbal and nonverbal aspects of communication to relate your ideas to an audience and help them understand what you are saying.

7.7

Printed texts of speeches are sometimes available in books or newspapers or on the Internet, especially of speeches presented by public figures. But they do not embody the speeches; rather, they are the written records of these speeches. It is the delivery of the speech that makes it come alive and that is ultimately the determinant of its success.

As we look at the process of preparing to deliver a speech, we will consider two types of performances: a live performance for an audience and a prerecorded or mediated presentation.

A Live Performance versus a Mediated Presentation

Delivering a speech before an audience is a unique event. To explore this notion, consider an analogy to how music is performed by an orchestra or a band. After the score has been composed, it's time for the musicians to prepare the piece for presentation to an audience. But what the composer hears in his or her head while writing the piece and what comes out as an actual live performance will likely be two different things. Similarly, if you ask performers about the difference between rehearsing and performing, they will probably tell you that every performance before an audience is a unique event. Even though the actual collection of notes is the same from one situation to another, how the piece is delivered and received will be unique with each new audience.

In Module One, we explored the channels of communication through which messages are transmitted. We learned about the views expressed by Bavelas, Hutchinson, Kenwood, and Matheson (1997), who believe that face-to-face communication should

delivery The performance of a speech for a live audience or a mediated audience.

FIGURE 7.20 Styles of Delivery

Manuscript delivery
Written out and
read aloud

Memorized delivery
Memorized and
recited word for word

Extemporaneous delivery
Carefully planned out
and rehearsed but
spoken "on the fly"

Each style of delivery has advantages and disadvantages.

be regarded as the standard for communication because it best integrates the verbal and nonverbal codes of communication. Bavelas and her associates also stress that the face-to-face channel of communication provides instantaneous collaboration between the speaker and listener in ways that allow for immediate feedback and adaptation of communicators to one another.

Perhaps the most distinctive element of a live performance, as opposed to a taped or mediated one, is the nature of the immediate connection between the speaker and audience. The audience provides direct feedback, and the speaker is able to adapt to it immediately, fine-tuning his or her message and delivery.

Three Styles of Presentation for a Live Audience As you prepare to deliver a speech before a live audience, consider three options for doing so (see Figure 7.20):

- Manuscript delivery
- Memorized delivery
- Extemporaneous delivery

Each of these has the potential to maximize the three dimensions of face-to-face communication examined by Bavelas and her co-writers.

The first two delivery options—manuscript and memorized—are pretty much self-explanatory. A speaker using a **manuscript delivery** has his or her whole speech written out and reads it aloud, and the speaker using a **memorized delivery** has committed his or her whole speech to memory and recites it word for word.

The **extemporaneous delivery** style requires somewhat more definition. In practical terms, when you deliver a speech extemporaneously, you will likely speak from a set of notes. Your notes may take the form of an outline, a series of bulleted points on note cards, or a presentation aid such as a PowerPoint slide or a poster. An extemporaneous-style speech is carefully planned out and rehearsed many times, as is true of a speech that uses the manuscript or memorized style of delivery. But each time you practice and deliver an extemporaneous speech, you will use a slightly different wording and a slightly different manner. This is where the concept of being extemporaneous can be loosely translated from the Latin word that means "from the moment." How you actually phrase and deliver the speech comes from the moment.

Each style of delivery has advantages and disadvantages. In discussing them in the sections that follow, we will use as criteria these five aspects of delivery:

manuscript delivery Performing a speech by reading aloud a fully written text.

memorized delivery Performing a speech by reciting it from memory, word for word.

extemporaneous delivery Performing a speech "from the moment"; the overall structure is carefully planned in advance but the final wording occurs at the time of delivery.

- *Wording:* How a speaker arranges words in a speech to achieve clarity, conciseness, concreteness, and creativity and to speak appropriately for the situation.
- *Voice:* How the qualities of vocal rate, pitch, loudness, variation, and pausing are used in order to communicate in a conversational manner.
- *Physical action:* How the speaker uses gestures, posture, location (at a lectern, for instance), facial expressions, and eye contact to communicate with the audience.
- *Collaboration:* How the speaker interacts with and adapts to the audience.
- *Other nonverbal elements:* The speaker's clothing, objects, presentation aids, and so on.

VIDEO
VIEW

7.15

Manuscript Delivery   The manuscript delivery style affords the best opportunity for crafting the language of your speech. By writing out your speech word for word, you will be able to carefully hone the language used, and by reading that written draft aloud to your audience, you will ensure that that language will be heard as intended.

Some of the qualities of effective wording that receive attention in preparing for a manuscript delivery, as well as for other types of delivery, are as follows:

- *Clarity:* Select the words that will best explain your topic and that your audience will understand. Sometimes, this may require defining words, especially technical terms and concepts that the audience has not heard of before.
- *Conciseness:* Phrase your ideas with an economy of language, never using more words than are necessary to make your point.
- *Concreteness:* Engage your audience by using words that appeal to the senses and thus make abstract concepts real and tangible.
- *Creativity:* Use figures of speech, such as metaphors and analogies, to express your ideas in creative ways. Some figures of speech employ repetitions of sounds, rhythms, and parallel structures to engage the audience in what's being said. Engaging your audience in this way will help you maintain their attention, appeal to them emotionally, and make your points easier for them to remember.
- *Appropriateness:* Use language that conforms to the audience and the situation. Your choices of words and content should be tasteful and sensitive to the demographic diversity of your listeners.

What are the disadvantages of a manuscript delivery? The primary drawback is that you may sound like you're reading aloud from an essay rather than delivering a speech. When you read from a manuscript, you may lose some of the qualities of effective vocal delivery that are vital for engaging the audience and creating a sense of dialogue with them. These vocal qualities are important in delivering any type of speech:

- The *energetic and forceful* use of vocal dynamics to express the intensity of the speaker's ideas and feelings.
- *Vocal variation* of rate, pitch, and loudness in order to sound spontaneous, help the audience understand ideas, and give dynamic expression to feelings. Effective speakers vary their vocal dynamics as they move from one idea to another.
- The use of *smooth pausing* to punctuate ideas and add emphasis. The use of pauses also serves the valuable function of giving the audience and the speaker alike the opportunity to reflect on what's been said. Effective speakers use silent pauses purposefully rather than clutter their speeches with unintentional "ahs" and "ums."
- Development of a *distinctive voice* that reflects the speaker's personality and is appropriately expressive of his or her role and status.
- A *vocal presence* that commands and maintains the audience's attention.

For successful delivery from a manuscript, you need to spend a substantial amount of time going over the manuscript in rehearsal while paying special attention to these dynamics of vocal delivery. Take a tip from effective newscasters, who read their material from a teleprompter: They are most effective when they create the illusion that they are just thinking of the thoughts as they are reading them. Winans (1938) addresses this idea when he notes that to achieve a sense of conversational engagement with the audience, the speaker should focus on the content of his or her ideas, rather than the words. After all, the words of the speech are merely the vehicle for expressing the ideas. It is also useful to rehearse a manuscript-type speech with a friend or coach, who will tell you when you seem simply to be reading words, rather than speaking ideas.

A speech delivered from a manuscript may also pose challenges for using physical action, especially facial expressions and eye contact, which may be undermined by excessive reading. Again, frequent rehearsal is required. Your goal is to gain enough familiarity with your text that you can look up from it to speak to the audience and make eye contact with them and then return to the text to pick up the next thought or phrase. The most effective speakers are able to look up and make eye contact with their audience about 75 percent of their speaking time.

A practical way to achieve this is to practice your speech with a coach who will provide feedback about your use of eye contact, facial expressions, and so on. Also get used to looking for feedback from your coach by reading the nonverbal responses he or she makes to your speech as you deliver it.

VIDEO
VIEW

7.16

Memorized Delivery   Speakers who use a memorized delivery style enjoy one of the same advantages as manuscript-style speakers when it comes to the wording of the message. That is, they can carefully craft the language of the speech and present it word for word to the audience. Another benefit of a memorized delivery is that it allows the effective use of various types of physical action, such as the following:

- *Gestures and movements:* Effective gestures and movements can be integrated with words, reinforcing and providing accents to the language.
- *A comfortable and relaxed posture:* The speaker's posture should fit the level of formality called for in a given speaking situation. A metaphor for posture is to think of where the speaker stands during his or her speech as the "home base"—for instance, behind a lectern. An effective speaker is comfortable at that home base, balancing his or her weight evenly and standing at his or her full height, rather than slouching.
- *A smooth and confident manner:* Just as the vocal delivery is most effective when it is smooth and used purposefully to express ideas and feelings, so can physical actions be used to communicate the speaker's confidence and poise.
- *Facial communication and eye contact:* The speaker's goal is to communicate a sense of immediacy with the audience, such that they are communicating directly, one on one.

For each style of delivery—manuscript, memorized, and extemporaneous—the above-mentioned types of physical action must be an integral part of how the message is presented. If you decide to memorize your speech, you will have some special advantages in this regard. Because you will have no need to rely on a set of notes or a manuscript, you will be free to move more extensively while speaking. In particular, you won't be confined behind a lectern but can make use of the entire speaking area. Memorizing the whole speech (or at least significant parts of it) also frees your hands to use visual aids. This is important in an informative-type speech that involves showing the audience how something works.

For instance, when Anna presented her speech on automatic external defibrillation (AED), she brought an AED unit into the classroom. Since she had memorized portions of her speech, she was able to move around the room at certain key points. At other points, she stood next to her PowerPoint display to highlight some quotations and statistics. When she arrived at the point in her speech for demonstrating the AED, she moved to the table where the unit was located. In sum, working with a manuscript or set of note cards would have made it very cumbersome for Anna to present her speech effectively.

Be careful, however, that you don't use *too much* movement. Perhaps you've taken a lecture class in which the instructor was a "pacer," who wandered back and forth across the room, or perhaps you've observed a speaker who gestures constantly. Many times, these types of excessive movements become distracting, largely because the pattern of movement is repetitive. Any time a speaker incorporates movement, it should be done with a purpose so as to enhance the delivery of the message.

As noted in discussing the manuscript type of delivery, one of the challenges of speaking to an audience is to engage them by using a style that seems conversational. Speakers who memorize their speeches have a special challenge in this area. It's all too easy to fall into rhythmic patterns when delivering a memorized speech, losing the conversational tone. In fact, the repetitiveness that comes with falling into rhythmic patterns has much the same distracting effect as the movements of a "pacer" or an exaggerated gesturer.

To be more effective when presenting a memorized speech, practice with a coach who will give you feedback. You might also find it useful to make an audio or video recording of yourself. Listen for places where you seem to fall into rhythmic cadences, losing a conversational style of delivery that is energetic, varied, and seemingly spontaneous and smooth.

To be sure, the downfall of many memorized speeches is that they lack spontaneity. In both the manuscript and memorized styles of delivery, it can be hard to depart from the script of the speech as it was written or memorized to interact in a spontaneous manner with the audience.

Extemporaneous Delivery   The sense of spontaneity and immediate feedback is truly the hallmark of the extemporaneous style of delivery. Recall from the earlier discussion that this type of speech comes "from the moment." Extemporaneous speakers can capitalize on the moment to practice all of the principles of good vocal delivery.

7.13

The extemporaneous speaker must beware, however, of one of the most often cited problems in vocal delivery: *vocalized pauses.* These are instances in which the speaker inserts filler phrases and sounds. An occasional "ah" or "um" is normal. The problem arises when vocalized pauses create a pattern. Once again, a pattern is repetitive, and that spells distraction for the audience.

Another problem for extemporaneous speakers is the use of *filler verbalizations*—for instance, excessive use of phrases such as "OK" and questions such as "You know what I'm saying?" These verbalizations disrupt the smooth flow of your presentation and clutter your speech, once again distracting the audience.

In order to deal with both these types of verbal clutter, we must first recognize why we use them: Silence is uncomfortable. We insert vocalized pauses and filler verbalizations in a speech to fill the silence that occurs when we're thinking of how to say something. We need to learn, instead, to appreciate the silence of uncluttered pausing and even to practice deliberate pausing. Recognize that a pause not only gives you a chance to think about your phrasing, but it also provides the audience with an opportunity to reflect. The use of well-paced pauses can add drama and impact to your speech.

Since you will not have prepared a manuscript and will not have memorized your speech, a key part of your preparation as an extemporaneous speaker will be to construct a *speaker's outline.* This is a skeleton version of the outline of your main points. It can be recorded on a few note cards or displayed for all to see as a PowerPoint slide or a poster.

An extemporaneous speaker follows the structure of his or her outline but creates the language "on the fly." This opens the door to two problems: failing

7.11

to speak concisely and rambling too far from the planned structure. To avoid these problems, you must rehearse extensively. By working from your speaker's outline a number of times, you will become comfortable with how one point leads to the next and thus be able to think on your feet more quickly.

Delivery with Presentation Aids   Earlier in this module, we observed that a variety of objects and presentation aids can be used in a speech as a form of evidence. Examples include charts, diagrams, pictures, and drawings, as well as sound and video clips, that you incorporate into your speech. You may create presentation aids in traditional formats or by using the capabilities of a multimedia computer.

Presentation aids enhance and dramatize what you are saying and offer visual reinforcement to your key points. For instance, graphs and charts are excellent tools for displaying the relative weights and proportions of statistics. Particularly significant quotations can be displayed on PowerPoint slides and posters. Likewise, a visual display is a useful means of posting an important date or address that audience members might want to know after the speech, perhaps to do some type of activity as a follow-up to a persuasive presentation.

Despite the usefulness of presentation aids, you should be on guard against some of the ways that using them can undermine your effectiveness as a speaker. Follow these guidelines:

Use Presentation Aids in Proportion   The dictum "Less is more" is appropriate in selecting presentation aids. Whether you plan on using PowerPoint slides in a presentation or a set of objects in a demonstration, be selective so that you don't use too many. For a PowerPoint presentation, one handy rule of thumb is to use one or two slides for each 3 minutes of the presentation. That means that a 10-minute presentation would not require more than six or seven slides. Cut that number in half if you are only speaking for 5 minutes.

The same guideline about proportionality applies to using recorded music and other audio and video clips. Keep these segments relatively short, such that they don't exceed more than 10 percent of your speaking time. So, 1 minute of a 10-minute speech might involve playing a segment of a song or video or just 30 seconds of a 5-minute speech.

Be Sparse with Text   One of the most frequent faults of PowerPoint presentations is having too much information on individual slides. Be concise in terms of the amount of text you present, and then present what text you use in an accessible manner by using a bulleted list format. Each bulleted point on a slide or poster should contain just three or four words, and there should be no more than four or five bulleted points per slide.

Following these basic rules will help you avoid another potential problem with using text in presentation aids: simply reading aloud what's on a poster or slide. Just as the manuscript for your speech should not be regarded as an essay to be read aloud, your PowerPoint presentation should not relegate your speech to a simple voiceover of your slide show. Your presentation aids should reinforce the ideas of your speech; they are not your speech, however.

Be aware of how much you turn away from the audience to look at slides and other text-type presentation aids. Plan to have a copy of the text or a hard copy of your slides in front of you so you don't have to read it from the display.

Don't Pass Objects around the Audience   In some speaking situations, the speaker may want his or her audience to see things up close, but it's not usually a good idea to pass objects around the room. It's better to display objects so everyone can see them at the same time. That way, the speaker can ensure that everyone in the audience will focus on a given object at the same time—namely, when he or she wants them to at the appropriate point in the speech.

To display objects effectively, they also must be large enough for everyone to see. Small photographs and drawings should be enlarged for this purpose, and complicated graphics should be simplified as much as possible.

The Speaker Is the Best Presentation Aid of All   The final guideline for incorporating presentation aids is to consider how the presence and delivery of the speaker are the best aids of all. When public speaking is considered from the relational view of communication, the speaker takes center stage to perform his or her role in tandem with audience members, who are playing their role.

To enhance your performance as a speaker, dress the part. In Module Four, we explored the concept of **impression management** with special reference to dressing for a part in order to enhance the favorable view that others will form of you. You will enhance the delivery of your speech by wearing clothing that's appropriate to the speaking situation and otherwise maintaining a professional appearance.

In deciding what to wear, choose clothing that is comfortable yet formal enough to fit the norms of the occasion. Your analysis of the speaking situation will help you discern the appropriate level of formality. If you are delivering your speech at a seminar or other professional event, you should present a fairly formal appearance and wear professional business attire. On the other hand, if you are speaking to an audience of your peers, whether in the classroom or on the job, you should dress like they do—more casually, in most cases.

Even so, there are some special considerations to keep in mind in deciding what to wear on the day that you speak in class. Be aware of those items in your wardrobe that might detract from your presentation. For example, something that has a slogan printed on it will likely be distracting, unless the slogan is somehow appropriate and intended to reinforce the ideas in your speech. If you speak about a subject related to your major or professional work, it may be effective to wear what is considered the "uniform" for that field.

7.13

Along with what you wear, you can communicate your presence as the most effective presentation aid by being willing to take center stage. That means speaking with your full authority and truly establishing your presence in front of the audience. Some speakers try to avoid being in the spotlight by overusing their presentation aids such as PowerPoint slides or objects for demonstration, seemingly hiding behind them. Resist that temptation. Challenge yourself to take control of the situation and perform.

In sum, your goal in speaking to a live audience should be to interact with them. Whether you deliver your speech using the manuscript, memorized, or extemporaneous style, you want to be conversational. To do so, use language that is clear, concise, concrete, creative, and appropriate to the situation. Also make sure your delivery is energetic, varied, and performed smoothly and that you integrate physical action with the language of your speech. The use of appropriate presentation aids can further add impact and reinforce your message as a whole.

Although we have discussed these elements of speech making in discussing speaking before a live audience, many of the same elements apply when delivering a speech as a mass-mediated performance. That type of speech making is the final topic of this module.

A Mediated Presentation

impression management   Efforts by a person playing a role to control the perceptions that audience members hold of him or her.

Let's start with an example: Robert Brown, who works as a multimedia designer for a community college in Virginia, was asked to do a presentation at a professional conference of educators and designers about how to produce DVD media for professional and home use. Rather than being in attendance at the conference and delivering his talk as a live, face-to-face performance, Robert delivered his speech as a **mediated performance,** which originated from his home and was broadcast over the Internet.

This example broadens the view of mass-mediated communication beyond what is commonly considered in studying mass-mediated speeches. Most people would think only about televised speeches given by public officials, such as the president, or about presentations by professional communicators, such as celebrities and journalists. Yet any of us could be called on to present a mediated presentation in our professional field using a wide range of new communication tools.

For instance, Robert's presentation about DVD technology was performed using a web-based conferencing system called *Centra Symposium.* His presentation illustrates how a speech can be broadcast from pretty much anywhere by way of the Internet to a live audience. That audience can hear an audio transmission of the speaker's voice or even see a digital video presentation. Additionally, tools like Centra Symposium permit the speaker to incorporate visual aids such as PowerPoint slides or a whiteboard, which is a sort of digital chalkboard that all the viewers attending the transmission can see and write on, too.

Audience members were all seated in the same room at the conference for the broadcast of Robert's speech, which was displayed on a large projection screen. However, tools like Centra Symposium can also be used for dispersed audiences—say, individuals in their own homes, seated at their own computers.

Clearly, presenting a mass-mediated speech offers great new opportunities for communicating but poses special challenges, as well. We will turn next to explore them.

Opportunities for Mass-Mediated Presentations   A mass-mediated speech can address a much larger audience than one delivered face to face to an audience. That was realized as far back as 1925, which marked the first time that a speech by a U.S. president was heard by a live audience and radio listeners simultaneously. President Calvin Coolidge was sworn into office on March 4, and his inaugural address was broadcast over the radio. As Baskerville (1979) explains, "Calvin Coolidge's voice reached more listeners than that of any previous American president—perhaps more than any speaker's in history" (p. 160).

In fact, there are some notable examples of presidential speeches that were *recorded* before the Coolidge inaugural. (They are available at the Library of Congress as audiotapes for historians to study, as is Coolidge's inaugural address.) However, what distinguished Coolidge's inaugural address was that

WEB
ACTIVITY
7.14

it was delivered to two audiences *at the same time.* Along with the audience gathered on the east side of the U.S. Capitol, Coolidge spoke to a much larger dispersed audience of radio listeners on the east coast the United States.

The filming and broadcasting of speeches also opened possibilities for addressing more than one audience at a time. During World War II, movie viewers were able to watch portions of important speeches as newsreel footage that preceded the main features in theaters. A particularly interesting example of such footage was President Harry S. Truman's announcement of the United States' dropping of the first atomic bomb on Hiroshima, Japan, which effectively brought about the end of the war. In viewing the footage of the president's speech, it appears that he was presenting several speeches simultaneously—or at least speaking to several different audiences. One was the immediate audience of American citizens. But another was the leaders of the Japanese government, who were being warned that the United States might drop another atomic bomb if they did not surrender. And still a third audience was a historical audience, which we are part of today. It seems reasonable that Truman recognized in delivering this speech that a new era of human history was being ushered in with the dropping of the bomb.

In addition to being able to be heard by audiences located anywhere (as long as listeners have access to the needed technology), mass-mediated speeches can be listened

VIDEO
VIEW

7.17

mediated performance   A speech that is transmitted by way of an electronic channel of communication; may be recorded and then broadcast or broadcast live to multiple audiences or to a dispersed audience.

to at any time. Namely, speeches can be recorded before they are transmitted and then broadcast and rebroadcast as desired. For example, the weekly presidential speeches that are broadcast on the radio each Saturday are often recorded on the preceding Friday. Future audiences can even keep recordings of speeches for much later use.

When a message is prerecorded, it is also possible to distribute a personal copy to anyone who wants one. For instance, a speech can be recorded on standard audio- or videotape or through various digital media, such as CD-ROM or DVD. Then, it can be mailed to an individual audience member by way of regular postal mail or e-mail for digital formats.

Thus, the speaker in a mass-mediated presentation is freed from the traditional constraints of time and place. This is also true in terms of the amount of time allotted for a speech. For instance, when students meet in a classroom to hear one another's presentations, very short time limits must be honored—usually, 5 to 10 minutes per speech. This allows the audience to hear a certain number of speeches during the class period or over several class periods. If these speeches were recorded and made available to classmates, the time factor would be less critical. Longer speeches would be possible, and students could view them or listen to them at their own discretion.

A final benefit of mass-mediated speeches is that speakers can choose one medium over another in order to capitalize on their particular speaking talents. For instance, President Franklin D. Roosevelt is often regarded as one of the most eloquent presidential speakers in the contemporary era. His particular strength was the quality of his voice, which projected a powerful image to listeners who heard it on the radio. Roosevelt was indeed an effective speaker in face-to-face situations, too. But these public appearances required a great deal of effort for him that was not required when he spoke on the radio. This is because Roosevelt spent most of his day seated in a wheelchair.

Afflicted with polio when he was in his thirties, Roosevelt was unable to walk without assistance for the rest of his life. So, when he gave speeches in public, he wore heavy leg braces that enabled him to stand. These appearances were physically taxing for the president, however. His radio addresses, by contrast, were more relaxed. During the Great Depression and World War II, Roosevelt perfected the "fireside chat," in which he presented a speech that was broadcast over the radio and into the homes of people across the United States. These chats emphasized the warmth and intimacy of the president's voice and were effective in building public support for his policies.

The medium of television may have contributed to John F. Kennedy's success in defeating then Vice President Richard M. Nixon in the 1960 presidential election. At the time of the initial televised debate between the two, reports indicated that Nixon was recovering from an illness. He had apparently lost weight and looked pale when he appeared on television. In contrast, Kennedy had rested the day prior to the debate and appeared robust and confident. Interestingly, those commentators who *listened* to the debate on the radio thought that Nixon had won, but those who *watched* it on television gave the win to Kennedy.

Challenges of Mass-Mediated Presentations   Using technology to present mass-mediated communications can also pose serious challenges. As you prepare to give such a speech, consider how you can meet those challenges by doing the following:

■ Adapt your delivery to the particular medium and its traditional audience.
■ Compensate for the lack of an immediate audience.

Don't think of a mass-mediated speech as just a tape recording of a speech that could be spoken for a live audience. You must adapt your message and approach to the qualities of the particular medium with which you will communicate—whether you are transmitting your message mainly as spoken discourse over the radio or as a more visual presentation over the television or through digital video. As discussed in the previous examples, you must write and practice your speech so as best to utilize the features of a particular medium. Follow these general guidelines:

Delivering an Audio Presentation   If your message is being carried largely through your voice, as is the case with radio transmission or communicating on the web with a tool like Centra Symposium, take special care to use clear and distinctive vocal articulation. In Module Two, we examined some of the ways that the enunciation and pronunciation of words are governed by phonetic rules. Applying these rules for careful production of each sound is vital when the primary means through which your audience is receiving your message is listening to your voice.

Delivering a Video Presentation   If your audience can see you by way of digital or traditional video transmission, you will also need to use clear and well-rehearsed physical actions. Keep in mind, however, that the types of gestures and actions that you use when delivering a speech in front of a camera will differ from those that you use in a face-to-face performance. The video image that appears on a television screen or computer monitor is two dimensional and contained within the rectangle of the display. When viewed in that context, gestures that feel natural and appropriate when made in a large room will come across as jerky or frenetic. Delivering a speech via a video recording requires a more relaxed physical presence than does speaking live in a big room. Nonetheless, the video speaker must still project enough energy to be dynamic. Achieving this is a difficult balancing act.

Compensating for the Lack of an Immediate Audience   Many mass-mediated messages are recorded and later presented without a live audience being present. As a speaker, you are thus communicating without feedback from your audience. As Robert began his presentation on DVD production, he referred in his introduction to the circumstances of not having feedback. He used an analogy, saying that he understood how a radio disc jockey must feel: lonely and isolated in a studio during the broadcast.

Absent audience feedback, the speaker in a mass-mediated presentation must rely more on **feedforward.** Recall from Module One that in using this technique, the communicator anticipates how the audience is likely to respond to his or her message. Feedforward strategies involve using a *set-up* to forecast what points the speaker will cover and how the audience should receive them.

Examples of this strategy of feedforward can be found in television news programs. An announcer will typically do a headline story and then highlight what other stories are coming within the half-hour before the broadcast or in the next segment following a commercial break. These forecasts might be used, in part, to keep the audience tuned until after the break. However, the same technique is also used in noncommercial programming, in which there is no break, in order to help keep viewers focused on the sequence of the presentation.

The speaker delivering his or her presentation through a mass-mediated channel might also find it helpful to imagine his or her audience. Sarett and Foster (1946) advise radio speakers to envision their audiences responding to the ideas of their speeches. Many effective communicators whose messages are recorded on video similarly use the technique of imagining that the lens of the camera is a person with whom they are having a conversation.

According to Sarett and Foster, effective media speakers also sometimes have a sample of their audience present for a broadcast. President Bill Clinton used this strategy on some occasions for recording his weekly radio broadcasts. While the president's primary audience was the American public, for some of his speeches, he invited a small group of

feedforward   A technique by which the communicator anticipates how the audience is likely to respond to his or her message.

listeners to the White House or went on location to record his speech before a small audience.

For instance, when Clinton decided to introduce legislation for giving financial assistance to college students, he went to a community college near Washington, DC, to record his radio message. A member of the select audience for that speech had thought it strange that listeners for the recording session were expected to arrive well before the actual taping. She was even more surprised when the president and his retinue showed up early, too. Clinton seemed to make personal contact with everyone in the audience, asking them about their college experiences.

When it was noon and time to deliver the speech, Clinton seemed more relaxed than he had been when he arrived. As he sat down to his microphone, an aide handed him the text for his speech, which he read as though he was having a conversation with each person in the room.

Implications for Communication: Relate to Your Audience

Whether you perform your speech for a live audience or as a mass-mediated presentation, the most important thing to remember is that speaking is relational. A speech is not the same as a written text. Rather, a speech is a dialogue with an audience, even one that is not physically present.

In particular, you will be a more effective speaker by following these four principles:

- Select the style of delivery that will be most effective for relating to your audience.
- Strive to create a conversational and spontaneous interaction with your audience.
- Integrate your words and your physical actions.
- Practice your delivery so it is dynamic, smooth, purposeful, and energetic.

ASSESSING YOUR SKILLS

7.6

RAPID REVIEW

7.7

Summary

Public speaking is a way of relating to an audience and engaging listeners in a public dialogue about ideas. An effective speaker goes through these six steps in planning and presenting a speech:

- Choosing a topic and identifying a goal
- Analyzing the audience
- Analyzing the speaking situation
- Conducting research
- Organizing ideas
- Deciding on a presentation style

The first step—choosing a topic and identifying the goal of your speech—involves considering the primary goals of speaking: persuading, informing, and entertaining. The persuasive speaker establishes desirability, justification, and motivation for audience members to change their position or behavior. The informative speaker aims to enhance his or her audience's understanding by providing them with a structure of accurate, complete, and comprehensive information. A speaker also may combine the goals of persuading and informing—for instance, with a speech that induces the audience to further inquiry or one that reinforces the audience's beliefs and feelings. Moreover, many speeches have an entertainment component, as well, which can be a means of motivating the audience to be attentive and responsive.

The second step is to assess the audience in order to develop a plan for the speech. The speaker should gauge the audience's views on his or her subject by doing a demographic analysis, which examines the social groupings of listeners, and a psychological analysis, which examines their attitudes, beliefs, values, and motivations. The speaker should then use those analyses to formulate a strategy for tailoring his or her speech to that audience. Along with analyzing the audience, the speaker should analyze other features of the rhetorical situation, including the occasion, the exigence and constraints that govern the situation, and how the audience perceives his or her credibility.

Researching the topic is a fourth step in the speech-making process. Research is the process of exploring the topic. It should be guided by research questions that enable the speaker to develop a more comprehensive perspective on his or her topic and thus consider alternative points of view. Effective research seeks a wide range of types of evidence and from a wide range of sources. The speaker should use critical judgment to assess the worth of types of evidence. The eventual goal of conducting research is to be able to narrow the focus of one's topic and develop a central idea and goal. The evidence that is gathered as proof or amplification of the main points should support that central idea and goal.

Organizing the speech is the fifth step. An effective speech employs a four-part organizational structure: an introduction, which gains the audience's attention and develops rapport with them; a partition, which clearly and forcefully states the central idea and goal of the speech and previews the main points; a body, which develops the main points; and a conclusion, which restates the main ideas and provides a sense of dramatic finality. Each part of the organizational structure should be carefully designed in order to relate the ideas of the speech to the audience.

The final aspect of speech preparation is deciding on a delivery style and rehearsing. The delivery is the performance of the speech, whether as a live event before the audience or as a mass-mediated performance before an assembled or dispersed audience. The style of delivery may be from a manuscript, by memory, or extemporaneous. Effective delivery integrates the language of the speech with effective vocal qualities and physical actions.

PRACTICE
TEST

References

Bavelas, J. B., Hutchinson, S., Kenwood, C., & Matheson, D. H. (1997). Using face-to-face dialogue as a standard for other communication systems. *Canadian Journal of Communication,* 22, no. 1, 5–24. Available online: <wlu.ca/~www.press/jrls/cjc/BackIssues/22.1/bavel.html>. Accessed May 17, 2002.

Bitzer, L. F. (1968). The rhetorical situation. *Philosophy and Rhetoric,* 1, no. 1, 1–14.

Baskerville, B. (1979). *The people's voice: The orator in American society.* Lexington, KY: University of Kentucky Press.

Burke, K. B. (1950). *A rhetoric of motives.* New York: Prentice-Hall.

Bryant, D. C. (1974). Rhetoric: Its functions and its scope. In W. R. Fisher (ed.), *Rhetoric: A tradition in transition* (pp. 195–230). East Lansing, MI: Michigan State University Press.

Cooper, L. (1960). *The rhetoric of Aristotle.* (trans.) New York: Appleton-Century-Crofts.

Doyle, T., & Barr, L. (2003). *ISearch: Speech communication.* Boston: Allyn & Bacon.

Fetsinger, L. (1957). *A theory of cognitive dissonance.* Stanford, CA: Stanford University Press.

Foss, S., & Griffin, C. (1995). Beyond persuasion: A proposal for an invitational rhetoric. *Communication Monographs,* 62, 2–18.

German, K., Gronbeck, B. E., Ehninger, D., & Monroe, A. H. (2004). *Principles of public speaking.* 15th ed. Boston: Allyn & Bacon.

Gernsbacher, M. A. (1997). Two decades of structure building. *Discourse Processes,* 23, 265–304.

Grice, G. L., & Skinner, J. F. (2003). *Mastering public speaking.* 4th ed. Boston: Allyn & Bacon.

Griffin, C. L. (2003). *Invitation to public speaking.* Belmont, CA: Wadsworth.

Labov, W. (1996). *The organization of dialect diversity in the United States.* Available online: <www.ling.upenn.edu/phono_atlas/ICSLP4.html>. Accessed August 27, 2003.

McConchie, A. (2002). *Great pop vs. soda controversy.* Available online: <www.popvssoda.com/>. Accessed August 27, 2003.

O'Keefe, D. J. (1998). Justification, explicitness and persuasive effect: A meta-analytic review of the effects of varying support articulation in persuasive messages. *Argumentation and Advocacy,* 35, no. 2. Available online: <ContentSelect: Communication>. Accessed April 24, 2003.

Petty, R. E., & Cacioppo, J. T. (1986). The elaboration-likelihood model of persuasion. In L. Berkowitz (ed.), *Advances in experimental social psychology* (vol. 19, pp. 123–205). San Diego, CA: Academic Press.

Putnam, R. D. (2000). *Bowling alone. The collapse and revival of American community.* New York: Simon and Schuster.

Richmond, V. & Hickson, M. III. (2002). *Going public: A practical guide to public talk.* Boston: Allyn & Bacon.

Richmond, V., & McCroskey, J. (1998). *Communication apprehension, avoidance and effectiveness.* 5th ed. Boston: Allyn & Bacon.

Sarett, L., & Foster, W. T. (1946). *Basic principles of speech.* Boston: Houghton Mifflin.

Sheldon, K. M., Elliott, A. J., Kim, Y., & Kasser, T. (2001) What is satisfying about satisfying events? Testing 10 candidate psychological needs. *Journal of Personality and Social Psychology,* 80, no. 3, 325–339.

Vatz, R. (1973). The myth of the rhetorical situation. *Philosophy and Rhetoric,* 6, no. 3, 155–160.

Wilson, J. F., & Arnold, C. C. (1964). *Public speaking as a liberal art.* Boston: Allyn & Bacon.

Winans, J. A. (1917). *Public speaking.* Rev. ed. New York: Century.

Winans, J. A. (1938). *Speech-making.* New York: Appleton-Century.

Zarefsky, D. (1999). *Public speaking: Strategies for success.* Boston: Allyn & Bacon.

GLOSSARY

allocentric Describes a person in an individualistic culture who subscribes to collectivistic values.

amplification Evidence that informs or reinforces the beliefs and feelings of the audience.

And Stance A response to a conflict situation that avoids blaming the other for a conflict or perceiving the conflict from one's own point of view, alone.

appraisal interview An interview in which an employee's job performance is evaluated; provides feedback to the employee and offers an opportunity for him or her to ask questions or explore concerns.

argument from analogy A claim that involves comparing two things and showing that one is substantially similar to the other.

argument from causality A claim that there is a logical connection between one or more effects and one or more causes that produces the effect(s) that are claimed.

argument from generalization A claim that suggests a logical connection between an example and a general conclusion.

argument from sign A claim that an observable or measurable indicator, or sign, is associated with a certain phenomenon.

articulation The production of the distinctive sounds of a language.

artifacts Personal objects and aesthetic elements that are used to communicate nonverbally.

asynchronous communication Occurs when a lapse of time occurs between when the sender transmits a message and when the receiver decodes it and provides feedback.

attitude A predisposition to respond favorably or unfavorably to a topic.

audience The spectators of a given communication situation; form impressions of the actors and the scene being played out.

authoritarian leadership A style of leadership that is characterized by a high degree of control and influence on the part of a leader.

belief A position or standard that is held to be valid and truthful.

blame game A dimension in an interpersonal conflict that goes beyond the content issue to accuse the other for being at fault or in the wrong in the conflict. Common strategies for the blame game include labeling the other as selfish, irrational, naïve, or controlling.

body The third part and essential core of a speech; develops each main point and demonstrates to the audience how it supports the central idea of the speech.

breadth Self-disclosures that include sharing of superficial information about oneself on a broad range of subject areas.

central idea A single sentence stated in the partition to synthesize each of the main points of a speech; the thesis sentence.

channel The medium of transmission used by the communicator; may be an electronic medium, such as the telephone; radio or television; the Internet; or face-to-face communication; or written communication.

channel capacity The amount of information that can be transmitted through a given channel of communication.

character and trustworthiness Aspects of credibility about which audience members judge the speaker's moral virtues.

chronemics Nonverbal communication related to the meaning of time.

chronological order A variation of the groupings pattern of arrangement in which a topic is examined by developing a timeline or presenting the sequence of steps in a process.

classical questions A category of research questions that frame research in terms of the type of speaking occasion: (1) a *question of policy* asks what course of action to pursue; (2) a *question of fact* asks what facts support the case at hand; and (3) a *question of value* asks whether the subject is good or bad, desirable or undesirable. (A fourth type sometimes identified is a *question of definition*, which asks what something means or how it should be named.)

closed questions Questions that address narrow areas of concern and provide little or no latitude of response.

closure The strategy of filling in information that appears to be missing so that an experience will be a whole and meaningful pattern.

codes Electronic signals that are used to transmit information through a channel of communication; verbal and nonverbal systems of symbols that are used for encoding and decoding messages.

cognitive complexity A measure of how many constructs an individual uses; persons high in cognitive complexity likely have a greater number of constructs and more insight into others.

collaboration The shared activity of creating meaning; a key element in the relational view of communication.

collectivism A cultural view that emphasizes the values of cooperation and group identification and in which achievement is considered a matter of group merit.

communication The process of creating meaning; involves exchanging information, using symbols, and creating and sustaining relationships.

communication situations The wide range of situations and circumstances in which most of us communicate each day.

competence An aspect of credibility that addresses the speaker's expertise and knowledge.

complementary relationship A relationship that is based on differences in power and control; one partner assumes the position that is superior, or "one-up," and the other partner assumes the corresponding inferior, or "one-down," position.

computer-mediated communication Communication that uses a computer as the channel through which the message is transmitted; used as a tool to transmit information, as a place for interacting with people, or for constructing a way of being online.

conclusion The fourth and final part of a speech; provides a summary as well as sense of closure by restating the central idea and main points and by offering a dramatic finish.

conditional positive regard An affirmation that is rooted in conditions of worth established by others, which an individual must fulfill in order to be regarded as worthy, competent, and lovable.

conditions of worth External criteria for achieving self-worth that are communicated to an individual as expectations that he or she must meet in order to be affirmed.

connection and autonomy An internal dialectic in which the contrasting value of togetherness or closeness is in tension with the value of independence.

connotative meanings The emotional level of meaning of a word; associated with the attitudes and values we hold.

constitutive rules Establish what behaviors must be performed in order to accomplish an intended communicative goal; what a speech act counts as in a given circumstance.

constitutive rules for relationships Establish patterns of communication behavior and reflect how members define the nature of their relationship.

constraints The limitations placed on a speaker in a given speaking situation.

content dimension The sheer information that is exchanged in a message.

control messages Relational messages that communicate power and status.

conventionality and uniqueness An external dialectic in which tension arises around being accepted and conforming to the conventions of a larger social network and having a sense of unique identity.

conversational maxims From Grice's model, which identifies four benchmarks essential to successfully coordinating communication; the benchmarks are quantity, quality, relation, and manner.

corporate culture The larger organizational context within which members of a small group work; members align with the views and vision of their culture, as articulated in its mission statement, policies, and manuals.

credibility The perception that members of an audience have of a speaker and that affects their response to him or her.

cultural dimensions view The perspective that cultural patterns influence how individuals form a sense of self by identifying with the values of individualism or collectivism.

cultural knowledge Insights about others based on their membership in a large cultural group. This type of knowledge is often used when relating impersonally to strangers.

cultural noise Interference with communication that occurs when cultural expectations are not met in communication.

decode/decoding According to the transmission view of communication, how the receiver receives and interprets the message sent by the source.

deduction A type of argument from generalization that involves beginning with a general conclusion and providing specific cases to support it; also called *syllogistic reasoning.*

defensive communication climate Patterns of communication that undermine the stability and well-being of an interpersonal relationship when interactions involve evaluation, control, strategy, neutrality, superiority, and certainty.

deliberative speaking Speaking that involves discussion and debate of matters of policy, as in a legislative assembly.

delivery The performance of a speech for a live audience or a mediated audience.

democratic leadership A style of leadership that emphasizes participation by all members of a group in shared decision making and control.

demographic analysis An assessment of the social groups that audience members belong to—for example, age, sex, cultural and racial/ethnic background, education, and so on.

demonstrating openness A strategy of relational maintenance that emphasizes self-disclosure and sharing needs and wants in a relationship as well as feelings about the relationship.

denotative meaning The objective or specific meaning of a word; typically among the first definitions found in a dictionary entry for a given word.

depth Self-disclosures that encompass sharing of personally significant information about oneself.

descending or ascending order A variation of the groupings pattern of arrangement in which a topic is examined by ranking ideas by familiarity or order of importance.

desirability A quality of effective persuasive speaking that is achieved when the speaker asserts a judgment, stating either implicitly or explicitly that something is good or bad or better or worse.

destabilized relationship Distressed relationships that are characterized by patterns of criticism and complaining, hostility and contempt, defensiveness and the avoidance of relational problems, which is termed *stonewalling.*

dialect A variety of a language; demonstrates systematic differences in how speech is spoken; may differ by geographic regions or correspond to differences in social or cultural groupings.

dialectical approach to communication A model of communication that examines how opposing goods or values create a dynamic tension.

direct questions Questions that are intended to evoke answers that are explicitly stated.

disequilibrium Being out of balance; occurs when components of a system are not experiencing equilibrium such as when a group's members are not able to resolve tension between competing values.

dramatistic view of self The perspective that an individual plays roles in his or her interactions with others and uses strategies and symbols to present himself or herself to others and to manage their impressions.

dynamic equilibrium The ongoing motion between poles of a relational dialectic.

electronic noise Interference with the transmission of information through an electronic system.

emergent leadership The theory that certain members of the group will be perceived as performing important leadership functions and therefore be accorded leadership status.

emotional intelligence The ability to monitor our own feelings and those of others, to discriminate among those feelings, and to use this information to guide our thinking and behavior.

empirical self What the individual sees through self-reflection; comprised of the material me, the social me, and the spiritual me.

employment interview An interview conducted in the workplace for a work-related purpose; for instance, a job-seeking interview, appraisal, or exit interview.

encode/encoding The act of creating a message by putting ideas, thoughts, and feelings into codes; according to the transmission view of communication, how the source creates the message using a symbolic form or system of signs.

environment The physical, psychological, social, linguistic, and cultural situation in which communication takes place.

epideictic speaking Speaking that addresses the particular concerns of audiences on special occasions, often celebrating shared values and giving voice to shared feelings.

equilibrium Translated literally from Latin, means "equal and in balance"; occurs when a group's members are able to resolve tension between competing values.

ethnocentrism The attitude that the value system, beliefs, and practices of one's own culture are superior to those of others and thus can be used as a standard for judging others.

evidence The supporting material a speaker uses to prove a point or to amplify one of his or her ideas.

evolution through exploration A response to conflict that involves understanding it. This entails examining oneself, the conflict, and the other.

examples A form of evidence that comprises illustrations, whether actual or literary; often expressed as narratives or as case studies.

exclusive relationships Relationships marked by one-on-one communication between two people or interactions with few people.

exigence A demand, burden, or expectation inherent in the speaking situation.

exit interview An interview conducted with an employee who is leaving his or her position; provides feedback about his or her work and brings closure to the work experience.

expert testimony A form of evidence that comprises quotes from people or organizations that the audience recognizes as having the authority to offer credible commentary on the topic.

extemporaneous delivery Performing a speech "from the moment"; the overall structure is carefully planned in advance but the final wording occurs at the time of delivery.

external dialectical tensions Dialectical oppositions felt directly by the primary partners in a relationship as they relate to a larger social network. External dialectics include the oppositions between inclusion and seclusion, conventionality and uniqueness, and revelation and concealment.

extrinsic gratification Rewards that come from outside the individual, such as gifts, material objects, and money.

fact questions Questions that seek specific factual details and examples or ask about trends and patterns of information; can be open or closed.

feedback The response that the receiver makes to the source.

feedforward A technique by which the communicator anticipates how the receiver is likely to respond to his or her message and makes adjustments in advance of encoding a message.

field of experience The set of life experiences, based on one's personal background and culture, that he or she draws on to encode and decode messages; shape how that person perceives the world.

focus group A group of individuals brought together to offer their perceptions of a product or a concept; participants are selected so that they represent a random sample of the larger audience to whom a product or advertising campaign is targeted.

follow-up questions Questions that seek additional information or clarification; prompt the interviewee to expand on what he or she has already shared about a topic.

forensic speaking Speaking that occurs in courts of law for determining issues of justice.

general procedural model for problem solving A five-step method of systematically solving a problem; entails (1) problem description and analysis; (2) generation and elaboration of possible solutions; (3) evaluation of possible solutions; (4) solution decision; and (5) planning for implementation.

general systems theory A theory that explains how the components of a system interact with one another in ways that enable the system as a whole to maintain equilibrium and to adapt to its environment; explains how work-related small groups are parts of larger organizational structures.

generalized others The culture at large; the attitudes, values, beliefs, norms, rules, roles, and expectations of an individual's larger relational communities, which he or she internalizes in defining the self.

goodwill An aspect of credibility that is linked with the speaker's building rapport and developing a relationship with the audience.

group cohesion An attraction that members feel toward the group and its task and the intensity with which they value their affiliation; dimensions include task cohesion and social cohesion.

group decision support systems (GDSS) A computer-mediated type of interaction that allows members to brainstorm ideas and discuss issues in a fairly anonymous manner.

groupings order A pattern of arrangement in which a topic is explained as a set of subtopics, developed as a chronology, depicted as a spatial map, or analyzed as a set of ideas in ascending or descending order.

groupthink Occurs when, in a rush to conformity, the prevailing majority of a group does not listen to alternative points of view and exercise critical thinking; results in bad decision making.

haptics Nonverbal communication through the use of touch.

helping/counseling interview An interview that focuses on problems and assists someone in dealing with them; for instance, an interview with a therapist, teacher, or clergy member.

horizontal perspective A cultural view that values equality, deemphasizing social class and downplaying status differences.

humanistic view of self The perspective that individuals experience self-esteem and seek to grow as individuals so that they can achieve their full potential as self-actualized persons.

hypothetical questions Questions that are intended to evoke less direct and more thoughtful answers. These are often phrased as imaginary situations.

I The part of the self that thinks and acts, sometimes impulsively and at other times with creativity and insight.

icons Symbols that resemble what they signify.

idiocentric Describes a person in a collectivist culture who subscribes to individualistic values.

immediacy messages Relational messages that communicate a desire for closeness or distance.

impression management Efforts by a person playing a role to control the perceptions that audience members hold of him or her.

inclusion and seclusion An external dialectic between the values of being integrated into a larger social network and maintaining separateness.

incongruity A mismatch between one's inner feelings of who he or she is meant to be and the outer expression of how he or she actually behaves.

individualism A cultural view that emphasizes the values of independence, self-direction, autonomy, and self-affirmation and in which achievement is considered a matter of individual merit.

inducing inquiry A type of speech in which the speaker explains a problem and then urges his or her audience to help solve it; combines elements of persuasive and informative speaking.

induction A type of argument from generalization that involves drawing a general conclusion after examining a number of specific cases.

information-sharing interview An interview that has the goal of obtaining or presenting information; for instance, an interview with an expert or a witness.

informative speaking Speaking in which the primary aim is to enhance the audience's understanding.

inner speech The interior dialogue an individual carries on inside his or her head.

intact work group A group that's formed to work together for an extended period of time and to accomplish many different tasks.

integrating into social networks A strategy of relational maintenance that is experienced when members of a relationship draw upon a larger relational community for support, affirmation, and recognition.

interdependence Describes how the members of a group need to pull together to accomplish a task in a cooperative and collaborative manner; one of the core concepts of general systems theory; sometimes referred to as the principle of holism.

internal dialectical tensions Dialectical oppositions felt directly by the primary partners in a relationship. Internal dialectics include the oppositions of autonomy and connection, novelty and predictability, and openness and closedness.

interpersonal communication Communication between people in a relationship that has been mutually defined as more or less personal, exclusive, and informal.

interpersonal conflict Expressed struggle between at least two interdependent parties who perceive incompatible goals, scarce resources, and interference from others in achieving their goals.

interpersonal needs The needs and expectations that individual group members bring to the group; basic needs are inclusion, control, and affection.

interpersonal relationships Personal relationships characterized by interaction between people who share a substantial amount of information about one another that has been communicated over the course of a relatively long relational history.

interview A specialized type of interpersonal communication that is organized around a specific goal; usually involves two people but can include several people participating as a group.

interviewee The person whose primary purpose is to respond to the questions asked of him or her; generally follows the lead of the interviewer.

interviewer The person who conducts the interview by organizing the structure, asking the questions, and generally controlling the exchange.

intrapersonal communication Communication within oneself that occurs by way of interior dialogues.

intrinsic gratification Rewards that come from inside the individual, especially as a sense of self-satisfaction resulting from perceptions of personal accomplishment and of being competent.

introduction The first part of a speech; engages the audience by gaining their attention and establishing their relationship with the speaker.

jargon A set of expressions, even common expressions, that are understood principally by members of a certain group.

job-seeking interview An interview conducted for hiring purposes; also called a selection interview.

journalistic questions Broad questions that frame research by encouraging the speaker to explore different aspects of his or her topic: Who? What? When? Where? Why? and How?

justification A quality of effective persuasive speaking that is achieved when the speaker provides the audience with a valid reason for change; may be based on self-interest, reasoning and evidence, or authority.

kinesics Physical nonverbal behavior, such as gestures, movements, and tensions of the body; facial communication is an important component.

laissez-faire leadership A style of leadership that delegates responsibilities and enables individual members to make decisions and work autonomously.

language A rule-governed system of verbal and nonverbal symbols used by members of a speech community to create meaning.

leadership Comprises those behaviors that guide a group toward accomplishing its goals.

listening The process of receiving information, constructing meaning from it, and responding to a verbal or nonverbal message.

logical order A pattern of arrangement in which a sequence of arguments is developed that justify the speaker's central idea and purpose.

manuscript delivery Performing a speech by reading aloud a fully written text.

mass-mediated communication Communication with a very large and usually impersonal audience with messages that are commonly transmitted by way of an electronic channel of communication.

material me The physical self; the perception of self that involves one's body as well as physical objects that are extensions of the self.

maxim of manner Concerns using the correct style for a given type of dialogue; in an interview, it's important to speak clearly and to organize your ideas.

maxim of quality Concerns making ethical responses to questions; an interviewee must be sincere and truthful in order to maintain credibility.

maxim of quantity Concerns the amount of information that a communicator shares; in an interview, means finding the right balance between saying too little and saying too much.

maxim of relation Concerns the relevance of the information shared; interviewees should not digress to talk about things that don't fit the focus of the dialogue.

Me The part of the self that has internalized the expectations and norms of the larger societal or interpersonal relational community of which one is a member.

mediated performance A speech that is transmitted by way of an electronic channel of communication; may be recorded and then broadcast or broadcast live to multiple audiences or to a dispersed audience.

memorized delivery Performing a speech by reciting it from memory, word for word.

message Information that is organized in symbolic form or in accordance with the rules for using a system of signs; a message is comprised of content and codes.

meta-communication Communicating about communication; may be used to explore the underlying assumptions, values, background and motivations for how we communicate.

metaphor Used to make a comparison between two things by transferring the meaning of one to another; a symbolic use of language, not a literal one.

method of residues A variation of the problem-solving order in which several possible solutions are identified and then eliminated until only the predetermined desirable solution remains.

mind reading Making judgments about how the personal constructs of a relational partner are similar to or different from our own.

motivation A quality of effective persuasive speaking that is achieved by addressing the needs and drives of the audience.

motivational order A pattern of arrangement in which a sequence of motives is developed for understanding information or adopting a course of action; the five steps include attention, need, satisfaction, visualization, and action.

motive clusters Affiliation, achievement, and power.

noise According to the transmission model of communication, an impediment to or breakdown in communication.

nonsummativity Describes how the whole is greater than the sum of its parts; a restatement of the principle of holism.

nonverbal code A rule-governed system of symbols expressed behaviorally by members of a relational community; includes physical, vocal, spatial, thermal, olfactory, and tactile components.

nonverbal congruency rule The expectation that verbal and nonverbal codes will reinforce one another.

norms Patterns of behavior that all or most members of a group are expected to perform; reflect the shared attitudes and values of the group's members; sometimes explicitly stated as rules.

objects and presentation aids A form of evidence that comprises concrete objects, charts, diagrams, pictures, and drawings, as well as sound and video clips.

olfactics Nonverbal communication related to how people exude and perceive smells.

onomatopoeia An iconic use of language in which a word sounds like what it signifies.

open questions Questions that afford the interviewee a wide range of options for responding.

openness and closedness An internal dialectic in a relationship in which the values of sharing information through self-disclosure is in tension with the value of withholding information.

opinion-centered questions Questions that ask for judgments.

organismic valuing Looking inward to tap one's intuitive sense of what provides the source of his or her value.

paralanguage Vocal nonverbal behavior that is produced through manipulation of the voice.

paraphrase To rephrase what another person has said; as an active listening strategy, allows checking comprehension and verifying common understandings and feelings.

particular others People with whom an individual has primary relationships, such as family members, lovers, and intimate friends, whose views he or she continues to internalize in defining the self.

partition The second part of a speech; focuses the audience's attention on the central idea and purpose of the speech and provides an overview of its main points.

passive-aggressive behavior A response to conflict that communicates a double message that appears to be positive and cooperative, along with veiled expressions of negativity and aggression.

patterns of arrangement Organizational plans or structures that guide the audience to follow the progression of the speech.

perception The process of creating meaning that involves receiving information through one's senses and then organizing and interpreting that information in a meaningful way.

perceptual set A previously determined view of an object or an event based on past experiences.

person centeredness The ability to understand the perspectives of others more clearly and thus become more competent in tailoring communications to other people.

personal construct A means of assigning meaning to a situation by perceiving how it is similar to a previous situation; enables people to assign meanings to situations and to anticipate events that are part of a history of similarly constituted communication situations.

perspective taking The ability to perceive concepts from another person's perspective.

persuasive interview An interview in which one party is advocating a position or urging the other party to do something; for example, an interview on a news program.

persuasive speaking Speaking in which the primary aim is to advocate a position or move the audience to change their behavior.

phonemes The particular sounds that make up a language; the sounds produced in accordance with the phonetic rules that describe the distinctive features of a language.

phonetic filter hypothesis Suggests that we recognize the phonemes that are part of our primary language and filter out or distort sounds that are not part of that language.

phonetic rules Guidelines that govern the creation of sounds of a language.

physical noise Interference with communication that comes from competing background noise, like music or loud talking.

plagiarism A form of academic dishonesty, in which one person presents another person's ideas as his or her own without acknowledging the original source.

plasticity The ability of the self to adapt to new relational contexts.

polyvocality The ability to hold multiple views, values, and sentiments, many of which may conflict on some level.

positive self-regard The realization of self-worth and an understanding of one's true potential.

postmodernism The perspective that living in today's technologically driven, fast-changing, and mobile world has altered people's sense of community and thus affected how they develop their sense of self. Postmodern thought rejects the concept of a stable core of identity.

pragmatic view of self The perspective that an individual gains self-awareness through self-reflection and by importing the perspectives of others he or she interacts with.

predictability and novelty An internal dialectic of a relationship in which the values of regular routine and the ability to anticipate the behavior of another are in tension with the values of being spontaneous and appreciating new experiences.

primary questions Questions that introduce topics; typically planned out carefully and thus used to structure or organize the interview.

problem-solving agenda A sequence of topics that is followed to organize a discussion; often phrased as questions; organized in a logical sequence for group reflective thinking.

problem-solving group A group formed to discuss a problem or issue for the purpose of resolving it.

problem-solving order A pattern of arrangement in which a problem is analyzed and a way of responding to it is advocated.

professional communication Communication in the workplace that is aimed at achieving work-related goals.

pronunciation How we actually make sounds and say words as we speak; in everyday use, demonstrates what dialect we speak.

proof Evidence that provides the reasonable basis upon which the audience can agree with the speaker; essential when trying to persuade.

proper meaning superstition The fallacy that there is only one correct meaning for a word.

providing reassurances A strategy of relational maintenance that involves expressing commitment and loyalty to the relationship and making investments of time, energy, and oneself in the relationship.

proxemics Nonverbal communication through the use of spatial distance; includes physical closeness and maintenance of zones of personal space.

pseudo-spontaneous nonverbal communication Nonverbal expressions that are intended to appear spontaneous; may involve imitating a certain feeling or attempting to mask a true feeling.

psychological analysis An assessment of the attitudes, beliefs, and values of the audience as well as the emotional response they will likely have to a subject.

psychological knowledge Personal information about another.

psychological noise Interference with communication that occurs when one's feelings, attitudes, values, and beliefs interfere with communication.

public discussion format A structure for discussing a problem or issue in the presence of an audience; may be a panel discussion, a symposium, and/or a forum.

public speaking Communication between a speaker and audience that is guided by principles of rhetoric for the creation and evaluation of formal presentations.

quantitative evidence A form of evidence that comprises statistics and probabilities based on statistics.

real self The sense of self-concept that is developed when an individual perceives himself or herself in light of his or her own unique self-worth and in accordance with his or her intuitive sense of organismic value.

receiver The listener or reader who interprets the message; according to the transmission view of communication, the person or group who receives the message.

regulative rules Govern what kind of communication behavior is appropriate or inappropriate in a given situation.

regulative rules for relationships Establish the boundaries of what is appropriate versus inappropriate.

regulators Types of nonverbal signals that communicators send to one another to govern the flow of conversation, back and forth; enable adjustments in the pacing of interaction and taking turns as source and receiver.

reinforcing beliefs and feelings A type of speech in which the speaker intends to intensify or amplify the audience's current position; combines elements of persuasive and informative speaking.

relational community The personal, social, or cultural context in which communicators interact with one another.

relational dimension The part of a message that communicates the attitudes and feelings each party has about the relationship; may be communicated explicitly through verbal language or implicitly through nonverbal language.

relational history The cumulative set of experiences shared by members in a relational community; develops out of the recurring types of communication situations that members repeat as part of their pattern of interaction.

relational self A sense of self that allows for multiple selves to relate to different people and relational communities.

relational view A theory of communication that focuses on how relational communities are created and how they provide a context for members of a community to share meaning with one another.

relational view of communication A theory of communication that focuses on how relational communities are created and how they provide a context for members of a community to share meaning with one another.

relational view of self The perspective that an individual constructs a complex sense of self, perhaps even multiple selves, as a result of participating in different relational communities.

research questions Questions that prompt deep exploration of your topic, going beyond what you already know or already think and looking at all aspects.

restatement A summary statement made during the conclusion to repeat and reinforce the main ideas and central idea.

responsiveness messages Relational messages that demonstrate interest in and attention to another person.

revelation and concealment An external dialectic in which tension arises over the value of sharing of information that is otherwise held in confidence within a relationship with parties outside the relationship or of not sharing the information.

rhetoric The academic study of public speaking; theories of rhetoric emphasize the philosophical and ethical foundations of speech making and provide grounds for the critical analysis of public |discourse.

rhetorical situation The speaking situation; includes the audience, the occasion, exigencies and constraints, and the speaker's credibility.

rhetorical theory The set of concepts that guide the practice of public speaking; also provides a philosophical and ethical foundation and methods for the critical examination of speech texts.

role identity The character and role that an individual creates for himself or herself; generally indicates how an individual likes to think of himself or herself.

role legitimation An individual's efforts to reinforce the legitimacy of the roles he or she plays and to get support and affirmation from the members of his or her relational communities.

role prominence The notion that people choose to play some roles over others, particularly those roles that are perceived as more important and thus desirable to perform.

roles Patterns of behavior enacted by an individual within the context of a particular relational community; the expectations for enacting a role are mutually defined by members of a relational community.

script Establishes the sequences of action and behavior that each party performs in his or her role in a given communication situation.

selective attention The act of making conscious and unconscious choices to pay attention to certain things.

self-actualizing tendency The perspective that an individual is motivated to fulfill his or her full potential.

self-centered roles Dysfunctional roles performed by group members that impede the group's progress.

self-concept The mental image an individual has of himself or herself; based on self-reflection and constructed through communicating with members of relational communities.

self-disclosure Intentional sharing of personal information about one's self.

self-disclosure as a dialectical process Sharing of information alternates between direct sharing and pulling back from disclosure.

self-esteem The evaluative dimension of self-concept, which is expressed as positive and negative judgments about the self; reflects assessments of competence and the need for recognition and respect from others.

self-fulfilling prophecy The idea that when we create an expectation for ourselves or for other people, we later communicate and otherwise act in ways that fulfill that expectation.

self-protection A response in a conflict that is motivated by the need to defend oneself. It may include adopting a stance of indifference, control, or compliance.

semantic features The mental categories of word meanings developed by members of a speech community; the set of attributes or characteristics of those categories.

semantic noise Interference with communication that stems from language differences and misunderstandings.

semantic rules Guidelines that govern the range of possible meanings for words.

semantic triangle A model for analyzing how denotative and connotative meanings are constructed; parts include a referent, a symbol, and a reference.

sensation The process of receiving information through the senses.

sharing tasks and responsibilities A strategy of relational maintenance that fosters interdependence and equality in a relationship by cooperative management of day-to-day tasks and responsibilities.

showing positiveness A strategy of relational maintenance that involves developing a positive attitude, optimism, and willingness to work constructively on resolution of relational growth or conflicts.

significant symbols The verbal and nonverbal expressions shared by members of a community that express a sense of collective meaning and identity.

signified The concept to which the signifier refers.

signifier What the listener hears and observes in its outward physical form; is perceived on the surface; can also be referred to as the sound image.

slang Specialized expressions that are unique to a certain group.

small-group communication Communication among members of a group that is organized to achieve the goals of solving a problem or making a decision.

social-centered roles Specific roles that contribute to the social cohesion of the group; sometimes referred to as group-maintenance roles, as they function to maintain the interpersonal harmony of the group.

social cohesion Reflects how much members are interpersonally attracted to one another and feel a sense of relational satisfaction and group unity.

social exchange theory The theory of behavior that suggests that individuals are motivated by efforts to maximize rewards and minimize costs.

social group A group that's formed for personal reasons; may be formed for socialization or to pursue individual growth intellectually, spiritually, or emotionally.

social me The perception of self in relation to other people and the value placed on those relationships.

social network Inclusive relationships that are usually larger than a dyad or a few people such as a group of friends or an extended family.

social noise Interference with communication that occurs when people communicate differently from one another because they have been socialized into groups that operate somewhat like cultures.

social penetration theory A model of self-disclosure that examines how relationships develop through the gradual sharing of information.

sociological knowledge Insights about another based upon his or her social grouping.

source The speaker or writer who originates the message; according to the transmission view of communication, the person or group who originates the message.

spatial order A variation of the groupings pattern of arrangement in which a topic is examined by creating a visual map of ideas.

speech act An utterance communicated to perform an action that is intended to achieve a specific goal, such as making a promise to do something; organized around an intention that the communicator is trying to achieve and includes a sentence or set of sentences and communicative behaviors that fulfill the requirements of performing the act.

speech community A group of people who share a given variety of a language, or dialect.

speech to entertain Speaking in which the primary aim is to evoke a pleasurable and aesthetic response from the audience; may be a secondary goal of an informative or persuasive speech.

spiritual me The perception of self that is the awareness of one's own mind; includes emotions, thoughts, desires, and intellectual ponderings as well as values and moral judgments.

spontaneous nonverbal communication Nonverbal expressions that are made involuntarily and thus reflect the underlying psychological states that evoke them.

standpoint theory The theory that a society is organized in terms of a hierarchy of power and status, and depending on the status of a social group in that hierarchy, its members will enjoy certain rights and privileges.

statement of dramatic finality The last line in the conclusion that is intended to give closure to the speech.

stereotype A way of grouping a whole set of people or events and then generalizing about the group as a whole.

structure building framework theory A theory that suggests that we receive and comprehend information by building cognitive structures.

supportive communication Patterns of communication that enhance the stability and well-being of an interpersonal relationship when interactions involve description rather than evaluation, a problem-orientation instead of control, being spontaneous rather than being strategic, empathy rather than neutrality, equality instead of superiority, and provisionalism rather than certainty.

symbolic interaction theory Term applied to George Herbert Mead's theory of communication to emphasize the importance of verbal and nonverbal symbols in the development of social relationships and identities.

symbolic nonverbal communication Nonverbal expressions that have symbolic meanings; governed by social conventions.

symbolic view A theory of how communication is a process of creating meaning; focuses on how communicators use symbol systems to create meaning.

symbols Vehicles of conception; enable humans to form conceptions that are abstractions of experiences and to generalize from one situation or circumstance to another.

symmetrical relationship A relationship that involves a mirroring of communication behavior and reflects the sense that communicators treat one another as equals in exercising control and power.

synchronous communication Communication in the here and now; occurs when the source and receiver are communicating without a significant delay between their sending and receiving of a message.

syntactic rules Guidelines that govern the arrangement of words into phrases and sentences; grammatical rules.

task cohesion Reflects how much members are committed to working together and to performing the type of work that they are involved in.

task force A group that's formed to work on a particular product or to study a particular issue; may exist only as long as it takes to complete the task.

task group A small group that's formed for a specific purpose; may be formed to solve problems and make decisions or to complete a specific project or job.

task-centered roles Specific roles performed by group members that enable them to work together to solve problems and make decisions.

territoriality A spatial aspect of nonverbal communication that deals with how people claim ownership of physical space.

topical order A variation of the groupings pattern of arrangement in which a topic is examined as a set of interrelated subtopics, or parts of the whole.

transaction The type of conversation in which one simultaneously plays the roles of source and receiver; often characteristic of face-to-face communication.

transactional leadership A form of relational leadership that involves an exchange between leaders and followers—a give and take.

transformational leadership A form of relational leadership that involves a higher level of motivation than self-interest; leaders and followers engage one another so as to raise levels of morality and motivation.

transmission view A theory for describing, explaining, and evaluating how information is conveyed or exchanged between communicators.

transmission view of communication A theory of communication for describing, explaining, and evaluating how information is conveyed or exchanged between communicators.

triangular theory of love Model for defining romantic relationships in key terms of passion, intimacy, and commitment.

typography and graphics Nonverbal aspects of communication that relate to how information is visually presented, whether on paper or onscreen; includes the arrangement of type and white space, the use of different type fonts, the colors used, the typewritten characters, the physical texture of the paper, and also the use of illustrations.

uncertainty reduction strategies Passive strategies involve indirect observations of others. Active strategies may include the indirect approach of asking others information about a party of interest or a direct strategy of asking for information from the person of interest or using small talk to learn information about the other.

uncertainty reduction theory Communicators seek information about others in an effort to predict and control communication. By reducing uncertainty an interpersonal communicator can anticipate how to communicate with others.

unconditional positive regard An affirmation that recognizes an individual's unique qualities and value without establishing conditions of worth.

value A deeply seated attitude that is commonly rooted in a core belief and usually establishes the intrinsic worth of something.

verbal code A rule-governed system of symbols codified as a spoken language that is used by members of a relational community.

vertical perspective A cultural view that respects the importance of status and hierarchy.

virtual work team A group whose members do a substantial amount of their interaction through electronic channels of communication.

INDEX